The Rebirth of Professional Soccer in America

The Rebirth of Professional Soccer in America

in America

*The Strange Days of the
United Soccer Association*

Dennis J. Seese

ROWMAN & LITTLEFIELD
Lanham • Boulder • New York • London

Published by Rowman & Littlefield
A wholly owned subsidiary of The Rowman & Littlefield Publishing Group, Inc.
4501 Forbes Boulevard, Suite 200, Lanham, Maryland 20706
www.rowman.com

Unit A, Whitacre Mews, 26-34 Stannary Street, London SE11 4AB

British Library Cataloguing in Publication Information Available

Library of Congress Cataloging-in-Publication Data Available

ISBN 978-1-4422-3894-7 (paperback: alk. paper)
ISBN 978-1-4422-3895-4 (ebook)

♾™ The paper used in this publication meets the minimum requirements of American
National Standard for Information Sciences Permanence of Paper for Printed Library
Materials, ANSI/NISO Z39.48-1992.

Printed in the United States of America

Contents

Acknowledgments

This book would not have been possible without the love, patience, faith, and encouragement exhibited by the following people: My wife, Alison Peppers Seese, and our son, Miles Francis (I can't express how much I love you both for carrying me through the small hours of fear and self-doubt); my brother, Andrew Paul (you helped me through one of the darkest times of my life and this book would have been impossible without you—I'll never be able to thank you enough); my fact-checking cuz, Michael Prosser (your eternal unending support and encouragement is and has always been invaluable— thanks for always lending your time and sharp editorial mind); the Seese family, my mother, Danette, and father, Dennis, my brother, Danny, my sister-in-law, Tiffany, and my lovely nieces, Ryann and Charlee (thank you all for picking me up when I was ready to quit and for believing in me when I didn't even believe in myself); my entire DePaulo family; the Perkarciks; Aunt Sharon; Kenny; the Abel Family; the Stank family; the McMinn family; Terry and Gloria Peppers; Keith J. Minnaji; Ryan Vok (for always believing and creating); my wonderful RTL colleagues at American University, particularly my friend Mark Winek (I can't thank you enough for your kindness and willingness to listen); my fantastic colleagues at Georgetown Day School, especially my good friend Aaron Pina (this past summer tied it all together, brother); my colleagues at *Managing Madrid*; and the editors at *In Bed with Maradona* (you all started and gave life to this beast).

Special thanks are reserved for Mr. Derek Liecty. Mr. Liecty, the general manager of the Oakland Clippers, was unbelievably kind and gracious with his time, sharing many insights, memories, and firsthand accounts of the events of the era that were indispensible in making this book come alive.

Finally, I'd like to thank my editor, Christen Karniski, for her endless patience and professionalism throughout this process. I'm so grateful for your insight and all the advice and counsel you've given me. Thank you so much!

Introduction

In *Small Is Beautiful*, E. F. Schumacher made the following observation about capitalism: "Call a thing immoral or ugly, soul-destroying or a degradation to man, a peril to the peace of the world or to the well-being of future generations: as long as you have not shown it to be 'uneconomic' [unprofitable] you have not really questioned its right to exist, grow, and prosper."[1] Most American journalists and tastemakers were already in the habit of depicting soccer as "a degradation to man" and/or "a peril to the well-being of future generations." But nobody had yet definitively proved in the postwar era that it was "uneconomic" or "unprofitable" in the United States, particularly as it flourished in the burgeoning global commercial and mass-media market that titans of American industry were increasingly moving and functioning within.

Thus it was then in the fateful year of 1966, coincidentally a World Cup year, that seed for the relaunch/rebirth of professional soccer in the United States would be sown by a brave and hearty band of wealthy American businessmen, many of whom already had interests and holdings in professional sports. By Schumacher's formula, the success (or failure) of this rebirth would determine whether the sport would have a legitimate chance or "right to exist, grow and prosper" in the United States, truly the game's reluctant, antagonistic final frontier.

To be clear, there were professional leagues in the United States before the mid-'60s, the American Soccer League (ASL) being most prominent among them. Formed in 1921, the ASL enjoyed a modicum of success before the Great Depression essentially wiped the league out of existence by draining money from its wealthy industrial patrons. The ASL averaged crowds of 4,000 to 5,000 spectators, with the Fall River Marksmen of Fall River, Massachusetts, drawing around 12,000. The ASL, though reasonably popular,

1

was concentrated almost exclusively on the East Coast and thus not national in its reach. The ASL operated on and off in many incarnations and iterations after the Depression, never enjoying the success or profile it had enjoyed during those few years before the crash.

If examined underneath the professional level, the game in America has accumulated a history far more rich and colorful than casual fans and armchair historians may realize. From all-conquering factory-based teams such as the Fall River Marksmen and Bethlehem Steel in the early twentieth century to the vast, complex networks of ethnically based amateur and semiprofessional teams that have thrived all over the country for decades in cities such as Chicago, Boston, and St. Louis, soccer has been a significant, if often silent and slippery, part of American cultural history. Those two prominent connections and associations—labor and ethnicity—have, however, conspired to engender an almost subconscious level of mistrust, paranoia, condescension, fear, and outright antagonism toward the game in the minds of many within the American establishment, particularly sports journalists.

Charles Parrish and John Nauright note that these feelings seemed only to increase in intensity after World War II, writing that "during the Cold War soccer faced an ideological barrier"[2] before ultimately being "branded 'un-American'"[3] and irredeemably foreign. According to Parrish and Nauright, these feelings solidified "as a conservative dominant discourse continued through the 1960s and into the 1970s and the idea of American Exceptionalism gained prominence again throughout the 1980s and 1990s, the subversive nature and historical legacy of soccer made it difficult for promoters to gain support"[4] for the game no matter how much they tried.

This introduces an interesting dichotomy of subversion and exclusion that cuts in both directions. Gary Armstrong and James Rosbrook-Thompson noted that soccer became subject to "fears that the game provided relay points through which a dangerous immigrant population would make their presence felt in American society."[5] It can also be argued that as time went on the game provided "relay points" through which women and other marginalized groups could and did "make their presence felt in American society." Conservative establishment forces likely recognized this to be at the core of soccer's "subversive nature and historical legacy," but the game was also viewed as a symbolic force capable of undermining or at least questioning and suggesting a viable alternative to U.S. hegemonic and cultural dominance, thus ironically they marshaled a uniquely American language of subversion against the game as it sought to create a foothold in postwar America. Traces of that language dot this story.

Scholars like Andrei Markovits and Steven Hellerman have written extensively about soccer's popularity in countries with a "large, well-organized, mass based working class movement headed by a political party.[6] " This closely held association is likely another major reason conservative

Americans ascribed a "subversive nature"[7] to the game, if for no other reason than the fact that American sports are stridently de-politicized. Markovits and Hellerman also view soccer's subjugation in America's cultural landscape and socialism's failure to make any lasting inroads into American politics as somewhat interrelated and essentially reverse examples of "American Exceptionalism."[8] Armstrong and Rosbrook-Thompson note that "possibilities for identity formation attached to soccer in the United States have been shaped by historical processes bound up with American exceptionalism"[9] and we see an example of that tense, typically antagonistic interplay when considering Markovits and Hellerman's examples as well as when viewing soccer as a valid cultural counterargument to or critique of American hegemonic dominance.

Soccer's very essence conjures up imagery of the collective in ways that makes comparisons to socialism effortless, making it an easy target for the rhetorical forces and voices of American exceptionalism. For even beloved American team sports like football and baseball were structured in ways to highlight the individual. Soccer's collective imagery carries sinister overtones and clashes fiercely with conceptions and images of individualism and individual freedom closely associated with free market capitalism, pillars that form the core of the American identity narrative.

Seizing on this connection, American journalists and pundits often explicitly and purposely labeled soccer "communist" and "socialist" throughout the Cold War era. The tension between the collective and the individual forms part of the aforementioned "ideological barrier"[10] that barred the game from mainstream acceptance, its intrinsic nature was/is depicted as antithetical to deeply held notions of what it means to be American. The other force at play here (and this dovetails with the issue of "reverse American Exceptionalism"[11] and global cultural hegemony) is that soccer represented a unique affront to powerful American cultural producers.

In Frank Deford's words, this was because soccer's presence in the United States presented a world "upside down, flying in the face of all other evidence, which tells us that in the modern world almost all entertainment tastes—from cowboys to Coca-Cola—have been exported from America, not imported to it."[12] This is a significant factor that surely contributed to the view that many powerful Americans undoubtedly held of soccer's "subversive nature and historical legacy,"[13] its very existence construed as a symbol with enough (soft) power and resonance to challenge rigid yet carefully crafted hegemonic notions of American primacy. The issue of soccer as a successful global soft power import would also represent a level of subversion to conceptions of "American Exceptionalism" and American business. American soft power and cultural exports were dominant, cementing America's preeminent position in the postwar hierarchy. To have soccer succeed in America as a cultural import would set a dangerous precedent, demonstrating to the world that there were still valid forms and symbols of mass culture outside of American hegemony. Soccer could provide a troubling alternative model (particularly since its cultural coding and symbolism was viewed to be so intertwined with socialism), a model that proved America did not have a monopoly on cultural cachet and legitimacy.

Interrogating these same issues of cultural hegemony, identity, and ethnicity, the scholar Michael Oriard has written extensively about American football, its relationship to the press, and its role in constructing and defining the dominant American identity. Oriard wrote that American football was long "an agent of 'Americanization' for immigrant groups but more tenaciously maintained its barriers to racial integration and equality."[14] Just as it represented a vital soft power counterargument against global American commercial and cultural supremacy, soccer also represented a vital inverse to the very need for immigrants, minorities, and other marginalized groups to "Americanize."

Sociologist David Trouille remarked in his survey of soccer's history in Chicago that the game "emerged as a significant vehicle for the construction and maintenance of collective identities"[15] in the city's ethnic communities. It represented a means of subversion to the very idea and necessity of "Americanization" by providing an alternative model of cultural communication, identity construction, and expression that allowed for and necessitated a different conception of what it meant to be "American" while bestowing a level of agency and control on the ethnic communities themselves as they renegotiated their identities.

This ability to help reconstruct identity paradigms was another (perhaps the most important) reason soccer was viewed, in Parrish and Nauright's formulation, as projecting a "subversive nature and historical legacy"[16] into a conservative-dominated discourse. Yet, as we'll see, United Soccer Association (USA), National Professional Soccer League (NPSL), and North American Soccer League (NASL) owners and administrators chased various conceptions of Americanization, often clumsily imposing a narrow, sometimes racialized, form of Americanization on the game to mostly disastrous results that both distorted the game and raised serious questions about what exactly Americanization entailed in the late twentieth century.

A common thread connecting all of the things thought to be intrinsically "subversive" within soccer are these interlocking issues of identity, agency, and access, with the game being unique in its ability to provide a canvas or prism for national and ethnic identity construction that was seized on by actors on both sides of the political divide: those more progressive or liberal forces who tended to support the game and wholeheartedly embrace its lexicon of collectivism and those conservative forces who viewed the game as ideologically incompatible with and antithetical to American values.

This story reveals a demonstrable and calculated pattern of efforts to systematically construct specific ethnic identities in American newspaper coverage of soccer, including the all-important "American" soccer identity, which was ironic, of course, because there were virtually no Americans playing in the NPSL and literally none on show in the USA. Americans (although essentially invisible on the field), Anglo-Saxons, "Latins'" (Italians and Spaniards), and South Americans were all ethnically constructed using a precise, highly controlled vocabulary that simultaneously invented and perpetuated stereotypes (both positive and negative) that solidified into a narrative composed of national or ethnic archetypes that persist to this day.

The negativity associated with specific ethnic identities—South Americans and people of color in general—and the language that codifies and communicates it were used to achieve a variety of purposes in the context of the USA. The language was used to mark soccer and the men who played it as alien and subversive, sabotaging the game outright when possible, controlling it always by dictating the terms and tone with which it was communicated. Consideration will also be given to British identity narratives and whether and to what degree they were imported comfortably along with the teams Great Britain lent to the USA. Many cities assigned their youngest, most inexperienced reporters to the soccer beat, leading some reporters to rely heavily on British vocabularies, signifiers, and their attendant identity narratives. Identity construction was a (and perhaps the most) powerful tool of control as we'll see.

Geoffrey Green of the *Times* of London wrote the following words on the eve of the NPSL's launch:

> All at once wealthy sponsors—already professional sportsmen in other fields—are jingling the almighty dollar. Here is a viable product they feel, and the whole operation is to be tackled as a promotional and merchandising effort on a scale comparable to what—to use their own words—a major automotive or soap company, for example, undertakes when it attempts to "condition" the public to its new product. [17]

This quote cuts to the heart of another major strand of the story, which concerns issues related to the corporate conventional wisdom of the time, a conventional wisdom whose flaws were starting to become apparent in many contexts and which in any case was uniquely unsuited to sell soccer as just another "product." The pervasive and ultimately damaging mind-set that viewed soccer as just another interchangeable product stems from what I've started referring to as the "psychology of standardization."

The psychology of standardization, ingrained after decades of mass production and promotion techniques yielded massive profits and an unchallenged status as the driver of the global economy, compelled successful American businessmen to view soccer as another widget with no intrinsic difference from tires, soap, or anything else trafficked on the modern market. This view allowed many otherwise savvy businessmen to essentially down-play or ignore entirely the need to examine and understand soccer as a unique cultural agent, one that could certainly be commercialized and commodified as a product, but as a product with a powerful, wide-reaching resonance that elevated it far beyond mere objects such as soap and razor blades.

And within this era of mass production and mass commodification there was actually a serious and significant difference between selling razors and soap and authentic pieces of culture like soccer. The psychology of standard-ization is also evident in the strange, baffling decisions made by USA/NPSL owners to award crucial, pivotal leadership positions to men who publicly bragged of their vast soccer ignorance to the press. The historian David Wangerin succinctly summed up these bizarre and quixotic choices in the following manner:

> More significant, though, was the breathtakingly naïve assumption that soccer was merely a commodity whose success in North America required little more than marketing. Too many executives and officials were hired on the basis of their understanding of North American sports rather than for any appreciation of the game, and in many cases, the "marketing" that took place was not particularly sophisticated. [18]

We will see these statements to be true at nearly every level of the following story, particularly with the quality of "marketing," some of which read more like absurdist anti-marketing. Soccer's cultural coding was untranslatable to American businessmen from this era, making marketing difficult in the best of scenarios. What was even more damaging was that most of them were too lazy to even bother deciphering it; such was their "naive" yet unshakable faith in their ability to launch "viable" [19] products, as Green so effectively put it. Part of the reason they couldn't read its coding was because the game spoke a global language of collectivity; it spoke to those in the chaos of the early postcolonial phase, those in the developing world, those within Brit-ain's underclass, and so forth. Ironically, those most sensitive to soccer's cultural charge and coding were the conservative critics who were able to discern right away (unlike the men who actually wanted to promote it) the game's "subversive nature."

Further compounding this already serious problem was the fact that USA and NPSL owners initially set their sights on ethnic or "hyphenated Americans" as their primary consumers. Yet the owners did not seem to possess the language or acumen to reach these specific consumers, as they were not part of the coveted white suburban demographic that most products were then still marketed to. In other words, the would-be American consu-mers of the game also existed outside of the mainstream channels of power, and not much consideration was given to fine-tuning extant marketing language or, more importantly, to devising language specific to their values and sensibilities. It was the perfect storm of misshapen language and broken codes.

Taken to its logical extreme, this pervasive psychology of standardization that viewed everything as a product and every product as interchangeable culminated in the selling/marketing of the Vietnam War, which raged on not so silently in the background during the launch of the USA/NPSL. To elaborate on this point, around the time his film *Full Metal Jacket* was released, Stanley Kubrick said the following in an interview with Penelope Gilliat: "Vietnam was probably the first war that was run—at least during the Kennedy era—as an ad agency might run it."[20] To make the connection even more explicit, Thomas Allen Nelson remarked that *Full Metal Jacket* was, at least in part, Kubrick and famous Vietnam chronicler Michael Herr's commentary on and satire of "America's 'corporate faith' in a war that could be won if it was handled as if it were just another ad campaign."[21]

Note the striking similarities in the language and psychology behind those quotes with Geoffrey Green's observation that the whole USA/NPSL "operation is to be tackled as a promotional and merchandising effort on a scale comparable to what—to use their own words—a major automotive or soap company, for example, undertakes when it attempts to 'condition' the public to its new product."[22] This is evidence of the psychology of standardization at its most deadly, dehumanizing form, where everything from war to global sports had become conflated in the corporate American mind by zealous adherents to a "corporate faith"[23] readily identified in both these drastically different yet simultaneously occurring quotes and contexts. The ultimate irony and fulfillment of this particular strain of thought came, of course, when the USA's Detroit franchise, backed by the Ford automotive empire, was dubbed the "Cougars" in homage to one of Ford's newest models. The New York Generals, too, would become a rather naked, artless advertisement for their owners, RKO General.

To be clear, I'm not comparing the sad, catastrophic carnage of the Vietnam War to the launch of the USA/NPSL. I'm merely trying to emphasize the striking similarities in the language used to sell and describe each endeavor and what that says about the dominant psychology of American power at this time, wherein both Vietnam and professional soccer were viewed (in some corners) as products virtually indistinguishable from tires or soap and could be merchandised accordingly. There was an effective, standardized template for advertising and marketing that had thus far not really failed in any meaningful way in the postwar era. These "products" were simply inserted into the template and rolled out like next year's Cougar. The impact of this overriding "corporate faith" (and its relation to the psychology of standardization) on the marketing and constitution of the USA/NPSL/NASL will be readily apparent.

Finally, nearly all of these theoretical and conceptual concerns are predicated on language. Language is central to this story on multiple levels, particularly within the varied and subtle ways it was used to construct and control not only the USA and NPSL as enterprises, but also individual teams and players as well. While discussing Tom Buchanan in his analysis of baseball's role in the *Great Gatsby*, Robert Johnson Jr. characterizes Buchanan "as a paradigm of the power structure"[24] and that "like a baseball owner or a business leader, Tom's racism will barely register in public." Johnson then chillingly observes that modern expressions of colonialism and racism "will be less about scuffles and name-calling than it will be about *subversive language and denied opportunities.*"[25]

Within this observation, Johnson Jr. articulates what will become a critical fulcrum of this book and "subversive language" will henceforth be analyzed as a tactic used to negate, subvert, and otherwise deny opportunities. Subversive language is designed to exclude and deny opportunities in contexts as disparate as those relating to the systemic, long-simmering socioeconomic problems in Newark and Detroit that erupted into violent civil disobedience in 1967 and the denial of the USA/NPSL's opportunity to sell their product neutrally due to what it represented and to whom it was ultimately designed to reach. It was used in both contexts to exclude African Americans, Italian Americans, South Americans, Catholics, women, and others from assuming a place in the dominant American societal structure. It was also used to further exclude and control these groups by constructing their identities on negative terms.

When I first started writing about this era, I was struck by and overcome with a sense of mystery and wonder. Actually trying to picture Gordon Banks making saves on the shores of Lake Erie for the Cleveland Stokers or Cagliari grinding down opponents with a calculated dose of Comiskey Park *catenaccio* seemed impossible, otherworldly, as if it occurred in some sepia-toned parallel universe instead of a convulsive America wracked with upheaval. It is my hope that this sense of wonder still permeates the pages of this book. I've often heard writers say that they don't know how their stories, songs, poems, or research will end once they begin. This uncertainty definitely occurred during the course of researching and writing this book. The interlocking theoretical and conceptual concerns outlined in the preceding paragraphs became so glaring, so frustrating, yet so fascinating that they began to overshadow some of the wonder and mystery I had initially felt.

I believe that these concerns offer a level of context that is indispensable and essential to properly understanding the era the USA and NPSL existed in and are inextricably linked to a faithful re-creation of their story and history. Having written that, I still hope and believe that there is enough talk of tactics, aging soccer legends, obscure teams from Dublin, Uruguay, Washington, D.C., and beyond to impart a semblance of the wonder I felt when I began thinking and writing of this era. I also feel that the overriding sociological concerns that are discussed here are all still relevant today. Even though the soccer landscape in the United States has changed drastically in the last two decades, many if not all of the currents, conversations, and concerns stirred up by the birth of the USA and NPSL are still being argued, reshaped, and renegotiated. Perhaps examining their origins will make us all understand the present with a little more clarity in hopes of building a more equitable future.

Chapter One

Risky Business

The year 1967 was a strange and tumultuous one in the United States. Cultural and political upheaval and generational realignments were galvanizing the nation in this most strange and troubled of decades. The *San Francisco Oracle*, an underground newspaper emblematic of the changing times, labeled the summer of 1967 the "Summer of Love" as a way to describe the warm and fuzzy psychotropic cultural explosion happening in California, even though, paradoxically, ugly race riots and acts of civil disobedience were simultaneously taking place in large urban cities like Detroit and Newark, in what was the culmination of a terrifying, convulsive period of civil rights struggle known as the "Long Hot Summer."

Vietnam hovered above everything like a specter in the night and poured through uneasy silences and cracks in the pavement with its sorrowful white noise of screams, sirens, and agony. "Strange Days" had indeed found us, as Jim Morrison would croon that same fateful year. Something else strange and tumultuous happened that summer as American sports entrepreneurial heavyweights Lamar Hunt, Jack Kent Cooke, and others undertook one of the latest attempts to reintroduce and import (literally) soccer into a roiling, reeling America. This is a look at that story. It's an attempt to understand why the narrative developed as it did. But above all else it's an attempt to recover this largely obscure and hidden chapter of America's sports history because its echoes still do reverberate to this very day.

PART 1: THE WORLD CUP NARRATIVE AND THE INFLUENCE OF THE INTERNATIONAL SOCCER LEAGUE

The World Cup final between England and West Germany on July 30, 1966, registered surprisingly strong television ratings in America, with *Sports Illus-*

trated reporting that NBC's broadcast of England's dramatic extra-time Wembley triumph garnered an estimated ten million stateside viewers.[1] The overwhelming reaction to this emotional, one-of-a-kind match prompted National Football League (NFL) and Major League Baseball (MLB) owners like Hunt, Kent Cooke, and Roy Hofheinz to pounce on the opportunity to establish a mass-marketed, aggressively promoted American professional soccer league that for the first time would be truly national in its scope. At least that's how the conventional narrative goes. But there is definitive evidence within the historical record showing that the wheels to form a professional soccer league in America were already well in motion months before Wembley held the world in rapt attention.

The initial impetus and rumblings for what would eventually develop into a "soccer war" between two dueling start-up American professional leagues in the summer of 1967 can be traced to March 20, 1966, a full four months before the 1966 World Cup finals, according to the *Washington Post*. Federation Internationale de Football Association's (FIFA) annual meeting took place at the Waldorf-Astoria in New York City and that was when *three* different groups of American sports moguls and assorted corporate heavyweights expressed interest in "establishing a major league on this continent."[2]

Soccer historian David Wangerin remarked that this new interest in soccer was spurred because "there were only so many established sports to go around, and the sudden rush to make money as a big league owner—or at the very least reduce tax liabilities—soon required aspirants to think in broader terms."[3] American sports owners were entering a golden age of prosperity, and they were zealously committed to extending the horizons of that prosperity as far as possible. There is no more perfect example of this than Canadian media-sports tycoon Jack Kent Cooke. Kent Cooke sold encyclopedias door to door before managing a radio station in Ontario. He eventually partnered with Roy Thomson, and before they were through operating and acquiring radio stations Thomson would be known as 1st Baron Thomson of Fleet Street. By 1966, Thomson's empire included the influential *Times* of London. Kent Cooke decided that owning sports franchises was his true passion after moving to the United States in 1960.

Kent Cooke emerges as the most active, significant early catalyst for what would become the United Soccer Association (USA), even though he demurely told the *Post* "he would not be particularly active in the venture, 'except to supply aid and comfort in the form of money.'"[4] The brash "sports empire builder" was on top of the world, owning a share of the Washington Redskins as well as owning the Los Angeles Lakers and the National Hockey League's brand-new Los Angeles Kings (not to mention the gleaming new building both teams would play in: the LA Forum), and he envisioned "a bright future for soccer" in America, particularly on television.

The symbiotic relationship between the increasingly lucrative power of television and successful West Coast expansion then being enjoyed by all of the major American spectator sports is one of the primary reasons Dave Brady's reporting on this fateful FIFA meeting is absolutely riddled with the names of American sporting royalty: the Rooneys (NFL), the Bidwells (NFL), the Allyns (MLB), and others, but it is perhaps more notable for who is omitted: Lamar Hunt and William D. "Bill" Cox.

Hunt, the owner of the Kansas City Chiefs and son of oil baron H. L. Hunt, had been instrumental in negotiating the then-impending merger of the underdog American Football League and the NFL and would soon become one of the most pivotal and important figures in the history of American soccer. Hunt's absence in this early account is surprising, but the omission of Bill Cox's name is shocking, particularly because his International Soccer League (ISL) is mentioned prominently by Brady, who writes that "until now the International Soccer League has presented the best attractions."[5]

Brady goes on to note that in 1964 the ISL "cracked the million mark in attendance for the first time," a significant milestone for a sport considered peripheral at best to many Americans. It would be more modest metrics such as this that began to catch the attention of the ravenous sports moguls as they sought to corner an ever-increasing share of the American leisure dollar prior to the 1966 World Cup. Cox's formation of the ISL was unquestionably the most important and influential development in American soccer since the end of World War II. So it is interesting to note that he is omitted by name from this account while his ISL accomplishments are lauded in glowing terms.

The curious case of Bill Cox intersects with so many of the following narrative's historical and conceptual concerns. He represents a figure on the shadowy edges of American power who seems to have made considerable enemies within the mainstream establishment. He was a Yale man of wealth and means who for some reason was unable to access the same levers and levels of power as his immediate social contemporaries. An inveterate dabbler, Cox initially accumulated his fortune by dealing in antiques and then through the timber industry in Oregon.

Perhaps this disconnect stemmed from Cox's ability to use his voice "to pass along—in strictest confidence—tales of stupefying chicanery in high places, face to face confrontations with the movers and shakers of the world,"[6] which placed him outside the circle of reverence typically reserved for people of his wealth in the newspaper chronicles of the day. Oakland Clippers general manager Derek Liecty, who'd worked closely with Cox during the 1961–1962 ISL seasons, described him as "very much a loner" and as "very driven. Once he got his mind set on doing something he was totally driven . . . the more antagonistic the other people got, the more fiery he got."[7]

Perhaps it was that "fiery" unwillingness to conform to the standard rules and strictures of his social class that made him feared, distrusted, and ultimately someone to be viewed as an enemy. It is extremely likely that this intrinsic "fieriness" fueled his clashes with organized baseball's old boy network led by commissioner Judge Kenesaw Mountain Landis, the United States Soccer Football Association (USSFA), and others during his journey up the river through American professional sports ownership's heart of darkness.

Years before starting the ISL, Cox, "a glib and convincing non-stop talker with the promotional instincts of a carnival barker,"[8] purchased the Philadelphia Phillies for $80,000 in 1943. In hindsight, he was almost comically ill suited to fit among the staid, regressive cadre of MLB owners. His tenure was perhaps predictably short-lived. Cox belligerently fired beloved Phillies manager Bucky Harris in July of that year through the press, ironically. This move earned him the fierce enmity of influential sportswriters of the day like Shirley Povich, who loved Harris and spent days trashing the Phillies owner in the pages of the *Washington Post*. But it was Harris himself who would prove a stubborn enemy.

According to *Sports Illustrated*, friends of the vanquished Harris began "saying that Cox bet daily on baseball games with his bookmaker."[9] Baseball historian Jerome Holtzman wrote that it was Harris himself who—after holding court with reporters at the Benjamin Franklin Hotel and famously calling Cox an "all-American jerk"—waited until the newspaper men were about to leave before saying, "He's a fine guy to fire me, when he gambles on games his club plays." Fittingly, Landis was alerted to Harris' comments "through a letter written to him by the sports editor of a Philadelphia newspaper."[10]

These off-the-record allegations were made after two earlier meetings with Landis, where Cox's ties to horse racing were discussed, with Landis giving him stern warnings to avoid associations with the track in particular and gambling in general. Ultimately, Cox was called before Landis once again to address Harris' accusations and after a few initial denials admitted his guilt, "citing ignorance of the rule as his only justification."[11]

As a result of this admission, Landis declared Cox "permanently ineligible" to hold any office in the Major Leagues, essentially banning him from the sport forever. Years after this, Cox rather implausibly told *Sports Illustrated*, "I never placed a bet of any sort on baseball games"[12] and that he figured his confession "would smoke out the person who had really done the betting, using our office phone." Cox also maintained that reporters as well as Landis' own office never could "find any evidence that I bet." Cox imagined that Landis felt "he had no alternative but to penalize me" after his confession.

This certainly made him a marked man in the eyes of most sportswriters of the era, men who grew up holding the sanctity of baseball in their hearts with an iron grasp. To drive home both the exceedingly close relationship between sportswriters and organized baseball, as well as the state of open antagonism that existed between these reporters and the deposed Cox, Landis "in a rare move"[13] opened his appeal hearing to the press.

Whether for all or none of these reasons, Cox, when actually mentioned, is nearly always depicted in a suspicious, sinister, or downright savage fashion in the newspaper-centric narrative of American sports history. Indeed, after his passing in 1989, his *New York Times* obituary opens with a reference to his banishment from baseball, with details of the then–forty-six-year-old incident consuming a surprising amount of space.[14] His long, fascinating life as an art dealer, successful entrepreneur, stamp producer/collector, and supplier of lumber that reinforced the Panama Canal during World War II is largely reduced and literally relegated to the margins at the overriding expense of the time that he abruptly dismissed a baseball manager.

In the end, Cox's entire existence was literally defined by his banishment from baseball thanks to his friends in the newspaper business. His omission from Brady's account is likely another small example of this bitter relationship. But Cox's influence on the rebirth of American soccer as the founder of the ISL is incalculable. "In my mind, he is the father of modern soccer in the United States as we know it today, and almost nobody knows this,"[15] according to Liecty.

Trying to understand why "nobody knows this" dovetails with the powerful discursive relationship that exists between soccer and baseball in the American consciousness and the central role that newspapers often play within it. For now Cox's role in creating the ISL and in the convoluted formation of the National Professional Soccer League (NPSL) is the primary focus.

Wangerin also highlights the importance of commercial airline travel as a reason why more American entrepreneurs increasingly began turning their attention to soccer. Wangerin wrote that "the development of jet travel and the creeping influence of television meant that the game's worldwide popularity had never been so apparent."[16] In an increasingly interconnected and globalized economy, Wangerin wrote that "it is not difficult to imagine an American executive in Rome or Buenos Aires switching on the television in his hotel suite and marveling at the enormous crowds."

Cox represented an actual flesh-and-blood embodiment of Wangerin's hypothetical "American executive," becoming a devoted soccer fan in the late '50s while trekking through Europe, tending to his mineral and oil concerns. Cox told Arthur Daley in 1960 that he was present at matches in London, Madrid, and Rio, where attendances had exceeded well over 100,000 and that he'd never been able to understand "why soccer hasn't caught on"[17] in America. This question inspired him to create the ISL and what he hoped would be a definitive answer and antidote to the overwhelming apathy of many American sports fans. Cox was so optimistic regarding the ISL's prospects that he boisterously proclaimed to Daley, "It can't miss."

The flip side of increased reliance on jet travel for business was that it also facilitated easy access to American dollars for famous European teams willing to fly over and tour the states during the summer. These tours had been occurring with evermore frequency since Liverpool's famous American tour in 1948, with the late '50s and early '60s seeing stateside visits from Manchester United, Celtic, Red Star Belgrade, and Napoli, among many others. Thus the method and magic of the ISL was born. Cox invited first division teams to fly to the United States and play a tournament in New York during the summer.

In what may have been a subtle tweak to Major League Baseball, Cox, a proud New Yorker, said he started "to toy with the idea after the Giants and Dodgers walked out on us and left a gap."[18] *Pitch Invasion*'s Tom Dunmore observed that in 1960 the "New York Metropolitan area's 16 million inhabitants had fewer options to spend their sporting dollar on than they would at any point later in the twentieth century."[19] It was a strange anomaly that such options would decrease in America's most bustling and glamorous city while increasing virtually everywhere else. Dunmore estimates the ISL's start-up costs to equal around two million dollars in today's money.

Cox, like many before and after him, thought that Americans were indifferent to soccer because they hadn't seen it played at its highest levels like those who flocked to matches in London, Madrid, and Rio. This strand of thinking—that an elevated quality of play was paramount (and in some extremes the only necessary component) in helping the game conquer America—would guide the decision making of Cox and others involved in the launch of the USA/NPSL. It would also eventually constitute one side of a philosophical divide between owners and promoters singularly obsessed with quality of play and those more concerned with establishing local fan identification and eventual full-blown "Americanization" of the game.

To emphasize the level of fanfare the ISL initially received, New York City Mayor Robert Wagner was on hand at city hall to officially announce the league's creation on October 28, 1959. The tournament would be divided into two sections with the winner of each section playing in the finals to decide the championship. The mayor was such an ISL booster that he donated a cup for the championship match. The ISL kept this basic format throughout its existence. Wagner stated, "Many of our citizens in the city are foreign born. They are all fond of soccer and they have instilled that fondness in their children. This new league will give us a chance to see the greatest players in the game competing against a New York team. The city will cooperate in every possible way to help this league succeed."[20]

Mayor Wagner's statement introduces issues of ethnicity into the narrative, as foreign-born, second-generation, so-called hyphenated Americans would loom large in the narrative construction of American soccer and as agents actually shaping the failures and successes of the game's relaunch in real time. The creation of a New York team was also an important acknowledgment of and concession to the need for the ISL to establish some form of local connection. It too would intersect with vexing issues of identity and identification. In what would be a recurring pattern in 1967 and beyond, the ISL's New York team, dubbed the "New York Americans," would ironically contain not a single native-born American. This tangled knot of dissonant identity reappears throughout the story and would remain problematic into the 1970s.

The New York Americans, coached in 1960 by Al Stubbins, a former Liverpool forward, would mix it up in section one with teams such as the legendary Bayern Munich, Scotland's Kilmarnock, and the reigning English First Division champions Burnley. The Americans were likely envisioned as a bridge for the ISL to ultimately transform into a legitimate American top-flight team. The team evolved into simply being called the "New Yorkers" and was stocked primarily with key players from New York's semiprofessional German American Soccer League. The New Yorkers would go on to score an extremely impressive victory over 1964 Football Association Challenge Cup winners West Ham en route to the ISL finals in 1965 before losing 5–1 on aggregate to Poland's Polonia Bytom.

After initially splitting ISL matches between the Polo Grounds in Manhattan and Roosevelt Stadium in Jersey City, Cox decided to rely specifically on the Polo Grounds, as attendance in Jersey were markedly lower. This became problematic when in 1961 the city of New York announced plans to demolish the dilapidated Polo Grounds, effectively rendering the ISL homeless. The difficulty securing proper, adequate venues to stage soccer matches would set a precedent that plagued American soccer into the '90s.

Perhaps following the mayor's lead, the ISL's media coverage was largely positive in its inaugural season, and the tournament even garnered a modicum of local and national television exposure. However, as the ISL's second section got underway, outbreaks of violence began to occur in what would be another ominous harbinger of things to come. According to Dunmore, eruptions of violence left Rune Lind, the goalkeeper for the Swedish side Norrkoping, "unconscious and with a broken tooth"[21] during a match with Sampdoria.

After a hard tackle in the box, "20 irate Italian fans ran onto the field and attacked the Swedish team."[22] Some, including the person who assaulted Lind, were brandishing sticks. Dunmore remarked that "amazingly, no arrests were made." It's eerie how the basic contours of this incident would repeat themselves during an almost identical incident in Yankee Stadium in 1967: a bad foul, an Italian team, enraged fans, violence, and astonishingly lax security. More trouble occurred when Sampdoria played Rapid Vienna and fans reportedly assaulted an official, marring what was by all accounts a riveting match that Sampdoria ultimately won 3–2.

The finals of the first ISL tournament in 1960 featured Kilmarnock (winners of section one) against Bangu from Rio (champions of section two) in a match that drew 25,440 fans to the Polo Grounds in addition to being broadcast on network television. It was an amazing crowd at that time in America's soccer development and it was rewarded with a thrilling, tense Bangu victory in "what was probably the best match played in the United States in a many a year,"[23] according to the *New York Times*. Both of these teams would reappear as characters in the USA, NPSL, and North American Soccer League (NASL) narrative. The ISL had made a small profit and looked to expand. Derek Liecty revealed what the atmosphere was like in the early years of the ISL, saying "we did everything. Arranging the hotels, arranging the buses, arranging the stadiums, arranging the field, getting the referees . . . dealing with USSFA, dealing with the press . . . getting these teams visas to get into the states in the first place. It was fascinating. It was wonderful."[24]

Cox continued growing and seeking more prestigious teams for inclusion in the ISL, even expanding into Chicago and Los Angeles in 1964 after an initial push into Montreal fizzled. The ISL, relatively solvent, seemed on the precipice of transformation. It was around this time, however, that perhaps the most crucial precedent of all was established and the ISL's demise was precipitated by a clash between Cox and the USSFA. The two had coexisted uneasily since ISL's inception, but USSFA grew increasingly weary of the ISL's growing presence as it had become utterly dependent on the revenue generated from scheduling exhibitions and friendlies. The ISL was now essentially dominating that market, siphoning all the crucial revenue. A confrontation was inevitable.

To provide a sense of how microscopic soccer was in the mid-'60s American consciousness, Zander Hollander's *The American Encyclopedia of Soccer* noted that the USSFA had a staff consisting of just two members: president Frank Woods and executive director Joseph Barriskill, while *Sports Illustrated* estimated the organization's entire operating budget to be $75,000 or less annually.[25] The tiny but aggressive organization increasingly viewed Cox as an outsider and feared his growing influence. Steve Holroyd aptly characterized the relationship between the two as "stormy" due to USSFA being overly suspicious "of an outsider like Cox" and his unwillingness "to take orders from individuals he knew were simply not businessmen."[26]

The fiery, headstrong Cox faced the monumental "challenge of working within the existing soccer infrastructure"[27] in America. Even if Cox were a less difficult, less abrasive personality, the contours of the conflict would likely have retained a similar shape, as the USSFA was a myopic organization mired in cronyism and ineptitude. Its shortsightedness was evidenced by its silly, stubborn view of Cox as an "outsider" intruding on its personal fiefdom rather than as a savvy businessman actively rebuilding the game in America. This sense of territoriality had guided USSFA's decision making at various points through the twentieth century, serving to hamstring the development of the very game it was charged with protecting and promoting. Still, it was the official imprimatur of soccer in the United States and a member of FIFA, vested with all the power that conferred.

The ISL would fold in 1965 after the USSFA forbade it to import any teams for that year's tournament. The organization threatened to label ISL an "outlaw league," language that served as a chilling precursor to what would soon occur. Foreign friendlies remained lucrative and the USSFA was never shy about wielding and withholding its power to authorize such matches when it suited its aims. The ability to designate entities as "outlaws" would loom large, as would the antitrust lawsuit Cox lodged against the group in the wake of the ISL's dissolution.

In all, the ISL was monumental within the postwar development of American professional soccer. Its immense influence was discernible in virtually everything that happened afterward, including the practice of importing foreign teams, stadium issues, often-problematic concepts of ethnicity and identity, disturbing flashes of violence, and, of course, the appearance of Bill Cox locked in perpetual conflict with a vengeful USSFA determined to perpetuate and solidify its power. Particularly since it would be USSFA that ultimately decided who would have official sanction to operate a professional soccer league.

The next major step taken in the reformation of American professional soccer occurred on May 10, 1966, when Cox, undaunted by the ISL's demise, convened a meeting at the Biltmore Hotel in New York, wherein he invited forty prominent people to lunch. These were "men of substance, the owners of baseball and football teams and other wealthy sports promoters."[28] After this fateful meeting a press conference was convened at the New York Athletic Club on May 11, 1966, and Robert Hermann of St. Louis emerged as the president of a sparkling new soccer venture to officially announce the formation of an eleven-team league that would become the NPSL.

Hermann provided another interesting yet more conventional portrait of American power, as he was the chairman of the Standard Container Corporation and the son-in-law of Augustus A. Busch. Saint Louis University's soccer stadium now bears Hermann's name. It is no surprise that powerful interests based in St. Louis would play a pivotal role in resuscitating professional soccer in America, being that St. Louis was one of the preeminent soccer cities through the 1960s in the United States. At this point, Cox is billed simply as a "spokesman"[29] and is later mentioned as being "among the owners of the New York franchise in the new league." He would soon take center stage.

Dean McGowen of the *New York Times* wrote that the "North American Professional Soccer League, if it receives sanction from the United States Soccer Football Association, will begin competition in the fall of 1967."[30] Even with the benefit of hindsight, the word "if" seems to leap ominously off the page. Sending out precarious announcements contingent on the approval of external forces such as USSFA and FIFA would become a hallmark of the NPSL and later the NASL, a nervous tic that would severely damage the league, signaling impetuousness and incompetence.

This is the only time the name "North American Professional Soccer League" appears on record, and it has led some to speculate (due to its similarity with the North American Soccer League's name, which was initially adopted by Kent Cooke's group) that perhaps the breach between Kent Cooke's syndicate and those constituting NPSL was not yet final. Details on that point are murky, but it seems by this point that they were likely separate. No records exist detailing exactly who was among the forty "men of substance" invited to lunch that day by Cox.

Fueled by fresh, specific animosity toward USSFA for derailing the ISL and a seemingly innate need to test boundaries, what happened next was critical. Cox boasted to the *Times* of the nascent league's "tentative approval of its operation from the Federation Internationale de Football Association (FIFA), the governing body of international soccer." Cox then openly acknowledged that the group "simply decided to take the bull by the horns and make our announcement now (prior to approval of the USSFA.)"[31]

The bold idea to force the USSFA's hand was underpinned by the fact that "several of our club owners flew to England last week for a personal meeting with Sir Stanley Rous of FIFA" and that "we have his blessing." Their explicit hope was that if FIFA approved the league "over the objection of USSFA, it would be a blow to the prestige of the governing body of the game in the United States."[32] This statement confirmed the level of personal animus between Cox and USSFA, and one must wonder if he let that animus override his business acumen in deciding to take "the bull by the horns." However, Cox had definitely established a working relationship with Sir Stanley, dating back to the formation of the ISL in 1960, and would not have been off base assuming that the group did have his blessing. It was an aggressive gamble.

The time line and status of the third syndicate remain somewhat murky. It was headed by Richard H. Millen, a lawyer from Los Angeles who had been affiliated with the amateur National Soccer League (which one is unclear, as there were several organizations operating under that name in Chicago, New York, and Canada). Who else was involved has been difficult to establish, but according to virtually all accounts, Millen's group was seeking USSFA's sanction along with groups headed by Cox and Kent Cooke. Amazingly, USSFA now had more wealthy suitors than full-time staff.

Frank Woods appointed a three-man committee to review the proposals, and James P. McGuire was one of those chosen to serve on it. McGuire was a craggy, abrasive fixture within the tiny American soccer firmament. McGuire immigrated to the United States from Scotland in 1926 and had played professionally for Northampton in England in addition to a stint with the Brooklyn Wanderers. McGuire served as the president of the American Soccer League and USSFA prior to 1954, when he began working directly with FIFA as an executive manager.[33]

The USSFA asked the groups seeking sanction to "present a brochure detailing what it would do to advance soccer in America,"[34] which they would consider before making their final decision, which would be handed down during their annual meeting on June 25 in San Francisco. Holroyd brilliantly summed up the atmosphere engulfing the USSFA at this time, writing:

> Somewhat dazed by the attention, the USSFA officials politely listened to the ambitious plans presented by people they had previously only read about. When all the talking was over, the USSFA offered a simple solution: all three groups should merge to form one league. Each of the delegations, in turn, informed the USSFA that a merger was simply out of the question.[35]

With a merger out of the question, USSFA sought the counsel of Rous' FIFA, who suggested that they "sanction individual clubs according to their merits," rather than en masse.[36] Rous' advice was later corroborated by Brian Glanville, who quoted him as advising USSFA to "forget the groups,"[37] while strenuously advocating for a merger that obviously would be in everyone's best interest. USSFA would ultimately not heed FIFA's advice. It was also around this time that all three groups started encouraging speculation (whether true or not) that they were seconds away from inking lucrative television deals.

While the USSFA was mulling over the competing proposals, the Cox/ Hermann outfit continued making power moves. Associated Press (AP) reports emerged on June 17, 1966, a week before USSFA's convention and more than a month before the World Cup finals, wherein the "acting league president" of the newly christened National Professional Soccer League, Richard H. Millen, officially unveiled the ten-team league. Millen grandiosely declared that "professional soccer in America is on the verge of a new era"[38] before acknowledging that the NPSL was expecting a decision regarding official sanction "to be forthcoming at the USSFA annual convention June 25–26 in San Francisco." It was an unsubtle attempt to increase public pressure on USSFA to choose wisely.

Undaunted, Millen confidently emphasized that "our membership represents the strongest combination of soccer experience, financial resources and sports promotional success ever assembled to promote soccer on a major professional level in this country." The league announced plans to start play the following April despite having no players or coaches.

League cities at this juncture were New York, Pittsburgh, St. Louis, Minnesota, Philadelphia, Chicago, Los Angeles, Toronto, and Vancouver. All would eventually field NPSL teams, with the exception of Minnesota and Vancouver. Millen's appearance in these press releases is confusing because it seems to indicate that his group had merged with Cox and Hermann's before the USSFA convention, whereas many historians, including Holroyd and Wangerin, indicate that the two groups joined forces afterward.

Indeed, a United Press International (UPI) report on August 9 confirms this, as well, announcing "the merger of two American soccer groups into a new organization called the National Professional Soccer League."[39] The report confirms that "the two groups had originally sought recognition separately" from USSFA. This stands as an example of how fluid the situation and the actors themselves truly were at this stage. It also demonstrates that the ability to merge was not out of the question, after all, at least for some of these rigidly powerful men.

Whether in reaction to the NPSL's provocation or, as Holroyd puts it, they "suddenly got hip to big business,"[40] it was around this time that USSFA decided to demand a $25,000 franchise fee, in addition to 10 percent of the sanctioned league's television revenue and 4 percent of their gates. To put these stipulations in perspective, the American Soccer League (ASL) was at that time paying USSFA an annual fee of $25 for its license to operate.[41] In perpetuating the overarching narrative that the 1966 World Cup finals sparked the leagues into existence, some writers incorrectly attribute the strong ratings garnered by NBC for the World Cup final as the primary impetus behind USSFA's decision to demand such figures. But the record clearly demonstrates that USSFA's conditions were set forth well before the final on July 30.

Despite their considerable collective wealth, the men behind the NPSL balked predictably at these demands, viewing them as a form of blackmail. The NPSL rejected them outright and as a result, the official sanction went to Jack Kent Cooke's consortium, which had no such qualms about outlaying the funds. The freshly sanctioned group officially became recognized and known publicly as the North American Soccer League. There are some like Holroyd who believe that Kent Cooke's group would have been awarded the sanction regardless, while others pointed to McGuire's dizzying elevation from USSFA's proposal committee to the presidency of the NASL within the blink of an eye as evidence of collusion. McGuire's maneuver was ultimately cited in the NPSL's lawsuit against USSFA and NASL.[42]

It's also very likely that personal animus between Bill Cox and USSFA, exacerbated by the NPSL's blatant attempts to force USSFA's hand, played into the decision irrespective of any alleged arrangement between the NASL and USSFA. This animus now clearly flowed in both directions. NPSL vice president Charles Houghton (also from St. Louis) emphatically stated that "we didn't feel that any organization had the right to give an exclusive franchise to any one soccer league."[43] Houghton warned that the NPSL had "appealed to FIFA," asking them "to examine the conditions under which soccer was being run over here. It's not compatible with our way of life. We feel that they've got to clean house."[44]

This language demonstrated clearly that the tone had changed. It also carried a vaguely palpable threat that would culminate in litigation between the two groups, à la USSFA and the ISL. To make this parallel complete, NPSL was now an "outlaw league." Wangerin brilliantly summed up this tension: "Were the millionaires merely piqued that they couldn't control the games as they liked? Or was the USSFA irritated by the forthright approach of individuals with far greater resources than their own?"[45]

Houghton was certainly not the first person to publicly question "the conditions under which soccer is being run over here" nor was he the first to feel that USSFA was long overdue for a housecleaning—but the fact remained that they were FIFA's official representatives in the United States. This structural relationship alone, wherein an international body tightly controlled a sport through national associations, would frustrate headstrong American businessmen not used to such convoluted and restrictive authority. The whole concept was foreign, metaphorically and literally, prompting the use of charged and interesting language such as Houghton's contention that "it's not compatible with our way of life."

After snidely commenting on the amount of money the NPSL was spending as it prepared to launch, Frank Woods couldn't resist gloating that the group could have used its resources "a little more wisely if they had agreed to our requests."[46] Woods affirmed that "FIFA strongly recommended that the leagues get together," placing blame for the failure to do so squarely on the NPSL, saying "they absolutely refused." The tone of Woods' comments lends credence to Wangerin's assertion that USSFA "had placed itself squarely behind the NASL." Woods was adamant that the money was not the only reason the NASL consortium won the day, telling the *Baltimore Sun* "most of the people in that league had a better background in professional sports."[47] Woods insisted that the requested money "is all earmarked for junior soccer, little leagues and clinics" so that "a base of fans and native-born players for the new league"[48] could be developed. The issue of "Americanization" obviously weighed on the minds of all involved from the outset.

Of course, the men behind the NASL weren't particularly enamored with these fees, either. Washington Whips general manager Jerry Cooper told the *Sun* that the USSFA "had no right charging each of the USA clubs a $25,000 fee just for the right to be sanctioned."[49] Cooper went on to assert that the league "had full veto power" over "how the money is spent," a somewhat astonishing claim. However, Chicago owner John Allyn sighed to *Sports Illustrated* that at least the "$25,000 fee is going back into soccer,"[50] which corroborates Woods' original comment.

So there were now officially two professional soccer leagues gearing up for war, although at this point in the story the NASL was still planning to begin operations in 1968, while the NPSL was steadfast in their determination to begin in April 1967. The term "soccer war" would slowly begin to enter the narrative being constructed around the two competitors. Amazingly, though, it seems that virtually nothing that happened during the late '60s—no matter how extraordinary—was actually unprecedented in American soccer history, as the riots, the foreign imports, and even a bona fide "soccer war" had indeed occurred before—way back in 1929.

As per usual, the United States Football Association (at the time known simply as USFA) was right at the center of it. According to David Litterer, the conflict stemmed from " the objections of the American Soccer League to the playing of U.S. Open Cup (National Challenge Cup) games during the league season."[51] The ASL was worried about the disruption of its schedule, the toll extra matches exacted on the players, as well as the "confusion" that cup matches sowed among its fans. But as Litterer notes, the "real underlying struggle was centered around who would be the controlling organization of soccer in the United States." And here distant echoes can be heard of what would again play out in America years later when USSFA feared that Bill Cox (via the ISL) was gaining too much influence over soccer.

The two entities had previously clashed a few years before when the ASL pulled its teams from the U.S. Open Cup and was subsequently suspended by the USFA. This time, however, as Litterer recalls, "when the League refused to allow its teams to enter the Cup competition, three teams, Bethlehem Steel, Newark Skeeters and the New York Giants defied the league and entered anyway." The ASL quickly suspended the three defiant squads. The teams then lodged an appeal with USFA, who duly threatened the ASL.

The ASL ignored the threats and, as a result, the entire league was suspended. "The ASL, unfazed, began the 1928–29 season as an outlaw league, minus the three suspended teams," according to Litterer. Sound familiar? In retaliation the USFA eagerly lent its assistance and support to the formation of the Eastern Soccer League, "which took in the three renegade ASL teams and several teams from the Southern New York Soccer Association." This, of course, led to the eerily familiar refrain of two rival leagues competing, spiteful alliances, conflicts with FIFA, and ultimately "a grim and contentious season with financial losses mounting on all sides,"[52] words that would eerily resonate for NPSL/NASL owners.

It is truly stunning that a precedent for 1967's self-destructive and point-less "soccer war" already existed in the annals of American history. Sadly, this history was so subterranean that none of the major parties in the NPSL or NASL can be criticized too harshly for not learning from it. USFA was the one constant. USFA's propensity to act on personal animus and take sides during a conflict is well established here, as is its precedent for giving a group or league, in this case the ASL, exclusive sanction to operate in the United States. This could be viewed as the first step in a pattern that would see the association's authority and decision making challenged numerous times in the 1960s, as the ISL, NPSL, and Oakland Clippers would all initiate lawsuits against the nominal governing body.

England's victory against West Germany in the World Cup finals that July, witnessed by a reported 400 million around the globe, certainly sent the late '60s version of the "soccer war" into overdrive as everyone involved had instantaneous visions of limitless profits, without stopping for a second to take into account the uniqueness of that particular match. Everything American business had touched up until that point in the postwar period had turned into gold, and there was no outward indication that soccer would be immune to their alchemy. Perhaps this overconfidence was the key to the many questionable decisions that followed.

But as we've definitively seen, the 1966 World Cup final, galvanizing as it was, was *not* the primary catalyst behind the rebirth of professional soccer in America. This is important to note and emphasize because the World Cup's supposed role as the primary instigator of these events has solidified into conventional wisdom, but the record clearly demonstrates that the two leagues that would compete against each other in 1967 were already estab-lished well before the final took place.

PART 2: CBS AND BEYOND

After the World Cup, the NPSL moved forward rapidly, stung but ultimately unbowed by the USSFA's denial of sanction. Setting a defiant tone, Robert Hermann told the *New York Times*: "We are opening in April and that is an irrevocable fact."[53] At this stage in late August 1966, the NPSL, although behind where it mattered most in terms of official recognition, was light years ahead of the NASL in terms of planning. The victorious NASL was taking its time and as summer faded into fall, the league still planned to begin operating in 1968. According to press reports, the NASL plan was to "open May-to-August season play in 1968" while staging "a series of exhibition matches in 1967."[54]

The announced intent to stage exhibition matches accomplished a few objectives. Perhaps most importantly it reintroduced the issue of lucrative international exhibitions that in many ways was at the core of the dispute between USSFA and the ISL. It was a not-so-subtle tweak to the NPSL, and to Cox in particular, that USSFA had reasserted its complete control over this vital revenue stream through its exclusive arrangement with the NASL.

The inability to stage or participate in international exhibitions due to its "outlaw" status and exclusion from the FIFA umbrella was likely just as—or perhaps more—damaging and frustrating than the NPSL's inability to use its considerable wealth to poach global talent without consequence. The NASL's pointed reference to staging exhibitions definitely had its desired effect, as almost simultaneously a curious statement emerged from the NPSL's board of directors meeting.

The statement, attributed to an unnamed public relations flak, was that the league hoped for FIFA "accreditation" so that it "could enter world cup competition."[55] This quote could be interpreted a number of ways. It could be viewed as damning evidence of NPSL ownership's complete lack of knowledge and nuance with regard to how soccer actually worked, particularly the major, easily discernible, distinction between domestic and international play. It could also have been a clumsily stated, misunderstood, or misattributed indication of the NPSL's obvious desire to play international friendlies and ultimately enter its teams into existing international competitions such as the European Cup or Copa Libertadores.

As far back as 1960, Cox had asked Sir Stanley Rous: "How can America get into international soccer at the highest level?"[56] Even at that time, Cox seemed to have a nuanced grasp of soccer's interlocking global structure, and it is likely that he foresaw an increased American presence internationally by building domestically. For example, In 1961 Cox publicly vowed that the ISL would support the struggling, barely extant U.S. men's national team (USMNT) by contributing "money, ideas and personnel toward the development of improved amateur players."[57] This assistance was granted with the aim of building an American soccer infrastructure and eventually a domestic topflight, thus increasing the United States' international status and presence. Viewed in this context, the statement could have been intended to communicate a similar desire on the NPSL's part to help resuscitate and rebuild the still floundering USMNT, supplying it with financial resources and ultimately quality American-born players. Whatever the real intent behind the quizzical statement, it telegraphed the fact that NPSL was already thinking internationally in scope.

A day after Hermann's declaration, the NASL announced that Detroit, Houston, and Cleveland had been awarded franchises, bringing their total to eleven overall. Art Allyn, owner of the Chicago White Sox and Chicago Mustangs franchises, also announced that the group hoped "to complete the league by granting a twelfth franchise"[58] prior to its next meeting on October

8. Allyn said that the league was reviewing "five different applications, including one from Milwaukee.

The new franchises were granted to ownership groups headed by Judge Roy Hofheinz, a larger-than-life Texas politico who had given birth to the Astrodome in Houston; a Detroit syndicate headlined by William Clay Ford, Edwin J. Anderson, and "other Detroit sportsmen"; and finally a Cleveland outfit "headed by prominent citizens whose names would be announced shortly,"[59] according to Allyn. The prominent citizens turned out to be Cleveland Indians owner Vernon Stouffer and Indians general manager Gabe Paul.

Returning to the international battlefield, things took a more serious tone on August 25, when the *Cleveland Plain Dealer* reported the English Football Association's (FA) public "warning" to English players considering life in the exotic new NPSL. The FA revealed that it had sent letters to "all our clubs" warning that "players who compete in this league are liable to be permanently suspended."[60] This was the first hint of the true depth of the NPSL's international restrictions. It was the same conundrum faced by the ISL, only the frustration was amplified tenfold by the fact that the NPSL actually had not just the desire but the resources to "take on the entrenched forces" of USSFA and "beat them dollar for dollar."[61] The ponderous USSFA had been able to outmaneuver the sleek NPSL, disarming it so that it couldn't effectively use its most valuable and effective weaponry: nearly unlimited financial resources.

Perhaps as a rejoinder to the FA's bluster, the NPSL responded by attempting to lure the secretary of the English Football League, Alan Hardaker, to America and a similar administrative role with the NPSL. This warning shot was almost certainly intended as an assertion of its financial might, as well as an attempt to reclaim a swath of space to wield it effectively. The NPSL dangled a reported "$30,800-a-year job offer"[62] to Hardaker. It was a particularly aggressive, symbolic piece of corporate headhunting, the boardroom a battleground where these men surely felt they could regain the initiative on USSFA. It was also emblematic of the ruthlessly competitive corporate ethos imbued within powerful American men unused to being marginalized.

Separate from its need to send a message, the NPSL also appeared desperate to add an established international soccer administrator for the purposes of bestowing a level of legitimacy on its enterprise. It's also likely that it envisioned this figure could or would provide a backchannel to FIFA and thus an alternate route into international waters. One week later on September 13, the NPSL approached Eric Taylor,[63] the secretary of Sheffield Wednesday, with the same offer Hardaker declined. Taylor too would pass. Eventually Sir George Graham, the former head of the Scottish Football

Association, would accept, only to immediately disappear into the void, probably because one of his duties was to focus on "intraleague affairs."[64]

Right in the midst of this heated rhetorical battle, the NPSL secured a coup, of sorts, on another front when the "Atlanta Braves" (the "Chiefs" would come later) franchise announced the signing of Aston Villa's Phil Woosnam. Woosnam was "a gifted inside forward with a pronounced football intelligence"[65] who had embarked on a professional football career after teaching high school physics until the age of twenty-six. Born in Wales, he was capped seventeen times for the Welsh national team. The cerebral Woosnam thrived during an era when "speed of thought rather than speed of foot distinguished the great creative players" and the *Guardian* considered him a contemporary of influential players like future USA stars George Eastham and Jimmy Baxter, who also embodied this slick style of play. He would go on to become one of the most pivotal figures in the history of American soccer.

The thirty-three-year-old Woosnam's time at Aston Villa was winding down, but he was still a good player and known quantity in the United Kingdom. His relatively high profile defection inspired headlines such as "Welsh Soccer Star Defies Ban,"[66] which gave the NPSL a huge public relations boost when it needed it most. The league's vulgar financial might was evidenced by Woosnam's reported annual salary of $16,500. To put that number in context, the average English First Division player earned £44 weekly, according to Sporting Intelligence.[67] The Woosnam transaction gave the UPI a chance to note that the "U.S. has created anxiety in many nations" that were "worried player salaries may soar when the U.S. league entered the race for talent."[68] Competing in an arena where money equaled leverage and power was natural terrain for NPSL owners determined to not go gently into that good night.

As the positioning and rhetoric between the two sides escalated steadily, the *New York Times* reported news of a meeting between league presidents James P. McGuire (NASL) and Robert Hermann (NPSL), where a potential merger was planned during a closed door session, according to USSFA's executive secretary Joseph Barriskill. In fact, the headline blared "Soccer Merger Is Planned"[69] and the *Times* stated without qualification that "the presidents of the two new and competing professional soccer leagues in the United States have worked out terms for a merger." Barriskill remarked vaguely that "the two league presidents exchanged ideas and suggestions" and "talked of getting together" pending a vote that each league would conduct within the next week. Since the news was obviously strategically leaked to the *Times* and Barriskill is prominently attached to it, it is reasonably safe to assume that the USSFA faction was confident in the merger becoming official.

The next day the Associated Press announced that "presidents of two United States professional soccer leagues have agreed to a proposed merger."[70] This time, the merger's breathlessly imminent completion was proclaimed by Walter Giesler, not Barriskill. Hailing from St. Louis, Giesler was a towering, beloved figure in the insular American soccer hierarchy. He had been the president of USSFA in the late '40s but was forever etched in history and lore as the coach of the USMNT that defeated mighty England 1–0 in the 1950 World Cup—an upset that remains one of the most shocking in World Cup history. Giesler, another figure indicative of St. Louis' stature as soccer's American epicenter, was drafted as "an intermediary" by USSFA to facilitate communication between the increasingly adversarial NASL and NPSL.

Giesler's appearance in the narrative at this point shows that an increasingly uneasy FIFA likely pressured USSFA to get the groups back to the table to hash out a merger before things got even more ugly and disruptive. It is telling that these semi-secret merger meetings happened directly following the sequence of events initiated by the FA's letter and culminating with the NPSL's relatively shocking capture of Phil Woosnam from Aston Villa. Woosnam's transfer proved that a potential arms race provoked by an unregulated, rogue entity such as the NPSL was not just a feverish by-product of arrogant American powerbroker minds, but an increasingly likely and highly destabilizing reality.

Sadly for all involved, the AP would run another piece just three days later on September 25 headlined "NPSL Nixes Merger Plan."[71] Dismissing earlier merger reports as "speculation," Hermann defiantly stated: "We think the best interests of major league soccer in the United States and Canada and the NPSL members are served by continuing to move ahead without delay to the launching of league play in April, 1967."[72] Also of note in the AP's report are the additions of Washington, D.C., and Philadelphia as NPSL cities. In the end, the NPSL's obstinacy constituted a hastily convened public relations embarrassment for USSFA and was another incident in what would develop into a pattern of similarly scattershot miscommunications on the parts of all involved.

On October 2, 1966, the *Washington Post* published an article by Dave Brady that is perhaps the first to highlight the mythic centrality of the 1966 World Cup final to America's "soccer war." Brady wrote that "the World Cup competition in London touched off the talent search by fat-cat Americans after they learned that 10 million persons in the United States had watched the overseas telecast."[73] This was highly ironic since it was Brady who wrote the earliest piece on record confirming the intentions of American businessmen to launch a national soccer league in March 1966.

Through Brady, McGuire blustered on about the NPSL being "outlaws," prompting Murdaugh Stuart Madden, the owner of the league's new Washington, D.C., franchise, to remark correctly that after fifty-three years of "nominal" control of the American game, USSFA had managed only to create a legacy where America is "the only country in the world that has not had professional competition in the most popular sport in the world." McGuire then laughably referred to the NPSL's launch as "a form of intimidation that isn't going to work."

Above all, Brady's piece confirmed that television was the next battleground the two leagues would bitterly contest, quoting Hermann, who revealed "his people had talked to a TV network about a contract."[74] Hermann then added that he believed both leagues were courting the same network—Columbia Broadcasting System (CBS). It was a delicious little ploy by a man who certainly had a card or three up his sleeve, as just two days later Brady and the *Post* returned to the American public with the headline "'Outlaw' Soccer League Lands CBS TV Deal."[75]

Brady characterizes the NPSL as having "won the first—and possibly the decisive—battle in its world-wide war with the North American Soccer League." Such language reflects simultaneously both the critical importance of television exposure as well as the level of contempt with which USSFA (and by extension FIFA) was viewed by American power unused to foreign oversight of domestic sports leagues. Brady also makes an interesting comparison between the NPSL and American Football League (AFL) regarding how television essentially "meant that the 12 team-National is in business to stay—as it was said of the American Football League."[76] This point also is picked up by Wangerin, who noted that when NBC paid $36 million for the rights to televise AFL games "almost at a stroke, the future of the league was assured."[77] The power of television eventually allowed the AFL to force the far more established NFL to the bargaining table, and the NPSL seemed to be following in its footsteps.

The deal, finalized on October 3, 1966, was announced as a "long-term multi-million dollar contract."[78] But, in reality, it was for ten years at one million dollars annually. Nonetheless, a victorious Robert Hermann gleefully emphasized once again that "the North American League had been negotiating with the same network, CBS." CBS's decision to award a television contract to the NPSL is a pivotal departure point in the narrative, establishing as it does the essential dichotomy that would exist between the two leagues until the merger at the end of 1967: one—NASL/USA—functioned with official international sanction and no television exposure while the other—NPSL—operated without sanction as an outlaw outside the existing international framework but in full view of the domestic public with its shiny new television contract. They were now officially two extremely imperfect (yet closely calibrated) fragments in search of a whole. Of course, this dichotomy was playing out in a nation where reception for one league was likely to be lukewarm at best, which would dictate the contours of everything that would happen afterward, including the decision to import foreign teams.

Perhaps following Hermann's cue, the wire services seemed to take great pride in emphasizing the NPSL's lack of sanction, writing: "The National Professional Soccer League, although not sanctioned by the governing bodies of the sport, took an important step towards permanency today as it announced it had sold television broadcasting rights for its matches to the Columbia Broadcasting System."[79] It is also interesting to note just how prominent the concept of television equaling "permanency" was in contemporaneous accounts of the deal, demonstrating how rigidly ingrained television, still a relatively new invention, was even at that point in America's cultural development and how it impacted every aspect of business, commerce, communication, and culture. The CBS contract was a form of sanction just as, or perhaps more, powerful than that of FIFA. Finally, the actual terms of the document itself would also influence the dynamic between the two leagues.

The international soccer community responded to this news by throwing down the gauntlet. On October 5 the *Washington Post* ran a UPI story emanating from Zurich under the luminously threatening headline "World Soccer May Retaliate against CBS."[80] Amazingly, FIFA was publicly threatening to boycott CBS in retaliation for its decision to essentially legitimize the NPSL. As part of its punishment, FIFA threatened to exclude the network from airing future World Cup matches, a threat that held more menace than ever before in light of the superlative World Cup ratings NBC had garnered in July.

Like clockwork, murmurs of imported teams started to emerge quickly in the days following the NPSL's CBS coup. For example, on October 13 the *Chicago Tribune* ran a piece by George Langford containing the first discernible mention about the possibility of bringing foreign teams to the United States the following summer to form a league "under the sponsorship of the fledgling North American Soccer League."[81] In typical *Tribune* fashion, the word "riot" is invoked in the very first paragraph when Langford notes "the world's finest soccer teams," which would be competing in this venture, "habitually stir their followers . . . to frenzy and occasionally to riot." It was a motif the paper seemed determined to write into existence over the next year.

Under the subheading "Imports to Compete for Two Months," Langford's piece contains no direct quotes from NASL brass but states unequivocally that the decision to import foreign teams was undertaken "admittedly to counteract the outlaw National Professional Soccer League, which has not received sanction from soccer's governing bodies, and to introduce first rate soccer to the United States."[82] This monumental decision was taken on October 12 during an NASL meeting at the Palmer House in Chicago. The seismic force exerted by the NPSL's television deal is evidenced by the incontrovertible fact that it took only nine days to force the NASL into a drastic, radical course correction.

The ungodly influence of the NPSL's television contract on NASL decision making rears its ugly head when unnamed league representatives revealed to Langford in the voice of jilted lovers "that they had turned down the same one million dollar contract offered by the Columbia Broadcasting System which the unsanctioned league accepted on October 3rd." The stipulations of the CBS contract would be criticized continually by NASL officials going forward, but it doesn't change the fact that they were obviously rattled by the NPSL's gambit.

The unnamed official continued, saying "the price was too low and the option terms were not suitable. We have negotiated with the other networks—NBC, ABC and Sports—and we are working towards a satisfactory contract." It's very interesting to consider that there are direct quotes about the television contract and nothing else in Langford's article, which serves to highlight the palpable sense of fear and anxiety engulfing NASL owners despite their attempts at bombast.

At this stage, the NASL still planned to "begin regular operations in 1968, playing a schedule of approximately 30 games from April thru Sept. 1."[83] But lest the NPSL get too far out in front of them, the new plan was to have foreign teams represent league "cities in competition only through July and August." Plans at this early juncture also envisioned a playoff "scheduled for August 6th and 13th consisting of the top four teams in the final standings." Obviously the identities of the visiting teams were not yet known, but the NASL divulged that it would be sending a "three man committee to Europe to complete arrangements with Sir Stanley Rous." The soccer war had found another gear.

An interesting aside: around this time the *Baltimore Sun* reported on a spot survey conducted by the NPSL that showed that sales of individual soccer balls had risen almost 50 percent throughout 1966. Various reasons are cited for the uptick, including the large number of schools and colleges that had begun playing the game, the "American public's new awareness of the sport—due largely to stepped-up coverage by news media, including the telecast of the World Cup final from England last summer,"[84] and the early age "at which a boy can begin to play the game." Not only is this a fascinating piece of information, it also shows that even then the influence of the 1966 World Cup Final was being used to fuel the NPSL/NASL narrative.

Things were relatively quiet through the end of 1966 as both leagues began the arduous process of assembling a professional sports organization within a compressed time frame. The next major happening was an NASL meeting at the Astrodome in Houston where it was announced that the "new North American Soccer League was officially sanctioned as the only major professional soccer league in the United States."[85] Although the sanction had been awarded by USSFA on June 25 in San Francisco and publicized and promoted regularly in the interim, this press release seems to indicate that the sanction was only officially granted on December 28.

Interestingly, it was noted that the "new league plans a home-and-home schedule from April through September next year, with each of the 12 cities being represented by a top-ranked foreign team."[86] This demonstrates that even at this relatively late stage the NASL's plans still appeared a little haphazard and ill-defined, as there were obviously no European teams capable of playing such a schedule due to blatant conflict with fixtures at the beginning and end of the domestic calendar.

The New York Times' Joseph Durso noted that Sir Stanley Rous was coming to New York a few days after the meeting in Houston in hopes that "from their combined deliberations may come a formula for peace between soccer's rival factions in America."[87] Rous' whirlwind stop through New York on the way back to England from the Pan Asian Games in Thailand reaffirmed his commitment to the facilitation of a merger between the two leagues. It's striking that a merger was still very much on the table less than four months before league play began in the NPSL, underlining the precariousness underpinning the entire enterprise. The other major piece of news to come from the meeting in Houston was that the NASL officially announced its hiring of Dick Walsh, formerly a vice president of the Los Angeles Dodgers, to be commissioner of the new league. The NASL's decision to hire Walsh remains perhaps the most baffling move during a surreal period filled with stupefying choices.

After signing a five-year contract that "paid him more than he received with the Dodgers,"[88] Walsh quickly became infamous, bragging publicly that he had only seen one soccer match in his life and that upon being named USA commissioner he trekked to the public library so he could check out books about the game. Andrew Beyer lends his portrait of Walsh in the *Washington Post* the absurdist details it begged for, noting that he "unabashedly"[89] checked out children's soccer books. Beyer is intuitively telegraphing the unabashed disaster Walsh's tenure as commissioner would be. The word is telling, as it indicates Walsh felt no shame, while subtly indicating that perhaps he should. Astonishingly but accurately, Beyer contextualizes Walsh by writing that "such groping for knowledge about the game is not unusual in the new world of American professional soccer." The fact that such lack of knowledge was cavalierly dismissed as "not unusual" would predictably come back to haunt the NASL and was a perfect example of why historians such as David Wangerin and Steve Holroyd attributed a collective and pronounced lack of ownership knowledge as one of the primary reasons the relaunch of American soccer failed so miserably in the late '60s.

Beyer notes that "the men who are laying out $11 million in the USA's first season of operation are not lifelong soccer aficionados. They are businessmen, most of whom have interests in other sports teams." Simple logic would dictate that with such considerable sums of money involved, the investment would benefit greatly from the appointment of a commissioner with a considerable level of soccer experience. Beyer then remarks, "So it is not surprising that they chose for commissioner someone who knew little about soccer." On the contrary, it was extremely surprising.

The psychology behind Walsh's appointment was revealed by Cleveland Stokers president Gabe Paul, who had chaired the commissioner selection committee. After Walsh confessed his complete ignorance about the sport, Paul remarked that "what we need is organization and an operation. We need someone versed in sports."[90] Jack Anderson of the Detroit Cougars told the press that Walsh "was the first man the committee considered."[91] This scene would play out almost identically at different points throughout the narrative.

Wangerin pointed out that such dogged insistence on and zealous overvaluing of North American sports experience in the executives they hired severely damaged the NASL and NPSL. That this damage was so predictable even without the gift of hindsight is what makes it so remarkable and incomprehensible. This is how far the psychology of standardization and what Michael Herr depicted as "corporate faith" in a doctrine of interchangeability had advanced, encroaching on the better judgment of ostensibly savvy men who should (in theory) have known better.

Walsh was the most perfect example of this folly, as well as the depth and pervasiveness of a psychology that viewed soccer as nothing more than a business proposal, nothing more than a product like a tire or bar of soap. A mind-set that held that a product was a product was a product and that anyone working in one sport, in this case baseball, was somehow uniquely qualified to seamlessly transition into another. Walsh was both a satiric example and practitioner of this way of thinking, publicly stating that the mechanics of creating a sports organization were "the same regardless of what sport you're in." This was after he bragged of not knowing "the difference between a soccer ball and a billiard ball."[92] Again, even without the gift of hindsight, it is difficult to read that comment without seeing quite clearly the disasters ahead.

Walsh had steadily navigated his way upward through the ranks of the Dodgers front office, but it remains unsaid why this experience made men like Paul and Anderson so bizarrely certain that he could run a soccer organization, not to mention one being built from scratch. His comments about the process of creating sports organizations being intrinsically the same regardless of the sport suggest a level of experience and skill he simply did not possess. His major accomplishment during his tenure with the Dodgers was overseeing construction of the team's stadium in Chavez Ravine, a process itself not without controversy.

Perhaps this experience is what prompted Paul and company to look so favorably on him. Otherwise it is exceedingly difficult to understand why someone like Walsh would be trusted with such a fragile eleven-million-dollar investment. It stands as a symptom of the all-encompassing arrogance exuded by the forces of American business that were enjoying an unquestioned peak in influence and prosperity during the mid-to-late '60s. Walsh and his almost defiant lack of soccer knowledge epitomized the owners' "corporate faith" in the idea that all soccer needed in order to succeed was marketing. And all Walsh had to do was stick to the script and adhere to the marketing templates that had been successfully selling everything under the sun for years. Another example of this psychological phenomenon was provided by Washington Whips owner Earl Foreman.

Foreman is a representative example of the type of man attracted to the prospect of conquering America's final sports frontier. Like many other powerful men in this story, Foreman was a real estate lawyer who while growing up "competed in track and basketball at Baltimore City College High School,"[93] his formative experience in athletics helping to cement sports alongside law as the "two passions" of his life. By the time he emerged as the Washington Whips owner in 1967, "upon the recommendation of Jack Kent Cooke,"[94] Foreman also owned the National Basketball Association's Baltimore Bullets and was co-owner of the NFL's Philadelphia Eagles. However, his ownership of both those enterprises would lead to varying degrees of drama and controversy during the next decade. His partnership with Eagles principal owner Jerry Wolman would sour as Wolman declared bankruptcy amid a mire of lawsuits and questionable business dealings. After a long journey through American Basketball Association (ABA) ownership that saw him traverse Oakland, Washington, D.C., and Virginia, Foreman would resurface as commissioner of the Major Indoor Soccer League in the 1980s.

Once again, as Wangerin would somewhat acerbically (yet accurately) note during his expert autopsy of the USA/NPSL era, "too many executives and officials were hired on the basis of their understanding of North American sports rather than for any appreciation of the game"[95] itself. Foreman directly illustrated that both in his own limited understanding of the game but perhaps even more so in his hiring decisions. Andrew Beyer provided a glimpse into his psychology shortly before the USA season.

While discussing his tendency not to "take an active role in the running of his teams," Foreman said "unless you've grown up with a sport . . . get the best possible people to run your team."[96] What was perhaps even more revealing was his philosophy that "the people who get in trouble are the people with a little knowledge. What right does an attorney have to start second-guessing people who have been in sports all their lives?"

The deference to "people who have been in sports all their lives" is perfectly indicative of the psychology Wangerin refers to, which held that a keen understanding of "North American sports" was somehow an easily translatable magic elixir that could instantly build solid, well-run soccer franchises. Even more startling is his nonchalant assertion that "a little knowledge" of the sport could be troublesome. That statement is a pitch-perfect encapsulation of the overriding corporate faith of the time as well as emblematic of the ingrained psychological standardization that saw everything as a product and every product as intrinsically the same. To give an example of this psychology within a sports context, an anonymous CBS executive insisted after the network had purchased the New York Yankees in 1964 that "I can't see the difference between Mickey Mantle and Jackie Gleason. They're both entertainers."[97] It was all "show business."

With this ethos predominant in the thinking of the men who ran the NASL/USA, it is no wonder that they relied so heavily on people with considerable but wildly incongruent knowledge of American sports. The nonchalance becomes even more maddening when Beyer notes that "Foreman's motivation for buying a soccer franchise was neither the hope for a quick profit, nor a tremendous love for the sport,"[98] but because he loved the idea of being able "to 'jump in the car and go watch a game.'" After reading this, it's not hard to see the Whips' inevitable demise flash clearly before your eyes. This is also a point where class definitely intersects with the story and we see a level of hapless power and callous affluence that thinks nothing of buying a sports franchise so clearly destined to founder on a bank of ineptitude and arrogance. How power looks and works among USA owners begins to become more apparent.

The effects of Foreman's psychology and mistrust of "a little knowledge" can be vividly discerned not just in whom he selected to be general manager (GM) of the Whips, but why. Jerry Cooper boasted a resume frighteningly representative of the times in American soccer. Cooper told Andrew Beyer he became the Whips GM in the following fashion: "Earl Foreman asked me, 'What do you know about soccer?' I said, 'Nothing.' He said, 'Great. You are going to run the new pro soccer team.'"[99] Perhaps it was meant to be humorous, and years later it is, but not in the spirit the two men intended. It's not even the fact that lack of knowledge apparently wasn't viewed as a hindrance but actually hailed as a positive virtue—it's also the vapid casualness with which it's relayed as if such ignorance is admirable. Again, the level of affluence juts through and you envision an ever-flowing stream of money bleeding from the Whips' coffers.

Cooper and Foreman had become friends "when Cooper headed a chain of supermarkets for which Foreman was the attorney," a perfect example of both the inner workings of the outer limits of the old boy network and the unbridled arrogance of American business at this time. A person demonstrated great ability running a supermarket chain? Well, he sounds *exactly* like the man we need to run our brand-new soccer outfit. When reading Foreman's statements in the '80s as Major Indoor Soccer League's commissioner regarding what he learned from the USA/NASL's early days, he offers some interesting insights—but never does he say that he shouldn't have hired a grocery store administrator to build and manage a soccer franchise from scratch.

Not only did Cooper hold a title of crucial importance with the Whips, he somehow (possibly due to Foreman's relationship with Kent Cooke) became responsible for the critical task of selecting and securing the twelve teams that would be imported into America to playact as USA franchises. Early accounts of his travels suggested that he had selected teams from Yugoslavia,[100] Leicester City,[101] Spain, Portugal, and Switzerland.[102]

In his book *Stars in Stripes*,[103] Sunderland AFC historian Paul Days reported that key figures involved in helping Cooper secure and select teams were the *Times* of London's Brian Glanville, the BBC's Kenneth Wolstenholme, former English international and Spurs legend Jimmy Greaves, ex–Nottingham Forest forward Roy Dwight (Elton John's uncle!), and London businessman Jim Graham. These men were all instrumental in brokering the NASL/USA tournament.

Beyer fleshes out Cooper's background, cataloging the numerous times throughout his past that the resourceful GM entered a business, such as retail grocery, knowing nothing of it yet somehow managing to become successful when all was said and done. It is an admirable and uniquely American story and another telling example of the psychology of standardization that permeated postwar corporate thought. Mass production had made interchangeability a supreme virtue, and this bled into other areas of administrative thought. Taken to its extreme, we see things like the head of a grocery store chain being tapped to lead a professional soccer franchise located in the nation's capital—because business is business is business.

With no prior knowledge of soccer history and lore, Cooper ended up becoming pivotal to the entire composition of the USA. Beyer noted that "when Cooper finishes lining up the teams for regular season play, the league will assign one to each city, based on that city's ethnic composition. Thus, Boston would likely be home to the Irish team, Cleveland a Hungarian squad etc."[104] This has been speculated on by researchers for years, and it's astonishing to consider that one of the prime movers behind recruiting USA squads publicly admitted knowing nothing of the game before being thrust into such a critical role.

The Aberdeen Dons were announced officially as the Washington Whips' surrogates on January 25, 1967. The announcement was made at a league meeting in New York. Stoke City and Sunderland of the English First Division were also officially announced as participants by the end of January. The two proud British clubs would represent Cleveland and Vancouver, respectively. The lesser-known "Glentorians of Belfast," actually the proud

Glentoran FC side from Belfast, were announced as surrogates for the Detroit Cougars. [105] In February, Joseph Durso emphasized (as if there was any doubt) that the NASL "did not expect to begin playing until 1968, but its hand has been forced by its rival. So in 1967 it will import entire teams from abroad, and they will represent each city." [106] Ultimately, the league settled on a twelve-match schedule.

It was around this time that another NPSL official made a strange comment that betrayed a serious lack of soccer acumen, particularly regarding the distinction between the international and domestic game. This time it was not an unnamed spokesman. New York Generals president John Pinto publicly lamented that the NPSL's lack of sanction would prevent them from playing in the World Cup, telling Durso, "we regret not having international sanction, which would be necessary for competing in the World Cup matches." [107] There is something so jarring and strange about this comment, coming as it does from an executive of a Generals franchise placed in the absolutely essential media hub of New York City. It remains jarring until you consider that much like Walsh, Pinto would publicly claim to know virtually nothing about soccer. Pinto said, "I hope by opening day I know enough about the game to enjoy it." [108]

It would be damaging enough having someone with that kind of knowledge deficit running what was ostensibly a marquee franchise, but what's unbelievable is that he was actually tapped to be on the NPSL's five-man executive committee. [109] One of this committee's major briefs was undergoing the complicated dance of signing players while being under international sanction.

What Pinto did seem to know about was television, as it was he who'd proclaim: "The Generals will wear hunter-green and gold uniforms. Just like the Green Bay Packers," adding that "these will be good colors for television." [110] These comments revealed many things, perhaps most importantly a true sense of the NPSL's priorities, which placed television and public relations at the tip of the pyramid. It makes their next move somewhat comprehensible.

On February 22, 1967, with their season less than two months from starting, the NPSL finally hired a commissioner. They chose a Manila-based newspaper publisher named Ken Macker. It was another exceedingly strange choice for commissioner but for different reasons. Whereas the NASL search committee decided on Walsh immediately, the NPSL selected Macker from a list of more than fifty candidates that included former MLB commissioner Ford Frick. [111] Macker embodied yet another shade on the expanding palette of American power, different from men like Hermann, Cox, and Walsh; he was a communication age Colonel Kurtz broadcasting the American prosperity gospel across the Pacific.

Why Macker? Robert Hermann said simply, "he was the most outstanding of those who interviewed."[112] In a press release announcing the hire, Hermann said, "we feel that Ken Macker brings to our league the experience, vitality and imagination so necessary to the introduction of top level professional soccer to the United States." Careful parsing of Hermann's words would reveal motivation, with the word "introduction" being particularly telling.

This is because Macker was a public relations veteran who also happened to be a close friend of NFL commissioner Pete Roselle. As a matter of fact, Macker and Roselle were partners in the former's San Francisco–based public relations firm: P. K. Macker & Co. Most notably, P. K. Macker & Co. "were commissioned in 1955 by the city of Melbourne to publicize the 1956 Olympic Games in Australia."[113] The ties between Roselle and Macker were so great that at one time Roselle left his job with the Los Angeles Rams to join Macker's firm.

But Macker was also an expat who'd spent the last six years in Manila "as publisher of three newspapers headed by the Philippines Herald." In addition to the newspaper holdings, "he also was president of a 12 station television and radio network." How he got where he was and why he was still able to figure so prominently on the radars of NPSL decision makers remains unclear. It is obvious that his public relations background was attractive, but it was also something that appeared to be entirely in his past. One UPI piece announcing his appointment was actually headlined "Filipino Chosen to Chair New Soccer League,"[114] while another labeled him soccer's "unknown civilian."[115] Macker would officially assume his duties at a league meeting on March 14, 1967.

On March 10, 1967, the *Washington Post* announced that the brand-new entity previously known as the North American Soccer League was officially changing its name to the United Soccer Association (USA). As always, Walsh took an opportunity to rub salt in the NPSL's wounds by saying that the change was made to "dispel any confusion which might have existed by reason of the similarity between our league name and the name of the unsanctioned group, the National Professional Soccer League."[116]

Walsh continued, "with its appealing initials of USA we hope that the new name will dispel any confusion or misunderstanding with the other new soccer league, the National Professional Soccer League. In addition it will make it easier for fans to remember that the league is sanctioned." While admiring the cheap garish audacity of the move, one must stop and wonder just how "the appealing initials of USA" would "make it easier for fans to remember that the league is sanctioned," particularly when the admittedly similar names had coexisted side by side for more than six months.

A few things the USA's appealing new name and initials could actually make easier to realize—if one thought about them for a few minutes—were the two bizarre strands of irony that the USA would contain absolutely *no* American-born players in 1967, consisting exclusively of foreign teams imported from around the world, *and* that the precedent for importing foreign teams into the United States was established by one Bill Cox, member of the "unsanctioned group," whose ISL was forced to shut down because of it. Now USSFA and McGuire, in his new role as USA chairman, were suddenly wholeheartedly supportive of the practice through the United Soccer Association.

Along with the monumental name change, it was announced the same day that Cerro of Montevideo would represent New York in "this summer's mini-league in which foreign teams will stand in for United States and Canadian cities."[117] Cerro was one of the last foreign teams secured and it would become the New York Skyliners. The Uruguayans were placed in New York in hopes of captivating the Big Apple's sizeable Spanish-speaking populations.

In yet another example of the obsession USA execs had with wildly incongruent figures from other sports, Muzz Patrick "former player, coach and general manager of the New York Rangers hockey team," was named the Skyliners' "acting general manager." Patrick is an interesting hire because he at least had strong New York connections that could be leveraged from a marketing and credibility standpoint, but once again, the lack of any soccer-specific knowledge seems to be entirely unimportant to USA decision makers.

Why weren't more men like Bill Cox sought out? There were a dearth of them and the soccer infrastructure at the professional level was nonexistent, hence the need to establish the USA/NPSL—but there were at least a layer of men who had run successful NCAA programs and amateur and semiprofessional soccer leagues who could have been recruited. In this context, the Chicago Mustangs' decision to poach Stu Holcomb from Northwestern,[118] despite his admission that he didn't know much about soccer, makes more sense due to his position as athletic director at what was then still a major collegiate sports school.

In late March with opening night of the NPSL season just over three weeks away, eleventh-hour merger reports began to leak out. On March 28 the *Los Angeles Times* reported that Walsh and Macker had met recently and "have been conducting a dialogue on mutual problems for some time."[119] Walsh added that "the meetings have been going on once a month for the last 90 days and have shown progress." Other owners involved in this negotiation process were Peter Block (Pittsburgh Phantoms) and Joseph O'Neill (Oakland Clippers) for the NPSL and their USA counterparts Earl Foreman, Roy Hofheinz, and Gabe Paul.[120]

As always, profitable foreign tours were never far from anyone's thoughts. An NPSL unnamed spokesman said "if we had recognition now the winning team from our league could play an 8-game European tour and come back with a million dollars."[121] Although Los Angeles Americans official Ed Fitkin said "a merger couldn't happen this year" because each league was so far along in their summer plans, the report sounded an optimistic tone and stands as an interesting testament to the fact that beneath the ego, bluster, and public relations, at least some on both sides of the divide realized the folly of what was about to transpire.

The next day Macker lamented the pressure that had resulted due to the premature, and in some cases misinterpreted, leaks that held that the leagues had already agreed to merge. The *Baltimore Sun* reported that someone at USSFA mistakenly leaked news of the talks.[122] In hindsight it can certainly be viewed as ominous that Macker, just two weeks into his tenure, was already losing control of the public relations cues when his supposed facility in this area is the only thing on his resume that could have suggested his fitness for the job. It also came to light that Walter Giesler, now chairman of the U.S. Olympic Committee, had resurfaced and "submitted a four-point proposal designed to bring the rival pro leagues together."[123] Macker closed by stressing his belief that there was a "definite demand for two soccer leagues."

On April 6, less than two months before the USA's season would begin, Wolverhampton Wanderers or the "Wolverhamptons"[124] were slotted to represent Jack Kent Cooke's Los Angeles Americans franchise. Other squads considered for this role were the Bolton Wanderers and more seriously, Club America from Mexico City, hence the appearance of the working title "Los Angeles Americans" in some recent press. Wolverhampton was the last team to fall into place and become reborn as the Los Angeles Wolves.

Also near the end of March, after "declaring for months that prosperity, in the form of a juicy television contract, is just around the corner,"[125] the USA was forced to admit that securing "any sort of nationwide television exposure appears very remote." "Frankly, we're hurting," admitted Walsh. The group had learned the hard way that "the television industry does not share its conviction that soccer is a sure thing to succeed in this country." Besides this considerable obstacle, the group seemed to have, perhaps due to the World Cup ratings, an overinflated view of its value, not to mention an obsession with getting a more favorable deal than the NPSL.

The USA was seeking a short-term contract worth $3.3 million a year, which would net each club around $75,000. The problem was, as with the NPSL's deal, the networks all wanted to lock USA into a long-term contract at a lower rate. The USA refused, believing that "once we have proven ourselves, we can get what want next year, rather than sign ourselves away now." It was a severe miscalculation that the group was now essentially conceding in public, with Walsh saying, "You better believe" that the group

would "settle for a less lucrative contract just for the sake of TV exposure."[126]

Sports Illustrated's Martin Kane reported that USA "refused to consider a
proffered CBS television contract, which, though it was announced as giving
the NPSL 10 years of television exposure at $1 million for the first year and
more on an upward sliding scale for the following years, also gives CBS the
right to drop the whole enterprise at any time."[127] An anonymous USA
owner told Kane that the NPSL's deal was "a unilateral contract, in which
CBS retains all the options. As I read it, CBS doesn't even have to put on one
game." This is important because it was reported that each NPSL club would
receive $50,000 if CBS televised a full season of matches. CBS's official
reasoning behind offering a contract to the NPSL and not the USA was
"because it was further along in the hiring of coaches, players and stadiums."

CBS executives were fairly assertive and transparent regarding their reasoning behind the structure of the NPSL's long-term deal. CBS vice president William "Bill" MacPhail, a man with deep connections to the New York
Yankees, which CBS happened to own at the time, told Andrew Beyer that
the NPSL deal was structured in such a unilateral, one-sided fashion in case
"the league were a complete fiasco and we couldn't sell anything."[128] Mac-
Phail recognized without a shadow of a doubt CBS's massive leverage in this
process, stating "soccer has no chance in the United States if there is no
television,"[129] after meeting with Macker in Manila. It was leverage the
network would manipulate aggressively in the months to come.

An inkling of the tenor and style CBS's NPSL telecast was provided by
MacPhail, who felt Macker's first job would be to "explain to the American
people that the National Soccer League is not illegal." Beyond that, Mac-
Phail "described CBS's planned coverage of the matches 'as an educational
program trying to educate the American people how soccer is played."[130] It
was a clear statement of intent.

CBS's onerous, vaguely ominous terms never looked better to the USA.
Not only would the group not be able to prove itself to skeptical networks,
but the entire rebirth of the game in American would suffer because the
cohesive, battle-tested and (in some cases) excellent teams the USA was
bringing over would be shrouded in darkness due to hubris and greed. A
skeptical, curious nation of sports fans would get to see the NPSL's cobbled-
together sides of middling quality but not a Stoke City outfit featuring the
magisterial George Eastham and Gordon Banks. Perhaps the opportunity to
see fully formed professional teams on CBS could have moved the needle in
a more pronounced fashion. It was a loss all around.

The USA's humbling public defeat in the all-important television derby
did not, however, stop them from sniping jealously at the NPSL's prize. For
example, the eternally quotable Jerry Cooper told the *Baltimore Sun*, "I
would prefer not to have one than to have theirs" and "We hate to think we

would have to give away rights to our game for nothing for ten years. CBS knows they have them on the hook. We even questioned the network about reducing the number of years in case there should be some kind of merger but they won't do it."[131]

The contract would remain a point of contention between the two leagues on a variety of levels going forward. CBS's decision to award the NPSL a television contract created the essential dichotomy that functioned between the two leagues: one was sanctioned and the other had a television contract and thus guaranteed exposure. This is the core dynamic that governed the entire existence and ultimate failure of the two enterprises.

On the eve of the first NPSL match between the Baltimore Bays and Atlanta Chiefs, Macker observed that the tangled relaunch and rebirth of American soccer was the only professional sporting enterprise that ever "started out on a national basis."[132] The urge to have the dueling leagues be national in scope was indeed present from the outset, making it the first time soccer had been aggressively marketed and promoted on a coast-to-coast basis in the states. It was also noted that "plans were rushed ahead after the World Cup soccer telecasts from last summer attracted 10 million viewers in this country." This put events in their proper chronological context. The magnitude of the 1966 World Cup final and its unquestionably strong television presence in the United States should not be underestimated, just better understood sequentially.

After a full year of corporate wrangling over sanctions, television contracts and rushed, radical decisions whose impacts were felt around the globe, the spring had arrived and for the first time in many years, professional soccer (and lots of it) would be played from sea to shining sea.

Final United Soccer Association Key

Boston Rovers = Shamrock Rovers
Chicago Mustangs = Cagliari Calcio
Cleveland Stokers = Stoke City FC
Dallas Tornado = Dundee United
Detroit Cougars = Glentoran FC
Houston Stars = Bangu Atletico Clube
Los Angeles Wolves = Wolverhampton Wanderers
New York City Skyliners = CA Cerro
San Francisco Golden Gate Gales = ADO Den Haag
Toronto City = Hibernian FC
Vancouver Royal Canadians = Sunderland AFC
Washington Whips = Aberdeen Dons

Final Roster of National Professional Soccer League Franchises

Atlanta Chiefs
Baltimore Bays
Chicago Spurs
Los Angeles Toros
New York Generals
Philadelphia Spartans
Pittsburgh Phantoms
Oakland Clippers
St. Louis Stars
Toronto Falcons

Chapter Two

1967, Part 1

Whip It Good—The United Soccer Association Season

TACTICS: TALES OF "DOUR, STERILE MASSED DEFENSE"

Brian Glanville and David Wangerin both noted that the general tactical trend in Europe during the mid-to-late '60s was that of boring, cynical, cautious football embodied by, in Glanville's words, "dour, massed sterile defense."[1] The contemporary side most associated with this style was Helenio Herrera's massively successful and thus massively influential Internazionale. Herrera's "La Grande Inter" were the scourge of European football, winning back-to-back European Cups (the Union of European Football Associations [UEFA] Champion's League title in today's parlance) in 1964 and 1965 and piling up a fistful of *scudettos* along the way.

The 1966–1967 European Cup final pitted "La Grande Inter" against Jock Stein's freewheeling Celtic squad in Lisbon, Portugal. This showdown became a pivotal, epochal match because Celtic's 2–1 victory was viewed (rightly or not) as an emphatic symbolic and philosophical victory for joyous, free-flowing attack-minded football that took risks. After warning that they would "attack as we have never attacked before,"[2] Stein's Glaswegian underdogs swarmed the pitch in Lisbon, handing Inter a bitter, decisive defeat that sent the Italians into a tailspin from which it took decades to fully recover.

In the manner of a prophet heralding an unprecedented era of light after lifting an interminable shroud of darkness, after the match Stein predicted that it was a "victory for offensive football and it will start a new trend in Europe."[3] Herrera himself would graciously concede that "Celtic deserved their victory. We were beaten by Celtic's force. Although we lost, the match was a victory for sport."[4]

Briefly considering this match is important to a better understanding of the United Soccer Association (USA), National Professional Soccer League (NPSL), and ultimately the North American Soccer League (NASL) for a variety of reasons, including how well it illustrates the tactical and philosophical tensions and trends of the times (primarily in Europe, but with some consideration given to South America), as well as the fact that no fewer than three USA squads (Aberdeen/Washington, Dundee/Dallas, and Toronto/Hibernian) played in the Scottish First Division (now Scottish Premier League) with Celtic, which adds an interesting level of contextual information regarding exactly where these teams stood in the European pecking order. Throw in a decent Cagliari side, boasting a handful of past and future Italian internationals coming off a sixth-place finish in Serie A, that had cut its teeth sparring with this historically significant Inter team, and it becomes clear that there was a considerable amount of class on display in America all those distant, humid summers ago.

But beyond Celtic and Inter, this match serves to illuminate the wider global football trends of the time so that the style of play in the USA/NPSL can be properly understood alongside what was happening elsewhere in the world. This understanding is important because the style of play and low-scoring or scoreless matches in particular become an important driver of administrative decision making that would exert a huge impact on the course of soccer's development in the United States.

Herrera's Inter were known for perfecting a particularly potent form of *catenaccio*, or bolt defense. Brian Glanville described it in the following manner for his *New York Times* readers: "It is a highly defensive tactic, whereby a player known as the 'sweeper-up,' or *libero* in Italy, operates behind a line of four backs, covering wherever he is needed."[5] Glanville observed that NPSL sides in particular "have plumped with such alarming unanimity for *catenaccio*," whereas Cagliari and Cerro, representing USA franchises in the pivotal media markets of Chicago and New York, were also known to utilize *catenaccio*.

In fact, after watching them, Glanville insisted that Cerro was playing a strained form of *catenaccio* despite the fact that its official program insisted the side was aligned in a 4–3–3.[6] Glanville's visceral disdain for *catenaccio* can be glimpsed in his characterization of a "wretchedly defensive" Inter vanquished by a righteous Celtic squad playing "flat-out sustained attacking football." Thus, Glanville noted, "it is a colossal irony that when, at long last, wealthy men have launched the game on a nationwide scale, it should be at a time when it is obsessed by defense."[7]

Despite the oasis of creativity offered by Brazil's electrifying 1958 World Cup triumph utilizing a 4–2–4, and more recent triumphs by Brazil and England in which both employed 4–3–3 systems, Glanville traces the inexorable drift toward defensive football all the way back to Herbert Chapman's

Arsenal of the mid-to-late 1920s and its development of the "WM" formation.[8] Indeed, the 4–2–4, as we shall see, was employed not only by the triumphant "Lisbon Lions" but by more than a handful of the teams chosen to represent the USA.

The 4–2–4 relied on the two midfielders or "link men" to have superior physical and mental abilities such as vision and a superlative tactical understanding of the game. To work to its full potential, the system also relied on wingbacks with the pace, quality, and stamina to exploit the space the system created for them. Designed for aggression and attack, the 4–2–4 required intense conditioning to work properly. All of these attributes—classy, determined midfield play (Whips/Stokers), devastatingly effective wing play (Wolves), and superior fitness levels—figure into the story of the United Soccer Association.

To whet people's appetites and flex their newfound muscles as the only sanctioned professional league in America, the USA had scheduled a handful of what it hoped would be lucrative exhibition matches in select league cities such as Houston (Real Madrid v. West Ham), Chicago (Athletic Bilbao v. Red Star Belgrade), and Washington, D.C. (Eintracht Frankfurt v. Cruzeiro), to name a few. The *Washington Post* lavished coverage on the Frankfurt/ Cruzeiro exhibition and in so doing shined a light on some of the general tactical changes and trends sweeping Europe, including the advent of the 4–2–4.

Eintracht had fallen on hard times, plummeting from the highest echelons of Europe into eighth place in the Bundesliga in 1965. Eintracht hired Elek Schwartz, a Romanian tactician who had previously coached Benfica and the Dutch National Team. The first thing Schwartz realized was that Frankfurt was wedded to the drastically outdated 5–3–2 alignment, which Andrew Beyer characterized "as passé as the straight T formation in American football."[9] Beyer remarked that by 1942 this formation had been discarded en masse in favor of the 3–2–5 system that put a greater emphasis on defense, which is another reason the general tactical trend in Europe had been slanted toward caution.

Schwartz immediately installed the 4–2–4 at Frankfurt. To demonstrate just how quickly this formation overtook Europe, when Schwartz implemented it in 1965, Frankfurt was the only club in Germany using it—by 1967 all sixteen First Division clubs were using some variation of it, according to Beyer.[10] Schwartz first observed the 4–2–4 in Sweden in 1958, becoming enamored with the flexibility it afforded. Beyer likened the drastic switch to the 4–2–4 from the predominant "WM" formation to a switch from "man-to-man play to a zone."

Schwartz said, "under the old system, it was kind of a military tactic" where the stronger player usually prevailed one-on-one. In Schwartz's view, "the old system took away initiative from the player, whereas the 4–2–4 "is more intelligent. It has more variations. Individual players can develop better under it, for it encourages them to play freely." Schwartz also noted that teams around Europe were starting to use the South American style "with its greater degree of finesse." Schwartz didn't see the shift in terms of finesse—that was and would be a preoccupation of the *Post*'s throughout its USA/NASL coverage; he saw it more in terms of psychology, saying "the South American player is a thinking man"[11] determined to win with creativity and guile, not just physical superiority and force. It was a bold admission and one that ran counter to much of the discourse and commentary focused on South American soccer in the late '60s. All of these tactical motifs and themes would play out to varying degrees when the USA season started.

Many in Europe, particularly in the United Kingdom, could not contain their glee over Celtic's triumph, with no less than the legendary Liverpool manager Bill Shankly reportedly telling Jock Stein that he was "immortal now."[12] It's true that Celtic was the first team from the British Isles to claim the coveted trophy, and there's no doubt that pride colored the commentary directed toward Herrera's Inter, but beneath the surface many (despite Glanville's caution toward oversimplification) seemed to view the match as a symbolic contest between two sides battling for the philosophical soul of soccer at a time when most were exhausted by cautious, cynical, trophy-generating displays.

Besides Inter's undeniable successes with the system and its centrality to their enviable position at the pinnacle of European football, many European squads deployed *catenaccio* as a matter of First Division survival—not as a ticket to glory—grinding out dull nil–nil away draws in desperate hopes of hoarding enough points on their travels to avoid the dreaded drop into the red ink–laden lower divisions. Although there was no infrastructure nor desire to implement relegation in the United States' brave new footballing world, the harried managers of hastily cobbled together sides of the NPSL most likely reached for *catenaccio* as a plug-and-play, quick fix that could be installed on the run to stave off embarrassment while scavenging as many points as possible, muddling through the dusty baseball stadiums of North America.

Winning was an American obsession, and most owners thought that fielding a winning team was the one true path to overnight success, which also helps explain why caution and its cousin *catenaccio* ruled the day in this context. Though this very caution itself would become a point of contention as owners feared dull, low-scoring matches, thus re-creating in the American consciousness (perhaps for the first time) the age-old philosophical tension in between success and beauty in soccer's psyche. This tension would become apparent again and again.

Caution itself on the part of hesitant managers unable to resist innately conservative urges to withdraw and defend leads will figure largely into the outcome of the USA's inaugural season. The owners were so afraid of this creeping defensive pallor, something Glanville referred to as "the blight of more sophisticated competition,"[13] that instead of implementing an arcane and inane scoring system like the NPSL, they decided to sweeten the pot and inspire daring the old-fashioned way, by dangling money. Commissioner Dick Walsh announced that "there will be a bonus of $400 to each winning team, and this will be split $200 for each, in tie games in which goals are scored."[14] Walsh added pointedly: "But there will be no bonus for scoreless ties."

THE 1967 USA SEASON: NEARLY BURIED BY TIME AND DUST

Celtic's dash to European glory was accomplished at least partially on the backs of domestic rivals such as the Aberdeen Dons. By the time the Dons arrived in the United States on May 23, 1967, their 2–0 defeat to the European Champions in the Scottish Cup final was still fresh in their minds, coming as it did less than thirty days before their plane touched down in Washington, D.C. The final was played before 126,102 in Glasgow's Hampden Park on April 29, with William Wallace's brace at either end of the half supplying Celtic's margin of victory. Perhaps the memories lingering from this setback are what prompted several of the "high-spirited, youthful clean-cut group"[15] to arrive toting liquor bottles ("for friends," they maintained) amid the blare and bleat of bagpipes at Dulles Airport.

Ironically, Chris Hunt, writing in *Four Four Two*, credited Celtic's five-week North American tour in the spring of 1966 as a significant factor in forging the legendary side's "indomitable team spirit."[16] The Dons transformation into the Washington Whips would occur with essentially the same salty team that had valiantly sparred with Celtic in Hampden onboard and ready to wreak havoc in the USA. Aberdeen brought a sixteen-member touring squad. It was a hearty group with one glaring absence, as manager Eddie Turnbull was too ill to make the trip. Turnbull, then forty-three, was suffering from an ulcer and would spend the first weeks of the tournament ping-ponging back and forth across the Atlantic, even after Earl Foreman invited Turnbull's personal physician to accompany him prior to the Whips' opening match.

In addition to being the first British player to ever score a goal in the European Cup, the grizzled Turnbull's playing days at Hibernian saw him form part of a feared attack known as "the famous five" alongside other Scottish greats such as Bobby Johnstone, Gordon Smith, Lawrie Reilly, and Willie Ormond. These men helped Hibernian win three Scottish League titles between 1948 and 1952.[17] Turnbull, primarily an inside-left, had also featured in Scotland's 1958 World Cup squad. The acerbic, no-nonsense manager, raised in a mining family near Falkirk, was never too shy to voice a craggy opinion and soon, ill health and all, he'd see to it that his men imposed their will on an unsuspecting USA.

Yet it almost didn't happen for the Scottish club. Sunderland AFC historian Paul Days noted that it was the Black Cats who were initially slated to represent Washington, D.C.,[18] but USA executives wanted to match teams with places where it was thought they could generate the biggest crowds. D.C.'s Scottish expat community and popular (predominantly) Scottish semi-professional teams like Britannica (indeed, Britannica founder Norman Sutherland's brother Alec was attached to the Scottish embassy) were likely what ultimately conspired to send the Dons to Washington.

In typical District fashion, the club's name was chosen by team officials after a public "name our franchise" contest netted more than 35,000 entries and 5,400 different suggestions.[19] A twenty-two-year-old American University graduate student named Alan F. Coffey suggested "Whips" for its alliterative allure and strong Washingtonian connotations after thumbing through his political science textbook one day. However, "Whips" was actually *not* the most popular name. That honor went to the nickname "Diplomats," which garnered 256 votes. General Manager Jerry Copper discarded that moniker over fears that the nickname would be shortened to "Dips" (late-period NASL history would demonstrate the prescience of such fears), which he felt "didn't sound too nice."[20] To further emphasize the name's uniquely Washington aura, it was publicly unveiled in the office of House Majority Whip Hale Boggs, with the three other congressional whips presiding as well as Coffey himself. President Johnson was gifted a season pass while meeting with Whips and USA brass before the season began.[21]

Perhaps due to 1967 being a headline-grabbing year for Scottish football wherein the exploits of its major teams would have been easier to track, the *Washington Post* and Andrew Beyer in particular did a consistently admirable job of providing ample background on and context to the Scottish teams appearing in the USA. For example, while previewing the Whips' opening night match with the Cleveland Stokers, Andrew Beyer noted that player-coach Harry Melrose, who was deputizing for the ailing Turnbull, along with Francis Munro, were "the 'link men' in the 4–2–4 alignment which Turnbull employs."[22] Munro was indeed a perfect example of the type of midfielder requisite to making the 4–2–4 function. He had vision, class, strength, and control.

Other observers would characterize the Whips' formation as a 4–3–3 with Munro playing alongside Jimmy Smith and Martin Buchan. Buchan would go on to accumulate thirty-four caps for Scotland and to enjoy a successful tenure at Manchester United, including a stint as captain after the retirement of Sir Bobby Charlton. He remains the only player to hold the unique distinction of having captained both a Scottish and an English side to Football

Association (FA) Cup glory, achieving the feat with Aberdeen in 1970 and United in 1977.[23]

The Whips boasted considerable firepower in the form of the two Jimmys: Jimmy Smith and Jimmy Wilson. Smith had scored twenty-one goals in all competitions, while Wilson tallied fourteen league goals as Aberdeen recorded a respectable fourth-place finish with an impressive 17–9–8 record. Known as "Jinky" due to his "languid style of play,"[24] Smith in particular captured the imagination with his serpentine runs and audacious nutmegs so much so that Turnbull characterized him as "the type of player you find once in a decade."[25] Sporting a *Revolver*-era Beatles' fringe and blessed with a magical right foot, the popular Smith would go on to become a Toon favorite after Newcastle paid a then–club record £100,000 for him in 1969.

As they prepared to square off with the Stokers to open the USA season, Melrose characterized Aberdeen/Washington's style of play as "very fast, very fluid" and employing a "set pattern," where the squad all tried "to be defensive players and attackers."[26] Melrose seems to be referring to a form of pressing, a tactic that was just starting to be more widely used and understood in global football thanks to Viktor Maslov and his dynamic Dynamo Kiev. Indeed, as the Dons grew more adept with this style, they were able to avenge their defeat to Celtic in the Scottish Cup finals with a resounding 3–1 victory over the Glaswegians in the 1970 final.

The USA started off strong on May 26, 1967, with huge opening-night crowds of 34,965 in Houston, 21,871 in Yankee Stadium, and 16,431 in Dallas, according to Steve Holroyd's American Soccer Archives,[27] impressive numbers all. No opening-night match drew fewer than 7,400 people. A great start, but as the novelty wore off in many cities, the crowds thinned. The league ultimately averaged a respectable 7,890 in attendance for the season.

To put that in perspective, after forty years of glacial, gradual growth, Major League Soccer now averages roughly 10,000 more in attendance per match. The Houston Stars, the reigning Champions of Rio de Janeiro Bangu Atletico Clube, would lead the league with an eye-catching 19,802 average attendance. In what was yet another sign of the poor planning that would be an unwelcome hallmark of 1967, the Chicago Mustangs lost 1–0 to Dallas in their first match largely because Cagliari was forced to field as many as seven reserves due to playing a rescheduled Serie A fixture in the middle of the USA's launch.

The Tornado riddled the undermanned Mustangs defense, outshooting them twenty to six, forcing reserve keeper Pietro Pianto into several fine saves to keep the score down on a cold, damp Comiskey Park night. The Tornado's Finn Dossing (labeled as "Dossing Finn"[28] in the *Chicago Tribune*) scored the sole goal in the sixty-fourth minute of a lackluster match on a feed from Tommie Millar. It was enough to earn the Tornado two valuable points, as the USA retained the then-standard 2–1 European system of awarding two points for a victory and one for a draw.

Like the Mustangs, the Stokers were also dealing with significant absences, none more prominent than the recently acquired Gordon Banks. After stealing the show the previous summer and earning great distinction as the best goalkeeper at the 1966 World Cup, Banks was transferred from Leicester City to Stoke in March for $145,000.[29] Banks would not arrive in the States until after he fulfilled his international obligations playing with a group of English FA all-stars in the 1967 Montreal Expo. Banks and the FA all-stars cruised through the Expo tournament, with the legendary keeper notably seeing action in a rematch between England and West Germany that the Brits won 3–2.[30] Also missing was Peter Dobing, an increasingly valuable member of Stoke's attack, who had just netted a solid nineteen league goals.

Stoke finished twelfth in England's First Division, producing a mediocre 17–18–7 mark, with their last match, a lifeless nil–nil draw against league champions Manchester United, occurring just over two weeks before they traveled to Washington, D.C. But such was the respect accorded to the English First Division, as well as the inclusion on its roster of internationals like Banks and George Eastham, that Stoke was considered by some favorites to win the USA.[31] According Stoke City's *Oatcake* fanzine, the historically plodding, physical side was actually chosen by British football experts Jimmy Greaves and Kenneth Wolstenholme due to their "attacking play."[32] Their relatively new creative gloss was largely due to the addition of the influential Eastham as well as the emergence of Dobing and Roy Vernon. Whatever the reason they were ultimately selected, the USA played host to one of association football's oldest clubs, a club started by railway apprentices in 1863, when America was wracked by a convulsive civil war.

Eastham had a large impact on the English game, partly due to his mesmerizing control and creative inside-forward play. He never seemed to lack for an incisive pass during a career in which he starred for Newcastle and Arsenal before moving on to Stoke in 1966, but his influence also cast a large shadow because he sued Newcastle for his release at the end of the 1959–1960 season. Eastham's case made it all the way to the high court in 1963, and his partial victory for undue restraint of trade dealt an irreparable blow to the onerous, hated "retain and transfer system" British players labored under at that time. It was a system similar to organized baseball's equally hated reserve clause wherein players had virtually no autonomy or control over where they could play. When he retired, Eastham became an assistant to Stoke City manager Tony Waddington and would ultimate succeed him in 1977 when the latter stepped down.

On a steamy night in the nation's capital with the temperature hovering in the 70s,[33] the Stokers' Maurice Setters scored the first goal in the United

Soccer Association's brief one-and-done history on a header against the Whips in the eleventh minute. It was one of three goals that the former Manchester United warhorse would score moonlighting as a center-forward in the states. Like so much that happened that summer, Setters' inclusion in Stoke's touring squad was in doubt until the time the team boarded the plane to Ohio.

Bad blood between the defensive stalwart and midfielder Calvin Palmer had erupted into open warfare during training and both were initially dropped from the traveling team. Setters apologized to Waddington and was reinstated, while Palmer refused and was left behind to stew in the Potteries. Setters had acquired a reputation as "one of the toughest players in English soccer,"[34] playing most of the previous campaign on damaged knee ligaments. Legend has it that he refused surgery until he drew a lengthy suspension in March.

A crowd of 9,403 was on hand at D.C. Stadium to see Stokers' outside-right Roy Vernon score the winning goal in the seventy-eighth minute as he lofted a looping twenty-yard changeup past the Whips' Bobby Clark. It was also Vernon's cross that Setters headed home for the opening goal. The Welsh international's late strike trumped Jim Storrie's forty-fourth-minute equalizer. Storrie slipped past Alan Bloor and slid a shot behind John Farmer—a goal the keeper sneeringly referred to as "lucky"[35] afterward. Storrie previously starred as a center-forward for Leeds United in England, scoring twenty-five goals in the 1962–1963 campaign before injuries and homesickness forced him and his family back to Scotland and the open arms of Aberdeen in 1967.

Storrie gave the *Washington Post* an excellent insight into the tactics of smaller European teams in the late '50s and early '60s, saying that at Airdrie, his first club, "you were never tied to a set position. Teams just played the game as they saw it. There were no tactics involved."[36] Storrie emphasized that "this was the trend at the time." His move to Leeds in 1962 demonstrated not only the evolution of tactical thinking, but also the dimensions involved in moving from Scotland to England, as well as from a small team to one with a much higher profile.

Storrie recalled that at Leeds he "entered method soccer" and that "individualism was out" because every player "had a certain part to do." This demonstrated the increasing sophistication of tactics and the general trends toward superior organization and collective thinking that would mark the great Dynamo Kiev and Ajax teams of the late '60s. Turnbull shifted Storrie to the perimeter, where he played on the wing as an inside-left, a position he favored earlier in his career as he considered himself "an old-fashioned inside forward"[37] playing one–twos and through balls for others to run onto. Storrie confirmed that Aberdeen was "basically an attacking, aggressive side" in contrast to Leeds' more calculated counterpunching style.

By all accounts the opening night Whips–Stokers contest was a brisk, physical affair that saw the talismanic Eastham withdrawn due to injury. The younger, more eager Aberdeen side effectively pressed the Stokers during the first half, denying them possession after Setters' goal and ultimately going into the break even and somewhat unlucky not to be ahead. Eastham admitted as much afterward, saying "they were unlucky on some shots" and that they had hit the post three times."[38] In Waddington's view, Stoke had enough veteran savvy to sense that much of the Whips' aggression and pace had dissipated as the humid night wore on. Stoke was able to regain control of the match in the second half and slow down the tempo en route to securing its first victory. Turnbull also could see that his side would have to learn to pace itself, not just in the heat, but as each individual match would dictate.

After the Whips' defeat, Beyer observed that the Scottish side had "lived up to their reputation as a hard-hitting team"[39] before gushing over the Whips' single-minded commitment "to get the ball to the goal." Such aggression and commitment was commendable and entertaining, but as a more astute tactician like Waddington noted, it would be increasingly unsustainable in the swampy, sweltering D.C. summer, particularly when fatigue due to the grueling amount of travel began to become a factor.

The Whips' next match was in Ontario against Toronto City, which was represented by Hibernian—the Dons' bitter rivals. Beyer does a great job expounding on the rich history between the two sides, a history that extended back into the nineteenth century.[40] Hibernian had also finished the previous Scottish league campaign with forty-two points, deadlocked with their long-time adversaries. Turnbull was unique in that his career would transverse the two, having successful stints at each club. Beyer noted that the Dons and Hibs had met four times in the previous year, the most recent being Aberdeen's convincing 3–0 defeat of Hibernian in the quarterfinals of the Scottish Cup.

Managed by Bob Shankly, Hibernian/Toronto boasted no less than three Scottish internationals: forwards Peter Cormack and Jim Scott and halfback Pat Stanton. Cormack would go on to become an important cog in a Liverpool machine that won a boatload of trophies in the '70s. Stanton came full circle after his playing days, managing Hibernian for a spell in the early '80s. As an interesting historical aside, Hibernian/Toronto would ultimately emerge from the USA unbeaten against teams hailing from outside the British Isles.

Toronto's first match was a 1–1 draw against the New York Skyliners in Yankee Stadium. CA Cerro of Montevideo, Uruguay, hit the lottery, such as it was, and was assigned to represent New York City, most likely an attempt to gain a foothold within the Big Apple's flourishing Spanish-speaking communities. Cerro was coached by Uruguayan national team manager Ondino Viera and was coming off an impressive third-place finish in Uruguay's First

Division, which saw it twice defeat the defending Copa Libertadores and International Cup champions Penarol. Viera's Uruguayan national side had impressively held the English to a goalless draw in the opening fixture of the previous summer's World Cup. Domestically, Cerro registered a 12–4–2 record and was filled with Uruguayan internationals such as Ruben Gonzales, Juan Pintos, Eduardo Garcia, and Ruben Bareno. Gonzales, a highly decorated center-half, was capped more than sixty times for Uruguay, earning player of the year honors six years running from 1959 to 1964. Pintos was coming to New York off a sterling campaign where he scored eighteen goals in eighteen league matches. [41]

In what would be the first of many clashes between radically different styles, the Uruguayans exploded "almost immediately with their carioca style of South American soccer," [42] before they too were "slowed to waltz time by the heat and the hard Yankee Stadium turf," in the eyes of Gerald Eskenazi. Already two themes begin to emerge rather starkly, the impact of the steamy American summer on the players' conditioning combined with aggressively ill-suited playing venues.

A crowd of 21,871 was on hand to see a "conservative, tight-playing" Toronto successfully negate the beautifully organized chaos supplied by the Skyliners in the first half. The temperature was in the high 60s and as such was expected to be an advantage for the South Americans. They attacked Toronto with a "studied freneticism, passing the ball almost blindly to players who would miraculously appear." The South Americans tormented the "solid and stolid" Scots with footwork but ultimately lacked an end product until Benedicto Ribeiro "an inside right and dazzling dribbler who seems to play the game with a sense of humor" opened the scoring in the forty-first minute. Ribciro, a Brazilian who'd be one of the stars of the summer, "took the ball from a swarm of Scottish defenders" [43] before punching it home with his back to goal.

To emphasize just how much the Skyliners carried the play initially, they ended up with fourteen total corners when all was said and done. [44] But just as the Stokers did in Washington, Hibernian weathered the storm early and began to slow the tempo of the match with veteran guile just as the Skyliners began to wane. It would be Cormack who manufactured the tying goal, as he set up Alan McGraw, who leveled brilliantly with a header. After the equalizer, Toronto set back and expertly defended its point, starting the Skyliners' descent into an oblivion of cynical, deadlocked, and increasingly physical matches with incongruently incandescent bursts of quality intermittently sprinkled in.

Perhaps the most interesting thing about Toronto City is the fact that it was the only USA franchise that had existed previously. Owner Steve Stavro formed the club in 1961 along with journalist Ed Fitkin to play in the newly formed Eastern Canada Professional Soccer League (ECPSL). Interestingly,

Fitkin would resurface in the USA as the general manager of the Los Angeles Wolves. Richard Whittall observed that "in Toronto in 1960, soccer was the sport of immigrants."[45] This placed it alongside other major North American cities like New York, which were also filled with bustling, diverse immigrant communities that would turn out in droves to support their ethnically based semiprofessional teams and international exhibitions. It was the same paradox faced by Bill Cox and the men behind the USA/NPSL.

This led Stavro and others to create the ECPSL in hopes of establishing a thriving, profitable domestic league in Canada. It was similar to the International Soccer League (ISL) in spirit and concept, as the ECPSL imported big stars such as Danny Blanchflower and Sir Stanley Matthews to play for the league during the summer of 1961.[46] By 1966, Stavro had essentially folded the Toronto City franchise into the USA wholesale, only now Hibernian was filling its uniforms.

It was Jimmy Smith who would torment Toronto as the two sides squared off for the fifth time in less than a year. Smith emerged from a cloud of defenders and played a beautiful give-and-go with Jens Petersen before burying the return pass to give the Whips a 1–0 lead. The Whips again dominated the first part of the match before relenting from sheer attrition, weather, or both, allowing Toronto to gain momentum. Peterson said afterward that the Whips "scored too soon"[47] and that may have caused the team to "let down" and focus on protecting their lead instead of building on it.

Once Toronto gained a foothold, the Whips were forced to rely on Bobby Clark to help withstand a withering Toronto barrage as they desperately sought to erase the Whips' 2–1 advantage. Ultimately, Clark's man-of-the-match caliber performance allowed the Whips to claim their first victory. Speaking to the press, Clark noted how different and distracting the huge game clocks erected by USA brass were, saying, "It's quite a thing here: you watch it ticking, ticking . . . you're counting the seconds"[48] It's a telling insight into the psychological impact that this particular attempt to "Americanize" the game had on the players.

Andrew Beyer displayed an impressive grasp of tactics when previewing the Whips' upcoming match with the Chicago Mustangs, speaking of the Italian side's "impenetrable defense and bashful attack."[49] Indeed Cagliari had yielded only sixteen goals in the preceding thirty-four match Serie A season, while scoring thirty-five en route to its impressive sixth-place finish. Cagliari's increasing strength within *calcio* was all the more impressive, considering that in 1963 it was still in Serie B, where it had resided exclusively for the first forty years of its existence. In fact, its trek through the USA was the midpoint of a journey that would see it rise all the way to the summit of Italian soccer in 1970 when it claimed its sole *scudetto*.

Cagliari brought a fistful of past, present, and future Italian internationals to the USA, including keeper Adriano Reginato, defender Communardo Niccolai, and forward Roberto Boninsegna. Reginato had kept goal for Italy's 1962 World Cup squad, while Niccolai would be on the side chosen for Mexico in 1970. All Boninsegna—also on the 1970 World Cup team— would do is pace the USA with ten goals in nine matches. Leading them into battle was Manlio Scopigno, an astute tactician known as "the Philosopher," who had a sophisticated understanding of the game as well as a considerable grasp of man-management skills and psychology.

Beyer, under the sway of the aggressive Whips, played up the prowess of the "offense minded Scottish first division" and predicted that the contest would be "a fascinating tactical exercise." The Mustangs were said to utilize a nine-man defensive wall, and a banged-up Jim Storrie said "with nine men back on defense, the wingers have to get across. It's no good to try and go through them." Beyer picked up the thread and outlined how the Whips would have to use their halfbacks and fullbacks to try and create space for shots and effective offensive opportunities. Despite saying that Chicago's fullbacks "would not advance toward the opponent's goal if Sophia Loren were beckoning," Beyer had a nuanced enough understanding of the game to realize that the aforementioned strategy would leave the Whips vulnerable to counterattacks, something Chicago could execute with deadly, ruthless efficiency.

The reserve–laden Mustangs were winless upon their arrival in Washington, D.C., drawing 1–1 with the Stokers on the strength of a Gerry Hitchens goal after dropping their first match to Dallas. Hitchens was an interesting addition to Cagliari, a one-time English international who had spent most of his professional career playing in Italy with Inter, Torino, and Atalanta. Atalanta had loaned Hitchens to Cagliari, where he'd spend the next two years. Hitchens revealed more tactical insight into the Mustangs' methods, explaining to Beyer that the Italians eschewed the common 4–2–4 formation in favor of a system that featured just two attacking players, a center-forward and winger.[50] Hitchens likened the team's approach to that of a boxer, probing patiently for an opening and then striking with a precise long ball to a streaking forward in lieu of a punishing jab.

The Mustangs had conceded only two goals, but that was enough to warrant legitimate concern for the stingy, well-organized outfit. The Whips would be the first team to have the pleasure of matching up with a full-strength Mustangs squad. The match, reinforcing once again the folly of playing soccer in the dead of the savage American summer, was dogged by 90-plus degree temperatures on the pitch. It got so bad that Wilson and Storrie "were treated for heat prostration during the game."[51]

Chicago's cagey willingness to play at a slow tempo actually served to undermine Clark due to his seeing precious little action during the match. Clark admitted, "it was much easier to play in Toronto"[52] because the sheer volume of shots denied you "time to think," forcing you to "play on reactions and instincts," whereas facing a more deliberate, unadventurous opponent in debilitating heat required far more concentration. Boninsegna scored in the seventeenth minute to give Chicago a 1–0 lead. Clark was then called upon to summon up all his concentration and save a penalty in the twenty-seventh minute,[53] which kept the Whips in the match. Clark's save allowed Storrie to equalize just six minutes later.

The grueling match ended in a 1–1 draw, the Mustangs' second consecutive result with that scoreline. Echoing Beyer's earlier prediction about a fascinating tactical clash, Melrose admitted that Italians' approach forced the Whips to "change our style" and "adapt." The USA, despite not featuring any Americans, was uniquely American in the sense that the league embodied a true melting pot ethos of soccer cultures, styles, and tactics, ultimately expanding all players' and managers' understanding of the game's many faces.

The Whips awaited a visit from the misfiring Skyliners desperately in need of some offensive balance, as Jim Storrie had netted three of their four league goals. The 0–2–1 Skyliners had just come off a punchless nil–nil draw against the lowly Boston Rovers in front of a paltry 3,850 fans in the Manning Bowl. Unexpected offense for the Whips would come in the form of a Julio Dalmao own goal just four minutes into the match. Down 1–0 the unlucky Skyliners carried the play to Washington, generating twenty-three shots on net and again demonstrating their ability to dominate stretches of a match without much to show for it.

Jens Petersen ignited the attack that led the Whips' second goal in the eighty-third minute. Petersen launched a long ball to Jimmy Wilson, who, according to sympathetic witnesses such as Andrew Beyer, was clearly offside.[54] Wilson wasted no time accepting the unseeing referees' gift and finished calmly to stake the Whips to a comfortable 2–0 lead. It would be just one of many instances throughout the summer when the substandard quality of officiating was either openly called into question or directly influenced the outcome of a match.

Three minutes later Storrie and Smith combined to remove any lingering doubt about the outcome when Smith slotted home a rebound from a dangerous Storrie shot to give the Whips a 3–0 victory. The result elevated the Whips to second place in the USA's Eastern Division at 2–1–1, a single point behind the Cleveland Stokers. Next up for the Whips were the surprising and unbeaten Detroit Cougars.

The Cougars were represented by Glentoran FC, a semiprofessional team based in Belfast. As much as Stoke City was favored due to its relatively stable existence in the middle of England's First Division, the Glens were lightly regarded due to its semiprofessional status and the quality of competition it faced in Northern Ireland—even though it had just won its eleventh league title. Beyer explained that the "caliber of Irish soccer is low"[55] because the maximum salary for Irish players was then $16.80 a week, leading "practically everybody with talent" to ply their trade in England or Scotland. This team was different. In the European Cup Winners Cup tie they actually held Celtic to a 1–1 draw in Belfast before succumbing 4–0 in Glasgow. In more than fifty league and cup matches from 1966 to 1967, Glentoran was beaten only *four* times, ripping off an amazing twenty-five-match unbeaten run during that stretch.[56] Like the Whips, Detroit/Glentoran utilized a 4–2–4 to great effect, racking up an eye-popping seventy-seven shots over the course of its first three matches in the USA. Overall, this Glentoran team is still recognized as one of the strongest sides in the team's illustrious history and its solid performance in this tournament remains a legitimate source of communal pride.

The Cougars boasted the presence of John Kennedy, reserve keeper of the newly crowned European Champions, as well as four other "guest players"[57] from assorted Irish sides, including Northern Ireland international Danny Trainor. The fiery John Colrain was Glentoran's player/manager and a major catalyst for the Glens excellent USA performance. The ex-Celtic and Ipswich Town inside-right was at the center of controversy almost immediately, as he was accused of punching linesman Bobby Jack in Detroit's very first match.

The Glens accepted the USA's offer on Boxing Day 1966 and when they left Belfast on May 23, 1967, hundreds of local residents and workers poured forth to say good-bye and wish them luck.[58] The team arrived in Detroit as champions of Northern Ireland and was feted by the Ford family, owners of USA's Motor City franchise. The Cougars derived their name from Ford's newest automobile, a brash, direct piece of corporate synergy and promotion that harkened back to the days of factory-sponsored teams in the northeast. The Glens were persuaded to abandon their traditional green, red, and white kits in favor of all-black stripes with garishly oversized numbers on the back that still couldn't mask the sense of pride, menace, and resolve that emanated from this gritty, decorated side. Right out of the gate, the team found itself thrust into an intense match against Dublin's Shamrock Rovers in Boston.

The *Belfast Telegraph*'s Malcolm Brody described the contest as "robbery with violence"[59] and once again poor refereeing and violence—the obvious correlation between the two took far too long to become clear to USA brass—would simmer to the surface when Bobby Jack negated a sure match winner by Trainor in the eighty-eighth minute. What happened next is controversial and largely lost to time, as Colrain was alleged to have struck the hapless linesman. He was suspended by commissioner Dick Walsh, but he steadfastly maintained his innocence throughout his time in America.

Comments about the quality of the USA's officiating began to emerge from angry, incredulous managers almost immediately and would solidify into a narrative rather quickly. After the Stokers' 1–1 draw with Chicago (in what was just their second match), Tony Waddington unleashed a withering tirade on referee Dan Lieberman, telling the *Cleveland Plain Dealer*: "Any

resemblance between this game and the game of soccer is purely coinciden-
tal."[60] Waddington praised the officials who handled the Stokers' first match
against the Whips but unloaded on referees that he felt were far too tolerant
of Chicago's physicality, noting that the referee seemed to think it was a
mistake to give more than one penalty. Going into overdrive, Waddington
said, "some of our guys who have been here a short time thought they were
drafted for Vietnam" due to fouls so brutal and blatant his guys needed steel
helmets. Two serious strands would emerge from this rant: the latent violence resultant from lax refereeing and Chicago/Cagliari's persistent presence at the center of it all. The Italians seemed to have a knack for getting
under the skin and into the heads of adversaries such as Waddington.

Like Chicago before them, the Cougars were set to face Washington at
full-strength with the addition of scoring ace Trevor Thompson. Thompson
had scored more than thirty league goals for the Glens the previous season en
route to racking up a club record 375 goals in 463 appearances.[61] To emphasize the perils and pitfalls of their semipro status, though, Thompson was
forbidden to leave for America by the firm he worked for as a salesman,
missing the team's first few matches. The Cougars also included inside-
forward Walter Bruce in their ranks, an international who just been named
Northern Ireland's player of the year, even though he had suffered a knock in
the previous match.

Prior to facing the Whips, the Cougars avenged their draw with the Boston Rovers in Detroit, edging them 1–0 in a return match they absolutely
dominated. Despite outshooting the beleaguered Rovers 36–11, the Cougars
had to rely on Arthur Stewart's successful penalty in the seventy-ninth minute to secure the result. According to reports, the "penalty was vehemently
protested against by virtually the entire Shamrock Rovers side,"[62] although
exactly why remains unclear. Controversial decisions aside, the major story
of this match was the torrential downpour that marred it, as thunder, lightning, and more than half an inch of rain blighted the pitch. It was so bad "that
Glentoran officials were forced to seek shelter in the press box only to find
that the roof of it also began to leak." In the end only 648 brave souls turned
up.

A far more respectable (and dry) 5,134 fans[63] were on hand to see the
Whips open the scoring after eleven minutes when Jimmy Wilson banged in
the rebound of a ferocious shot from Pat Wilson that had initially deflected
off the crossbar. Trevor Thompson answered almost immediately for the
Cougars, getting in behind the defense and drifting a shot past Clark, who'd
come out to challenge. Thompson then put Detroit in the lead with a thumping header in the twenty-seventh minute, showing the delighted local fans
exactly what they'd been missing. The Whips had chances to go level and
Jimmy Smith actually did score, but the goal was nullified by an offside call.
The match teetered back and forth until the eighty-fifth minute when Jim

Storrie broke free in front of goal and slid a pretty pass to Pat Wilson who finally equalized for the Whips.

Despite their eye-opening performances in the USA, some were still convinced that the Cougars were a pushover and that a draw was akin to a loss for the more battle-tested Whips. Beyer noted that people had even attempted to console Harry Melrose after the match "with the comment. . . . 'You were clearly better than Detroit,'"[64] which prompted the surprised captain to ask, "We were?" Detroit had earned the Whips' respect. The same, however, could not be said of the Stokers, as the Whips felt "to a man they can lick Cleveland."

The 2–2 draw put Washington into a decent position ahead of their rematch with the Stokers in Cleveland, but in what was certainly a variation on an eerily familiar theme, they would be facing the already-solid Stokers with the addition of Gordon Banks and Peter Dobing. Dobing was so sorely missed that the gangly, gimpy Maurice Setters was plodding through at center-forward for Cleveland. Dobing answered the bell with authority, scoring twice in his debut, a 4–1 thrashing of a decent San Francisco Golden Gales side. The dynamic duo of Setters and Roy Vernon had once again conspired to net two points for the unbeaten Stokers a few days before that when a Setters goal in the waning moments consigned the Boston Rovers to a 1–0 home defeat on June 4. The Stokers applied constant pressure on Rovers keeper Pat Dunne while marinating in the fury inspired by a disallowed Alan Bloor goal (also off a feed from Vernon) that surely set Waddington's pulse racing.

Vernon had become a pivotal figure for the Stokers in the United States, garnering glowing praise in the Cleveland press where he was dubbed the "Soccer King."[65] It was the culmination of a long road back for the forward who famously captained Everton to a First Division crown in 1963. Vernon suffered a severe knee injury that limited him to only fourteen appearances for Stoke from 1966 to 1967 but had rounded brilliantly into form alongside the mist of Lake Erie. Vernon could not, however, overcome the elements that conspired to make the Municipal Stadium pitch a soggy mess when the Los Angeles Wolves paid a visit in early June.

It was the first meeting between the longtime English rivals in more than two years, as the proud Wolverhampton Wanderers had spent that time languishing in the Second Division until their promotion back to the topflight in May 1967, mere weeks earlier. Rain swept in causing the players to skid "around like roulette pills in the first few minutes,"[66] according to the *Plain Dealer's* Dan Coughlin. Once the footing solidified, the twin scourges of crippling humidity and awful officiating conspired to make the match a scoreless affair, even though both sides had chances to score.

This time it was Wolves manager Ronnie Allen's turn to blast the referee, saying that "Ninety-nine out of 100 English referees would have allowed"[67]

Dave Wagstaffe's goal in the thirty-fifth minute. Instead the crafty outside-left's industry was washed away, leaving Allen to ponder why, since typically "when a fellow pulls the ball back from the dead ball line he can't be offside." One wonders about Waddington's thoughts on the matter, because the Stokers also had an apparent Roy Vernon strike nullified in the forty-first minute.

In a philosophical mood afterward, Allen said that "when you score, you talk about the goals. When you have a nil–nil tie, you talk about the weather." Waddington would only grudgingly concede that his side had played conservatively due to a depleted bench.[68] The disappointing 0–0 result was the Stokers' third straight draw in Cleveland, with both of their victories coming on the road away from their "home" support. It was still enough to keep them ahead of the Whips and atop the Eastern Division.

The Stokers had scored only four goals in four matches before the highly anticipated arrival of Peter Dobing prior to a visit by the San Francisco Golden Gales, which was represented by the Eredivisie's ADO Den Haag. According to the *Washington Post*, the initials ADO stood for Alles Door Oefening, which translated into "Everything as a Result of Training."[69] This credo obviously communicated all one needed to know about ADO's standards regarding conditioning and preparation.

Perhaps the most obscure team selected to participate in the USA, ADO was undergoing a mid-'60s resurgence under the highly regarded Austrian tactician Ernst Happel. Happel was the perfect manager for ADO, implementing a "highly aggressive pressing game"[70] that relied on superior stamina and fitness levels. ADO finished third in the Dutch topflight in 1965 and had suffered some agonizing losses, most recently to the mighty Ajax, in the KNVB Beker (Dutch) Cup finals, a trophy they would at long last claim upon their return home from the USA with a 2–1 victory over Ajax in the spring of 1968. The Austrian would ultimately go on to become the first of only four men to win the European Cup/UEFA Champions League with two different clubs, achieving the feat with Feyenoord and Hamburger SV.[71]

The Gales had stormed out of the golden gate, racking up an impressive ten goals in their first three matches, including a 6–1 demolition of the Vancouver Royal Canadians and 4–2 triumph over the Houston Stars. Their only loss had come against Toronto, where paradoxically they were blanked. Inside-right Henk Houwaart was proving to be a prolific scoring threat, notching a hat trick in his first USA action against lowly Vancouver. Houwaart went on to a relatively successful coaching career after his playing days, particularly during the 1980s at Club Brugge KV, with whom he won the Belgian league in 1988. Center-forward Lambert Maasen was living up to his colorful nickname as "the man with the golden head,"[72] to the tune of three goals in three matches, adding some balance and a lethal aerial threat to the Gales' attack.

The visit from the high-octane Gales, as well as an increasing pressure to produce more goals, prompted a wary, weary Waddington to acknowledge that "according to the reaction of the fans and what I read in the papers, they want us to score more goals. We'll do just that, although it may be at the expense of victories."[73] These thoughts highlighted the deep-seated philosophical tension between aesthetics and results in soccer, a tension exacerbated by the zealousness of neophyte USA owners desperate to showcase a high-scoring product for largely skeptical, uninitiated fans. In some instances, NPSL owners directly intervened and overruled managers' technical/tactical decisions in their haste to promote scoring. In light of these comments, it is worth pondering whether similar pressure was applied to Waddington by Cleveland's ownership group, although no definitive evidence exists.

Waddington would keep his promise. After displaying their trademark guile and veteran savvy by adopting a clever rope-a-dope strategy that saw Cleveland patiently absorb frantic San Francisco attacks in the opening part of the match, the Stokers—reinvigorated by the prodigal Dobing—exploded. Sadly, only 4,138 saw the pitch-side pyrotechnics in Municipal Stadium. After letting the Dutchmen extinguish their initial fury and initiative in the oppressive 90-degree heat, the Stokers put on a passing clinic. Dobing created the first goal with his pace, screaming down the left side of the pitch and finding Vernon, who lobbed a beautiful cross into the box for a wide-open Setters to dispatch it, giving the Stokers a 1–0 lead.

Becoming ever more influential, Vernon also set up Dobing's first goal of the campaign, using his superlative vision to pick out Dobing, who seemingly emerged from thin air to neatly tuck a shot inside the left post. The degree to which the weather and their own aggressive precision had rattled the Gales had to have surprised even this battle-tested Stokers squad. To their astonishment, Setters and Dobing were essentially able to play one-twos all the way into San Francisco's goalmouth, "seemingly undecided about who should put it in"[74] before Dobing eventually slid it home to make it 3–0.

Eastham was the catalyst for the final Cleveland strike, supplying a pretty pass for Vernon to register his second goal of the season. Kees Aarts got a measure of consolation for the Gales when he closed out the scoring on a rebound from a corner-kick scrum in the seventy-second minute. Afterward, Waddington acknowledged the difference that Dobing had made while praising his side's conditioning, saying, "it's good to know that the fitness is still there." Even though, strikingly, it had taken only ninety minutes for the Stokers to equal their entire scoring output for the season, Waddington still sounded uncertain and vaguely uncomfortable, once again referencing the public's desire for goals. Waddington observed that "until the people of the United States become more experienced in watching soccer, they want goals." He acknowledged that his awareness of this desire dictated his decision to attack to "the very end rather than fall back into a defensive game,"[75] with such tactics and psychology being almost second nature to such a traditionally cautious squad.

Reservations aside, Waddington would surely have been heartened by the frightening fluidity of his 4–2–4 attack with Dobing restored to a dangerous frontline consisting of Vernon, Eastham, and Setters (who would be rested against the Whips due to his wonky knee). The understanding and interplay among these men would continue to yield serious dividends during their pivotal showdown with the Whips. Indeed, the Stokers picked up right where they left off, scoring twice in the opening half while threatening to deal a severe, perhaps irreparable, blow to the Whips' title hopes.

The white-hot Dobing opened the scoring in the twenty-third minute, converting an Alan Bloor cross into a 1–0 lead. Eastham was up next, displaying his magical dribbling along the left side of the goal line before spotting John Mahoney, who coolly flipped the ball over the head of a defender for Eastham to punch into the right side of the goal. With Eastham at his majestic best, Andrew Beyer labeled Cleveland's attack "a thing of beauty,"[76] marveling at its "short, accurate passes," which had completely bewildered and undone the Whips' defense, while Washington's forays forward consisted of "clumsy, non-effectual lunges." The Stokers took a dominant, well-deserved 2–0 lead into halftime.

The second half of this match would prove absolutely critical in determining the remainder of the season for each team. The Whips doggedly sought a foothold, slowly becoming ascendant but meeting stiff resistance from Banks. With less than twenty minutes to play, their hopes of a division title ebbing away, Martin Buchan launched a long, optimistic cross to Ally Shewan who blasted it into the net from about twenty-five yards out. Beyer observed that after Shewan's goal, Cleveland shrank palpably, bunching its defense while (even more crucially) abandoning its initiative.

Sensing this, the Whips kept chipping away until finally Pat Wilson engineered a gilt-edged chance for Jim Storrie, whose "shot at the open net practically carried into Lake Erie."[77] Surely this wasted chance would haunt Washington throughout the rest of the summer, yet the determined, undaunted Whips kept pouring forward. Miraculously, with less than two minutes to play, Pat Wilson would reappear, this time slotting home a rebound that bounced to him after Jimmy Wilson frantically crossed the ball into the crowded penalty area. The Whips had somehow salvaged a hair-raising and miraculous 2–2 draw, a result so improbable after Cleveland's imperious first half performance that Beyer swore "such a situation could not have been imagined by the most wild-eyed optimist." An exasperated Banks pronounced himself "disappointed in my performance."[78]

It was a bitter result for Cleveland, particularly because it played out in many ways as an eerie inverse of its previous victory over San Francisco.

Waddington was forced to concede that the Whips "deserved a point because of their fitness at the end." This concession came only a few days after Waddington had singled out the Stokers' superior fitness levels as a primary reason they beat the Gales so handily. Tony Allen also admitted openly that the Stokers "ran out of steam the last twenty minutes."[79] Eddie Turnbull was long obsessed with fitness, believing wholeheartedly that "condition is 75 per cent the secret of success."[80] His team was certainly a hardened, tireless reflection of that ethos. Aberdeen's emphasis on fitness and the pronounced advantage their superior conditioning gave them in the USA made such a huge impression on the Whips' organization that it would become a neurotic, obsessive hallmark of the homegrown 1968 Whips under coach Andre Nagy. After virtually singlehandedly defeating the Whips 3–1 in July 1968, an impressed Pele remarked: "I have never seen a team run like that."[81]

The other direct inverse for the Stokers was a conscious reversion to their cautious nature. Again, just days after securing a result against San Francisco—a result achieved partially because Waddington's team refused to withdraw into an unambitious shell after building a lead that came about largely due to its admirable attempts to satisfy the goal lust of neophyte American fans—the Stokers almost instinctually chose to indulge their conservative inner selves. It proved to be a monumental mistake. Ironically, the imposition of the desires of impatient goal-seeking American fans into Waddington's tactical psychology (something he took great pains to point out repeatedly) was a blessing against San Francisco, a lesson demonstrating the value of remaining positive no matter the score. It was a gift that would go unheeded, allowing an on-the-brink Washington side to survive and continue challenging for the Eastern Division.

To illustrate the stark divide in approach and psychology, Storrie said the Whips made a conscious decision to be more offensive in the second half, to attack relentlessly without fear of conceding more goals. This overwhelming fear of the counterpunch was apparently a significant component of Waddington's psychological makeup; he even cited it in a boxing analogy while lecturing American fans about the perils of chasing goals. It's fascinating to see how it damaged him from both ends.

In comments that had to have stung Waddington to his core, Storrie explicitly implicated the manager's overtly cautious approach, emphasizing that "the Stokers helped us by laying back on defense in the second half,"[82] proof positive that Cleveland was complicit in enabling the Whips' great escape. It was truly a tale of two halves (or, more precisely, two halftime talks) and these decisions would dramatically alter the trajectory of the USA season. To add final insult to injury, Cleveland had now played four of its home matches, leaving it with just a two-point cushion over the Whips and only two home games remaining.

It was all falling into place for the Whips. The Detroit Cougars blew an opportunity to tie them for second place in the Eastern Division when they lost 2–0 to the Houston Stars in a match that had to be halted after seventy-three minutes when it erupted into violence and a "player riot flared"[83] in the Motor City night. The Glentoran FC fan site referred to the simmering encounter as "a roughhouse of a match,"[84] which saw referee Eddie Clemons steadily lose control of the mounting tension, resentment, and aggression.

It finally exploded when "Houston's fullback Luiz Alberto laid out Detroit's Tommy Jackson cold with a kick to the kidney."[85] Clemons awarded Detroit a free kick about ten yards from the net that prompted the players to start scuffling. Some Houston players allegedly used the corner flagpoles as spears in the melee. It escalated even further when "officials of both teams rushed into the fighting" as well as "about 20 of the 7,196 fans" on hand at Detroit's University Stadium. To further illustrate the folly of using woefully inexperienced and unprepared officials in USA matches, Clemons officially blew the match dead but astonishingly never reported any of the players to the league or to USSFA for official discipline.[86]

Complaints about the quality of officiating had been mounting steadily, but this incident served to dramatically underline the dangerous situations that occur when the latent yet explosively contagious violence residing beneath the surface of a given match is nourished by a series of ever more egregious, unpunished fouls that lead to brawling and ultimately a full-fledged riot. As Glanville would remark, soccer is able to "reflect, quite intimately, its surroundings"[87] and the already extant violence permeating the summer air in bitterly divided American cities like Detroit provided a fertile atmosphere that fed symbiotically off the frustrations of disgruntled players unaccustomed to weak, incompetent officiating.

This is yet another area where the owners' abysmal collective lack of soccer knowledge conspired to hurt themselves and others. They didn't seem to realize that blown offside calls and wrongly allowed or disallowed goals were only one aspect of the increasingly vocal frustrations with the league's officiating. Had they understood the culture and nuances of the game more clearly, they might have realized sooner that, as unfortunate as a blown call is, it pales in comparison to the damage that can result when a referee fails to maintain proper control of a match. This too was ironic because what most sportswriters wanted to talk about as the USA launched were the riots that had taken place at soccer matches around the world. It's not as if violence in the game was unknown, specifically in the American press. Perhaps owners more acquainted with soccer would have had a better grasp of why such things happened. This incident was only the beginning.

Meanwhile, the Whips were awaiting a visit to D.C. Stadium from the surprising Los Angeles Wolves. The undefeated Wolves occupied first place in the USA's Western Division with an impressive 4–0–2 record, and the swaggering, freewheeling side arrived in the District having scored fourteen goals while conceding only five through their first six matches. The Los Angeles Wolves were actually Britain's historic Wolverhampton Wanderers. The Wolves came to the USA after a brilliant season in England's Second Division that saw them earn promotion in style, going 28–8–6 and ultimately finishing a scant one point behind Second Division champs Coventry City. As Beyer noted, many "USA officials were a little embarrassed and defensive about having a second-division club in their lineup."[88]

These fears were naive and misguided. With a rich, decorated history dating back to 1877, the Wolves had indeed stumbled into the Second Division at the end of the 1964–1965 season, but their history would reveal a dominant stretch through the 1950s that saw them win the First Division title no less than three times (1954, 1958, 1959). They would ring in the new decade by claiming the FA Cup in 1960. Ronnie Allen arrived as manager in 1965, quickly guiding the Wolves back to the topflight within two years. Allen was a talented, productive center-forward in his day, starring for West Bromwich Albion in a decorated career that saw him score two goals in the 1954 FA Cup final to secure the trophy for the Baggies during a 3–1 victory over Preston North End. Interestingly, Allen would go on to coach Athletic Bilbao after his time with the Wolves, leading the Basques to a Copa del Rey triumph in 1969.[89]

Like the Whips, Allen's Wolves almost didn't wander over to the states in the first place, according to a 2003 reminiscence published by Brian Glanville in the *Times* of London. He remembers speaking to Jack Kent Cooke on the phone and recommending the Wolves to the Canadian sports magnate.[90] Kent Cooke had already lined up Club America from Mexico to represent his Los Angeles franchise but instead decided to pursue an English squad at the last minute. The irony of the inclusion of Club America, based in Mexico City, in the United Soccer Association (USA) would have been delicious indeed, but conceding to the gods of irony would have been profitable, as Club America would certainly have drawn well in Southern California's burgeoning Latino communities.

Glanville noted that Allen was keen to go to the United States but that the BBC's Kenneth Wolstenholme, a major player in the USA's bid to secure teams from the United Kingdom, told him that the team wouldn't go so soon after securing its valuable promotion to First Division. Into this void of confusion and mixed messages stepped the Bolton Wanderers, who were reportedly so sure of their imminent arrival in Los Angeles that they bought new flags and kits.[91] Bolton was thus spared the ignominy—as indeed were the Wolves in the eleventh hour—of becoming the Zorros, Kent Cooke's initial choice for the Los Angeles franchise's name. The *Los Angeles Times* reported that Kent Cooke finally relinquished the name to avoid being confused with the crosstown rival Toros.[92] They were known simply as the "Americans" for a brief time until "Wolves" saved the day.

Wolves forward and all-around English football cult hero Derek Dougan recalled the team being accorded "film star treatment" as soon as it arrived in California. Dougan, Dave Wagstaffe, and the boys immediately became poolside fixtures at the Beverly Wilshire Hotel or Sheraton-West whenever they were in town during the next six weeks.[93] Incredibly, just like the Stokers, only fourteen days separated the end of Wolves' successful promotion campaign and their 1–1 draw against Houston in the Astrodome. Dougan, a Northern Ireland international and bona fide Belfast legend, described the team's mind-set by saying "in effect, we were demonstration salesmen and we piled on the sale pressure in 14 matches. In every game, we played superb football."[94]

Superb it was. After drawing with the Stars in Houston, the Wolves beat the Skyliners 2–1 in a bruising match in front of just over 7,000 Angelinos who saw them called for twenty-eight total fouls. The Skyliners actually got on the board inside of two minutes when Benedicto Ribeiro, "the slickest player on the field,"[95] marauded down the right side of the pitch and launched an inch-perfect cross for New York's outside-left Ruben Bareno to slam into the net behind Phil Parkes. Minutes later, Wolves inside-right Ernie Hunt, who had paced the team's promotion campaign with twenty-one goals, capitalized on a goalkeeping error by Eduardo Garcia to level for the shaky Wolves.

Brian Glanville was in attendance and he lamented the Skyliners' unwillingness "to commit more than three men to attack"[96] the Wolves' "vulnerable defense" after it had conceded the early goal. In a dichotomy almost identical to that which played out between Cleveland and Washington, Glanville noted that like the Whips, the Wolves were a "very young, enterprising side" who wanted to score goals while the Skyliners wanted only to prevent them. New York would also pay for its caution.

The Wolves settled into the game and began to control the tempo with their 4–2–4 formation, "using both their wingers out on the touchline"[97] to supply width and defensive cover. Peter Knowles in particular began to influence the match, finding incisive passes as a link-up man alongside Dave Burnside. It was Burnside who pounced on a rebound after a skirmish in front of the goal, giving the Wolves a 2–1 lead they would never relinquish.

The Wolves would grind out another close 2–1 victory over Toronto City in front of a paltry 3,363 in Canada. Wolves legend Bobby Thomson scored on a long-range effort with less than a minute remaining in the first half to give Los Angeles the advantage. The Wolves then conceded a penalty to Toronto's Joe Davis, who knotted the score at 1–1 in the second before Derek Dougan swept in to save the day. Dougan scored the winning goal on a pretty feed from center-half John Madsen. This match was notable because the Wolves lost so many players to injury that the thirty-eight-year-old Allen was ultimately forced to suit up.

The colorful Dougan's legend had proceeded him to America, with Beyer noting "'the Doog' long has had the reputation of being one of the kookiest players in English football."[98] Kookiness aside, the towering six-foot-three Dougan was a prolific goal poacher and aerial threat, with massive size and a pure nose for the net. Acquired from Leicester City in March, Dougan made an immediate impact on the Wolves' bid for promotion, scoring five goals in the club's next six matches. He would remain the focal point of Wolverhampton's attack into the early '70s, scoring ninety-five goals for the Wolves during the next eight years. It was the start of a long, strange trip that saw Dougan ultimately became the Wolves' chairman in 1982.

Before making the trek to Washington, D.C., the Wolves annihilated an undermanned Vancouver squad that fielded seven players under twenty years of age by a 5–1 scoreline. Even though the young Canadians went ahead on a Brian Heslop goal after twenty-nine minutes, the Wolves smelled blood and reacted accordingly. Again using the stellar, effective wing play of Dave Wagstaffe and Paddy Buckley to control the match, Los Angeles scored a bucketful of goals, starting with a beautiful Wagstaffe cross to Ernie Hunt. The two wingers teamed up for the second when Buckley scored off of Wagstaffe's corner delivery.

Once again the enigmatic Knowles, "the bobby-sox idol of Wolverhampton fans,"[99] beguiled the opposition with an elegant array of dribbles, tricks, and flicks that bordered on devilish mockery before setting up another Buckley goal after a serpentine jaunt down the length of the pitch. Clearly enjoying one of "his days of grace,"[100] Knowles would finally get on the board himself, scoring on a pass from Dougan. The Doog would close out the scoring with a punishing header after more sublime service from Bobby Thomson. Taken together, Knowles combined with the devastating wing presence of Wagstaffe and Buckley served to illustrate the effectiveness of the 4–2–4 formation when a team had the proper players to utilize it. The comprehensive 5–1 thrashing was sadly not even Vancouver's heaviest defeat of the tournament, as they had also fallen 6–1 to the Golden Gales.

Los Angeles kept rolling, manhandling the Cougars 4–1 in a convincing fashion that the tiny Belfast outfit hadn't yet encountered in America. Thomson and Knowles were once again instrumental in devising a pulsating Wolves attack that prompted Allen to gush over the "fine overlapping by fullback Bobby Thomson who is the best fullback in football when he plays like he did today. Peter Knowles in the first half was pure champagne."[101]

The Whips dominated the first half of their showdown with Los Angeles, barraging the Wolves defense with fourteen shots. Jimmy Wilson scored in the twenty-third minute to give Washington a 1–0 lead. The Wolves would equalize before the break, largely against the run of play after the typically excellent Bobby Clark misjudged a ball amid heavy traffic in front of goal, allowing Dave Burnside a chance to slam it home. The score would remain deadlocked, but the second half of the match turned out to be eventful anyway because the Wolves made and the referees allowed what the Whips alleged to be an illegal substitute.

With thirteen minutes remaining, Allen withdrew Dave Wagstaffe for Gerry Taylor. It was the Wolves' third substitute of the match, but USA rules clearly permitted only two substitutions for outfield players per game. Washington's Jim Storrie protested while it was happening, only for referee Miro Roguly to say that "he didn't know any such rule."[102] This had particular bearing on the match because both teams were playing with ten men and Taylor's fresh legs definitely gave Los Angeles an unfair competitive advantage. Whips general manager Jerry Cooper threw down the gauntlet in front of commissioner Dick Walsh, saying publicly that "anything short of awarding us 2 points . . . isn't going to be of help to us."[103] Walsh announced that the league would investigate.

The Whips had no time to dwell on this bizarre state of affairs as they traveled to San Francisco and a date with the Golden Gales. Despite their thorough, comprehensive defeat in Cleveland, the Gales had remained a force in the Western Division, carrying a 4–2–1 record and steadily keeping pace with the high-flying Wolves. The goals kept going in for San Francisco, which had now scored twenty-three times in seven matches. Henk Houwart led the USA's goal-scoring race with eight. The Gales' problem was a porous defense that had conceded fifteen times for one of the worst defensive records in the league.

It was a match stuck in neutral, a scoreless tie defined by disputed, disallowed goals and lackadaisical football. The Whips thought they had snatched two points on the way out the door when Whips sparkplug Pat Wilson found Dave Johnston wide open for a tap-in that linesman Bela Palfalvi ruled out. The Whips protested Palfalvi's offsides call "vehemently and at length but to no avail."[104] San Francisco's Rene Pas, who came from nowhere with six goals as a reserve, also had one nullified early on. It would be the Whips' fourth straight draw. The Whips were "booed angrily several times" for their "rough play." Beyer observed that this "rough play" had escalated to a point where "half a dozen times it appeared the Dutch-men and the Scotsmen would come to blows."[105] Thankfully it didn't escalate, but the sulky air was ominous and heavy.

The Whips were now awaiting the arrival of hapless Vancouver and needed at least a draw against the 2–4–2 Royal Canadians to keep pace with the steady Stokers. Sunderland AFC had fallen on hard times and was trying to weather an overall low point in the club's historical trajectory, finishing a disappointing sixteenth of twenty-two in the First Division as it limped meekly into British Columbia to assume the role of the Vancouver Royal

Canadians. The Canadian franchise was owned by Brigadier General E. G. Eakins. According to Paul Days, Sunderland's Cecil Irwin recalled being headquartered at the Tower Hotel in Vancouver where Little Richard was the resident entertainer.[106]

Perhaps this loose Little Richard ambience explains Vancouver's abysmal start. The club had been ravaged with injuries as well as being in the midst of a significant roster overhaul; this was also evidenced by its overreliance on rookies and squad players against the Wolves. Still, their roster featured players like Jimmy Baxter, a wing-half considered by many to be one of the greatest Scottish players of all time. Baxter played for Scotland thirty-four times between 1961 and 1967. The gifted winger was blessed with exquisite control, "delivering the ball to teammates with a touch that made it appear weightless."[107] Baxter was on the Scottish side that triumphed 2–1 at Wembley in 1963, scoring both goals against his country's bitter rivals, yet when reduced to ten men and clinging desperately to a tenuous lead, Baxter joked that he had seriously considered putting one through his own net so he could say that he had scored a hat trick.[108]

The mischievous, hard-living Baxter, known to suck on peppermints in training as a futile attempt to cover the booze that was usually still oozing from his pores, had starred for Rangers, racking up an impressive trophy haul in the early '60s before being sold to Sunderland in 1965 for £72,500. Other Scottish internationals playing for Vancouver included the enigmatic, influential George Herd, who had starred for Inverness Thistle before moving to Wearside, and center-forward Neil Martin.

Recently they had lost 4–2 to Toronto in Vancouver to sink all the way to the bottom of the Western Division. Toronto used a "fast breaking, short-passing attack"[109] to pile up three second-half goals against an overrun Vancouver backline. Despite being a side clearly in flux, playing a strange tournament in a strange land, Baxter's workrate was exemplary and he never stopped running against Toronto. Martin opened the scoring for Vancouver in the twenty-seventh minute and nearly struck again minutes later but was unlucky when his shot rung off the woodwork.

Vancouver manager Ian McColl referred to that moment as the "turning point," as a two-goal lead would have put immense pressure on Toronto. A Brian Heslop own goal put Toronto level, and the game remained deadlocked at 1–1 until Colin Stein scored Toronto's second at the end of a beautiful sequence of passes with Eric Stevenson and Bobby Duncan. Stein and Jim Scott would add Toronto's final two goals in a frenetic space of four minutes. Toronto manager Bill Shankly called the 4–2 victory "the best game we've played in this league."[110] In the return fixture four days later on June 25, the Royal Canadians earned a respectable 2–2 draw against Toronto on their way to Washington, D.C.

Herd would be rested against Washington, and a banged-up Baxter started on the substitutes' bench. The Whips controlled the first half of the match with relative ease, taking a 1–0 lead into the break on the strength of a Francis Munro goal off a beautiful Jimmy Wilson cross in the fourteenth minute. Less than four minutes into the second, Vancouver scored off a set piece when Alan Gauden nudged the rebound of a corner past the frozen Bobby Clark. It was the second time in three matches that the reliable Clark was caught off guard or out of position at a critical time. After gaining an equalizer, the Royal Canadians were content to sit back and defend, and the Whips were unable to break them down any further. Vancouver's general manager John Pickburn was so impressed by his team's organization that he labeled it "Sunderland's best defensive game thus far."[111]

The disappointing 1–1 draw was the Whips' fifth straight stalemate and sixth in nine league matches. Luckily for the Whips, the Stokers had also begun to slump, leaving the Eastern Division title within reach. The Englishmen had spent a lazy week soaking up the sun in Ft. Lauderdale, yet after handily beating the Dallas Tornado 4–1, the Stokers dropped two straight, once again giving the deadlock-prone Whips a lifeline. Strangely, the Stokers had only gotten stronger on paper with the addition of a healthy Harry Burrows. The flashy outside-forward injured his right knee on May 31 in Cleveland's match with the Chicago Mustangs and he had struggled to regain the form that saw him become the club's second-highest goal scorer the previous season.

Burrows described himself as an "old fashioned winger."[112] In a fascinating piece of tactical information that reflected the game's rapid evolution, Tony Waddington referred to Burrows as a "rarity in the game today." Waddington added: "at one time wings were speedy, able to rush past the fullbacks. They outflanked the defense. Then a revolution came. Outside wings became players who rarely shot on goal."[113] Burrows was an exception, possessed with blazing speed and a powerful shot. He had scored twice in the Stokers' victory over Dallas and seemed to be rounding into form at the perfect time.

The Stokers welcomed a New York Skyliners side that had struggled mightily away from Yankee Stadium, losing three away matches. Despite fielding an impressive team, the Skyliners were perhaps the most disappointing squad in the tournament, going winless in seven straight contests, losing no less than four of those by 1–0 scorelines. Waddington rather forthrightly told the *Plain Dealer*: "I don't know anything about Cerro."[114] One thing that people around the USA had learned about the Uruguayans was that they'd forged a "reputation as a bruising opponent," relying on brutal tackling that stretched the outer limits of legality and sportsmanship. One such tackle against the Chicago Mustangs touched off the frightening Yankee Stadium melee. This match would be no different.

It was a contest brimming with "fisticuffs and boiling tempers"[115] that eventually saw the Stokers reduced to ten men when right halfback John Mahoney was ejected for fighting with eight minutes left. Dan Coughlin described the match as "a brewing tempest that erupted in a semi-controlled brawl at the corner of the field near first base."[116] There had been a series of minor incidents that began to gain in frequency and intensity. Referee Richard Giebner placed the blame squarely on Mahoney, saying, "the game wasn't that dirty" and that "Mahoney was ejected because he was the cause of a small riot, if you care to call it that." It *was* interesting who labeled these incidents "riots" and why.

The Plain Dealer depicted Cerro/New York as a club possessed of "speed and skill with hard tackling and aggravating arrogance." The Stokers struck first, when Setters crossed to Dobing, who scored easily. Whether they switched off in an effort to protect their 1–0 lead or they were undone psychologically by the Skyliners' physical assault, the Stokers demonstrated defensive vulnerability that New York was able to exploit. Benedicto Ribeiro scored the equalizer on a brilliant one-on-one move that saw him deftly outmaneuver Banks to slip the ball into an empty net.

Juan Pintos scored on a similar burst of individual skill in the sixtieth minute to give New York a 2–1 lead; amazingly it was the first time Cleveland had trailed through eight USA matches. After securing the lead, "Cerro dilly dallied away the last 20 minutes, squandering precious seconds with exaggerated injuries." Waddington, refusing to be drawn in, said, "once they got ahead, their tactics were perfectly legitimate and justifiable."[117] The 2–1 result was the Skyliners' first victory of the tournament.

Despite the Stokers' surprising setback against the Skyliners, optimism in and around Cleveland remained high, with the *Plain Dealer* writing, "barring World War III, the Stokers are headed towards a championship showdown on July 16th with Wolverhampton."[118] The paper also provided interesting context to officiating's role in the recent outbreaks of violence, noting that language barriers were a problem but that "the catalyst for the reaction are American referees."

On that point, Maurice Setters noted that "referees in different countries interpret the rules differently . . . and then the players can't understand what the others are saying." This exacerbated the pain of clumsy fouling, because it eliminated any chance for a player to say "I'm sorry" or "My mistake," leading to an escalation of bad blood. Setters concisely summed up this state of affairs, saying that all a player could do under these circumstances was "react."[119] The tenor of these reactions would be increasingly raw and violent.

Next up for the Stokers were the enigmatic Houston Stars. The Stars were a true reflection of their mercurial owner, the legendary Judge Roy Hofheinz, a uniquely American figure who could only have sprung from the soil of

Texas. Hofheinz "was a shrewd and sophisticated operator in the Lyndon B. Johnson genre—country boy geniality mixed with a gimlet-eyed grasp of reality."[120] At twenty-four, he became the youngest county judge in American history, before managing one of President Johnson's earliest political campaigns.

The Astrodome housed Hofheinz's—and Major League Baseball's—Houston Colt .45s before it completely subsumed their identity and transformed them into the Astros. An engineering monument whose interior reflected American wealth and opulence, the offices in the $37 million Astrodome complex featured "yards and yards of deep gold carpet, lush velvet scarlet-and-gold chairs supported by rampant Austrian lions or gold metal frames, specially designed gold telephones on every gold-trimmed Louis XIV desk." The bathrooms featured "yellow gold plush" toilets. There would be an abundance of gold china cups and gilded ashtrays, leading some locals to derisively dub the judge "Giltfinger." Details like these led *Sports Illustrated*'s Liz Smith to dust off her Kubla Khan references.[121]

The stadium itself was every bit as lovingly garish and over the top. The two-million-dollar scoreboard roared to life whenever the Astros hit a home run, projecting a frontier fantasia with gunfire, cowboys, bulls, and other symbols of the eternal Texas mind or, as Miller put it, an electronic reimagining of "the Battle of San Jacinto." It was a vulgar, distinctly American display of ostentation. This is the tableau Bangu Atletico Clube found itself thrust into as it became the Houston Stars. The reigning champions of Rio de Janeiro, Bangu claimed the Campeonato Carioca for the second time in 1966, six years after it had won the inaugural ISL tournament with a victory over Kilmarnock.

The Stars, perhaps the most technically gifted side in the competition, prompted Sunderland's John O'Hare to rave that their "skill level was superb" after they had thrashed the Black Cats 4–1, giving them a proper "football lesson.[122] The Stars' lineup included Paulo Borges, a player some considered the second or third best in the world after Pele and Eusebio. Also featuring for the Stars was veteran Brazil international center-back Mario Tito and Carlos Roberto Cabral, better known as Cabralzinho. Cabralzinho, who scored twice in the USA tournament, would go on to a well-traveled, relatively successful managerial career with stops at Santos (one of his clubs prior to Bangu) and Al Ain.

Bangu used a deadly, rhythmic short-passing attack to lull teams into lethargy before attacking with surprising pace and penetration. The Stars' match with the Stokers in the Astrodome was a strange affair marred by "another of those aggravating snafus that have scarred the first nationwide professional soccer season."[123] This particular snafu saw the game end abruptly, bizarrely, and with no real explanation, as the referee suddenly blew the final whistle with 5:48 remaining on the oversize game clock.

The Stokers, trailing 2–1, protested vehemently to no avail. The Stars had dominated the stolid Stokers with their pace and workrate, leaving an already frustrated side to ponder the referee's baffling decision. Jair opened the scoring in the fortieth minute, when he sailed a powerful shot over Banks' head to give the Stars a 1–0 lead. Dobing scored his sixth goal in five matches to equalize for the Stokers in the waning moments of the first half. The goal was illustrative of the intricate possession-based football of which Cleveland was also capable, as Alan Bloor started the move down the right flank, setting in motion a sequence of passes between Setters and Vernon that culminated in Dobing's goal. Dobing would end the tournament with seven goals in eight matches. The Stars' Noberto scored the winning goal with less than seventeen minutes to play, supplying Houston's margin of victory while handing the stumbling Stokers their second straight 2–1 loss.

With races tightening up—the Stokers, Whips, Cougars, and Toronto all still had a chance to claim the East and the West was essentially a two-horse race between Los Angeles and San Francisco—a coin flip (yes, a coin flip) was held to decide which division leader would host the USA title match. The West won the toss, virtually ensuring that the game would be held in California.[124]

The Stokers led the Whips by a single point in the East as Washington geared up for its own trip to Texas and a date with the Dallas Tornado in the Cotton Bowl. Again delving into the Scottish First Division's recent past, Andrew Beyer noted that Dundee United had finished the previous campaign in ninth place and, further, had lost five of their previous six matches against Aberdeen/Washington.[125] However, Dundee United had scored an impressive sixty-eight goals in thirty-four league matches, quixotically dealing the all-conquering Celtic their only two defeats as they stormed through their legendary trophy-laden season, including a nail-biting 3–2 decision at Celtic Park.

Unfortunately for Dundee—not to mention Lamar Hunt and the primordial strata of fans in the Dallas Metroplex—the goals dried up drastically upon the side's stateside arrival. The club had managed only ten in its first nine matches heading into its clash with the Whips, with four of those coming against the lowly Boston Rovers. Beyer also noted that, amazingly, despite its offensive futility, the Tornado were actually leading the USA in shots with 211, thirty of those coming in a game they lost 4–1 to the Stokers in mid-June. This match perfectly illustrated the disconnect between high shot totals and low goal output.

The Tornado had actually dominated the Stokers in terms of possession and initiative but were undone by their toothless attack and wobbly defense. According to Bill Lace of *The Fort-Worth Star Telegraph* "most of the game was played in Cleveland's end of the field as Dallas mounted attack after attack with mad abandon."[126] Lace emphasized that "there was little method in their madness," illustrating the problem with the "harem scarem type offense." Many of Dallas' thirty shots were far off target and failed to trouble Banks in the slightest.

The chaotic, whirlwind, yet ultimately fruitless nature of the Tornado's offense was illuminated in stark contrast to Cleveland's deliberate pace and "classy ball handling." Peter Dobing and company were able to weather early Tornado pressure to seize control of the match. Harry Burrows supplied a brace and fullback Ernie Skeels added a fourth before Dallas' Jackie Graham scored off a corner to give the Tornado scant consolation in a 4–1 defeat. The Stokers relentlessly sought and found openings to operate within, and George Eastham pulled the strings masterfully, orchestrating quick, decisive breaks. Manager Jerry Kerr said afterward that his team "ran with the ball too much," [127] again demonstrating the perils of possession without invention.

Kerr had guided Dundee into European competition on the strength of its sixth-place finish in 1966. The club then shocked Barcelona, scoring an astonishing 2–1 victory at Camp Nou, in the now-defunct Inter Cities Fairs Cup, before ultimately losing to Juventus. Playing on the narrow Cotton Bowl pitch likely hampered Jerry Kerr tactically, but the lack of firepower from a team that had averaged two goals per match in a world-class league was puzzling.

Kerr, who spent two years playing for the Rangers after World War II, was a Scottish football renaissance man. The manager became an agent of modernization, finding new ways to finance Dundee United so that they could not only compete financially with Scotland's Old Firm, but also so that they could survive and flourish "despite attendances which were some of the poorest in the land." [128] *The Independent* credited the forward-thinking Kerr with being one of the first to realize that the game "could not survive through the turnstiles alone." [129]

The manager was also one of the first to look to Scandinavia for talent. Under Kerr, the Scandinavian influence "took root more strongly in Dundee than anywhere else." The Dundee side that played in the USA featured Scandinavian players such as Finn Dossing, Mogens Berg, outside-right Finn Seeman, and Orjan Persson. This would be perhaps the part of his legacy that most influenced the early years of the NASL, as both Dallas, his host city, and Washington would also look to Nordic lands to fill out their rosters when the imports returned home.

Dallas showed erratic flashes of the team it had once been in Scotland, particularly when it ripped the Rovers 4–1 under granite gray skies in rainy Boston. On this night, the Dallas attack "included fancy dribbling, deft fast breaks," [130] and a deadly accurate long ball that Doug Smith launched downfield for Jackie Graham to run onto and score. Finn Seeman opened the scoring for the Tornado and Mogens Berg bagged a brace to provide the 4–1 margin of victory, with the gritty Liam Touhy adding scant consolation for the Rovers in the thirty-ninth minute.

Around a week before their match with the Whips, the Tornado lost 1–0 in Detroit to the Cougars on June 25 in another match dominated by quizzical officiating. Kerr referred to it as "bloody scandalous,"[131] largely for their unwillingness to "let the teams play." Writing in the *Dallas Morning News*, Bob St. John likened referee Michael Wurtz and linesmen Tom Syme and Ed Clements to "toy soldiers who automatically raised their arms at intervals."[132] This led to Dallas piling up eleven offside violations.

Detroit's volcanic player/manager John Colrain reportedly benched himself near the end of the match "because he felt he couldn't keep his 'cool' regarding the officials." It was a lesson Colrain had learned the hard way after being suspended for his mysteriously uncorroborated altercation with an official in the Cougars' USA debut. Complaints about the refereeing aside, Kerr bluntly characterized his team as "bloody awful." The game's lone goal occurred in the fifty-second minute when Detroit's Danny Trainor headed a pretty pass for inside-left Tommy Morrow to slam past keeper Sandy Davie.

The Whips' superior fitness levels would again play a decisive factor in the showdown with their longtime rivals in Texas on July 2. Beyer singled out "superb physical conditioning"[133] as one of Washington's greatest virtues before noting its tendency to be "the stronger team at the end" of matches. This fact was also lamented by Tony Waddington. The Whips harnessed their conditioning to a relentless workrate and devotion to pressing that enabled them to secure results such as this. With less than twenty minutes to play, Jim Storrie stole the ball and set up a Jimmy Smith goal that cemented two points for the Whips, who easily blanked the Tornado 2–0.

With a decent 4–3–3 mark, the Stars awaited the Whips in the Astrodome. Despite their impressive record, the Stars had just been knocked out of the Western Division chase after a stunning loss in Boston to the previously winless Rovers. The League of Ireland's Shamrock Rovers were drafted as the USA's Boston representative and were certainly the league's most lightly regarded team. The Rovers were so poor that they'd only managed three draws heading into the final weeks of the USA season. Still, they were managed by ex–Newcastle United inside-right and Republic of Ireland international Liam Touhy, a fierce competitor who would prowl the pitch himself that summer.

All in all, the Rovers did indeed prove to be the league's weakest link on and off the pitch, propping up the table and registering the league's poorest attendance. Interestingly, Glentoran FC notes that Kenneth Wolstenholme had initially wanted the Rovers to combine with Linfield to form some sort of Irish Select XI, an idea that likely would have appealed to USA administrators. Linfield declined for various reasons "but primarily because their rules then prohibited Sunday football."[134]

Owned by Weston Adams of the Boston Bruins, the Rovers entered the USA on the back of a fourth straight Irish Cup victory, their sixteenth in the previous twenty-two years. Their stadium, the Manning Bowl, was a high school football stadium fifteen miles outside of Boston. Much like their Glentoran counterparts, the Rovers were a part-time outfit. Touhy explained exactly what this meant to the press: "we're always at a disadvantage against teams such as Stoke. They live it year-round. We're only part time professionals." [135] Touhy's admission was followed by context regarding soccer's place in Irish culture when he remarked that the truly big sports in Ireland were Gaelic football and curling. To emphasize this point further, Touhy revealed that the Gaelic Football championship drew around 70,000 spectators on average while the Irish Cup final drew only 30,000.

Like the Cougars, the men on the Boston Rovers had to maintain full-time jobs and were able to train only twice a week. Touhy was a mechanic in Dublin, for instance. Also like Detroit they were allowed to field four "guest" players to strengthen their lineup. The Rovers' guests included John Brooks and Dougie Wood, a left-half who was named the Ulster player of the year for 1964–1965. Another of these guests was the Brazilian born Carlos Metidieri. Metidieri had featured for the ECPSL's Toronto Italia Falcons and would go on to star for the Los Angeles Wolves and the Rochester Lancers in the NASL. While playing for the Lancers, Metidieri won back-to-back NASL MVP awards, [136] the only player to do so consecutively. Such was the state of the U.S. men's national team in the early '70s—Metidieri was eventually capped twice for America, most notably in a 4–0 loss to Bermuda.

The conditions for the Rovers–Stars match definitely favored Boston, as rain soaked the field, making it difficult for Houston to find the proper tempo and control for their intricate passing game on the muddy track. Despite being outplayed, the Stars struck first on a header by Jaime about twenty minutes in. Undaunted, the Rovers kept pressing and finally broke through in the forty-first minute when Bobby Gilbert scored on a pretty pass from Wood. Metidieri caused havoc among Houston's backline and helped the Rovers take the lead when Billy Dixon banged in the rebound of one of his shots. The grizzled Touhy closed out the scoring, giving the Rovers a much-needed victory.

For once, the Whips were facing a team *weakened* by national team obligations, as Stars leading goal scorer Paulo Borges was unavailable. Borges had notched six goals for Houston before returning to Brazil. Strangely, the forward was slated to return to the Stars before the Whips game but had yet to resurface, [137] leaving baffled club officials at a loss. At 3–1–6, the Whips remained a point behind the sputtering Stokers.

The Stars established their passing rhythm against the Whips early but were unable to translate their possession into concrete chances. The Stars operated at a slow tempo, which worked against them by allowing Washington to conserve its energy for the second half. By the time the Whips finally increased the tempo of play, Houston had tired, allowing the Whips to dictate the match. Washington players noticed that Houston began shying away from its aggressive, tough-tackling physical play and also seemed to be pursuing "loose balls with less vigor."[138] This realization caused to the Whips to step "up the pressure a bit," according to Jim Storrie.

The increased tempo and physical pressure finally caused Houston to "throw in the towel," according to an unnamed Whips player. So demoralized were the Stars that Francis Munro picked up the ball in Washington's penalty area and barreled all the way down the pitch into Houston's end before finding Jimmy Smith, who wasted no time burying it for a 1–0 lead that carried the day. The result had given the Whips a point lead over the Stokers for first place in the Eastern Division with one match to play.

The Stokers squared off against the Detroit Cougars on July 5, the night after the Whips took control of the division. Cleveland would be without the services of Gordon Banks who, in the words of Stokers assistant manager Frank Mountford, was rested after "two hard years of football."[139] Paul Shardlow would be guarding Cleveland's net. The young Irishman Terry Conroy was inserted into the Stokers' front four. Conroy had been transferred from Glentoran to Stoke in March and was excited to play against his old teammates.

The twenty-year-old Conroy was a force for the Glens, catching Stoke's eye after scoring twenty-four goals in thirty-six league matches. Conroy's story reemphasized the trials of being a part-time player in Ireland, as the young forward held down a job as a printer in Dublin. This forced Conroy to drive the two-hundred-mile "round trip from Dublin to Belfast and back just for games,"[140] which he did for fifteen months before moving to Stoke.

The contest was a chippy, scoreless, slow-motion grind most notable for the ejections of Danny Trainor and Tony Allen for fighting in the eighty-fourth minute. A wasteful Detroit actually carried the play, outshooting the Stokers thirty-eight to eighteen, according to some accounts. Although only 4,729 showed up at University Stadium, the Cougars were given a "rousing ovation all the way to the changing rooms"[141] in what was their last "home" match. The Cougars' determined, inspiring performances prompted franchise moneyman Jack Anderson to say afterward: "You know, I had been told by everyone that Glentoran would not live with the opposition when they came here. Even some people in Belfast assured me they would get hiding after hiding. The results have made nonsense of those statements."

The nil–nil draw drew the Stokers level with the Whips in the Eastern Division hunt. It also left them perilously thin at goalkeeper, as Paul Shardlow separated his shoulder. Gordon Banks already had one foot on the plane back to England. To make matters worse, the Stokers' slips had left them with no real control over their destiny heading into the final week of the season. This was because on July 5, the USA announced that the disputed 1–1 draw between the Whips and Wolves on June 20, wherein the Wolves made an illegal substitution, "must be replayed in Washington if its outcome would affect the final league standings."[142]

Due to the tightness at the top of the Eastern Division, this decree gave the Whips a definitive advantage heading into their last match against the Rovers. This trouble can be traced back to the Stokers' decision to play conservatively with a 2–0 lead against the Whips in Cleveland, thereby giving them a lifeline instead of burying them for good. The solitary point the Whips earned in their pivotal 2–2 draw now loomed larger than ever.

The Whips were unbeaten since losing to Cleveland on the USA's opening night (although most of their results had been ties), gaining momentum and confidence as they barnstormed through Texas with their "nonstop hustle and relentless attack."[143] The Stokers had faltered since their second fateful meeting with Washington, winning only one of their previous four matches. They faced a daunting, draining trip to British Columbia.

Bobby Clark had been immense for the Whips during this unbeaten stretch, yielding only one goal in the last 410 minutes of play as he awaited a visit from the unimposing Rovers.[144] Perhaps their victory over a talented Houston squad gave them confidence or perhaps they had finally adjusted to the USA's pace and travel. Whatever the reason, the Rovers came to Washington, D.C., to play—not just for the ride. The Whips brought everything that they had spent the last month honing to bear on the Irishmen, attacking keeper Pat Dunne with withering pace and aggression in front of 9,760 of the District faithful. Afterward a ruminative Turnbull suggested that his side was perhaps "too offense-minded,"[145] which made them vulnerable to Boston's counterpunching forays.

Dunne turned in one of the performances of the tournament, stopping shot after deadly shot, keeping the Rovers on level terms. For the increasingly influential Francis Munro, it was the best and worst of times. Munro instigated the Whips' long-awaited breakthrough after receiving an immaculate long ball from Jens Petersen (more evidence of Scottish soccer's increasing Scandinavian influence) and blasting a shot into the net from distance. Just three minutes later, however, Munro would bring down Mickey Leech in the penalty area, allowing Frank O'Neill to convert from the spot. Unable to recover, the Whips fell 2–1.

The Stokers weren't faring much better in Vancouver. Jimmy Baxter was definitely in the mood to spoil the Stokers' summer, scoring twice in the first half to stake Vancouver to a 2–0 lead before Harry Burrows found Alan Bloor with a delightful cross to put Cleveland on the board. Colin Suggett added to Vancouver's lead less than twenty minutes into the second half, allowing the Royal Canadians to slow the pace and protect their two-goal lead. This surprising 3–1 victory, only their second of the tournament, effectively ended the Stokers' hopes of playing for the USA title.

Creeping slowly along in the background was Toronto City, which also had a chance to qualify for the USA title match if it could beat the Cougars in Toronto. Unfortunately for them, the match was played in absolutely frightening, abysmal conditions, as torrential rain and powerful winds pummeled Toronto. The conditions were so bad that John Colrain reportedly asked the officials to abandon the match.[146]

The tenacious Cougars, relishing their role as spoilers, played hard despite the deluge, striking first on a Jim Weatherup goal in the forty-seventh minute. Toronto, just seconds away from losing outright, snatched defeat from Detroit when Colin Stein crossed to Jim Scott who equalized in the small hours. It was a frantic finish to the season and a gigantic missed opportunity for Toronto, which could have won the Eastern Division outright over Washington and Cleveland due to number of goals scored with twenty-three.

Amazingly, it was announced that Glentoran was to be suspended by the Irish League for playing on Sundays throughout the USA season.[147] Such was the Glens' size, centrality, and standing in the Irish League—club officials basically shrugged. The people of Belfast welcomed their conquering heroes home with raucous pride, staging a celebratory procession from city hall after a formal reception.

As it stood, the Stokers were 5–3–4 with fourteen points and nineteen goals scored, while the Whips, pending the result of their now-mandatory replay with Wolves, were 4–2–5 with thirteen points and sixteen goals. Washington, of course, still needed to beat a tired, disinterested Wolves team but could also still win the division with an improbable 4–4 tie. The entire topsy-turvy Eastern Division race would come down to one match.

The Houston Stars definitely underachieved relative to their skill level but still were able to light up the night. They met fellow South American travelers, the New York Skyliners, in Yankee Stadium for their USA final match. It was a match, with no stakes or bearing on the championship, wherein the two proud sides managed to put together a "dazzling technical display"[148] in a frantic 2–2 draw, according to Gerald Eskenazi.

As was his creative, speculative wont, Eskenazi peppered his recollection of the contest with allusions to the two clubs suffering from "homesickness" and preoccupations with other times and places before noting that "Bangu were flawless in the first half opening half." The heads of their backline "would strike out cobra like, to break up enemy passes," while "their skill at dribbling and movement gave them a flowing attack."

The Skyliners answered the bell in the second, summoning their own potent South American majesty. It was, as it had been throughout, Benedicto Ribeiro who got things rolling, bringing "gasps and laughs from the fans with sudden stops and starts." Ruben Bareno finally scored after a series of New York corner kicks. Bareno was also instrumental in Sergio Silva's equalizing goal, which closed the scoring in this lost gem of a match, a bittersweet monument to two underachieving yet undeniably talented teams. [149]

The Wolves and Gales continued to battle for the Western crown, with the persistent Gales refusing to fade away as Houston had. The Wolves made it harder on themselves, stumbling to an ill-tempered 2–2 draw with the Chicago Mustangs in a match they led twice. It was made more frustrating by the fact that the Mustangs played for more than thirty minutes with ten men after fullback Martin Tiddia was ejected for kicking Peter Knowles. Referee Lawrence King wasted no time in sending off Tiddia, but the Mustangs leveled minutes later on a wobbly strike from halfback Guiseppi Longoni. [150]

The Wolves' damaging, prolific wing play was on full display again as Gerry Taylor tore down the right side of the pitch and found Dougan who headed to Ernie Hunt to opening the scoring. It was a concise sequence that demonstrated the effectiveness of the Wolves' relatively simple approach working out of their 4–2–4. Much like the Stokers, the Gales had shot themselves in the foot the very same evening, losing 2–1 to Dallas at the Cotton Bowl.

At this point in the season, grueling travel and punishing heat had reduced even the most fit, robust teams, and home teams were playing with an ever-greater advantage. The Tornado unleashed one of their most cohesive performances of the year, as the possession and voluminous shots suddenly began finding the target. It started ominously enough when Henk Houwaart scored his ninth goal for the Gales less than two minutes into the game.

But the Tornado bore down, allowing inside-right Jackie Graham to decisively put his stamp on the match. It was Graham's shot that caromed off a defender before falling to Finn Dossing to boot home, tying the match at 1–1 in the twentieth minute. Graham appeared at the end of a latticework move inspired by great passing between inside-right Dennis Gillespie and outside-left Ian Scott. Working down the left flank, Graham blasted in the winning goal, delivering the Dallas faithful their first victory in the Cotton Bowl. [151]

The Wolves had to earn only a draw with this unpredictable Tornado squad to clinch the West, while the Gales needed both a Wolves loss and a victory over the Chicago Mustangs. The Wolves' trip to Dallas was a fittingly wild affair. Dallas got on the board first when the red-hot Graham scored in the fourteenth minute. The Wolves scored twice in relatively quick succession to take the lead before the end of the first half. Peter Knowles struck first, lofting in a long shot that eluded Dallas keeper Donald MacKay. Bobby Thomson scored from a corner to put the Wolves in the lead, 2–1. Before heading into halftime Knowles was sent off for arguing with the referee, consigning the Wolves to a tense second half.

According to Bob St. John, Dallas "did about everything but wipe the Los Angeles goal off the Cotton Bowl turf"[152] in its furious quest for an equalizer. Playing with only nine men in front of him, Phil Parkes was forced to make a handful of difficult saves. The breakthrough came with less than fourteen minutes to play when Jim Cameron scored to give the Tornado a much-deserved draw. The point was enough for the Wolves to clinch a spot in the USA championship match—a match that, thanks to the whim of a coin toss, would be played in their own stadium.

The Gales played out an ultimately irrelevant, mostly invisible scoreless draw with the Chicago Mustangs in Kezar Stadium to close out their season. The only outstanding piece of business for the Wolves was a meddlesome trip to Washington, D.C., for a rematch with the Whips that would determine their opponent for the July 14 title showdown.

The disinterested Wolves flew across the country to play Washington to decide the Eastern Division title. A cagey Los Angeles side played resolute defense without being too ambitious going forward. The match remained scoreless ten minutes into the second half before the dam broke when Francis Munro crossed to Jim Storrie who notched the first of his two goals. Martin Buchan added the second before Storrie closed out the scoring. It was a sixteen-minute onslaught that arrived with the sudden power of an intense summer storm. The Whips secured a hard-fought 3–0 victory to finally decide the Eastern Division.[153] Their reward would be a trip to Los Angeles and a high-stakes rematch with the Wolves.

"NOT QUITE AS GOOD AS THIS ONE"

On July 14, 1967, the Los Angeles Wolves and Washington Whips clashed for the USA title. Going into the final, the Whips had conceded eleven goals in twelve matches, the Wolves fourteen. Andrew Beyer once again noted that the Whips' reliance on wing play, writing that their favorite tactic was having their "fullbacks advance the ball down the field along the wings."[154] Beyer remarked that this tactic "forces opponents to spread out their defense making them more vulnerable." It would definitely be a match decided down the flanks, with both teams relying on width and pace as integral parts of their identity and approach. The crossing of Wolves' outside-forwards Dave Wagstaffe and Terry Wharton had been methodical, even a tad predictable, but altogether deadly throughout this celebrated summer.

By this time, the teams had played twice in a little more than a month, becoming a bit too familiar with each other as the Dons grew weary of the "English side's robust approach."[155] Indeed, a total of forty-eight fouls had been called between the two teams in the contests that took place before their title showdown. This was ironic because the Whips drew the ire of other

USA teams and supporters (they were booed lustily in San Francisco for extras and rough play[156]) with a robust style of their own, so much so that the *Washington Post* reveled in the incessant promotion of their nature as a "hard hitting, hard-tackling team."[157]

The Wolves, on the other hand, were viewed, at least by Beyer, as a little more traditional (or primitive), preferring to "let their outside forwards loop passes into the middle of the penalty area," where the incomparable Derek Dougan could use his size and positional awareness to cause havoc in the air and create goals. There was an element of simplicity in what the Wolves were doing, partially because Dougan was such a prototypical target man. But there was certainly more to Ronnie Allen's Wolves than just "the Doog," as the USA performances of Peter Knowles, Ernie Hunt, and Dave Wagstaffe would attest.

Whips manager Eddie Turnbull appraised their tactics and philosophy harshly, saying "the Wolves have only got one approach. It's simple they throw a high ball into the middle to Dougan. He has no ability, but they rely on his forcing defenders to make mistakes."[158] But for someone with "no ability," the Whips continually and deliberately fouled Dougan. Public bluster aside, they recognized his threat and made him the focal point of their defensive strategy during the team's previous meetings. Turnbull bluntly concluded that the Dons had "nothing" to fear from the Midlands boys.

For his part, Wolves manager Ronnie Allen began working the referees through the press, saying that he thought "the key to the whole game is the referee."[159] Allen, like virtually every other football veteran, referred to USA officials as being "impartially bad." Complaints about American officiating from British managers had been circulating since at least 1965, when then–West Ham manager Ron Greenwood told United Press International that "the officials aren't up to European standards simply because they can't get the experience."[160] The trials and tribulations during the summer of 1967 shed a massive spotlight on the problem, revealing its immensity like never before.

Far too many times during the short five-week tournament was poor, incompetent refereeing the marquee story, overshadowing the good-to-excellent soccer being played by a kaleidoscopic gallery of legends past and present. Allen was likely angling for an advantage but also laying down a marker and essentially pleading that the title match not be ruined or made a mockery by substandard officiating.

The match, played in front of 17,824 in Los Angeles Memorial Coliseum on July 14, 1967, would turn out to be "one of the most exciting in U.S. Soccer History,"[161] according to Steve Holroyd and others. Whips player Jim Whyte recalled the atmosphere, remembering:

I'd never seen anything like it. For a start, the teams did not come out together as usual. Each player was introduced one-by-one to the crowd and we walked through a pipe band. It was like the Super Bowl! [162]

The violent contest had an overt rugby feel as the overfamiliarity and accumulated bad blood spilled over into a storm of elbows and extras, particularly during the first half, when the Whips were called for twenty fouls. Eventually, the tempestuous Jimmy Smith was ejected for going after the Wolves' Dave Wagstaffe, who allegedly spat on him. Referee Richard Giebner admitted afterward that Smith's foul "wasn't worse than any other foul" [163] committed up until that point, indicating that something had to be done to maintain a semblance of order and control before the match descended into utter chaos. It was a lesson learned far too late, but better now than never. Giebner had evolved more quickly than most USA decision makers, as it was he who had thrown the Stokers' John Mahoney out of a match against the Skyliners before things escalated. Beyer absolved Giebner from any blame, noting perceptively that "referees' tolerance of such situations led to riots in three USA games this season." [164]

Perhaps no more clearly is the connection made between violence and poor officiating than here and although this connection was perceived far too late, it was heartening that it was perceived in enough time to prevent the championship match from degenerating into farce or worse. Echoing Ron Greenwood, Allen noted that "poor refereeing was the main obstacle the USA must overcome." [165] The ejection achieved its objective, and the match settled into a superb, tense encounter, a match Beyer characterized as being "filled with incredible drama."

Things really ignited after the sixty-third minute when four rapid-fire goals split the humid afternoon in half. Suddenly it was 3–3. In a minor bit of foreshadowing, Beyer had continually lauded the Whips for their "superb conditioning" in the weeks before the match, only to have them wilt in overtime, "bedraggled," [166] and run ragged after playing ferociously with ten men for more than ninety minutes. The Wolves outshot the Whips twenty to three in overtime, putting an exclamation point on their extra-time dominance. However, it would be an unlucky bounce, an unfortunate—considering the crazed overall climate and tenor of the USA—yet perfectly surreal and fitting twist of fate that would decide the championship at the end of this epic match.

Dougan scored deep in extra time, prompting the Whips' excellent goaltender Bobby Clark to admit (likely to Turnbull's chagrin) "that big boy Dougan really took me to the cleaners." Clark saved a penalty in the waning moments, a save that initially seemed pointless until the Whips were awarded a penalty that Francis Munro converted with no time left. Amazingly, Munro's hat trick made such an impression on the Wolves in this match that they purchased him from Aberdeen the following January for £55,000. Whyte remembered fondly that "after extra time it was 5–5 and then it was like the school playground, next goal the winner."[167] After 120 grueling, graceful minutes, the teams were knotted at 5–5. This set the stage for sudden death and Ally Shewan's bad bounce, or as Whyte would put it, "a classic own goal to end it."

After three penalties and two separate hat tricks (Burnside recorded the other), the USA title was decided after thirty-six minutes of extra time when Bobby Thomson's cross caromed into the Whips' net off the unlucky Shewan. It was almost as if the league had to end this way, Shewan's miscue a perfect symbolic amplification of all the unforced errors made by hapless American soccer entrepreneurs during the previous year. It was a fittingly madcap end to a madcap season. Whyte summed up the feelings of the exhausted players toiling in the steamy Southern California night "with all the stoppages, it felt like we'd been on the park for three hours." To complete the narrative circle, Bobby Clark told the *Post* after the match that "the World Cup final between England and Germany was not quite as good as this one." The Wolves grabbed the $3,000 winner's share of the spoils, while the Whips' boss, Earl Foreman, who referred to the match as "one of the greatest sporting events ever played in this country,"[168] was so moved that he awarded the defeated Whips $3,000 as well.

For his part, Jack Kent Cooke was so excited about the USA title victory and so enamored with the Wolves personally that he approached Wolverhampton Wanderers director Wilfred Sprosin and offered him one million dollars for the historic Midlands franchise. Kent Cooke told Sprosin that he "wanted to run Wolves as a brother club with Los Angeles,"[169] to which Sprosin dutifully replied, "there wasn't enough money in the world to buy Wolves." Years after the euphoria of the victory had long since vanished, Kent Cooke called the USA a "farce,"[170] saying "we won the North American Soccer League Championship but it cost me three-quarters of a million dollars."

The Washington Whips final paid attendance for the 1967 USA season was 54,846, a figure that was the third highest overall in the USA. The Cleveland Stokers drew 36,501. The paid attendance for all seventy-three USA matches in 1967 was 521,787, with 118,813 coming from the Houston Stars alone.[171] Factoring in the six exhibition matches staged by the league, the attendance rises to 690,256.[172] Interestingly, attendance after thirty-eight matches (the halfway point in the schedule) was 332,485, which shows that the league took a demonstrable nosedive in the waning days of the season—just as the quality of play was increasing.[173]

United Soccer Association (USA), 1967 Season Final Standings (W: win; L: loss; D: draw; GF: goals for; GA: goals against; TP: total points)

Eastern Division	W	L	D	GF	GA	TP
Washington Whips (Aberdeen Dons)	5	2	5	19	11	15
Cleveland Stokers (Stoke City FC)	5	3	4	19	13	14
Toronto City (Hibernian FC)	4	3	5	23	17	13
Detroit Cougars (Glentoran FC)	3	3	6	11	18	12
New York City Skyliners (CA Cerro)	2	4	6	16	17	10
Boston Rovers (Shamrock Rovers)	2	7	3	12	26	7
Western Division	**W**	**L**	**D**	**GF**	**GA**	**TP**
Los Angeles Wolves (Wolverhampton Wanderers)	5	2	5	21	14	15
San Francisco Golden Gate Gales (ADO Den Haag)	5	4	3	25	19	13
Chicago Mustangs (Cagliari Calcio)	3	2	7	20	14	13
Houston Stars (Bangu Atletico Clube)	4	4	4	19	18	12
Vancouver Royal Canadians (Sunderland AFC)	3	4	5	20	28	11
Dallas Tornados (Dundee United)	3	6	3	14	23	9

POSTSCRIPT: BACK FOR THE FUTURE?

With teams like Wolverhampton, Aberdeen, Stoke, Hibernian, Bangu, and Cagliari slated to represent the USA, the league had the quality of play market cornered initially, with even NPSL commissioner Ken Macker conceding that "we obviously couldn't play against the other league this year. We have imported individual players and they have borrowed entire teams."[174] Thus the dichotomy caused by the USA's audacious short-term gambit was laid bare. The league enjoyed a marked advantage in terms of quality in 1967, even with tired teams making the trek over to sightsee after marathon domestic campaigns. But what about the following season? Conceding ground in the short term while fashioning rosters from scratch would have given the NPSL a significant long-term boost when the foreign teams went home at summer's end and the USA franchises would undertake the arduous roster construction process already completed by NPSL teams. The effects of the NPSL's structural advantage and headstart would have been interesting to observe over a longer period of time had the leagues stayed in direct competition with one another.

Two of the more enduring and perplexing questions surrounding the United Soccer Association are: (1) How structurally sound and well developed were the USA owners' plans to construct their own franchises from scratch in 1968; and (2) Did they really think that the resultant vertiginous drop in quality of play wouldn't be noticed? Shav Glick of the *Los Angeles Times* underlined the perils of this haphazard approach as well as the marked advantage the USA enjoyed in terms of quality of play in a column recapping the Los Angeles Wolves' season-opening 2–1 victory against the New York Skyliners.

Los Angeles, being one of five cities with a franchise in each fledgling league, Glick was quick to pose "the obvious question": How did the Wolves compare with the Toros? Ralph Crosby, an official of Southern California amateur soccer, delivered an eloquent warning to the USA:

> The Wolves are going to spoil their fans by bringing in these top foreign teams. Next year the fans will be disappointed when the Wolves play with a team picked up from everyone like the Toros have. Naturally the Wolves look better by comparison; they have played together for years and know each other's moves. Next year the team may not look as good as the Toros[175]

Thus was the folly of the USA's hazy, hasty, long-term strategy laid bare. Perhaps the USA would have been better served seeking the counsel of people like Mr. Crosby, who were already involved in soccer at some level in the United States instead of the baffling plethora of baseball executives, hockey general managers, college football stars, and grocery store magnates they zealously pursued.

It has become clear that at least a few USA owners and administrators had *no* concrete vision with regard to how they would proceed once the foreign teams left. Cleveland Stokers general manager Gabe Paul essentially confirmed these long-held suspicions when he told the *Washington Post* that he "would like to see soccer follow the same format next year and again bring in entire foreign teams to represent our cities."[176]

Paul went on to provide the most frank and frighteningly clear evidence that many, if not all, of the USA's decision makers had no idea what to do about league play in 1968, saying, "I haven't the slightest idea what system will be followed in 1968 to field teams but we should give serious thought to bringing our foreign affiliates back to the United States again." Brian Glanville recalled others hearing Judge Hofheinz speculate "on the prospect of buying a foreign team en bloc,"[177] another startling piece of evidence that lends further credence to the notion that there was no long-term plan for developing the USA.

When considering this it seems to reflect a more tenuous state of internal affairs than the public bluster that USA figures outwardly projected, particularly as they arrogantly entered into merger talks with the NPSL in August 1967. It shows a startling lack of vision as well as the fact that in reality, USA owners needed and were just as desirous to merge as their counterparts across the great divide.

Chapter Three

1967, Part 2

The National Professional Soccer League — Bay City Rollers

ORIGINS: THE D.C. CONNECTION

Thanks to an association with Jack Kent Cooke, nascent Washington Whips owner Earl Foreman had been involved in the rebirth of American professional soccer since its genesis in March 1966. Washington, D.C., was plainly his territory, and when the factions seeking to start a professional league fractured, with Kent Cooke's group ultimately gaining the United States Soccer Football Association's (USSFA) exclusive sanction, the District appeared to be off the board for the rival, rogue National Professional Soccer League (NPSL) until August 1966, when whispers of a new NPSL franchise based in Washington D.C., began creeping into the historical record.[1]

Minnesota and Hartford, CT, were connected with the NPSL throughout the first part of 1966 but ultimately didn't receive franchises when league play began in 1967. The record remains unclear with regard to what ultimately doomed these ill-fated outfits. Hartford's demise is particularly perplexing because it was commonly associated with the mercurial William D. Cox. Oakland Clippers general manager Derek Liecty, an associate of Cox's, recalled that "There was a meeting in Chicago where I learned that Mr. Cox was not going to have his franchise in Hartford; it was out. Finished."[2] No other details from this meeting have emerged. The elimination of Hartford left a hole in the NPSL's burgeoning infrastructure that needed to be filled.

On September 22, 1966, the NPSL awarded a franchise to Washington after merger talks with the North American Soccer League (NASL) had fallen apart.[3] The team was awarded to a group headed by an attorney named

89

Murdaugh Stuart Madden. Madden had also secured the backing of legendary National Basketball Association coach and longtime District resident
Red Auerbach, along with other power brokers, such as St. Louis Blues
owner Stanley Rosenweig. The franchise was known as the Washington
Internationals throughout its brief existence.

Both Foreman and Madden had their eyes on D.C. Stadium, becoming
engaged in an arbitration process that culminated with their appearance before the D.C. Armory Board to present dueling proposals in hopes of securing the stadium. While awaiting the board's decision, the Internationals had
advanced far enough in their preparations for the upcoming NPSL season to
hire a coach named Dan Ekner,[4] a Swedish journeyman who'd spent time
with Marseille and Fiorentina during his playing days.

As an example of the many ways in which stadium policy has historically
impacted American soccer, D.C. Stadium, under the auspices of the armory
board, ran a "vast annual deficit,"[5] which seemed to indicate that it might
look favorably on the group that had "access to the best players and promises
the biggest contribution to the stadium deficit." On November 3, the armory
board deferred its widely anticipated decision, asking the applicants to sub-
mit proposals in a more "comparative form," namely "sealed bids which will
be opened publicly."[6]

Foreman's USA franchise, then operating under the working name the
"Washington Lancers," was declared the winner when the bids were finally
opened. The Internationals' $102,600 bid was trumped by the Lancers'
$109,000.[7] Foreman and the Lancers were awarded a three-year lease at
$109,000 annually. In hindsight it was probably a contest Foreman wished he
would have lost, as this lease would almost immediately become an albatross
around his franchise's neck. Even around the time the lease was announced,
expenses were estimated to amount to $7,800 per match. In addition, Fore-
man's team was prohibited from playing within seventy-two hours of the
Redskins or Senators.

To put the flat annual guarantee of $109,000 in perspective, the Washing-
ton Senators' lease arrangement called for them to pay 7 percent of their
gross gate receipts, or a minimum of $65,000; 1965 saw them pay the mini-
mum. When the smoke cleared in July 1967, Andrew Beyer noted that the
Whips "paid more in rent for eight home games last season than the Senators
have ever paid for 81 games."[8] Foremen told Beyer that "most athletic clubs
pay about 15 percent of their revenue for use of a stadium. The Senators pay
7 percent. The Redskins pay 12 percent. The Whips last season paid 66
percent." When operating expenses were figured in, that number rose to 90
percent for the Whips.

Upon being outbid, Madden said it was "likely" he would "operate his
franchise in one of several other cities which have indicated interest."[9] Within a week Madden was meeting with J. Frank Cashen, executive vice presi-

dent of the Baltimore Orioles, about "Orioles management joining forces with the Washington group."[10] Cashen said the Orioles "still have an interest in soccer" but emphasized "no decision had been made" or would be for some time. Initially, Baltimore Colts general manager Donald Kellet had considered bringing an NPSL franchise to Maryland, but he "lost interest"[11] sometime around August, likely when he found out the NPSL would be "outlaws."

Cashen had become interested in soccer the previous summer upon talking to Arthur Allyn, owner of the USA's Chicago Mustangs franchise, at a baseball meeting. His interest deepened when Orioles vice president Joe Hamper Jr. met with St. Louis Stars president Robert Hermann in September. Hamper later recalled to the *Baltimore Sun* that it was the day he first learned "soccer is governed by a body called the United States Soccer Football Association,"[12] such was that organization's presence in mainstream American sporting circles. This was also when the men learned about the NPSL's lack of sanction, but Hamper remembered being impressed and feeling that the NPSL was more "aggressive and progressive" than its sanctioned counterpart. With the Orioles in the midst of a pennant race, the curious execs decided not to invest any money at that time. Fate, in the form of the D.C. Armory Board, would soon intervene.

Perhaps more than some of their ownership compatriots, the Orioles group noticed the bigger contextual picture, acknowledging soccer's subtle yet sizeable presence in their local community as a decent investment. Orioles owner Jerry Hoffberger noted "More people have played soccer in Maryland than any other sport except baseball. Every high school, state-wide, has it. Even the parochial grade schools have it. Why, it wasn't until last year that Baltimore County schools had football, but they've had soccer for years.[13] Hoffberger added that the "challenge was to turn this interest into ticket sales." It was the intractable dilemma: how to cross the divide from active participation to compulsive consumption. A variation of this dilemma had plagued promoters and would-be owners for years, typically, though, they were dealing with ethnic communities that obviously loved the game but for a variety of reasons remained aloof and uninterested in efforts to launch a domestic league.

Hoffberger was one of the first people to spot the changing landscape, identifying the game's increasing influence, particularly in suburban areas outside the game's traditional inner-city roots. As Franklin Foer would note so eloquently in *How Soccer Explains the World*, soccer's ascendancy to suburban dominance grew partially from its widespread adoption in relatively affluent middle-class suburban communities in the Beltway area. These suburban areas were highly coveted consumer demographics and when they adopted products, cultural or otherwise, Madison Avenue took notice. Once it conquered these areas, it spread like wildfire.

By November 25 Madden stated publicly that a deal to relocate the franchise to Baltimore was nearly complete. According to the *Post*, Madden's group "proposed sharing ownership of the soccer franchise with the Orioles"[14] but that the Orioles preferred to buy out Madden's group. To clear the way for the transaction, the Orioles "obtained consent to use Memorial Stadium by a unanimous vote of Baltimore Park Board." The franchise was about to become a wholly owned subsidiary of Baltimore Orioles Inc. To once again emphasize how onerous Foreman's D.C. Stadium lease was, the Orioles agreement with the park board consisted of a "minimum guarantee of $2,500 for each game or 7 percent of the total receipts."[15]

The transaction was made official on November 28, when it was announced that the Baltimore Orioles had purchased Murdaugh Stuart Madden's NPSL franchise.[16] The Orioles ultimately persuaded Madden's group to sell for the cut-rate price of $60,000.[17] It was also announced that Joe Hamper, with his now comparatively comprehensive soccer knowledge, would run soccer operations as executive vice president in addition to retaining his baseball duties. The still nameless soccer franchise was officially in business. Almost a month later, it hired Clive Toye as vice president and general manager.

BETTER BAYS AHEAD: PREPARING FOR THE NPSL SEASON

Toye had spent the previous decade writing about soccer for the *London Daily Express*, which at the time had a circulation of around four million. This experience gave him a wealth of important connections in England and beyond, prompting Joe Hamper to remark that Toye "knows just about everyone in international soccer."[18] He would need every one of those global connections to put together an entire franchise in less than four months while operating as a rogue entity. Toye had initially been slated to work for the mysterious Hartford franchise but quickly became a highly sought free agent when that outfit was tabled.

Toye's first order of business was to finesse the removal of the unfortunate Dan Ekner as coach, a maneuver he pulled off with considerable aplomb, sliding the Swede into a position as director of player development. Toye had his heart set on St. Mirren manager and ex–Ipswich Town man Doug Millward. Millward had spent his time in Ipswich Town playing under Sir Alf Ramsey, the man who guided England to the World Cup promised land in '66. Toye quickly arranged a meeting between the two parties in London and within hours Millward was on board. Before their meeting, Toye recalled telling Hoffberger "the best coach available is Doug Millward."[19] The two men would form a tempestuous union. With Millward in place, Toye immediately began scouring Europe and South America for players.

The crafty ex-journalist provided expansive insight to the *Washington Post*'s Andrew Beyer regarding the team's "far-flung"[20] recruiting and the resultant mash-up of "Latin and European players." Toye said "the Brazilian characteristic is a lot of fancy ball play" while "the European characteristics are strength and vigor." This is also an instructive example of how the stereotypes that contribute the symbolic grammar and heft to ethnic identity construction are so easily introduced within this narrative.

Toye expounded further on these thoughts, telling the *Post* "my image was of team with a European kind of defense, with men who do not shirk physical contact. We wanted a Latin-style attack with a great deal of artistry, fluidity and skill, not just long passing and hard running."[21] Toye was so committed to this specific vision that he spoke of turning down players "who didn't fit into the image we had of the kind of soccer we wanted to play."

On January 10 the franchise officially adopted the Bays moniker "in recognition of the Chesapeake Bay"[22] and to "draw upon the heritage and prestige of Baltimore and Maryland," according to Hamper. The team had even considered using the name "Chesapeakes." Toye felt so confident that his radically ragtag collection of players from all over the globe was jelling after training began in March that he predicted "in a month's time"[23] the Bays could take on their neighbors, the Aberdeen Dons/Washington Whips, "with utter confidence of beating them." This was a bold statement, considering the Dons had just spent a season sparring with the likes of Celtic, the European champions.

On the other hand, Toye had reasons to be confident, as the primordial Bays featured a tantalizing mix of aging stars, such as Juan Santisteban, a member of the fantastic, dynastic Real Madrid teams of the late '50s, who would go on to a decorated managerial career, including a stint with Spain's U21 team, and Zemaria, a center-half on Brazil's 1958 and 1962 World Cup–winning squads. Signing Santisteban was a legitimate coup, even at his advanced age, and Toye predicted that as a midfield "engineer,"[24] the Spaniard would be one of the best "in the whole of the American continent."

The Bays also featured upstart internationals such as the twenty-year-old Israeli defender David Primo, a player Toye and the Bays were "expecting to blossom quickly." Primo was so highly regarded in Israel, where he'd been a full international since the age of seventeen, that "some 500 fans showed up at Tel Aviv airport"[25] to try and coax him to stay, ultimately delaying his departure for three hours. He would feature in the 1970 Israeli World Cup squad that competed in Mexico. While scouting Primo, Toye and Millward noticed his countryman Shimon Cohen and sensed immediately that "he was too good to leave behind."[26]

Cohen gave the *Baltimore Sun* valuable perspective on the state of Israeli soccer at the time, saying, "There is no such thing as a professional in Israel. You get paid by a bonus system."[27] Cohen said that this system could net

good players as much as $200 a month but that average players made as little
as $35. Like the part-time professionals from Ireland playing for the USA,
Cohen too was saddled with a day job. Low wages and lack of full professional status caused Cohen to shrug off threats of a suspension by Israeli
officials.

Other signings included the Argentine Constantino Tejada, an ex-Depor-
tivo player with a powerful left foot and excellent vision who Toye predicted
would lead the NPSL in assists,[28] and a pair of twins, Art and Asher Welch,
from Jamaica. An outside right, Art had played in Jamaica's World Cup
qualifiers prior to the 1966 tournament, including a match against Mexico
where he notched a brace in a 3–2 loss, and would remain an NASL fixture
until 1980, when he returned to the Beltway as a member of the Washington
Diplomats. More recently, Art had recorded yet another brace in Jamaica's
2–1 victory over Cuba. Toye tapped the Jamaican to be "one of the best
players in the United States this year."[29] Millward and Toye continued to
strengthen the squad, poaching the Brazilian Fernando Azevedo from St.
Mirren. Fernando was a crafty inside-right known for his dribbling and close
control. The Bays then signed center-forward Karl Minor, who spent the
previous campaign playing for West Ham.

Finally, the team produced a local boy, Joe Speca, who would become
one of only a handful of native-born Americans playing soccer in the sprawl-
ing, crowded summer of 1967. Speca had just won the American Soccer
League (ASL) title with the Baltimore St. Gerards after starring for Patterson
High School while growing up. The NPSL set a $5,000 minimum salary and
early word was that the average league salary would fall somewhere around
$10,000. There was talk of a "gentlemen's agreement"[30] among NPSL own-
ers not to pay players more than $20,000.

Doug Millward emphasized the versatility of his nascent squad, telling
the press "we have some players who can play five or six different positions
and one who has played as many as seven."[31] Millward also declared "we
will have an attacking team, one that will be pleasing to the fans." Sounding
an eerie warning that would define many of the teams he'd soon compete
against, Millward remarked that it was "easier to destroy than create especially at lower level of ability." Fresh from scouring ten different countries
for players, he assured the public that his Bays were being constructed with
"attacking players who can overcome, create problems for the defense." As
an aside, the bubbly Toye remarked "we will train our players one third for
soccer and the other two thirds practicing how to fall down"[32] in response to
a question about how teams would deal with stoppages in play for "all-
important" television commercials. These playful, off-the-cuff remarks
would assume a more ominous tone shortly after the season began.

Meanwhile Major League Baseball (MLB) commissioner William D.
Eckert had suddenly become sensitive to the issue of field conditions in light

of the fact that ten out of twenty Major League parks were to be used for NPSL matches. Eckert was so troubled by the thought of chewed-up, unsuitable fields that he added the topic to baseball's ownership meetings that March. [33] This unwanted scrutiny and interference by outside forces, along with the protracted and onerous lease commitments that ultimately sent the Bays to Baltimore, are major reasons why stadium policy and Major League Soccer's (MLS) virtual insistence on soccer-specific stadiums have always been important determinants in the development of the American game. Perhaps hitting even closer to home for the Orioles, the commissioner was also interested in opening up a dialogue regarding potential conflicts of interest, since no less than six baseball ownership groups now owned soccer franchises.

The NPSL publicly unveiled its "revolutionary scoring system" [34] on March 21. Also known as the "6–3–0," the scoring system awarded six points for a victory and three for a draw in lieu of the common 2–1–0 format, where teams accrued two points for a win and one for a draw. The system also awarded bonus points for goals to encourage scoring, with each goal, up to a maximum of three, contributing to the overall point total. An NPSL team winning by a score of 3–0 could gain a whopping nine points in one outing. This was done expressly to encourage and reward scoring, with the added bonus of serving to further "Americanize" the game with its uniqueness.

The *Baltimore Sun* characterized Toye as "instrumental in getting the system approved at the league's recent meeting in New York." [35] Toye believed that the scoring system would begin to erode "the defensive mentality" that had taken root in the game. The general manager noted that England had only narrowly voted down a bonus system a few years back, with the forces of tradition marshaling to defeat the proposed change. Toye claimed that if the NPSL could "establish a precedent. The rest of the world could well copy us." It turned out to be a widely derided and despised system.

This was also an inflection point where television was exerting both overt and subliminal pressure. NPSL owners would have to present an attractive product for CBS to sell, particularly due to the sport's innate structural antagonism toward television commercials, which itself caused the league intense public humiliation when it was revealed that fouls were being called for the express purpose of creating interruptions for advertisements.

While scrimmaging against the New York Generals, Millward got an inkling of what was to come when officials allowed an exhibition match turn into a "no holds barred" [36] slugfest, where players "freely shoved, pushed, tripped and tackled throughout the slow moving match." Millward said afterward that the Generals "would be lucky to finish with nine players in Europe the way they fouled," before emphasizing "the referees let the match get out of hand in the first half. This is no good for anybody." Perhaps if the NPSL had hired a soccer man instead of a newspaper mogul as commissioner somebody would have heeded Millward's prophetic words.

One also wonders why Sir George Graham, hired to give the league credibility on football matters, was nowhere to be found when incidents like this began occurring in scrimmages. Poor refereeing was perhaps the one thing that truly united the disparate leagues in 1967. Besides lack of adequate infrastructure to properly train American referees, pay was likely also an issue, with local linesmen getting $35 per match and referees reportedly getting as much as $75.[37]

The Bays played an exhibition match against their opening-night opponents, the Atlanta Chiefs, on April 2 in Richmond. Phil Woosnam had by then already added the title general manager to his resume but was still "the best player on the field,"[38] according to Clive Toye. Atlanta's roster was "loaded with English players" and with players from all over the globe who happened to speak English. Woosnam was not the only player with Aston Villa connections, as the Chiefs roster also featured former Villans Vic Crowe and Peter McParland, giving the team a healthy dose of English First Division grit and guile. First Division veteran Ron Newman, formerly of Portsmouth and Crystal Palace, had also found his way into the Chiefs' lineup. After watching the Chiefs' practice, Toye felt strongly that Atlanta, unlike the clumsy, ponderous Generals, would approach the season in a similar fashion as the Bays: with enterprise and positivity.

The Chiefs were buzzing about a young midfielder from Trinidad named Everald Cummings. Woosnam compared him to "a baseball pitcher with an exceptional fastball"[39] due to the power of his shot and his ability to strike from distance. The Chiefs were expecting big things from the eighteen-year-old with blazing speed. Cummings would go on to feature for the New York Cosmos and Veracruz before becoming the coach of Trinidad and Tobago's national team.

Amazingly, the Bays didn't actually practice on Memorial Stadium's field until a mere two days before their first match. Millward admitted "it was very foreign for the boys"[40] because "they wanted to kick it in a certain direction and they had difficulty with the angle." This was likely due to the exceedingly poor dimensions of the stadium as a soccer venue. Regardless, it seemed a strange decision on the part of Bays management and could certainly be read as a symptom of Commissioner Eckert's concerns about soccer's impact on MLB playing surfaces.

In addition to owning the Orioles, Jerry Hoffberger was also the president of the National Brewing Company, and as such it was decided that the Bays' kits would be a living, breathing athletic advertisement for National Brewing's regal red-and-gold color scheme. It was another perfect piece of corporate synergy, similar to Ford's decision to name the Cougars after its latest auto. Both stood as towering symbols of their time, a time when marketing, advertising, commerce, culture, communication, and business were blending together in an amorphous mass where boundaries became blurred.

THE 1967 NPSL SEASON

The NPSL opened on April 16, 1967, with much fanfare, as the first five matches drew a respectable attendance of 45,210. The governor of Pennsylvania, Raymond P. Shafer, was on hand to ceremonially kick out the first ball of the match between the Philadelphia Spartans and Toronto Falcons at Temple Stadium. That contest, a 2–0 Spartans victory, attracted an eye-popping 14,163 fans, a figure that so caught the Spartans off-guard that team vice president Jerry Lawrence jumped into a ticket booth and reportedly sold 400 tickets himself.[41] Incidentally, this match also outdrew a baseball game between the Philadelphia Phillies and New York Mets by 5,000. In a mélange of strange, uniquely American scenes, the actress Julie Christie was in Oakland to throw out "the first ball for the game between the California Clippers and Pittsburgh Phantoms" while a band played "Dixie" to herald the arrival of the Atlanta Chiefs and Baltimore Bays for their CBS debut.[42]

Commissioner Ken Macker was on hand in Memorial Stadium with his old friend Pete Roselle as the Bays kicked off the NPSL season, with a 1–0 victory against the Atlanta Chiefs. The players were introduced carrying the flags of the countries from which they hailed, adding to the pageantry and creating an overwhelming sense of optimism. Guy St. Vil notched not only the match-winning goal five minutes into the second half, but also the first goal of the tournament and of that entire turbulent summer of American soccer. St. Vil launched home a hard shot from six yards out on a pretty pass from Asher Welch, who had raced into open space down the left flank.

The Haitian celebrated his goal by racing into the net and rolling "on the ground deliriously."[43] As fate would have it, St. Vil was likely on the field due to a thigh injury suffered by Fernando Azevedo. Most accounts of this match describe a cagey, slow-tempo slog, with brief explosions of class and excitement as Atlanta slowly gathered steam, forcing Bays keeper Dennis Connaghan, who Millward referred to as "the best goalie within 3,000 miles of here,"[44] to make "several sensational saves" as they sought an equalizer. The Chiefs concentrated on hard running, utilizing long, looping passes, while the Bays focused on a more controlled short-passing approach.

The match was CBS's much-anticipated debut telecast and the network pulled out all the stops. The network's technical staff actually practiced in Memorial Stadium more than the Bays (once again demonstrating the balance of power in the NPSL–CBS relationship), scouting the stadium in late March and choosing no less than six camera locations. There would be a roving camera placed on a golf cart, cameras in precisely chosen vantage points on the upper decks facing both goals, as well as cameras in sections four and thirty-five.[45] It was practically a panopticon when compared to the crude setups of earlier eras.

It was also the debut of the CBS's legendary Jack Whitaker and Danny Blanchflower broadcast team. Whitaker was a smooth, seasoned play-by-play vet who had covered everything from horseracing's Triple Crown to the first Super Bowl. Blanchflower was a Northern Ireland international who captained Tottenham Hotspur to glory during the North London side's legendary double-winning season in 1961. Blanchflower, a right-half, made his professional debut for Glentoran, who was then crisscrossing the United States as the Detroit Cougars, and developed into a slick passer with a metronomic ability to set the tempo of a match. He had also written a well-regarded column for the *Sunday Express* and was brought in to add insider knowledge and color. He would not disappoint.

In what would foreshadow the Peter Rhodes incident (more on this later in this chapter), the *Baltimore Sun*'s Bob Maisel spoke to referee Eddie Pearson after the contest about the need to create time and space for commercials. Like Rhodes, Pearson was an Englishman from Doncaster with more than fifteen years of experience. Pearson said, "they had me wired up, with a microphone under my shirt, and they told me when to take the timeouts."[46] This tech setup has since been confirmed multiple times by numerous referees and journalists. Pearson said the signal was when he raised his hands in the air over his head. He also remarked that the forced timeouts "slowed down the action and momentum" of the match, which is likely why many felt it to be so lugubrious. Finally, he said, "I had to tell the boys to stay down a while longer to get the full 60 seconds in."[47] The similarities between comments by Pearson and Rhodes, whose were far less blunt, are startling.

Already television had imposed itself in ways that sometimes overshadowed the action on the pitch that it was designed to capture and project. Blanchflower wrote eloquently about this after leaving, noting that

> TV is an intruder at a sports event and should always be kept in its place. It should not be allowed to change important details of the event to suit its own ends. It should stand back at times and be critical about what is going on. But because it is a very presumptuous being, television thinks the world belongs to it.[48]

In the United States, this balance skewed perilously toward television, particularly in the relationship between the NPSL and CBS, where the network clearly felt no qualms about calling the shots. Television was no longer an "intruder"; it was as integral as the players. This creeping sense of unequal power would manifest itself in various ways throughout CBS's partnership with the NPSL.

The victorious Bays readied themselves for a visit from the St. Louis Stars and their eccentric boss Rudi Gutendorf. The German disciplinarian had made it to the Midwest via his native Stuttgart and wasted absolutely no time becoming deeply unpopular with his players. Gutendorf had rules and protocols for everything, from $3 fines for being late to practices, to obsessing over player injuries no matter how small. Gutendorf succinctly summed up his philosophy to Ken Nigro of the *Baltimore Sun*, saying, "All my players have to give their entire working power and way of living into their service of their new job."[49]

Gutendorf had already alienated the Stars' Pat McBride. McBride was a hometown hero who'd starred for a St. Louis Billikens squad that won two straight NCAA titles. McBride was generally acknowledged as one of the best American players at the time, as well as an embodiment of St. Louis' exalted position in the history of U.S. soccer. The two men clashed vociferously during a practice match in Arizona. Gutendorf ultimately told McBride to go home. The German publicly voiced his respect for McBride afterward, saying he "didn't want to lose him" and that perhaps it was "just a matter of him learning our European style of play."

It seemed like McBride would relent and repent, but shortly before the Stars' opening match in Chicago, he said, "I don't feel I can play for him."[50] Already engulfed in controversy, the Stars lost their first match 2–1 to the Chicago Spurs and were staring down a 0–2 hole as they trekked to Baltimore. Nigro noted jokingly that a second straight loss might compel Gutendorf to take away his players' meal money. After the NPSL, Gutendorf would go on a national team world tour, holding the top job for a whopping eighteen different countries during his lengthy career.

The night before, the Spurs won their second consecutive match when forward Willie Roy scored in the dying seconds of the match to beat the Toronto Falcons 1–0. Roy scored the first of what would be a lofty seventeen league goals on a pretty feed from Wolfgang Glock. Roy, born in Treuberg, Germany, moved to Chicago at the age of six, becoming a fixture in the Windy City while starring for the powerful Hansa squad in the National Soccer League of Chicago. His growing stature earned him a spot on the U.S. men's national team (USMNT) in 1965, when he received the first of his twenty U.S. caps against Mexico.[51]

He became a successful coach at Northern Illinois University, winning two national titles during an eighteen-year tenure, and was elected to the National Soccer Hall of Fame. McBride and Roy offered two different portraits of American soccer "stars" from the pre-USA/NPSL era, one a native-born collegiate who had no arena to show off his skills after graduation and the other a naturalized American who thrived in one of the many amateur semipro leagues that dotted the Midwest and northeast.

The Stars didn't conduct themselves much better in the Charm City dusk, yet they somehow managed to claim an ugly 3–1 victory against the Bays in a match where the 4,400-plus in attendance were gifted a booklet explaining the rules of this exotic game called soccer.[52] St. Louis victimized the Bays with goals from two Bora Kostic free kicks to cement the victory despite being outshot twenty-four to eleven. Kostic was a grizzled thirty-six-year-old Yugoslav international, a warhorse who scored 158 goals during a long spell with Red Star Belgrade.

The Bays controlled the first half, but went into the half down 1–0 after Kostic's first goal in the twenty-second minute. Hipolito Chilinque and Shimon Cohen had spurned decent chances, but it was an Asher Welch shot that hit the goal post instead of equalizing early in the second that turned the match over to St. Louis, according to Millward. "If the shot goes in we tie the match and who knows,"[53] he said afterward. St. Louis played almost strictly on the counter, getting an amazing four goals waved off for offside calls.

Like many of their counterparts in the USA, the Bays were trying to stay within in a rough 4–2–4 formation while cultivating a fluid short-passing attack that could dictate the tempo of a match. They were wasteful and not completely in sync against the Stars, but Millward noted that the squad "had plenty of inside chances," which he felt would translate into goals soon enough.

Local product John Speca was benched for the Bays' short trip to Temple Stadium and a date with the Philadelphia Spartans. Many thought Memorial Stadium was a narrow field, but the Bays now had to contend with a cramped Temple Stadium pitch only seventy yards wide. The Spartans were owned by Art and John Rooney, members of the family who had owned the Pittsburgh Steelers for decades. Philadelphia had managed to construct an impressive roster filled with quality players such as Ruben Navarro, a gritty Argentine international who had played in the 1962 World Cup. Navarro also starred on the backline of an Independiente side that won two consecutive Copa Libertadores crowns in 1964 and 1965. After scrimmaging against the Spartans in April, Clive Toye remarked, "Philadelphia played blood and thunder soccer"[54] and they're "not going to win in this league if they keep it up." Temple Stadium's narrowness made the Spartans' physicality that much more difficult to handle.

The Spartans had beaten the Toronto Falcons on the strength of burgeoning chemistry between forward Peter Short and inside-left Walt Chyzowych. Chyzowych, a local product who was an All-American at Temple as well as the 1965 ASL most valuable player, later would coach the USMNT from 1976 to 1981. But before that, Chyzowych would begin the 1968 season as the Bays' East Coast scout.[55] Short had been toiling for Toronto City in the Eastern Canadian Professional Soccer League. The pair linked up beautifully for both Spartan goals.

Spartans manager John Szep drilled his squad to attack the opposition in what the *Trenton Evening Times* labeled a 3–3–4 formation, breathlessly noting that "on offense the halfbacks virtually become forwards and on defense, fullbacks."[56] This speaks to the flexibility offered by more modern tactical approaches, such as the 4–2–4, and seemed more ambitious than the "blood and thunder" epithet Toye hurled at the Spartans. With this emphasis on pressing, the Spartans would score fifty-three goals and battle the Bays for the NPSL's Eastern Division title until the final weeks of the regular season. This would be their first encounter.

Late in a scoreless match, the rugged Navarro fouled Art Welch in the area to concede a penalty. However, the spot kick by the Bays' Nelio dos Santos was saved by Spartans keeper Ernesto Lopera. The rebound fell to the unlucky dos Santos, who promptly sailed it over the crossbar. It would have snatched six unlikely points for the shorthanded Bays, who had been forced to play with ten men for more than fifty minutes when Shimon Cohen was ejected late in the first half for kicking Philadelphia's Tibor Szaly in the stomach. The Bays defended with resolve, keeping everyone back save for Welch and St. Vil, and got excellent goaltending from Dennis Connaghan to keep it scoreless. Millward singled out the work of Israeli defender David Primo, who locked down Short, as a major reason why Philadelphia recorded only six shots in the second half despite their man advantage.[57] The match ended 0–0.

In these early weeks of the NPSL, Los Angeles Toros player Ron Crisp, who played six years in England's Football League, judged the startup NPSL's caliber of play to be "about the same standard of English Third Division at the moment."[58] Crisp's sentiment was echoed in *Sports Illustrated* by Eric Barnett, who was described as "a young Australian in the U.S. studying television techniques who has played soccer at club level in Australia, New Zealand and England."[59] Observing the NPSL's debut match in Baltimore, Barnett too judged NPSL play as equivalent to Third or Fourth Division play in England. Barnett characterized the midfield dribbling by the Bays and Chiefs as "now and again brilliant," saying that it fleetingly "approached first-division quality, but that the chaps seemed a bit confused when they got within the 30-yard line."[60]

The Bays were hoping to continue their solid defensive play against Willy Roy, who scored all four of Chicago's goals through three matches, and the banged-up Spurs at Soldier Field. Spurs boss Al Rogers lamented having only fifteen players available before giving a somewhat frightening appraisal of the NPSL's minimalist mien, saying, "we don't even have a full-time trainer or equipment manager."[61] The cold realities of a shoestring budget become baffling in light of the incessant talk about wealth and resources during the run-up to league play. In contrast, the Bays had both of those in addition to such amenities as a director of player development. There were reasons, other than personnel, ensuring that the Bays would contend.

The Spurs dropped their most recent match 2–1 to the previously winless New York Generals, which prompted the cranky Rogers to note that the Generals "used two players who just got off the plane"[62] and that perhaps this was because New York "needed" a win in the eyes of the league. One of those players was a young Argentine man named Cesar Luis Menotti. Menotti made an immediate impact, opening the scoring on a cross from Warren Archibald in the fourteenth minute. Menotti had seen stints with Rosario Central and Boca Juniors before seeking his fortune in America. Menotti would go on to enjoy global renown for coaching Argentina to World Cup glory on their home soil in 1978.

The clash with Chicago was the Generals' first home match at Yankee Stadium. It was dubbed "the Day of the Generals" and featured a parade of young men proudly bearing the flags of more than nineteen nations. While covering this spectacle for the *New York Times*, Gerald Eskenazi remarked, "ethnic appeal has been sought to stimulate interest within America's sizeable foreign born population," yet the Generals were hoping to bring the game "to the wider—and probably more affluent—portion of American sports fans."[63] It was a naked articulation of what many in the game would often couch in ambiguous, antiseptic terms, if referring to it all. Eskenazi is very clearly speaking of issues of class and ethnicity, issues that intertwine so intrinsically with the game of soccer, which is a major reason it was so unloved by large segments of American power. It was also a prescient articulation of an "Americanization" process that would begin in earnest during the '70s.

Speaking proudly of what Toye had termed "blood and thunder" soccer, Rogers said "we play it real Chicago style—rough and ready. We run over people through walls."[64] Chicago didn't disappoint as "the second half nearly deteriorated into a pier six brawl on many occasions." This approach turned out not to be much of a problem for the Bays, who ran out easy 2–0 winners. The ex-Cruzeiro man Hipolito Chilinque notched both strikes, the first on a nifty setup from Uriel Da Veiga. He banged in the second on a rebound with less than five minutes to play. According to Ken Nigro, "except for a short spell near the end of the first half and in the opening 15 minutes of the second, the Bays dominated the match."[65] The team's short passing was crisp and effective, while keeper Dennis Connaghan kept his second straight clean sheet.

The victory put the Bays at 2–1–1, two points behind their next opponent, the Pittsburgh Phantoms, who had just suffered a comprehensive 4–1 defeat to the St. Louis Stars. Owned by attorney Peter H. Block, the Phantoms were living up to the more sinister connotations of their name. They were already on their second coach of the season, with Janos Bedl drafted to replace Herb

Vogt before the games even began. Vogt's departure was allegedly due to illness[66] but remained shrouded in mystery.

The Phantoms then made waves by signing "the Flying Dutchman" Co Prins. A Netherlands international, Prins had a decent run for Ajax in the early '60s, scoring sixty goals in a little more than six years. But despite being a talented, prolific contributor, the erratic Prins wore people down personally, so much so that "Ajax shed no tears when he left,"[67] according to sources in Holland. It was said of Prins that "his play, like his moods, varies from top-rate to poor as poor can be." This was all bubbling to the surface when Prins was arrested for kidnapping after a messy, public domestic dispute wherein he chased his wife to Germany and "allegedly roughed up his father in law."[68] The kidnapping charge was dropped and Prins was freed on bail.

Despite leading the Eastern Division, the shambolic Phantoms were on their third coach of the season when they visited Baltimore—none other than Prins himself. In what proved the most blatant and direct case of NPSL ownership's penchant for tactical interference, Janos Bedl was fired for being too cautious and defensive. It was another direct manifestation of the pressure for an attractive product being brought to bear on managers from overzealous owners who didn't really know much about how the game was played. Amazingly, pressure of this sort seemed to pay off on a macro level, considering that the NPSL averaged 3.4 goals per match, a higher average than both the English First Division and the Bundesliga that year, according to David Wangerin.[69]

In a head-scratching move, Peter Block elevated Prins to player-coach. An Associated Press report about the incident noted that Bedl's firing "came as no surprise,"[70] since he had "been feuding with the front office since last week when Block ordered him to open up the team's offense." Even more explicitly Block "said he told the coach to concentrate on the attack throughout the game rather than sit on a lead." Phantoms publicity director Jim Bukata told the *Sun*, however, that Bedl's firing had been discussed as far back as the preseason and that the coach was viewed as undisciplined. As evidence, Bedl had apparently done things like introducing a sub without telling him "where to play."[71]

Not surprisingly the Phantoms were among the first wave of franchises to fold before the merger in 1968, averaging just 3,100 in attendance, the second worst in the league next to the Spurs. Bedl would go on to coach the Kansas City Spurs to the NASL title in 1969. He also enjoyed a short tenure managing Borussia Dortmund in the early '70s. Prins, too, would move on in North America, spending 1968 with the New York Generals.

Prins had already implemented significant tactical changes, switching the Phantoms from a 4–2–4 to a 4–3–3, likely in hopes of stabilizing a defense that had already conceded a league-leading twelve goals.[72] The Phantoms, like the St. Louis Stars, relied on a counterattacking, long ball strategy to generate offense, averaging more than thirty shots per match. A missed penalty would again doom the Bays in a wild contest at Memorial Stadium.

Down 4–3, Art Welch sailed his penalty wide left in the eightieth minute. Just six minutes later the Phantoms' Manfred Rummel closed out the scoring with his second of the night to make it 5–3. Down 2–1 the Bays battled back to even terms thanks to an own goal credited to Pittsburgh halfback Herb Finken. It was the NPSL's first credited own goal.[73] Prins figured directly into the Phantoms' first two strikes, scoring the first himself on a penalty and facilitating the second with exquisite delivery on a corner that Theor Laseroms thundered home. Suddenly Baltimore was riddled for five goals after recording shutouts in three of their first four matches. The last-place Generals were next to roll into town.

New York City was obviously an immensely important NPSL market and Wangerin accurately observed what this meant regarding expectations for the New York Generals, writing "for the Generals in particular this was critical, operating as they did in a city which knew good soccer from bad, and whose hugely influential media was likely to make or break the entire venture."[74] The man tasked with shaping the New York Generals was Freddie Goodwin. A grizzled Mancunian and gnarled First Division veteran who'd logged time on the pitch as a Manchester United player before a relatively successful spell managing Scunthorpe United, then in England's Third Division, Goodwin handpicked a motley assortment of men from England, Denmark, Austria, Hungary, Jamaica, and Trinidad and then set about the grueling task of fashioning them into a unit.

Some of the players had topflight experience, including Geoffrey Sidebottom, who had played for Aston Villa and Wolverhampton, and Barry Wright who, like his manager, once played for Leeds United. As an example of the strange nexus of players, nationalities, and experience levels that defined the NPSL, the Generals also featured an Austrian named Paul Freitag who had been playing for Hota in New York's well-regarded German-American League. Trinidad and Tobago international Warren Archibald was projected to be one of New York's primary offensive threats due to his pace.

Goodwin told the *Times* that one of his main objectives was having the men "get to know each other and blend the different styles of play,"[75] a positively herculean task as their inaugural campaign would prove. Goodwin was optimistic though and hoped "we'll have a team that will be as good as the teams in the lower part of the English First Division or in the upper part of the Second Division." Despite Goodwin's positivity and hard work, anecdotal evidence suggests that Brian Glanville was right about the Generals' desperate turn to *catenaccio*, when the *Times* quoted a young Generals fan lamenting the side's cynical 5–2–3 formation, saying "when you've got a lousy team, you need the defensive stuff."[76] After his sojourn in America, Goodwin would go on to manage Birmingham City.

The sputtering Generals had only scored four times, two of those coming in their lone victory against Chicago. Goodwin attributed the Generals' halting start to a lack of cohesion. The Generals' first visit to Baltimore would ultimately be rescheduled due to inclement weather. Undaunted, the Bays made news anyway by signing ex–Manchester United star Dennis Viollet as player and assistant coach.[77]

Viollet scored thirty-two goals for the Red Devils in 1960, earning himself a place on England's 1962 World Cup squad. Viollet was one of the few survivors of the tragic Munich air disaster that decimated a promising young United team in 1958. More recently the crafty attacker had been plying his trade for Stoke City. Stoke would eventually contest the validity of Viollet's contract with the Bays. Toye told the press he hoped Viollet, in his role as assistant coach, would be able to free Millward for more scouting.[78] On the pitch, Viollet was viewed as a perfect complement to Juan Santisteban. The Spaniard was proving to be Baltimore's primary offensive catalyst. He was an excellent passer and with a finisher of Viollet's pedigree alongside him, the Bays' attack would, on paper, be stronger and more balanced. Shimon Cohen and Nelio dos Santos had been playing with Santisteban, who now would have the luxury of playing with a polished, natural goal scorer.

Viollet made an immediate impact, scoring the tying goal in a cynical 2–2 draw with the Chicago Spurs that saw David Primo ejected and both sides finish with ten men.[79] Willie Roy scored twice and had now accounted for all seven of Chicago's goals. Inside-left Wolfgang Glock would score for the Spurs in their 1–1 home draw with the Los Angeles Toros a few days later, becoming the first player other than Roy to score.

The Bays lost both Uriel da Veiga and Hipolito Chilinque to injury after the bone-jarring clash, with da Veiga suffering a separated shoulder. This gap in the lineup allowed local boy Joe Speca to shine. He took full advantage of it by scoring the winning goal in the final minute of a pulsating 3–2 victory over the Philadelphia Spartans on May 19.[80] It was the Bays' first home victory since opening night against Atlanta.

When the Bays traveled to Yankee Stadium to finally meet the struggling New York Generals, they would be facing the ninth different Generals lineup of the season. Though seeking cohesion, Freddie Goodwin was "signing, releasing and switching players at such a rapid rate it's almost impossible to tell the New York team even with a scorecard."[81] The Generals had just signed three more players from Boca Juniors and plucked Herb Finken from Pittsburgh's discard pile.

In news that would have made Spurs boss Al Rogers cringe, the Generals had already dropped Adilson Silveira, one of the players who helped New York scrape out a victory against the Spurs on April 22 after signing the day before. The Generals signed Bruno Siciliano from the Serie A's Bari as well as a promising Israeli named Zeev Zeltser. Zeltser too had already been released amid this blur of transactions, landing in Los Angeles, where he scored the winning goal for the Toros in their upset of a strong California Clippers side.

The Generals earned a hard-fought 2–2 tie with the Atlanta Chiefs in their previous match after going scoreless in the three contests prior to that. Regressing all the way to the fiery molten fundamental core of wing play where wide players mechanically fired crosses into the box, the Generals created two goals against Atlanta in two minutes, both by Michael Ash in front of a paltry 3,938. Warren Archibald set up the first with a looping cross to Siciliano, whose shot deflected to Ash. Archibald figured into the second, as well, passing to Barry Mahy, who hit the woodwork only to have it once again fall directly to Ash.

Again emphasizing how much television itself had become part of the narrative, the *Times* spent considerable column space analyzing whether referee Eddie Pearson seamlessly signaled for his ten allotted commercials. [82] Despite high attrition and acute offensive woes, Goodwin insisted that "the spirit is high."[83] Millward felt that playing on the road could be a blessing due to the "other pitches being smaller," which could allow the Bays to "break better." Millward offhandedly illustrated the absurdity of playing in baseball stadiums, saying, "they tell me New York has a good pitch, but you have to go over the pitcher's mound."[84] The mounds and base paths would indeed claim their fair share of ligaments, tendons, and bones.

Besides playing surfaces, baseball was inextricably linked to the Generals' stadium plight in other ways. In keeping with the general pattern of hiring a "sports executive"[85] to run a brand-new soccer franchise, the Generals named Bill Bergesch as their general manager. Bergesch had previously worked as the Yankee's stadium manager since 1964. It was a textbook NPSL/USA hire in its emphasis on superfluous experience in American sports, but it dovetailed directly into another issue that would plague American soccer for decades: adequate venues.

Showing great deference to his former colleagues, Bergesch wrote clauses into the Generals' rental contract that forbade "the field to be used for soccer within 48 hours of a baseball game,"[86] giving the Yankees the power to refuse use of the stadium in such instances. This arrangement illustrated not only the precarious nature of adequate venues for staging soccer matches, but also the unequal partnership many teams endured as tenants in baseball stadiums that didn't really suit the game to begin with. It also showed the downside of recycling executives from other sports. Luckily for the Generals, the Yankees only exercised their option to cancel once in two seasons.[87] But between agreements like this and the exorbitant rent franchises like the

Whips were paying, it's easy to see why soccer-specific stadiums would become a pillar of MLS expansion in the future.

The Bays were wary of facing Cesar Luis Menotti, who'd quickly acquired the nickname "the Cannon" on the strength of his tremendous shot. Los Angeles Toros goalie Blagoje Vidinic said that Menotti's shot "comes in like a bullet"[88] and that he was in pain after stopping one with his stomach. They needn't have worried, as the two sides played a lifeless, lackluster 0–0 draw that thankfully only 2,351 bothered to see.

Toye and Millward blasted the Generals for their negativity, with Toye accusing New York of playing with a "mass defense" where "no more than four of them ever crossed midfield."[89] Toye branded it the "kind of stuff you would see in Italy." This performance definitely reflected the level of pressure Goodwin was under to produce results. Less than a month before the Bays' match, he told the *Times* that "European Soccer has become so defensive minded that now the games are barely being played for the spectators. A team is satisfied to come away with a tie."[90] The only thing that changed in the interim was a five-match winless streak.

Meanwhile the Toronto Falcons were also struggling mightily. They had just been thrashed 7–2 at home by the Philadelphia Spartans on the strength of a hat trick by Tibor Szaly. Orlando Garro added two goals of his own. To put Philadelphia's eruption in perspective, they had scored only eight times in the previous seven matches. The humiliating loss dropped the Falcons to 1–8–1, with their sole victory coming against the Los Angeles Toros. Falcons coach Hector Marinaro, a holdover from the old Eastern Canada Professional Soccer League, was named the team's general manager by owner Joseph Peters. His replacement as coach was Ferdinand Daucik, father of Falcon's star Yanko Daucik. Ferdinand was a formidable manager who had won multiple La Liga titles with Barcelona[91] and Athletic Bilbao during his career.

Yanko had also made a name for himself in Spain, playing for Real Betis and ultimately Real Madrid. He missed the first four NPSL games but quickly scored five goals in the last six to lead the league in scoring. With the addition of Daucik's father, Ferdinand, the Falcons were becoming a legitimate family affair because the team also featured Daucik's brother-in-law, the legendary Ladislao Kubala. Kubala's life and career read like a map through the dark corridors of twentieth-century European history.[92]

Born in Budapest, Kubala joined Ferencvaros at the age of eighteen and scored nineteen league goals. He escaped Hungary's Communist regime in 1949, turning up in Italy. The Hungarians sought reparations and repatriation, leading FIFA to ban him for a year. In Italy, Kubala formed a touring team of Hungarian exiles called Hungaria. Kubala's home base at the time was in Cinecitta, the mecca of Italian film production, so it was only natural that a film about Hungaria's travails was made called *Kubala: Stars in Search of Peace.*

Eventually he settled in Barcelona, under Ferdinand Daucik, and became a bona fide Blaugrana legend, scoring 280 goals for the Catalan giants[93] as they collected trophies at a feverish clip. Kubala was so revered by *cules* in Catalonia that he was voted the best Barcelona player of all time in 1999.[94] He was despised throughout the rest of the Primera due to shadowy allegations of communism and subject to often blatant physical abuse that culminated in a staggering seven knee surgeries. As a naturalized Spaniard, he soon began scoring goals for the Spanish national team, becoming the only player to ever be capped for three nations: Hungary, Czechoslovakia, and Spain. At this time, he was so feared that as Spain prepared to play Turkey in a playoff for World Cup qualification, FIFA actually faked a telegram to "put him out of the match,"[95] according to Brian Glanville. Spain, of course, lost without him.

He was forty years old in the summer of 1967, "thick-thighed as always, scarcely mobile, but loping into good positions, giving intelligent passes; some of them to Branko, his son."[96] Branko was the final member of the Kubala/Daucik family quadrant but was yet to make an impact for the Falcons. All of the excitement and flux paid off, at least for one night, as the Falcons recorded a 2–0 victory over the suddenly listless Bays.

The Bays' success was predicated on pace. Tactically they were always looking to use that speed to score first and to draw teams out, leaving their defenses exposed and vulnerable to the explosiveness of players like Art Welch. However, if the other side scored first, it could retrench and defend with six players or more, making it next to impossible for the Bays to exploit open space with their speed, which is what happened against the Falcons.

The Bays were struggling, having been blanked in three of their last four matches. Their defense remained solid, conceding a league-low fourteen goals. Millward had switched the team's formation to a 4–3–3, which some were blaming for the drought. Toye defended the switch, characterizing it as a positive since there were now upward of "six men shooting at the goal."[97] Toye blamed a lack of accuracy and a tendency to run with the ball too much as underlying reasons the goals dried up, saying, "when you run too much, defenses become even more packed." This again showed how important open space was for a Bays team designed to gobble up space with speed.

Atlanta returned to Baltimore in early June. Phil Woosnam, amazingly, was leading the team in scoring with eight goals in nine matches to pace an Atlanta squad that was coming on fast as Baltimore faltered. In the Chiefs lineup since their second match against Los Angeles, Woosnam "supposedly only inserted himself because Peter McParland was out with kidney trouble."[98] The Chiefs had lost once in their previous seven outings, a 3–2 defeat to Philadelphia that Woosnam was forced to miss due to a sore knee. The

Bays came out swinging against the Chiefs, overrunning Atlanta throughout the first half.

For the first time in weeks Baltimore's quick-strike approach yielded dividends when Fernando Azevedo dribbled past a handful of defenders to flick a shot at Vic Rouse, who deflected it to the waiting Shimon Cohen. Cohen, a man with much on his mind, since Israel was once again embroiled in war, finished smartly to give the Bays a 1–0 lead. Both Cohen and David Primo were in continual contact with the Israeli embassy to see if they were needed for military service. It was a timely reminder of the turbulence engulfing the world. Santisteban, pulling the strings for Baltimore as always, floated a ball into the box that caromed around before finding the net off Atlanta defender Gordon Ferry's heel. Although Atlanta would be the far better side after the break, the Bays held on for a much-needed 2–1 win. [99]

The wavering Bays found themselves in third place in the East. Their lack of consistency was troubling and had Millward grasping for answers. The coach felt that the inability to string together a few positive results had left the team tight and prone to mental lapses. "If we can win a few in a row it will give us some breathing space and then the boys will play with a bit of relaxation. Right now, they're still pressing a little," [100] Millward said.

Their next opponents were a suddenly revitalized Toronto Falcons squad. Since Ferdinand Daucik took over, the Falcons had won three straight, including victories against Chicago and New York. Becoming ever-more influential as the match played out, the slick Santisteban stole the ball in Toronto's end and found Uriel Da Veiga tearing down the left flank. Da Veiga launched a perfect cross to Art Welch who headed it home with a vengeance. It proved a timely strike, as the erratic Welch had become a lightning rod for fan discontent, even getting booed during warm-ups. [101]

Daucik leveled for Toronto on a brilliant individual effort. A little later, Welch struck again after some nice work from Baltimore native Speca to make it 2–1. Daucik pounced to equalize once more, marking the third time he'd scored a brace in league play. The seesaw match remained poised on a knife's edge. Santisteban ultimately scored the winner off a corner with less than six minutes to play, giving the Bays a 3–2 victory. The goal marked a pair of firsts: it was the first goal Baltimore had scored from a corner and it was the first time the Bays would record back-to-back victories.

Baltimore was now awaiting the return of the Pittsburgh Phantoms and the never-ending saga of the combustible Co Prins. The Phantoms were on their fourth coach. Prins had stepped down as player-coach, which left general manager Ted DeGroot in charge until the team secured Pepi Gruber as a permanent replacement. Gruber was an Austrian who, like Prins and four other Phantoms, had connections to Ajax. Prins' stormy tenure started out with four straight victories, but in keeping with his topsy-turvy nature, the team lost their next three. The pressure of playing and coaching quickly got to him, and he had a full-blown meltdown during a match with Los Angeles. Prins was sent off for excessive arguing and almost touched off a melee leaving the pitch.

The scene was bad enough that the "game had to be halted for 10 minutes and both teams were ordered off the field for a cooling-off period before action was resumed."[102] Prins' outburst even caught Ken Macker's attention, and he received a one-game suspension for his troubles. The wobbly, wacky Phantoms had lost five of six and DeGroot "told Baltimore officials that he fined each Pittsburgh player $100 for their poor effort in Los Angeles."[103] Like clockwork, owner Peter Block promptly denied it. The disorganization and dispiritedness manifested itself in Baltimore, as the Phantoms were easy pickings for the focused Bays who rolled to an easy 4–1 victory.

The Bays headed west and lost 3–1 to the Oakland Clippers. It was their first loss away from Memorial Stadium. However, the Oakland Coliseum was an unfriendly place in which no team would win during 1967. Under the tutelage of the two-headed tactical monster that was Dr. Aleksandar Obradovic and Ivan Toplak, the Clippers were a finely constructed machine cruising through the NPSL's Western Division like a low rider down East Fourteenth Street. Both men were veterans of the prestigious Red Star Belgrade squad and along with general manager Derek Liecty had fashioned a cohesive unit with a strange but effective Yugoslav/Central American core.

Obradovic and Toplak loved to press the opposition, and their Clippers' sides were models of disciplined, organized movement. Obradovic's "strategy of flooding the penalty zone with seven or eight players paid off with the game less than a minute old"[104] when the Clippers' Edgar Marin punched in a close-range shot, giving Oakland the lead and knocked the Bays into a tailspin. Baltimore was now unable to utilize its pace, which was perhaps the one advantage they had over Oakland. Obradovic particularly favored this tactic at home, as weary teams traveling into Oakland were quickly overwhelmed and pressed into submission with superior awareness and organization.

The exact opposite occurred in Los Angeles. The Bays were able to stick to their preferred script, scoring three minutes into the match in front of 3,463 fans in the monolithic L.A. Coliseum. Santisteban found St. Vil with a lovely pass from midfield and St. Vil streaked to the right side before unleashing a laser past Los Angeles keeper Lothar Spranger. It was the only goal the Bays would require. At 1–0, the Bays dropped into a shell of their own. They needed a man of the match–caliber performance from David Primo to hold on, however, as the Toros played much of the contest in Baltimore's end.[105]

At this juncture, the East was shaping into a wild race between Baltimore, Atlanta, Pittsburgh, and Philadelphia. However, people around the Bays were getting nervous thanks to the "revolutionary" new scoring system that Toye had raved about. Baltimore had the best win-loss record, but, with only twenty-five goals, was lagging behind Atlanta.[106] A trip to Forbes Field and a date with the Phantoms lurked in the shadows.

After kicking a player during a recent victory against Philadelphia, Co Prins was once again ejected from a match, and he was expected to be suspended by Macker. His status against the Bays was uncertain. The Phantoms had already managed to give up an eye-popping forty-two goals. A black cloud seemed to engulf the club, as stories emerged of a player walking out of a bar in Georgia with a broken jaw during preseason. The club's fourth coach, Pepi Gruber was also still trying to decide whether he could cope long term with the madness of Prins and the club's darkly comedic carnival atmosphere.[107]

The Phantoms roared out to a 2–0 lead only to get cautious and careless, allowing the Bays to hang on. Pittsburgh spurned a handful of worthy chances and could have increased its lead. Prins somehow avoided suspension and was eligible to play after paying a $500 fine. The Bays threw everyone forward in attack throughout the second half as they sought a chance to get back into the match. Finally, the Phantoms' resistance broke and the Bays scored twice within a span of eighteen minutes to knot the score at 2–2.

The second goal came with less than ten minutes remaining when the electrifying Guy St. Vil once again beat a defender cleanly around the box before lifting a pinpoint cross to Azevedo who banged it home. Even the ambience at Phantoms matches seemed to convey a sense of warped, surreal menace, as Ken Nigro reported that the kickoff was delayed because officials were unable to locate their recording of "The Star-Spangled Banner." When they did find it, they managed to play it at the wrong speed—a recollected image that conveys a deeper resonance within the context of 1967 on the pitch and beyond. Fortunately, only 2,236 were there to take home the tale.[108]

From Pittsburgh the Bays traveled to Toronto and another date with the Falcons. Ladislao Kubala had started playing in earnest and recorded two assists in a recent 3–1 triumph over the St. Louis Stars. Clive Toye and Dennis Viollet raved about Kubala's legacy and still-superb fitness and vision, with Toye calling him "one of the best I've ever seen."[109] Kubala admitted that he "played all out against St. Louis," but felt he still needed two or three matches to acquire a rhythm.

The Bays again fell behind 2–0 and were left to chase the match. This time they would fall short, losing 2–1 and dropping to second place in the East behind Pittsburgh, which somehow accrued ninety-two points to the Bays' ninety. The Phantoms played a rabble-rousing 3–3 draw with St. Louis that earned them six points while Baltimore was consigned to defeat for the second time by a mediocre Falcons side. Yanko Daucik and the great Kubala supplied the margin for Toronto's victory. The torrid Daucik figured in on Kubala's goal, heading the ball to him at the left post, where Kubala beat David Primo, twenty years his junior, to the punch. Strangely, Daucik, already with ten goals to his name, was "razzed every time he made a wrong move by most of the 3,016 who turned out at Varsity Stadium."[110]

This was a good stretch for Toronto, which had won three straight and six of nine. The team played its first six matches on the road because it was impossible to use Varsity Field before May 10 due to the weather, according to general manager Hector Marinaro. Marinaro called Baltimore the best team he had seen in the league besides Oakland, a sentiment heard more often as the two teams separated themselves from the pack. For his part, Dennis Viollet considered the Falcons "one of the best clubs in the league."[111]

The Bays ground out a 1–0 win against the Clippers in Baltimore and talk gathered apace that the two were perhaps destined to collide in the NPSL championship. Before that talk could become reality, Baltimore had to contend with a brutal stretch in July that saw them play four matches in eight days. Heading into this crucial part of the schedule, the Bays with 112 points enjoyed an eleven-point advantage over the Phantoms on top of the Eastern Division standings. This was after the Bays had blown a winnable game against the sorry New York Generals, losing 2–1 "in a game that had only the slightest resemblance to soccer."[112]

Nigro labeled referee Ken Stokes "the star" of the proceedings, a label seldom affixed to a referee in a positive context. Bad blood between the Bays and Generals had been simmering since the two met in spring scrimmages. Stokes had made the error of "letting the match get out of hand in the first ten minutes."[113] From there the game degenerated into an abject ballet of elbows, trips, and ornately feigned injuries. Juan Santisteban, excellent all season, completely lost his cool and had to be restrained from going after Stokes by goalkeeper Terry Adlington.[114] It is amazing to consider the parallels occurring as these scenarios played out across both leagues: poor, lackadaisical refereeing leading to increasingly violent matches and ultimately spreading like a dull contagion into the stands. The NPSL was lucky in that it largely avoided the conflagrations the USA endured in New York, Detroit, and Toronto.

Suddenly news broke that the NPSL was considering changing its playoff format midseason. Sponsored by the Chicago Spurs, the idea was to include the top two teams from each division in a playoff to decide the championship. This idea seemed to appear from nowhere and was heartily voted down by a 7–3 count at a recent league meeting. St. Louis and Toronto, teams that had essentially been buried by the runaway Clippers in the Western Division, were the only other clubs to support the motion.

Yet as Toye, Hamper, and the Bays were watching CBS's broadcast of the Pittsburgh–St. Louis match, they were absolutely stunned to hear Ken Macker publicly announce that he was resurrecting the idea. Nigro likened the announcement's impact to a bomb. Toye said he was "absolutely horrified" and "could have leaped through the television,"[115] characterizing the idea as "grossly unjust" before adding the coup de grace: "This is major league?" It was a venomous yet fair rhetorical question.

Was the NPSL a major league? You can almost sense Toye's horror when reading those words years later, the sudden vertiginous flash when he realizes the truth. The league featured marquee franchises with no trainers and equipment managers (Chicago), teams playing in ill-suited stadiums with potentially dangerous playing surfaces under onerously one-sided leases, and poor refereeing that was detrimental to players and fans alike. Toye's question was and is certainly worth investigating. Macker's ham-fisted, tone-deaf approach is also worth considering. For a man with a public relations background, it's mystifying that he would blindside franchise owners on national television with a proposal they had swiftly and overwhelmingly rejected only days before. Upon closer examination of the NPSL's public relations record—and Macker's in particular—it is truly difficult to find a single success. Even lowering the standards from "success" to "competence" or "adequacy" yields scant few examples.

The Chicago Spurs were a team transformed. They fired Al Rogers after suffering through a fourteen-match winless streak, replacing him with Janos Bedl, one of a handful of men who had coached the Pittsburgh Phantoms in just over three months. The arrival of Bedl coincided with the arrival of Scottish forward Ernie Winchester, a longtime fixture within the Aberdeen Dons side, which happened to be playing in D.C. Stadium right down the road. According to Nigro, Winchester's transfer "has probably done as much to slow the proposed merger between the National League and United Soccer Association as anything."[116]

This was because Winchester had another year left on his existing contract, and not only were the Dons not notified of the move, but they didn't receive a fee. Not finished scouring Scotland for talent, the Spurs also managed to add Pat O'Connor from Kilmarnock. Transfer drama aside, the rejuvenated Spurs were now unbeaten in their last six.[117] Winchester would return to Scotland with the Hearts in 1969, but the core of this team would contend strongly in the NASL during the next two years, culminating with a title victory in 1969. Sadly for the few Windy City faithful, the club would achieve these feats as the Kansas City Spurs.

Winchester opened the scoring for Chicago during another uninspiring first half for the slow-motion Bays. The rough-and-tumble, mid-paced Spurs even seemed quicker than the lackadaisical Bays. During the second half Millward made a pivotal adjustment, deciding to use his wingers more aggressively. He also sent more men forward to attack and receive crosses from the unleashed wingers.[118] The moves paid off and Baltimore started pushing the tempo. Shimon Cohen got the equalizer on a shot that deflected off an unlucky Chicago defender. The real breakthrough came when Badu du Cruz hit Viollet, who was moving with surprising swiftness on his wonky hamstring, in stride for the match winner. It was his third goal of the season and it gave the Bays a deserved 2–1 result. Millward was finding ways to adapt while always maximizing the strengths of his talented, yet uneven, squad.

As the Bays prepared to face the Los Angeles Toros, a small item buried in a much larger *Baltimore Sun* piece about Toros keeper Lothar Spranger would change the fate of both NPSL Division leaders: the Los Angeles Toros had sold halfback Dragan Djukic to the Oakland Clippers.[119] In what was perhaps the match of the season, the Bays and Toros put on a clinic for the 6,422 fans lucky enough to be in Memorial Stadium. It was described as a "game of brilliant passing, continuous movement and few penalties."[120] Veteran official Walter Crossley was reported to have remarked, "that's the best game I've ever worked in."

Leading 1–0 after a frantic first half that saw Spranger make a number of huge saves to keep Baltimore off the board, the Toros switched off briefly and it cost them. Viollet scored to tie the match at 1–1. The teams exchanged goals again and looked to be headed toward a highly entertaining yet ultimately unresolved match when Fernando Azevedo scored with thirty-eight seconds left. The influential defenseman Badu du Cruz, who had figured in both Baltimore goals, found the regal Santisteban, who slid a dagger ball to Azevedo: 3–2 Baltimore. It was over. The exhausted Toros sank to the ground in disbelief.[121]

Seeking to lock up the Eastern Division title, Baltimore traveled to Atlanta. The Chiefs had lost only one of their ten home matches and were now in second place behind the Bays.[122] Incidentally, the Chiefs' sole home loss was a 3–0 drubbing at the hands of the Oakland Clippers. Atlanta had coalesced into a potent mix of gritty, lockdown defense and blazing, counterattacking speed. It was a strange match in which the Chiefs dominated possession and flustered Baltimore with the pace of their attack yet somehow went into the break down 2–1.

Atlanta outshot the Bays nineteen to eleven but was prone to overpassing near the goalmouth, their lack of directness costly. The speedy Zambian playmaker Emment Kapengwe screeched down the left side of the pitch before spotting Peter McParland, who easily headed home for a 1–0 Atlanta advantage. Atlanta graciously opened the scoring for their hosts, as well, when Art Welch's shot wrung off a tangle of Chiefs, giving the Bays an equalizer that was very much against the run of play.

It was and is typical of the type of bounces that division- and title-winning teams need and, more importantly, receive along their journey. Despite some close calls near the end when the Bays were counterattacking with deadly intent to exploit the space afforded by Atlanta's aggressive pursuit, the match ended deadlocked at 2–2 in what was ultimately a huge missed opportunity for the Chiefs. Baltimore was one step closer to wrapping up the East. [123]

The Bays traveled to New York with Oakland in their thoughts, as the Eastern Division crown was so close they could almost graze it with their fingertips. Similar to the Spurs, the Generals had undergone a dramatic renaissance after their early struggles. Also like Chicago they were somehow able to skirt the sanctions of their rogue status and import midseason quality in the form of English center-forward George Kirby. Kirby had forged a decent legacy in the English Football League, including a season with Plymouth Argyle, where he tallied eighteen goals.

Kirby joined the Generals on June 28 and had scored an impressive ten goals in twelve matches. This output inspired a run that saw the previously inept Generals lose only two of thirteen matches. [124] As an example of the Bays' consistency, not losing consecutive games all season, the Generals were still twenty-three points behind Baltimore. Unlike their last meeting, this match had a decent tempo and was a tightly contested affair.

Demonstrating his considerable versatility, Dennis Viollet did an excellent job frustrating the in-form Kirby. The contest went back and forth in the rainy Manhattan night until Geoffrey Sidebottom fouled Leif Klasson as he barreled in on goal. The Bays were awarded a penalty, which had haunted them throughout the campaign, as the side had missed three of four—including one by Shimon Cohen in their most recent encounter with the Generals, which likely would have yielded a victory instead of a 3–3 tie.

Badu du Cruz stepped up to spot, and as 5,807 held their breath, he blasted the ball into the left side of the net for a 1–0 Bays advantage. Millward said afterward that he'd decided at halftime to use Du Cruz if Baltimore was awarded a penalty because "he hits a hard, low ball and since it was wet it didn't figure that anyone would stop the shot." [125] Millward also admitted that he considered using the more experienced Viollet at the last minute. He decided to hold firm and Du Cruz rewarded his faith.

The 1–0 result stood and, with Atlanta losing 3–2 to St. Louis that same evening, the Bays' division lead was a considerable twenty-five points with only four matches remaining. The victory, the Bays' first in four attempts against the Generals, meant that Baltimore had recorded a victory against every NPSL squad, something to build their confidence as they eyed the NPSL title. Fate kept handing Baltimore golden opportunities, the latest being a home date against a reeling, decimated St. Louis side that had just been demolished 9–0 by the Oakland Clippers.

Before running into the Clippers juggernaut, the Stars had won three straight and were looking to climb back into Western contention. Gutendorf made a huge mistake before the match, saying, "Oakland is not that good that we can't beat them." [126] The Clippers were as sensitive as they were talented and that statement was sure to inflame their borderline belligerent pride. Down 3–0 at halftime, the German told his team to attack in hopes of gaining goals and thus points. With their defense joining the attack, they were exposed and annihilated by a ruthless Oakland side. Gutendorf said, "we lost our rhythm, our system. We were like a machine with the wheel broken." The heavy defeat left the Stars' hopes in tatters as the Clippers and Bays began a seemingly inexorable march to the championship.

The vulnerable St. Louis side was easily dispatched by the Bays, who recorded a 3–1 victory to put themselves within seven points of clinching the Eastern Division. Perhaps still rattled from the Clippers' drubbing, Gutendorf made the exceedingly strange decision to put his leading scorer Rudi Kolbl in goal after the Stars, without substitutes, saw their keeper, Bronco Topalovic, fall to injury late in the match. Kolbl, the former TSV 1860 Munich forward, had scored thirteen goals for the Stars and was an interesting choice as keeper when the Stars were desperately chasing what was then a one-goal match. [127]

On August 14, 1967, fresh reports of a possible merger between the rival leagues again began to surface. The expansion committees of each league had been meeting to discuss a union. The USA season was over and the owners had had time to mull their considerable financial losses, while NPSL owners certainly could see where their fortunes were headed even though the season hadn't ended.

The Bays had a chance to clinch in Baltimore against the Philadelphia Spartans. During the season, Ruben "the Hatchet" Navarro assumed the role of player-coach while continuing to maintain his high standards of defensive disruption. Since taking over for John Szep, who had resigned abruptly after management refused to sign a player with visa issues, the Spartans had won three of four under "the Hatchet." Pele once referred to Navarro as "the greatest defensive player in all of South America. [128] At thirty-four, the wizened center-half's positional instincts were stronger than ever and he still possessed enough mobility to be one of the NPSL's best defenders. When the Spartans folded after the season, Navarro stayed in America with the Cleveland Stokers.

A season-high 11,329 turned out at Memorial Stadium to witness what they hoped would be the Bays' coronation. [129] The Spartans had become more conservative under Navarro, playing effective defense and patiently waiting for openings on the counter. Philadelphia's "blood and thunder" defense stifled the Bays and after thirty-one minutes, the chance they were waiting for materialized. The typically reliable David Primo, voted the Bays' most popular player, misjudged—as countless outfielders playing on Memorial Field's diamond had doubtlessly done—a long ball that sailed over his head and found the waiting feet of Tibor Szalay. Szalay fired past Terry Adlington to give the Spartans a 1–0 lead. It was enough for Navarro and company to grind out a victory.

Toye referred to the Bays as the "most dejected group in the world" after the loss, as in his view, the team would "have spit blood to win before that many people."[130] It was a missed opportunity, certainly, but the Bays also knew it was a matter of time before the title was officially theirs. The impressive crowd lifted the Bays' total attendance for sixteen home matches to 90,041. The Bays were now forced to win the Eastern Division title on the road in Atlanta.

The Bays took their impressive 5–3–6 away record to Fulton County Stadium, where the Chiefs had been tough to break down. The Bays needed only five points to finally win the crown. Despite stretches of inconsistent play, Millward felt "our speed to the ball and our reason were good"[131] and when those two facets of Baltimore's game were strong, the team liked its chances against anyone.

The match was broadcast on CBS, creating a nice bookend with their season-opening clash. However, the television audience as well as the 4,361 in attendance witnessed an anticlimactic scoreless draw that saw the Bays back into the Eastern Division title.[132] Amazingly, the New York Generals had played themselves back into contention and were the only division team still mathematically alive after the disappointing 0–0 result between the Chiefs and Bays. New York was playing the Clippers in Oakland so the Bays had to wait into the night until the Generals were beaten 4–2 for their title to become official. It was ironic that Oakland had given the Bays one final push; the adversaries who'd been circling each other since Baltimore's 1–0 victory over Oakland in July now prepared to meet for the NPSL title.

POSTSCRIPT

The Philadelphia Spartans claimed second place in the Eastern Division on the strength of a raucous 2–1 victory against the New York Generals at Yankee Stadium in the last match of the season. Ruben Navarro's high level of play and stellar job managing the Spartans—who lost only once under his stewardship—combined to make him the NPSL player of the year. Navarro was selected for this honor in a poll taken by his peers.[133]

Philadelphia's second-place finish earned it a spot in the NPSL's Challenge Cup where it would play the Western Division's runner-up, the St. Louis Stars. The match was set for September 13 and the winner would go on to face the NPSL Champion. Philadelphia lost the second-place playoff to St. Louis in what would be the franchise's last match. The Spartans had lost upward of $500,000 and president John Rooney asked the newly merged

NASL for a yearlong "leave of absence."[134] The NASL denied Rooney's request and the Spartans faded into oblivion. The team would be ransacked for parts by the desperate, hollow franchises that had competed in the USA, with many of the best players ending up on the Cleveland Stokers.

The Pittsburgh Phantoms also folded rather quickly, perhaps mercifully, as they managed to lose $750,000 in less than a year. Strange decisions, exceedingly poor attendance, and a rental agreement at Forbes Field—similar to the one the Yankees and Generals had—that allowed stadium officials to postpone games—which had occurred twice in the season's first month alone[135]—in order to protect the stadium for the Pittsburgh Pirates were factors that contributed to the Phantoms' short existence.

Something shocking happened while the Bays were navigating their tricky two-legged championship tie with the Clippers: Doug Millward was fired. The decision had been made sometime in August when Millward asked Clive Toye and Joe Hamper for clarification regarding his future. He was offered a contract for 1968 but was also told "it was felt that the best interests of the club would be served if Millward were employed in a capacity other than head coach."[136] The news, kept secret for weeks, had now mysteriously leaked the day after Baltimore's 1–0 victory against the Clippers in the first leg of the NPSL title series.

According to the *Sun*, Millward was fond of saying, "My problem is that I'm too blunt."[137] It appears that a $200 fine Millward earned "for using foul language to referee Ken Stokes" is partially why Bays' management soured on him. If that wasn't silly enough for a team in first place, they asked him to resign for "personal reasons" when he asked for a better contract. Another alleged Millward indiscretion occurred in a scene that recalled the dark, poignant absurdity of *Death of Salesman*. While on an early season trip to Philadelphia, Hamper "became upset when Millward permitted the players to sing on the bus."[138]

Hidden deep in the background here are issues of class. Compare the gruff Millward to the erudite Toye. Millward was ultimately considered part of the undesirable classes of folk that American businessmen were determined to pry the game away from so that they could simultaneously sell and neutralize it. Millward was an embodiment of the foreign, blue-collar people who constituted the game's image in America, an image USA and NPSL owners were desperate to recast and reconstruct. As if the Baltimore Orioles status as a publicly traded company was not already an obvious factor in this decision, the *Sun* removed all doubt, writing "Owner Jerry Hoffberger also was reportedly upset over the image Millward was creating."[139] It was an uncomfortable reminder that from CBS on down, the NPSL was coldly, callously, and clinically about business. These reminders and intrusions were apparent in the USA if you paid attention, but in the NPSL they were blatant, Technicolor monuments to corporate priorities and power. Toye glimpsed this icy cold reality himself when Ken Macker announced on national television that the league was revisiting a playoff plan that had been soundly rejected.

It's one of the cruelest paradoxes in modern American life that corporate titans like Hoffberger expect a scripted, inflated level of decorum from everyone in their orbit due to a narrowly defined conception of "image," while in many cases the actions of corporations themselves—the entity the image is designed to protect—often reflect a level of hypocrisy and malevolence that mock the very concept of decorum. This reflects the ascendancy of artifice in the American psyche. As long as the veneer was polished and friendly, the essence, the inner core, could be insidious and contradictory. As an example, Hamper told the *Baltimore Sun* that the Bays stuck to their "principle" of not abandoning/firing the people they hired from all over the globe in midseason, piously adding they might have been the "only club in the league to do it."[140]

Men like Millward, who grew up with soccer pulsing through their veins, were only useful until their accents or knowledge of the sport inevitably ran afoul of business interests, and they were coldly discarded. Macker's selection as commissioner and the slavish deference to CBS showed that the slant would always be weighted toward business, not the game itself. The trouble was that American business didn't know how to properly interpret or sell soccer, and as time went on, it was proven that soccer and American business traveled on incongruent paths. Hamper referred to the tension between "customs"[141] that people from different cultures must navigate when interacting. He was referring to differences between American culture and those embodied by the foreign men representing the Bays, but in actuality he's describing the incompatibility and incomprehensibility of newly retrenched corporate "customs" that people all over the world were rebelling against in the '60s.

But with all the power vested in its hands, business, in the guise of the NPSL, was free to make fantastically poor decisions regarding the game of soccer. Men like Hoffberger and Hamper were so far out of their element that they made decisions, like firing a first-place manager, that were blatantly counterintuitive to what they supposedly knew best—business. The fact that Millward, while operating under sanction and outside of FIFA's umbrella, still managed to select good players from all over the globe, players who were used to drastically different styles and levels of play, and to successfully shape them step-by-step into a cohesive, championship-contending unit within the space of six months was a staggering accomplishment, the scope of which can't be overstated.

Toye was the one person who could have appreciated the magnitude of what Millward accomplished, but something had changed between the two men. Gone were the days when Toye thought Millward was the "best coach available," which, again, is astonishing considering the Bays were only a draw away from the NPSL title. What had changed? Even stranger was the

Bays' decision to also prematurely dismiss their leading goal scorer, Fernando Azevedo, until you realize that he too asked for a better contract. Toye's opinion in regard to the NPSL's dense scoring system evolved, as well. Initially an evangelist who was "instrumental" in its adaptation, he later told Bob Maisel, "I don't think we've proved a thing this year with the scoring system." [142] It was another drastic change in tone and mood.

Fulham manager Gordon Jago was chosen as Millward's replacement. Jago's hiring was announced in the same clumsy, embarrassing fashion as Millward's dismissal, when a leak in England forced the club's hand. They had planned to announce the move the day after Jago resigned from Fulham, but the reverse happened. In what were also eerily familiar words, Toye said, "Gordon is the coach I had in mind when I left for Europe." [143]

Millward resurfaced as Toye and Jago's Bays crashed out of NASL contention in August 1968 to give a scathing interview to the *Baltimore Sun*. Millward finally decided to speak out because "he felt too much criticism of Baltimore's fourth-place standing this year was being heaped on him." [144] Millward placed the blame squarely on Toye, saying: "Clive speaks very well, very persuasively. But what has he done. He has no real knowledge of handling players and decisions. I handled negotiations for most of the players last year. Clive just doesn't talk their language."

It's incredible how language intersects with and shapes the conflict between Millward and the Bays. Millward's blunt, plainsong speech was viewed at its extremes as damaging the "image" of the Bays' (and by extension, the Orioles') brand while Toye's slick, persuasive, ultimately hollow speech ("It wasn't a question of firing the coach, but rather a question of organizational alteration") fit perfectly with the brand but was extremely ineffective in achieving essential objectives, like communicating with players. In a sense, Millward represents someone empowered to use subversive language, insomuch as his ability to communicate uncomfortable truths plainly were seen as subversive to men like Hoffberger obsessed with constructing images that not only subverted and concealed reality but ultimately existed almost solely to perpetuate their power and wealth.

Another man, of a similar pedigree and background, who went through similar travails with CBS and the NPSL was Danny Blanchflower. Blanchflower recalled a conversation with Jack Dolph, a high-level executive within CBS Sports, where he was told, "You're a spellbinder with words, I'll admit it. But, to be honest, you frighten me." [145] Blanchflower also recalled a reporter telling Bill MacPhail that he'd "ruin" Blanchflower.

The former Spurs legend remembered being summoned to CBS not long after the season started and criticized for his commentary. Blanchflower's honesty was quickly becoming legendary, and he had correctly come down hard on a goalkeeping error but was instructed next time to instead emphasize the positive by playing up how good the shot was. He replied that doing so would not be truthful. This prompted the CBS execs to say, "we think there are two truths: a positive truth and a negative truth."

This remains an astonishing admission that illuminates why interrogations of language and image are so important within the history of American soccer. The concept of having two truths is akin to admitting that the very construction of objective reality was itself at stake in the new era of mass communication and corporate consolidation. Multiple truths not only protect power but excuse it. Multiple truths always cast carefully constructed and preferred images in the most favorable light.

Blanchflower remembered lucidly realizing right then that "there was a conflict in the land, and I was in the middle of it." By land he meant America, but this conflict was quickly becoming global. He *was* in the middle of it; he was an actor empowered with language that frightened powerful interests due to its penetrative perceptive abilities but also resonated with ordinary people not empowered to speak in such fashion. But on a larger level the conflict he sensed occurring was centered on soccer itself, and its uncomfortable relationship with America.

This discomfort stemmed from the fact that soccer was uniquely positioned at the absolute center of messy, dynamic issues of power, image, ethnicity, and class that were already being violently, vehemently renegotiated in 1967. Blanchflower's rejoinder that he knew "only one truth to which a man takes either a positive or negative attitude,"[146] represented grave danger to those who wished to monopolize truth so that it could be distorted and disseminated into multiplicities of truth (or "truthiness" as Stephen Colbert would have it years later) and competing versions of reality that could ultimately be manipulated to serve the needs of the moment. The erosion of language, truth, and reality were all interconnected, their sinews visible in the NPSL experiment.

The examples of Blanchflower and Millward illuminate a great divide, a divide between the dominant strains of corporatized thought and language at cross-purposes with and ultimately antagonistic to the players and consumers that drove the game. Not only were the two unable to communicate across the divide, corporate language was eventually used to reshape the landscape, excluding undesirables such as Millward and the "frightening" Blanchflower as much as possible. More and more this divide would intersect directly with issues of class, an issue that dare not speak its name in the United States.

Far from being noble folks bound to "principle," as Hamper would have it, Millward contended that "considerable front office promises to the players were broken last year."[147] He specifically singled out the case of Fernando Azevedo, labeling it "diabolical" before noting that his absence could have cost the Bays the title. Millward mocked Toye and Jago for publicly announcing that the Bays would play an attacking, aggressive style of soccer, tracing this impetus directly to owner Jerry Hoffberger.

Millward criticized the two for inexperience "bordering on stupidity" and emphasized his belief that Jago and Toye said what "Hoffberger wanted them to say." The fiery coach perceptively noted that Toye's "continued alibi" that a higher standard of play in the NASL was largely responsible for the Bays' regression was "laughable." "It sounds more like a sales pitch from the league office," he added. There is a difference between being blunt and speaking uncomfortable truths. Uncomfortable truths have a habit of damaging carefully constructed images and narratives. Millward was right, and Toye would ride those silver-tongued sales pitches all the way into the upper echelons of NASL leadership, becoming the aptly named director of administration and information.

Finally, Millward observed, "the Bays seem more concerned with image. They forget that actions speak louder than words." It could have been an epitaph for the entire NPSL experiment, and the NPSL's actions *did* speak louder than words. Their actions showed that soccer, particularly the people who played and coached it, was completely ancillary (and in some cases a nuisance) to the television spectacle that they wanted to erect around it. The NPSL was completely in the service of the corporate images and brands underwriting their enterprise as they sought to reconstruct the image of the sport, the very life's blood of players and coaches toiling on the pitch in 1967, within class and ethnic boundaries that ultimately would negate and exclude said players and coaches in the name of "Americanization."

Millward and Blanchflower emerged from the wreckage of the NPSL as avatars of a language and psychology that showed a way forward in the ongoing battle to construct reality, identity, and image through the medium of soccer. They stood out as undesirable due to their stubborn refusal to be "mechanical idiots," with Blanchflower remarking that a "TV producer fears an announcer with a mind of his own."[148]

Much to CBS's consternation, his refusal to peddle two truths was popular and "refreshing" to many fans watching NPSL broadcasts. Blanchflower observed that this feedback demonstrated "that the public know most sports television has a deliberate phoniness about it." This phoniness underpinned the carefully constructed, lucrative hyperreality the networks and NPSL/NASL owners were determined to protect at any cost, making him a singularly "frightening" outlier.

The NPSL's obsession with corporatized image and spectacle, while troubling for the reasons outlined here, cannot erase the fact that their one, solitary season encompassed plenty of bad, mediocre, and sometimes brilliant soccer played by a cavalcade of global figures both known and unknown. This history should be celebrated and enjoyed for all the simple joys, moments, players, and symbols of the *beautiful game* it embodied.

THE PETER RHODES AFFAIR

In March 1967, Georg N. Meyers, the sports editor for the *Seattle Daily Times*, wrote a column entitled "TV Invents a Sport, Call it Soccer."[149] In it Meyers wryly observed that "most sports—even barrel jumping—make cracking good shows. Television cannot find enough of them. So it has 'invented' one. It will be called soccer." The way Meyers wields the word "invent" so pointedly is shocking at first glance. Did the game really have to be "invented" because it didn't exist on any meaningful level for Americans such as Meyers?

But a closer reading reveals something extremely interesting in the next sentence: his emphasis on the point that the same game was "called football everywhere else on the globe." This seems to imply that Meyers can intuit the degree to which American television will actually distort the game in its efforts to reinvent and reconstruct soccer to conform to a more recognizable, more suitably corporate American image. It would be a reinvention so radical that were it to be accepted and successful, it could alter the very nature of the game, rendering it unrecognizable: thus, in a sense, ultimately "inventing" a new American sport. Meyers' parting words were those of caution, invoking the grave damage "the profit oriented camera" inflicted upon the once beloved American sport of boxing.

Exactly one month after Meyers' column and just one day before the NPSL season was due to start, NPSL commissioner Ken Macker made a blunt, honest observation to the *Associated Press* that "we came along at a time when TV needed another sport.[150] Macker's statement dovetailed with Meyers' column to an almost frightening degree, because it seemed to confirm television's role as an unequal partner in the process with license to aggressively shape the contours of this newly "invented" sport, a sport it needed to support its growing hunger for profits and control. Taken together the two combined to starkly illuminate a point where the muddy, naked nexus of corporate power, media, and commerce telegraphed plans to squeeze soccer into uneasy, distorted shapes in the name of "Americanizing" it. This was also another way of reconstructing the game's image along more preferable, profitable terms.

With television all to itself, the NPSL had to find a way to keep CBS's patrons happy during soccer matches that were completely antithetical to the stop-start rhythms of popular American sports, many of which were purposely engineered to coexist with consistent, relentless advertisement breaks. Those in charge at the highest levels of CBS and NPSL would not be subtle in their determination to wedge scads of banal commercial poetry into their Sunday afternoon NPSL match of the week broadcasts.

To accomplish this, the referees—already an inflection point in the turbulent scenes of violence and disorder that summer—would have to be integrated into the flow of the commercial infrastructure. So seriously overmatched and undertrained officials would not only be monitoring the action on the pitch, something they were struggling to do adequately from the outset, but also facilitating the dictates of cloying, skeptical television producers and sponsors. Ivor Davis set the scene like this in the *Los Angeles Times*:

> The referee packs a gun—not to defend himself, but to signal two minutes to go. He wears a receiver around his waist so that the TV producer can bleep him to pause for commercial breaks. He carries a golf counter to keep tab on the advertising timeouts and also has a notebook, pencil and whistle. That latest gimmick is for him to carry a red handkerchief, to wave for commercial timeouts. On top of that he still has to control the game. [151]

Certainly a CBS/NPSL invention, this system was so bizarre, so rich with uniquely American symbolism, so unashamed in its frantic, brutal haste to sell, sell, sell that it was almost automatically the most authentically "American" facet of the entire NPSL package. It was also only a matter of time before the system malfunctioned.

A British official from Yorkshire named Peter Rhodes was charged with refereeing a CBS match of the week between the Pittsburgh Phantoms and the Toronto Falcons on May 14, less than a month into the NPSL season. Rhodes had been officiating for more than thirty years and had worked in America since at least 1964, when he'd served as a linesman in numerous International Soccer League matches that summer. After the game he told the Associated Press that "11 of the 21 fouls he called in the nationally televised Toronto Falcons–Pittsburgh Phantoms soccer game were made to allow the Columbia Broadcast System to work in its commercials." [152]

Expounding on what Ivor Davis had written, Rhodes said that he "has an electronic unit strapped on his back for televised games." Rhodes explained the mechanics further, saying, "I get three beeps on the radar thing and then I hear the producer saying 'A commercial is coming up,' so I have to get the play stopped." Perhaps even more damaging, Rhodes admitted to stopping by the dressing rooms and telling the players "to fall down or feign protest at his call when he blows the whistle." Rhodes said that the players "all cooperate because it gives them a breather and at the same time is making money for the league." [153]

Rhodes also said that "the maximum number of commercials is ten" before mentioning a referee who had only gotten in three earlier in the season. "I don't think he's around anymore," [154] he noted. This was the ultimate subversion, the ultimate symbolic assertion of Americanization and corporate control: a CBS television producer recasting, repackaging, and reprogramming the organic rhythms of the game to conform to a stuttering, consumerist pulse peddling first-world baubles. It was a supreme act of negation and control.

With uncharacteristic speed and decisiveness, Macker announced the very next day that he had "ordered an investigation of statements attributed to Peter Rhodes."[155] Confusingly, nameless "other league officials" are then cited as attributing the following quote to Rhodes: "I did not call any false fouls. It would violate the laws of the game and would be dishonest and unfair to the players." These quotes allegedly uttered by Rhodes contradict the tone, tenor, and cadence of the ones initially attributed to him by the Associated Press. It's odd that the second set of statements is attributed to him by unnamed NPSL officials and resembles the stilted, clinical language of scared public relations flacks issuing ghostwritten confessions and not the unscripted colloquial tone reflected in his original remarks. Both the content and tone of the remarks were dramatically different. The phrase "false fouls" would become pivotal.

However, Macker admitted that the league had been "experimenting for several weeks with methods of providing time required for television sponsors of our games." He then said that going forward "all timeouts called by the referee to enforce such commercials will be clearly indicated by the referee." Macker assured the public that these "timeouts will be rigidly limited as originally conceived"[156] by CBS and the league. These statements indicated clearly that artificial timeouts were indeed mandated as part and parcel of the television deal and were being systematically injected into the American version of the game. It seems that Rhodes, like Millward and Blanchflower, was just a little too blunt and forthcoming about it.

Macker took great pains to absolve CBS of any involvement or blame for pressuring Rhodes, emphasizing that "at no time did CBS ask us to do otherwise." Macker's statements then dissolved into more phantom comments from "the league," which "quoted Rhodes as having said that 'this did not interfere in any way with the outcome of the game.'"[157] This poses a series of legitimate questions: Why was Macker commissioning an investigation of Rhodes' comments if they were already being refuted or qualified by the man himself? Why were Rhodes' refutations and clarifications not directly attributed to him? Why weren't the league officials to whom he issued these clarifications named publicly in the NPSL's press release?

The gravity of the situation can be glimpsed in the league's aggressive and ham-handed response. It also prompted other NPSL figures not directly involved, such as Phil Woosnam (who was perhaps even then eyeing a position of power), to publicly declare that the Chiefs weren't "involved in any phony fouls"[158] when they played Baltimore on CBS in April. Rhodes' allegations had garnered such intense publicity that on May 18 the Federal Communications Commission (FCC) requested an official response from the network within ten days. CBS's response, written by vice president and general counsel Leon R. Brooks on June 2 and made public by the *New York Times* on June 7, stridently assured the commission "that CBS has not participated, directly or indirectly in false fouls, in telling players to lie down or feign protest or injury or to propel the ball out of bounds or in telling the referee to call timeouts for pretend injuries."[159]

A closer examination of the letter revealed CBS's admission "that it was quite possible that players may sometimes deliberately feign injury for their own purposes" and that "on occasion a referee has waived the trainer on the field for broadcasting a commercial announcement." The network was adamant that it "never suggested to referee Rhodes or any referee that they call timeout for pretend injury or for the purpose of providing opportunities for the broadcast of commercial announcements."

That sounds rather clear: CBS didn't signal for or pressure referees to signal for timeouts in order to insert commercials into matches. Until you read on and discover CBS's concession "that it had 'on occasion' indicated to a referee that at the next natural stoppage of play following legitimate injury or the kicking of the ball out of bounds, it would broadcast a commercial." This notification was done so that the referee could, if the timeout was not long enough for commercials, "extend it himself the few seconds necessary."[160] This also sounds rather clear: CBS did "on occasion" indicate that referees carved time out of matches for commercials.

CBS's statement was an example of legal obfuscation and linguistic manipulation that ultimately did not at all deny the basic setup outlined by Ivor Davis and Rhodes himself. The underlying absurdity of the situation—magnified greatly by the reactions of CBS and the NPSL—was captured by columnist Milton Richman in a column entitled "Ref Toted a Gun."[161] Richman duly noted Rhodes' initial comments about phony fouls before writing "after a hurried talk with league officials, Rhodes, who comes from England and isn't entirely familiar with the ways over here yet, denied he said the fouls were phony. That shows he's learning." Richman used the colloquial phrase "ways over here"; powerful men like Joe Hamper and Robert Hermann preferred the word "custom."

Rhodes would indeed learn about American "customs," ways in which "the world of established wealth, which though contemptuous of . . . blatant kinds of corruption . . . itself indulges quietly in bribery, blackmail and manipulation (preferably legal) to maintain and consolidate its power."[162] CBS, in particular, seemed to inhabit a murky boundary on the outer edges of legal manipulation to consolidate and extend its power. In 1964 the network purchased the New York Yankees and was thus now a major force at the center of the growing intersection of sports, media, advertising, and commerce, a fact that is relevant to this story for numerous and increasingly complex reasons.

In May 1965 Bill Veeck wrote an article for *Sports Illustrated* called "Octopus under the Big Eye,"[163] wherein the bitter, maverick once-and-future MLB owner unloaded on the blatant hypocrisy and subtle corruption surrounding the sale of the Yankees to CBS. Among his many valid complaints are those concerning the trail of linguistic subversions surrounding antitrust law and the ever more complex and entangled corporate allegiances controlling American sport in the age of mass media and economic diversification. Veeck traces this all the way back to 1922, only three years after the Black Sox scandal, when the Supreme Court granted baseball an antitrust exemption "on the grounds that baseball was 'not a commercial enterprise.'"

With great disdain Veeck writes, "of course not. Baseball, like loansharking, is a humanitarian enterprise." Veeck then juxtaposes this legal absurdity with Justice Felix Frankfurter's minor opinion in a 1955 Supreme Court decision to deny boxing an antitrust exemption similar to baseball's. Frankfurter noted that "it would baffle the subtlest ingenuity to find a single differentiating factor between other sporting exhibitions and baseball." Veeck then remarks that "one of the troubles with discussing a subject like this is that nobody ever says what he means. No one really believes that baseball isn't a business."

This is illustrative of the versatility of the subversive language and its ability to sustain beneficial fictions and lucrative hypocrisies on behalf of those who are powerful enough to utilize it. Traces of this type of language can be glimpsed in CBS's letter to the FCC. It also underpins CBS's philosophy of having "two truths,' a psychological process that was capable of draining the very meaning from language itself when used to project the opposite reality of what was actually occurring as well as what the words conveying the message meant at their core. Veeck was similar to Blanchflower in his adherence to one truth.

Veeck would also note the other ways the Yankees–CBS partnership showed that, in Robert Johnson Jr.'s formulation, baseball was still "a microcosm of American capitalism,"[164] due largely to the inconsistencies, hypocrisies, and potential illegalities reflected in some of its business practices. Indeed, it was indicative and reflective of contemporary American corporate practice that *Sports Illustrated*'s William Barry Furlong referred to the actions of the American League owners during the Yankee sale as exhibiting "a thoroughly reckless mood of laissez-faire."[165]

Just as baseball functions convincingly "as a microcosm of capitalism," Brian Glanville observed that "Soccer reflects, quite intimately, what is going on around it, and in an age of safe young corporation men in grey flannel suits, soccer plays safe, too."[166] An argument can be made that the intimate reflection of the "safe young corporate American men" through the expression of the NPSL/USA enterprise revealed far more, or at the least a dramatically different message than Glanville realized. The Peter Rhodes incident reflected a ruthless desire to reconstruct and reinvent the game of soccer as a means to mitigate its "subversive nature"[167] as a tool of progress and agency, to render it just another commodity producing profits for huge corporations like CBS.

Veeck observed that "baseball considers its own rules eminently collapsible where powerful interests such as CBS and the Yankees are concerned." So too did the NPSL, which obviously had far less stature and leverage than baseball and graciously seemed to let CBS help coauthor its rules and procedures at their origin so that they need never be "eminently collapsible." Veeck acerbically depicted the absurdity of CBS's position as the owner of a Major League franchise: "It should be clear enough by now that in negotiating any contract with baseball—and certainly any contract with the Yankees—CBS is sitting on both sides of the table at the same time. It is both buyer and seller." This, along with the Rhodes incident, provides an example of the shadowy, "preferably legal" world within which American power often functioned. It also demonstrates that as an avatar of this particular world, CBS had established a pattern of being involved in situations that required the obvious use of sophisticated legal manipulation and linguistic subversion, such as its letter to the FCC regarding Rhodes, which also seemed to stake out positions on both sides of the question at hand.

All of this is important to consider contextually, but the story becomes even more complex and directly connected to the NPSL when you consider the role of the Baltimore Orioles, owners of the Baltimore Bays. The Orioles provided the swing vote for CBS to officially acquire the Yankees. At that time, Joseph A. W. "Joe" Iglehart was the Orioles chairman of the board of directors and "the largest single stockholder of the Baltimore baseball club." Iglehart also happened to be "director and chairman of the finance committee at CBS" and owner of "40,000 shares of CBS stock worth $1,720,000." Iglehart resigned from CBS just in time to cast the deciding vote among American League owners finalizing the sale of the Yankees.

As Veeck noted, "thus it was his vote—the vote of a major stockholder of CBS—which put the deal through." This was the most egregious of a fistful of serious conflicts of interest Orioles brass had to acknowledge and untangle after deciding to deal with CBS as business partners *and* fellow American league owners. Other major conflicts included the fact that then–Orioles president Lee MacPhail (previously of the Yankees' front office) was also the brother of William "Bill" MacPhail, the sports director of CBS, both then and during the negotiations that saw the NPSL emerge with its television contract.

This transaction wherein "CBS bought a ball club and joined an organization with which it was already doing business" and all its attendant conflicts of interest on a personal and structural level (CBS was already broadcasting the Yankee game of the week before the sale, a contract that paid New York $550,000 annually, to which Veeck observed they were now paying to themselves) is important to emphasize because it demonstrates CBS's willingness to work the margins of legal and ethical behavior.

The tangle between the Orioles, Bays, and NPSL can best be understood against the backdrop of the obvious necessity of television and what was seen in the late '60s as the increasing need for economic diversification on the part of sports franchises. David Wangerin wrote, "but there were only so many established sports to go around, and the sudden rush to make money as a big league owner—or at the very least reduce tax liabilities—soon required aspirants to think in broader terms."[168] Wangerin's observation that there "were only so many established sports to go around" connects directly with Meyers' assertion that new sports such as soccer needed to be "invented."

In 1967 the Orioles were one of the few publicly traded baseball clubs, and Baltimore Orioles Inc. purchased the Baltimore Bays with the expectation that "their success or failure also will be figured in the profit and loss statement of the baseball club,"[169] a clear example of Wangerin's comment about the need for baseball owners to seek "economic diversification." The ramifications of the Bays' successes or failures and their direct impact on the Orioles were the result of a decision made solely by Jerry Hoffberger. The *Sun* introduced the idea that the city would perhaps get behind a new soccer club quickly and more zealously if it could buy stock. Hoffberger rejected that notion out of hand, emphasizing that "he would get into soccer only if the Orioles had a controlling interest."[170]

More on how the Baltimore Orioles club was incorporated: the company was two different entities—Baltimore Baseball Club Inc. and Baltimore Orioles Inc.—with separate, distinct stocks. The latter, Baltimore Orioles Inc., consisted of the Orioles and Bays. The Baltimore situation provides a fascinating example of this new-fangled "economic diversification," particularly when such diversification resulted in significant losses.

On December 24, 1967, the *Baltimore Sun* published an article about Baltimore Orioles Inc.'s annual report, which saw the company record a net loss of $57, 412.[171] The executive vice president of the Orioles, J. Frank Cashen, "attributed the loss to three basic factors: the Orioles performance on the field and unprecedented bad weather which collaborated to reduce home attendance by 342,972, plus the expense of setting up the Bays."[172] The *Sun* notes that "actually, the operation of the Bays was the dominant factor in the loss"[173] because separately the Orioles "would have shown a net profit of $200,000 after taxes had it not been for the substantial loss suffered by the Bays."[174]

It must be emphasized that this occurred exclusively because Hoffberger insisted on ensuring that the Orioles, not the public, had a controlling interest in the Bays. The paper also estimated that the Bays lost around $400,000 in their first year of existence. Obviously that is a significant loss and overall drain on a company's finances, but it is striking how it seems to be elevated so quickly above the vertiginous Orioles attendance drop of 342,972. All in all this is a great case study of what happened when "economic diversification" took the shape of NPSL/USA ownership.

The *Washington Post*'s Bob Addie referred to Major League ownership of NPSL and USA teams as "the Great Tax write-off" in a column entitled "Expensive Subsidiary"[175] before citing the Orioles as a cautionary example. He noted indignantly that "it could come as something of a surprise if you invested your money in the Baltimore Orioles baseball team some time ago and now find out you are in the soccer business and not doing too well."[176] Addie, as he would do numerous times, provides an interesting example of the uneasy discursive relationship between soccer and baseball that exists on many levels in the American consciousness. This particular relationship between the Orioles and Bays, however, was a tangible one reflecting a different kind of unease. It was also emblematic of how interconnected CBS was with the NPSL—most publicly as its television provider but also on a more subterranean level as the owner of a New York Yankees franchise, whose closely associated American League business partners, the Baltimore Orioles, had a vested, demonstrable financial interest in the league itself—thereby making those scripted, unnatural CBS advertisements that much more important.

Unsurprisingly, CBS was ultimately exonerated by the FCC on charges that it asked Peter Rhodes to call "false fouls" in the Toronto–Pittsburgh match on August 2, 1967. The Associated Press report seemed to indicate that Rhodes' strangely unattributed remarks, overheard by league officials then embedded in Ken Macker's press release the next day, were partially responsible for the exoneration, writing, "Rhodes later denied them in news stories."[177] This is a startling example of the versatility of subversive language and its ability to deny opportunities and to paradoxically create silences that beg further explication. It also illustrates that only powerful and privileged actors such as Macker and high-level CBS executives can access and successfully wield this subversive language, whereas actors such as Peter Rhodes—and to a lesser extent Bill Veeck, Bill Cox, Danny Blanchflower, and Doug Millward—are diminished and ultimately undone by it.

In this case, its subversive force lies in its powers of obfuscation and dilution, the ability to weaken language itself. Macker's statement with words attributed to Rhodes by phantom, unnamed league officials served to immediately muddle and simultaneously reconstruct the record of events, possibly becoming the very evidence to exonerate CBS for its intrusions, even though it essentially admitted to the FCC that it engaged in at least some form of pressuring referees to orchestrate and extend timeouts. Macker virtually canceled Rhodes' words by inscribing a new reality (or "second truth") atop them, in real time, creating a silence.

Even though it ultimately prevailed and was exonerated, CBS was clearly concerned enough about the implications of the Rhodes incident to remain extremely sensitive about it. In March 1968, as an aside within a piece titled "Why It's Better to Watch," the *New York Times'* Leonard Shecter wrote, "It was television too (CBS), which faked injuries in soccer so that commercials could be fitted into this no timeout sport."[178] Shecter struck a nerve, prompting an angry response from none other than Bill MacPhail.

Bill MacPhail was at the outer edges of the early USA/NPSL narrative, surfacing most notably to tell Andrew Beyer that CBS was having trouble selling NPSL airtime to sponsors because "no sponsor wants to commit himself to something so brand new,"[179] thus underlining the need to hotwire referees with radars, golf counters, and starter pistols. Here he emerged to call Shecter's allegation "erroneous" in a letter to the editor in the March 31 edition of the *Times*. As evidence he cited a "printed refutation by Mr. Rhodes,"[180] which of course was Ken Macker's May 16 announcement wherein Rhodes' words were uttered secondhand through the mouths of "other league officials." MacPhail indignantly questioned Shecter's research methods and chastised him for failing to "take note" of the allegation's "subsequent refutation."

Shecter eviscerated MacPhail in his reply, noting that "the reason this 'refutation' never caught up to the 'allegation' is that it had so far to go."[181] Shecter correctly noted that Rhodes only denied that he called "false fouls"— and in a superimposed voice at that, which also explains why CBS clung so vigorously to that phrase when defending itself to the FCC. Here again is the intersection of subversive language and the semantics of privilege—Shecter is able to intuit and note publicly the strange inconsistencies within CBS's story. This incident is instructive for many reasons, not the least of which is that it provides an authentic example of how subversive language is used to construct a more favorable, beneficial record of events while simultaneously silencing any inconvenient truths or allegations.

Rhodes' voice was not only silenced, it was apparently reconstructed through the words of other "officials," creating a new testimony that delicately managed to both destroy him and to exonerate CBS. The mechanics of the Rhodes incident are visible and they demonstrate the step-by-step erection of a sophisticated, fictional edifice that solidified slowly into nonfiction and then into history. It's an apt example of how "established wealth . . . indulges quietly in manipulation (preferably legal) to maintain and consolidate its power."

As for Rhodes, he retired from officiating in early June 1967 and returned to England. Shecter noted sardonically "that the National Professional Soccer League denied that he was fired"[182] and that this was "another denial that had to huff and puff to catch up to allegations." Who has access to subversive language is something that dots this narrative, intruding at crucial times and begging for further explication.

Chapter Four

Press Play

The sixties was a time for screams and grunts.—Bill Veeck[1]

As the United Soccer Association's (USA) debut season began simmering, the fresh, young beat reporters covering this strange game being played by foreign teams pretending to be fresh new American franchises took different approaches regarding how to communicate and (perhaps more importantly) interpret what was happening on the pitch and in the stadiums. How reporters negotiated the strange structural and cultural dissonance created by the true identities of these teams added another layer of interest and intrigue to the already fascinating USA enterprise. The concept of identity is fundamental to consider while examining press coverage of the league, as the structure gave reporters opportunities to insert subtly coded language to shape and ultimately control the construction of the bewildering assortment of identities on show.

For instance, the relationship between USA's Chicago Mustangs and the *Chicago Tribune* is particularly interesting. The *Tribune*'s coverage was probably the most negative and subversive of all the USA cities and thus certainly worthy of further interrogation. The Mustangs themselves, Cagliari of Italy's Serie A, were a proud, colorful squad with a handful of internationals, past and present, just three years away from the only *scudetto* in team history. They also ended up at the center of a handful of scuffles, riots, and pitch invasions that inspired a rush of fascinating writing, also worth investigating. The National Professional Soccer League (NPSL) is also considered when relevant, particularly with regard to the concept of fan identification, but the USA's foreign teams and lack of television exposure made newspaper coverage indispensible.

133

The strange interplay of identity and ethnicity was particularly acute in the USA due to the imported team format that allowed for a myriad of confounding identity construction possibilities that were unavailable to reporters and critics covering the NPSL, which explains why issues of class are more discernible in the record of that particular league.

Also revealed is the antagonistic tone utilized in many instances by sportswriters determined to use their uncontested power (in the USA's case) to intentionally render the game as foreign and alien as possible by deliberately using subversive language to interpret it. In their quest to emphasize the foreign, many writers also undermined, whether deliberately or not, any sense of local connection with the team by doing so.

The subversion was often subtle but there are overt instances of subversion when it appears as if the newspapers or perhaps the powerful interests controlling them are deliberately trying to sabotage the game's growth. Why some powerful entities in America were so opposed to the game's reawakening in America is considered, as is the decision to consciously shift soccer's image away from its close ties to ethnic communities in America.

The *Chicago Tribune* decided to publish much of its USA coverage with no bylines, signaling perhaps that the Mustangs were inconsequential when they weren't being ignored entirely. This happened despite the Mustangs being owned by the Chicago White Sox ownership group headed by Arthur and John Allyn. In keeping with its history, the *Tribune* seemed to consciously take a more acerbic tone when covering the USA. The paper deliberately played up the confusion and dissonance inherent in asking consumers to pledge their allegiance to an alien game played by foreigners representing a "local" franchise under the auspices of an organization ironically branded with the literal essence of American patriotism.

The *Tribune*, a longstanding and firmly entrenched "establishment voice," started out by espousing "nativist, anti-immigrant views,"[2] according to the *Encyclopedia of the Chicago Literary Renaissance*. Perhaps the weight of institutional memory helped color the overwhelmingly dismissive tenor of the paper's USA coverage. After all, the USA was nothing if not a foreign enterprise on virtually every level, save for the corporate titans on the top floor.

The *Tribune*'s example provides an interesting inflection point where the tension between being an "establishment voice"—the support typically expected for a product launch undertaken by local establishment giants like Arthur Allyn—and the paper's historic tendency toward nativist sentiment is awkwardly negotiated. The tension produced among contrasting segments of the mainstream corporate mind are greatly illuminated by analysis the *Tribune*'s work.

Soccer, as always, provided a perfect symbolic locus to attract scorn, ridicule, and fear from writers principally opposed to the game's reintroduction to the United States. Since its inception the *Tribune* has come by its former masthead motto, "an American paper for Americans" honestly, remaining stalwartly conservative through the 1970s. Numerous scholars such as Thomas M. Keef have closely examined the paper's belligerent nativist period where special scorn was reserved for Catholics, particularly the Irish, and this history is worth considering contextually when interrogating the tendencies and tics of the *Tribune*'s coverage of the USA and other tumultuous events during the summer of '67.

A true statement of intent regarding the *Tribune*'s USA coverage can be glimpsed in David Condon's "In the Wake of the News" column (the great Ring Lardner actually wrote this long-running column from 1913–1919[3]) nearly a month before the Mustangs' first match. A beloved and respected "Chicago legend,"[4] Condon would write "In the Wake of the News" for twenty-seven years and was lauded for his wit, versatility, and "humorous style."[5]

Condon was tasked with covering the exhibition match between Athletic Bilbao and Red Star Belgrade, part of a series of such contests that the USA scheduled to generate excitement before its inaugural season. Condon observed vaguely that "there were reports that the exhibition would draw so poorly that each fan could have his own personal Andy Frain usher."[6] One wonders about the source and nature of these vague, secondhand "reports" and why they're mentioned in an *actual* news report. He then remarked with a modicum of surprise "that the press box was packed with writers, some of whom spoke English." Already a pattern is emerging, predictions of doom followed by a direct allusion to the foreign nature of the proceedings; naked nativism concealed under cheap humor. Condon then notes "that there had been apprehension that fans not familiar with soccer would be bored with all of the kicking and head play."[7]

It must be emphasized that the Windy City had, even at this time in the late '60s, a rich, thriving soccer culture and tradition that dated back more than fifty years and was filled with the exploits of storied amateur and semiprofessional teams such as Hansa and the AAC Eagles. Sociologist David Trouille, who has written extensively about soccer's history in Chicago, noted that after the creation of the Chicago Soccer League in 1921 "over 60 teams were competing in four Chicago leagues[8]" by 1924, "in addition to the multitude of youth, church and recreational leagues also operating in the city."

Trouille also observed that these leagues "received substantial coverage in mainstream newspapers like the *Chicago Daily Tribune*," and further that "it was not uncommon for soccer to be the lead sports-page story.[9] " It's interesting and telling that a sportswriter like Condon, so connected with the city, would fail to be aware of this tradition on at least some level, not to mention his paper's history relative to said tradition.

Condon gushes that "the action was continuous" and that you didn't "have to be a soccer expert to appreciate the fancy dancing of the athletes."[10] The use of the word "fancy" is an example of the deliberate, consistent word choices that denote not only the otherness of the game, but that suggest a level of femininity or, at the very least, a lack of an American conception of masculinity. "Fancy" is used exclusively in the press narrative to depict and ultimately construct the identities of players with brown skin and is often applied specifically to South Americans. Never is it used in association with players from the United Kingdom.

Referring to the Belgrade and Bilbao players as "fancy dancers" also cuts right to issues regarding tone that Vadim Furmanov aptly characterized as Condon's propensity to view "soccer as a curiosity, as if he were observing a demonstration of a tribal ritual at the world's fair in Victorian Britain rather than the world's most popular pastime."[11] In this guise, subversive language amplifies soccer's foreignness while adding elements of mockery and condescension that encourage readers to gaze from afar and laugh at "fancy dancing" foreigners as they "skidded over the turf and sparred around."

The tone becomes more subversive and nativist when Condon refers to Don Jose Jesus del Arenal Martinez de Bedoya as the "secretario of the Spanish eleven."[12] Coincidentally (or not) every member of Athletic Bilbao is christened Don Jose by Condon, save for "several other fellows named Pancho." Here is Athletic Bilbao, a football institution and proud beacon of Basque identity and culture deconstructed, reduced to a collection of cheap, lazy stereotypes that ultimately represent nothing more than a silly faceless gaggle of "fancy dancing" men named "Pancho."

Upon further examination, as it if were necessary, no one on Bilbao's 1966–1967 roster was named Pancho. Lengthy Basque names are catalogued in painstaking detail, seemingly for laughs and to play up the "tribal ritual" nature and "almost satirical tone"[13] of the piece as noted by Furmanov, only to be then cast aside as meaningless, the players carelessly and dismissively conflated when Condon remarks "that no one in the press box agreed as to whether Rojo got two goals and Uriate only one, or vice-versa,"[14] their true identities unimportant save for the value of the "humor" they provide.

Condon's piece demonstrates the versatility of the language of subversion, its ability to subtly confer and suggest otherness, its capacity to reduce powerful cultural symbols like Athletic Bilbao to a set of interchangeable, hapless, carnivalesque characters, thus neutering or negating outright its considerable ethnic and cultural resonance. It was used in full register to negate, control, and sabotage. In this instance, to negate soccer's relaunch, to control the narrative by making the game and the men who played it seem silly and foreign by crudely deconstructing Bilbao's identity, and finally, to sabotage it as a cultural force capable of challenging existing mainstream paradigms.

As a parting shot, Condon remarked, "there was one good fight on the field, none among the fans, although this oversight will be corrected." Sadly, this ominous prophecy would be fulfilled numerous times during the tempestuous USA season, but it is worth noting that it appears completely out of context with regard to the actual events being reported on the peaceful, relatively well-attended (9,786) exhibition between Bilbao and Red Star.

In yet another commentary on how things had changed, Trouille noted that in the 1920s "exhibition games with foreign teams were special events for the city and often entailed an official meeting with the mayor and a variety of special events with the visiting team's ethnic group in the city."[15] In 1967 there seemed only to be tumbleweeds and condescension. This is likely because Trouille characterizes it as occurring near the end of Chicago soccer's "ethnic period," which he dates from 1938 to 1971, wherein the game slid away from the mainstream and was nurtured exclusively within the Windy City's bustling, diverse ethnic enclaves.

The resulting mockery was emblematic of Gary Armstrong and James Rosbrook-Thompson's contention that consumption of soccer at this time brushed up against the "exclusive boundaries of a hardening United States class hierarchy" where the "most trenchant expressions of exceptionalism and exclusion were directed at those posited outside this hierarchy altogether: America's migrant population and the symbolism of the British game that was its preserve."[16] The *Tribune*'s coverage of USA is a textbook example of what "the most trenchant expressions of exceptionalism and exclusion" looked like.

While previewing the first actual Mustangs match, Condon continues playing the rote American journalist "soccer-is-foreign" trope to the hilt, explaining to readers that the game is *so* foreign he has to enlist Ray Huber of National Soccer of League of Chicago powerhouse Hansa to decipher the mysterious "tribal ritual" and wizardry that occurs on soccer fields. Although it must be noted again that it takes a healthy dose of willful ignorance and laziness to have a local player "explain" a game that was established enough in the city of Chicago to support its own flourishing, multi-tiered league infrastructure.

The various ethnic and amateur leagues—of which the National Soccer League of Chicago was just one example—demonstrate that even at this stage, the soccer-is-foreign trope was not entirely true in cities like Chicago, but the stubborn ignorance underpinning it would not be rigorously challenged until the twenty-first century. The game was only foreign to writers like Condon because its currency resided in marginalized ethnic communities whose narrative was usually crowded out of mainstream vehicles like the *Tribune*. In this case it merely fits the pattern of otherness and exclusion the *Tribune* was consciously trying to push. Ultimately, soccer's general "ethnic period" in the United States would be openly renegotiated in the early days of the North American Soccer League (NASL) when the game's image would be consciously shifted away from ethnicity under the guise of "Americanization."

For all the public pronouncements indicating that rolling out the USA would be just another product launch—a business endeavor the high-rolling oilmen, lawyers, and media moguls bankrolling the league had significant experience with—USA owners ultimately undermined themselves with their panicked, confusing imported team format. Importing foreign teams did little but amplify the clumsy irony that, despite the blaring patriotism garishly projected by the league's name, it contained no American cultural symbols and, perhaps more importantly, it encompassed no American players. The NPSL tried, with varying degrees of failure and ignominy, to at least customize or "Americanize" its product as much as possible with its unique (yet vehemently disliked) 6–3–1 scoring system.

Condon blithely acknowledged the irony of the USA's aggressively patriotic acronym with the line, "So we've all imported teams to play as American clubs this year."[17] Condon announced that the Mustangs are getting set to host the Dallas Tornado at Comiskey Park, except "that the Chicago Mustangs are not really the Chicago Mustangs." Condon then had Huber explain that the Mustangs are actually Unione Sportiva Cagliari of Sardinia, Italy. Condon utilized the Italian squad's entire official designation for maximum "Midwest otherness" effect, just as he did when emphasizing the full names of the men on Bilbao's roster to similar effect. Their foreignness is emphasized pointedly and once again the tone switches to the cold, clinical curiosity that feels as if, as Furmanov noted, Condon is remarking upon participants in a tribal ritual, not a soccer match.

Condon then wrote sarcastically "a sneaky suspicion crossed our mind: very likely the Dallas Tornadoes are not the Dallas Tornadoes."[18] And again Huber was left to reveal the club's true identity as Dundee United. Condon managed to highlight the dense irony and inspired absurdist flair of the entire USA enterprise in the next paragraph, writing "now this much is clear: The three stars of the Dallas Tornadoes, who are really Dundee United of Scotland, are two Swedes and a Finn."

Condon signed off with some delicious Italian American stereotypes (pizzas, Jimmy Durante, the college of cardinals[19]) that contained murmurs and echoes of the paper's anti-Catholic past. Once again we see a proud, rich ethnic culture, Italian American in this instance, deconstructed and reduced to a pile of lazy stereotypes—and there you have the core essence of the *Chicago Tribune*'s United Soccer Association coverage. The "college of cardinals" reference in particular harkens all the way back to 1859, when *Tribune* editorial writers argued that a truce in hostilities between Italian provinces and Austria signaled a troubling "triumph of Jesuitism, over which the College of Cardinals will go mad with joy."[20] Why that institution holds such resonance in the paper's psychological lexicon can only be guessed and is noted simply to highlight trends that have apparently occurred throughout its existence.

Condon largely ignored the NPSL's Chicago Spurs, with one notable exception. While sympathetically profiling Spurs' co-owner Will Cutler, Condon can't resist asking, "But why does Cutler have to be ape over soccer? Why couldn't it be football, baseball, golf, or even wresting?"[21] Condon spent the rest of the column wondering why this "healthy, well-scrubbed young man" and "gentlemen executive" with "plenty of fine associates" is sullying himself and "risking the grocery money in something like soccer."

The snapshot of Cutler is filled with details (prep school, investment banking, well-married, etc.) that demonstrate the stark contrast between the game's true consumers and advocates in U.S. ethnic communities and the men trying to sell it to them in the late '60s. Standard marketing language and psychology could not bridge the gulf. Men like Cutler dot this story, and the image they project, so fawned over by Condon, was that of clean-cut, all-American power. The symbolic grammar of such power was an accurate reflection of the lily-white tenor of America's dominant social class. Eventually the game would be awkwardly recast and reconstructed in their image, another step in what Armstrong and Rosbrook-Thompson termed the "hardening of social divisions along lines of ethnicity and class."[22] The game would for a time be re-appropriated.

The *Tribune*'s dismissive tone can be further glimpsed in the recap of the aforementioned Mustangs–Tornado match, the tenor of which can be easily discerned by the blaring headline "Soccer? Wrestling? Football?" slapped across a photo of Finn Dossing "shaking off a body block or wrestling hold."[23] The paper could not be troubled to find out which, but the implicit ridicule embedded within the question marks speaks volumes. Yet it must be emphasized once more that soccer had been played at every level in Chicago for more than fifty years and many readers would certainly have been able to distinguish the game from wresting or football.

Written by James Fitzgerald, the recap continues Condon's sarcastic overselling of the dissonance surrounding the Mustangs' identity, as the piece begins by letting the readers know that "A Dane scored the winning goal for a Scottish team representing Dallas which defeated an Italian team wearing Chicago's colors."[24] The purposeful obfuscation here can be read as an example of the *Tribune*'s nativism resurfacing to prevent professional soccer from encroaching upon the shores of Lake Michigan. The paper's continual reinforcement of the otherness permeating the USA provided a steadfast barrier that prevented the development of local fan identification in a major American city that could have been crucial to ensuring the league's survival. Other newspapers would be more subtle.

Cagliari was often represented in interesting ways outside Chicago as well. For example, the *Dallas Morning News* made a conscious decision to consistently reveal the Chicago Mustangs' true identity as Cagliari. Within the confines of the *Morning News*, the Mustangs were uniformly referred to as "the Chicago Mustangs, nee Cagliari of Italy."[25] The *Oxford English Dictionary* (*OED*) defines *nee* as being "placed before a married woman's maiden name: originally called" and "born with a name."[26] Obviously the usage is correct in the sense that the Chicago Mustangs were indeed born with the name Unione Sportiva Cagliari Calcio, as the *Chicago Tribune* so helpfully pointed out. The OED further defines *nee* in the extended use context as being "Placed (often humorously or for effect) after the current name or title by which a person, place etc. is known."[27]

But considering the emerging pattern of subtle and overt feminization of Cagliari specifically (and the so-called Latin and South American teams generally) in USA's press narrative, it's hard to downplay or ignore the feminine connotations implied by the word's deliberate and repeated usage with regard to Cagliari, and seemingly only Cagliari. Even within the OED's examples of the more "humorous" extended use of *nee*, the contextual effect is that of feminization, with a particularly telling example within the common American lexicon provided by the *New York Times*' William Safire. Safire, a noted wordsmith, is quoted in a 1970 piece, writing that "The flight attendant, nee stewardess, singsongs over the loudspeaker."[28]

Safire's example confirms not only that *nee* was definitely in the lexicon of the era's American newspapermen, but also that it subtly communicated something very specific. The deliberate use of the word *nee*, a relatively uncommon word at that, appears too calculated to not be read as a subtle renegotiation of Cagliari's masculinity. Perhaps it was intended as a comical, lighthearted method of "othering" the Tornado's opponents to gin up identification with the local community as the *Dallas Morning News* was apt to do, but nevertheless it appeared to contain a coded message that's hard to dismiss as coincidence.

Los Angeles Times reporter Shav Glick did consistently interesting work covering the Los Angeles Wolves, often breaking the USA's exceedingly selective and tenuous fourth wall by quoting Wolves manager Ronnie Allen as he referred to "the Wolverhampton boys"[29] playing "British Football at its best, long passes, short passes and excitement in the goal mouth." Andrew Beyer of the *Washington Post* also acknowledged the Washington Whips' true identity as the Aberdeen Dons throughout most of his stint covering the USA.

For instance, after the Whips' season-opening 2–1 loss to the Stokers, Beyer wrote that the "Whips played as an American team might be expected to, when this country produces home grown stars." Beyer's words also offer an intriguing view of the concept of identification (local, tribal, and consumer) and how it intersected with other issues throughout the existence of the USA/NPSL, while the *Chicago Tribune* provided the textbook example of how a paper could actively undermine such identification.

Beyer also produced the opening salvo in what would be the *Post*'s obsessive quest to construct an "American" soccer identity using the Whips as a canvas. Beyer projected Aberdeen's rough-and-tumble style onto hypothetical American teams, establishing an immediate contrast in the narrative with teams like Cagliari, Bangu, and Cerro whom, it was continually emphasized, played a selfish, individualistic, and even "soft" style. The question of an "American style" of soccer would preoccupy the *Post* as well as many NASL execs in the years ahead.

Glick brought a multiplicity of perspectives and techniques to his coverage of the Los Angeles Wolves. Interviewing knowledgeable spectators and utilizing strange baseball metaphors were just two of the many tricks in Glick's arsenal. The thorny, tangled concept of identity was always dealt with in a unique fashion in Glick's writing. For example, he refers to the Wolverhampton Wanderers as "an English professional soccer team which has been calling itself the Los Angeles Wolves while playing a post-season schedule in the United States."[30] This is a strange construction, as it appears that Wolverhampton suddenly had an identity crisis and haphazardly showed up in California randomly looking for games.

Glick varied this theme of nebulous identity when he wrote of "Jack Kent Cooke's Los Angeles Wolves, who have been playing together as the Wolver-
hampton Wanderers in England's Second Division."[31] Again, a casual sense of vagueness and confusion is deliberately affixed to Wolverhampton. Casual readers would have no sense of the team's rich, storied past as founding members of England's Football League, not to mention its more recent period of First Division dominance in the late '50s. Were they the Wolverhampton Wanderers or the Los Angeles Wolves?

Glick may as well have introduced the Wolves as an improv troupe that also happened to play football, such is the vague, unfixed character of their introductions in the previous examples. Glick certainly chose bizarre ways of reporting about what was ostensibly a "local" team. The day after the Wolves' exhilarating 6–5 title victory against the Washington Whips, Glick glibly noted that their "lend-lease arrangement"[32] with Jack Kent Cooke was at an end.

Glick further undercut any sense of local attachment by referring to the United Soccer Association as the "USA Tour League." An interesting question can be posed here: Was Glick committing a particularly brutal form of honesty, laying bare the flimsy, ill-conceived, intrinsically temporary nature of the USA enterprise? Or was he practicing a subtle form of subversion, less insidious and charged than the *Tribune*'s, but every bit as deliberate in its design to further muddy the already opaque waters surrounding the league?

The USA was, however, ostensibly conceived as a permanent enterprise, so it was worth questioning—no matter how strange its inaugural season—the wisdom and motives behind depicting it in such fashion. Could that coverage have been achieved without insulting the readers' intelligence and perpetuating a sense that they were marks and victims of an elaborate trick?

Although Glick's tone is not as acerbic as the *Tribune*'s, it seems that he too is uninterested in allowing soccer to establish an uncontested rebirth in the national consciousness. Perhaps he (like others) could sense the game's unique cultural charge and possibility to grant agency to those excluded from mainstream American narratives. It is also glaringly apparent that—although Glick may be skeptical of the enterprise and uninterested in maintaining any threadbare fictions about the Wolves' identity—the Wolves are constructed positively; they are never emasculated. With no language barrier—another factor that allowed for greater space to construct identities in the USA—the Wolves have control over the presentation of their identity, as evidenced by Glick's willingness to let Ronnie Allen brag about the Wolves' distinctly "British" football.

Glick was fond of using the word "masquerade" to describe the roles played by foreign teams within the USA. For example, his account of the Vancouver–Los Angeles match referred to "Sunderland of England, masquerading as the Vancouver Royal Canadians soccer team."[33] The word *masquerade* was employed by numerous journalists tasked with covering the USA, and its deliberate use must be taken into consideration, as it pointedly implies a level of deception.

To give another example, Brian Glanville, writing for the *New York Times*, introduced a match recap by observing that Wolverhampton was "representing" the Wolves of Los Angeles, while Cerro of Montevideo were "masquerading as the New York Skyliners."[34] In the Merriam-Webster Thesaurus, *mask* is a direct synonym for *masquerade* under the definition "an outward appearance that seeks to obscure an underlying true character."[35]

Midway through his recap of the Wolves' 2–2 draw with the Chicago Mustangs, to whom Glick consistently had been referring to by their USA franchise name, he jarringly references "the Italians from Cagliari"[36] who had "dominated the late stages of the game." There is no context provided in the column as to who "the Italians from Cagliari" are or why they very suddenly appeared in recap of a United Soccer Association match between Los Angeles and Chicago.

Thus their "underlying true character" was obscured and subsequently revealed in the most drastic possible way. A casual reader would likely have been baffled by Glick's decision to shift Chicago's identity in midstream. Not only is the selective acknowledgment of identity confusing and hard for observers to grasp, but it is compounded by the sudden, sharp intrusion of an explicit jolt of otherness. Lamar Hunt would later publicly lament the implicit confusion wrought by this format.

Glick took great pains to emphasize the British nature of the Los Angeles Wolves as well as the overtly British character of the Wolves' fan base. Glick's coverage is filled with references to the Wolves "British accented crowd," Los Angeles "anglophiles," and the "knowledgeable Britishers" on hand to watch the Wolves demolish Vancouver/Sunderland 5–1. The implication of foreignness—even a notion of foreignness broadly sympathetic to and closely aligned with the United States—is continually foregrounded by Glick.

Perhaps the colorful crown jewel of the USA's press pantheon can be glimpsed in *New York Times* reporter Gerald Eskenazi's work covering the New York Skyliners. Eskenazi had a tremendous gift for making the mundane compelling and dramatic, as well as a unique voice capable of finding dark, absurdist humor in otherwise ominous occurrences. Eskenazi seemed to have a genuine sympathy for the star-crossed men of CA Cerro who were tasked with representing the pivotal New York Skyliners franchise, but it was a playful sympathy laced with devilish dashes of melodrama and parody.

Recounting the Skyliners' 4–1 victory over the Dallas Tornado, one of only two wins they would record, Eskenazi wrote that the victory had "also lifted them out of the condition of self-pity and embarrassment that had engulfed them"[37] before noting that the side had "suffered through collective guilt feelings" for thus far letting down their august Madison Square Garden sponsors with listless displays that had resulted in draws and defeats.

Unfortunately for the homesick Cerro players, the Uruguayan postal service went on strike during the summer of '67, leaving the exhausted players isolated in Manhattan. Eskenazi wrote melodramatically that "without a letter from home and ashamed of their efforts on the field, the Cerro soccer club has become melancholy."[38] The *Times* reference to the postal strike is a small detail that establishes a surreal tone as the Cerro players transform suddenly into heartsick athletic troubadours anxiously toiling in Yankee Stadium without a word or whisper from home, perhaps making it easier for jaded New Yorkers to identify with and hopefully to value their efforts.

Conversely, the decision to highlight their shame and "melancholy" coupled with Eskenazi's depiction of Cerro's perceived "condition of self-pity and embarrassment" and "collective guilt feelings" can also be situated within the wider pattern of overt and subtle "othering" of the South American teams playing in the USA, with these particular characterizations reeking of feminization and standing in polar opposition to the far more masculine, albeit stereotypical, ethnic identity construction the press accorded teams from the United Kingdom, such as Wolverhampton and Aberdeen.

In a June 17, 1967, column titled "Referee Chased by Soccer Fans" Eskenazi described the riotous events of the previous evening's New York Skyliners–Chicago Mustangs match at Yankee Stadium, wherein "40 partisans of a 'wronged' Italian team chased the 5-foot referee around the infield."[39] Eskenazi actually characterizes the event as a "United Soccer Association match between Cagliari of Sardinia and Cerro of Montevideo, Uruguay," before noting that the Italians were "playing under the name of the Chicago Mustangs in the league, while Cerro, under lease to Madison Square Garden, is known as the New York Skyliners."[40]

This demonstrates that even the most creative, sympathetic reporters often deliberately chose to play up the inherent identity confusion of the USA enterprise. Eskenazi was fairly consistent in this regard, referring to the team as "the Uruguayan players of New York"[41] in his recap of the Skyliners' 2–2 draw with the San Francisco Golden Gate Gales. Imagine reading this as a casual fan. Imagine how easy it would be to get confused among the shifting tangle of identities.

Press accounts of NPSL matches required no such negotiations and even the most motley and incompetent franchises legitimately belonged to the communities they played in, making the fans' collective ability to identify much easier. The cognitive dissonance built into the USA's press narrative, a narrative made infinitely more important by the league's lack of television exposure, was difficult for fans to navigate from the outset, making the role of reporters such as Eskenazi, Glick, and Beyer more pivotal and influential than they would otherwise have been.

Their words were the league's main conduit to those outside of the stadiums, and the choices made by these reporters both confirmed and provided necessary color to the USA's existence. They literally interpreted the league to the outside world, and this marks perhaps the last time in the history of sports journalism that writers had such exclusive license to shape the identity, narrative, perception, and thus ultimately the reception of a professional sports league. The centrality of their roles in writing the USA into existence is why their choices bear such close examination and scrutiny. Their decisions to construct the various ethnic identities of the people involved within certain parameters and following certain patterns also bears further investigation.

Alas, in true Eskenazian fashion, the real hero of the largely theoretical Skyliners–Mustangs recap is the aforementioned "5-foot referee" Leo Goldstein. The column is in fact subtitled "Goldstein Gains Tie Here against 40 Partisans,"[42] and Eskenazi chose to interpret the mayhem of this contest through the prism of the besieged referee. Eskenazi's character sketch begins by describing Goldstein as "a 42-year-old Brooklynite who has been subjecting himself to emotional players for 20 years."

Goldstein was in fact a miracle made flesh, a Polish Holocaust survivor who reportedly saved his life en route to the gas chambers in Auschwitz by volunteering to referee a match between two teams of SS guards. Goldstein had already etched his name in global football lore by the time he ended up in Yankee Stadium on that fateful night due to his participation as an assistant referee in the infamous "Battle of Santiago" between Chile and Italy in the 1962 World Cup.

"The Battle of Santiago" was fueled largely by unflattering stories about the earthquake-damaged Chilean capital written by the Italian journalists Antonio Ghirelli and Corrado Pizzinelli, stories inflammatory enough to cause the writers to be deported on the eve of the match after they were picked up and disseminated by the local media. The first-round clash took place on June 2, 1962, in Santiago's Estadio Nacional. A replay of the match was famously introduced to British audiences by the BBC's David Coleman, who referred to it as "the most stupid, appalling, disgusting and disgraceful exhibition of football, possibly in the history of the game."[43]

The first foul was called less than twelve seconds into the contest and the situation only descended further into a violent maelstrom of filthy tackles, fisticuffs, and dropkicks. When yet another ugly melee kicked off in the waning minutes of the match Goldstein was alleged to have told referee Ken Aston (later the chairman of FIFA's referee committee and inventor of red and yellow cards): "Ken, don't bother sorting this mess out."[44] Goldstein would never have been involved if it were up to Aston, who later remarked that he had "asked for my own linesmen" but was stuck "with a Mexican and little American from New York. They weren't very good, so it became almost me against 22 players."[45] Aston ultimately compared refereeing the match to "acting as an umpire in military maneuvers."[46]

Whether Eskenazi knew the true extent of Goldstein's brushes with disaster and infamy can only be guessed. He notes that the "fiercely pro-Cagliari" crowd of 10,089 became increasingly angry and demonstrative as the grinding, humid, scoreless match wore on, its fervor culminating over a perceived non-call against the Mustangs' Communardo Nicolai around the eighty-seventh minute of play. The foul by the Skyliners' Jose Rotolo against a member of what was ostensibly the away team caused the crowd to vehemently berate Goldstein, an indicator of the paltry level of local identification the Skyliners inspired. The tension escalated steadily from firecrackers and "about 1,000 fans" edging toward the box seats to a scene where finally a fan "dashed on the field, where Goldstein was running from team to team, and punched the referee."[47] Strangely, the police let the man return to his seat.

Another fan then "chased Goldstein in a little circle" before our Chaplinesque hero "stopped and kicked the man in the chest." This only made it worse for Goldstein, as "a wave of fans followed and Goldstein took off to the first base dugout. One Goldstein apparently was more than a match for the crowd, for no one caught him until he tripped over the first base line. [48] Eskenazi renders this ominous scene of actual and implied violence in such a way that it is skillfully transformed into a spectacle so ridiculous, so whimsically absurd, that the reader becomes slightly disarmed.

Some details of how potentially horrible this incident could have been do float to the surface. Eskenazi notes again the shockingly lackadaisical police response wherein "officers watched several fans pummel Goldstein before they waded in" and began clubbing "one of the gang members." Ultimately Goldstein emerges unscathed, "his thick chest was red." The end. Such a carnivalesque tour-de-force was this portrait of Leo Goldstein that Eskenazi never definitively discloses the match result, other than to note it was scoreless before the violence kicked off.

Incredibly, the incident between the Skyliners and Mustangs wasn't even Goldstein's *first* soccer riot in the United States. Goldstein was deputized as an emergency linesman in the 1963 International Soccer League Championship (ISL) match between West Ham United and Poland's Gornik after the referee was injured as a result of rioting by "more than 200 fans." [49] In a far uglier incident, the referee, James McLean, was actually replaced after suffering "damaged bridgework and a cut on the face" when fans poured onto the field to protest an offside call. Officials and players alike were struck by fans invading the pitch at Randall's Island, setting a precedent of violence that reaffirmed the worst things written by American journalists about the game.

Strikingly, when reviewing Real Madrid's 3–2 victory over West Ham in the Astrodome as part of the USA's inaugural series of exhibition matches, the *Dallas Morning News*' Gary Cartwright remarked, "by soccer standards this was obviously a tame crowd. Nobody kicked the referee in the head," [50] an amazing and frightening piece of foreshadowing (à la Condon's throwaway remark) that prefaced exactly what would happen less than two months later in New York.

Contrast Eskenazi's work with the Associated Press's (AP) account of the Yankee Stadium incident titled "Fans Assault Referee in Mustang Duel" published in the *Chicago Tribune*, wherein the spectacle was artlessly described as an "uprising." [51] The AP has Goldstein being chased by "10 spectators" not the "40 partisans" witnessed by Eskenazi. Gone are the Felliniesque details of Goldstein holding his own before tripping over the first base stripe. The AP's tone is authoritative and mechanical, removing any detail that could possibly make the events at Yankee seem like anything other than an "uprising," a dangerous affront to order that would not be tolerated. But between the lines of the AP's recap, one can imagine the voice of authority trembling slightly as it ponders the true strength of its grasp before the bloody, anarchic deluge of 1968.

Did these two drastically different accounts of the same event parallel the growing unease within our national psyche as it struggled to find ways to deal with the creeping violence, cultural ferment, and generational upheaval that seemed to permeate everything in America that summer? Was Eskenazi's absurdist, Three Stooges–style take on the event a way to make something terrifying like mob violence palatable or at least a little *less* terrifying? Was it a comedic attempt to convince readers that the wolf wasn't at the door after all (the Newark riots were less than twenty miles and a month away)? Or was it simply the only way to make a scoreless soccer match sound interesting? These are legitimate questions to consider as the USA was an entity very much of its time, a time in American history that would become known as the "long hot summer."

According to the *Encyclopedia of American Race Riots*, "the Long Hot Summer is the name given to the riots that occurred in the urban ghettos of the North between 1965 and 1967."[52] Many historians consider the Watts Riots in 1965 to be the beginning of this period, which culminated in the cauldron of the summer of 1967 with the riots in Newark and Detroit being particularly destructive and deadly. The "long hot summer riots" were significant for a multitude of reasons, but their collective shock to the establishment can be best understood when considering that "these riots signaled an unprecedented shift in the pattern of racial violence that had occurred previously in the United States."

The "unprecedented shift" was due to the fact that "prior to the 1960's, most race riots or incidents of racial violence were instigated by whites,"[53] with blacks invariably the victims. These disturbances were different in that they were violent expressions of long-suppressed pain and frustration emanating from urban black communities. It is worth briefly exploring the language used to interpret these riots as a counterpoint to the incidents occurring on the field during USA matches. In some cases the similarity of the language used will intersect and diverge in interesting ways.

As with most things involving the USA, a spiritual precedent for the chaos in New York was established the previous August during an exhibition match between Santos and Benfica at Downing Stadium in a contest that was repeatedly interrupted by a variety of colorful disturbances. Once again Eskenazi was there to chronicle the events when a "thousand men, women and children took the field . . . carrying banners and flags, singing and jumping"[54] and thus delaying the start of the second half. Play resumed "only to be halted as beer cans started to fly for no apparent reason at the hundreds of spectators bunched on the sidelines." Eskenazi wrote that at one point "it appeared that most of the record crowd of more than 28,000 was hurling cans."

Delving further into the color of the chaos as only he could, Eskenazi noted that "foam-rubber cushions and even Panama hats rained down" on the field and "a blond hit a man on the head with one perfect pitch."[55] The "fights and shouting, hysterics" resulted in numerous people being treated for injuries. Eskenazi capped off this dispatch with the most Burroughsian of details: the officials at Downing decided to blare polka from the public address system to quell the swelling beer-fuelled rancor.

H. Rap Brown famously said that "violence is as American as cherry pie," and no matter how one views that statement, it was certainly true during the '60s, when violence seemed to be the answer to every question. Indeed, Brian Glanville referred to violence in the American game as if it were an already-established fact by the time he crossed the Atlantic to cover the USA in 1967, and it's hard to argue with or take exception to that notion when evidence like this and earlier accounts of ISL violence like the West Ham–Gornik incident are considered. The heady tension in the air certainly exacerbated it during the summer of 1967, but it was already there throughout the ISL's existence as well. Why it was there is more difficult to understand. Reducing it all simply to notions of tribalism is too simplistic.

While recounting the Yankee Stadium incident to the *Times* of London in 2003, Glanville characterized that summer's violence as "all too frequent." To emphasize the point he recalled the words of an unnamed English goalkeeper who uttered in indignant exasperation, "You ought to see them! Animals, some of them, animals!"[56] Glanville had initially shared those words contemporaneously in his *New York Times* column, attributing them, however, to an anonymous NPSL keeper and using them to illustrate the "problem of violence"[57] that he felt already existed just more than a month into the NPSL season—before the USA season had even begun.

In its original *New York Times* context, it appears that the unnamed player is referring to other players as "animals" and that the violence Glanville is remarking upon was happening on the pitch due largely to poor refereeing but (thankfully) not yet pouring forth from the stands. Having already introduced the word *animals* into the lexicon himself, Glanville remembers with the benefit of hindsight, almost as an affirmation, that it was also a word "the chief of Yankee Stadium Police" used after the torrid events of the match between Cerro and Cagliari to describe "those Italian fans."[58]

Glanville is likely recalling an Eskenazi column a few days after the melee wherein a Yankee Stadium security official named Anthony DiGiovanni was quoted as saying, "Those fans were animals."[59] Nowhere in the *Times*' original account are "those Italian fans" singled out as animals. Perhaps it was the fog of memory or perhaps Glanville's slip in 2003 is something far more telling. Regardless, the use of the word "animals" to other and to essentially dehumanize players and fans—almost uniformly players with brown skin or those with so-called Latin temperaments—was prevalent during the late 1960s and can in large measure be traced to England.

Meeting in the quarterfinals at Wembley the previous summer, Argentina and England played one of the earliest entries in what would grow into a legendarily contentious series of World Cup matches. At this point in its historical development, being closely aligned with pervasive global trends of cynical, defensive football, the Argentine national team and successful Argentinian club sides such as Estudiantes and Boca Juniors were known (or at least perceived by Europeans) to practice a particularly virulent strain of aggressive, negative, and sometimes violent football. When considering this, it is ironic that South Americans in particular were frequently portrayed as "fancy" or "soft" in American discourse.

It was a match so ill tempered that papers released in 1997 under the auspices of Britain's thirty-year rule indicate that it "strained"[60] diplomatic relationships between the two nations. England ultimately triumphed 1–0 after Argentina's captain, Antonio Rattin, was sent off. Rattin initially refused to leave the pitch, stalling and stoking the crowd's ire to volcanic levels before stopping "to wipe his hands on the miniature Union Jack that served as a corner flag."[61] The Argentines menaced the referee en masse when the final whistle sounded and security had to form a cordon to whisk the beleaguered official away.

Sir Alf Ramsey allegedly told his men not to exchange shirts with the furious Argentines. In the aftermath of this ugliness, Ramsey remarked that England hoped to meet a team interested in a football match and not "act as animals."[62] This comment would shadow Ramsey for years, providing as it did one of the most crucial, high profile introductions of the word "animals" into soccer's vernacular.

Glanville was in Wembley that afternoon, and he steadfastly maintained that the vanquished Argentines did act disgracefully, allegedly banging and ultimately urinating on the door to England's dressing room. No matter what happened that day, Ramsey's injection of the word "animals" into football's lexicon to "other" Argentines added a level of acidity to the discourse that can be felt in the coverage of the USA/NPSL. The "animals" characterization coupled with the fraught "Latin temperament" signifier proved to be a significant double-barreled way to code and perpetuate racialized frames. It didn't take long for the "animals" descriptor to enter the USA/NPSL's narrative, coming less than a year after Ramsey's outburst and with British writers like Glanville all too willing to spread its currency.

Glanville retained a particular animus for Argentine teams and players, never missing an opportunity to show disdain and perpetuate the "animal" frame when constructing their identities for his American readers. However, Glanville, a gifted writer, was usually far more subtle and cerebral in his attacks, never using the word *animal* himself, save for paraphrasing Ramsey.[63] In 1968 alone, Glanville wrote numerous columns denouncing Argentine football, culminating, perhaps, with his view that "The Argentines . . . might almost be characterized as the SS men of contemporary football."[64]

An element of this discourse was introduced into the NPSL narrative by none other than Clive Toye, a man universally lauded for his eloquence and erudition. Eager to spread the gospel at his introductory press conference, Toye remarked, "Soccer is a sport that a boy of any shape or size can play. You don't have to be 7 feet 6 inches or a Gorilla to compete."[65] Besides unnecessarily bestializing athletes, this comment seems to subliminally invoke dangerous, toxic stereotypes that had a long, shameful history in American racial discourse. However, being English, Toye legitimately might not have known the depth and nuance of such history in the states. But as a "great Civil War buff,"[66] it seems less plausible that Toye, a journalist specifically interested in that particular time in American history, a man who named his children Gaynor Lee and Robert Alexander Grant, would have no inkling that such words were ill chosen at best. Shortly after a brutal, dirty scrimmage between Toye's Baltimore Bays and the New York Generals, Bays coach Doug Millward was quoted as telling Generals boss Freddie Goodwin, "why don't you put your animals in a cage now and give them some raw meat."[67] This virulent form of othering was definitely circulating far too much in an already charged environment.

The explicit conflation and construction of soccer players and fans, specifically ones with brown skin, with animals and animalistic behavior also had a sorry precedence in American letters, predating Ramsey's ugly declaration by a handful of years. It can be traced back to an Arthur Daley column that appeared in the *New York Times* in 1960. The column was ostensibly a profile of Bill Cox, who had just announced the formation of the ISL. Taking a dismissive, paternalistic stance, Daley sets the tone by noting that "soccer is the No.1 sport throughout the world, but in the United States it ranks not quite so high as bird-watching." Daley then indulges in the sinister, doomsaying, riot fixation that American sportswriters never missed a chance to comment on throughout the 1960s.

In a sense they were prescient, as incidents began to mount in the USA, but they never missed an opportunity to remind Americans that in the dark recesses of the world, people of color wrought all kinds of violence over a silly game no more interesting than bird watching. Running through a list of outrages in South America, Daley wrote of the infamous "moat" that encircled the pitch in Rio's Maracana Stadium, saying: "This is the same principle used in the famous Berlin zoo. A moat protects the customers from the ravenous beasts. In Brazil, the moat protects the performers from the ravenous spectators."[68] Daley constructed a wondrous blend of both explicit and subtle othering, overtly comparing the Maracana with a zoo designed to protect the performers from the "ravenous," animalistic fans. This goes beyond the mere condescension that characterized American soccer reporting up to that point into explicitly racist and derogatory colonial frames made even more disgraceful considering America's concurrent racial posture.

Lest readers wonder about Daley's preoccupation with crude, violent brown-skinned people, he wrote "not all of this can be blamed on explosive Latin temperaments," which was his cue to list the violence soccer instigated behind the Iron Curtain in the Soviet Union. So in one column the blueprint was set—quite masterfully, as it announced the ISL's launch—to construct soccer as a pastime reserved for poor, uncivilized, violent communist animals, a "tribal rite"[69] to be observed and mocked à la Furmanov.

The discernible stain of colonialist frames was acknowledged and explicitly brought to the surface by Glanville while discussing the random, ragtag nature of the 1967 Atlanta Chiefs squad assembled by Phil Woosnam. Glanville wrote incredulously of Woosnam's confidence "that the colored colonial players he has signed will, despite their obscurity, astonish us all."[70] It is a revealing glimpse at the sinews of the psychological framework that many (if not all) of the writers interpreting the USA/NPSL enterprise were functioning within. Glanville's comments seemed to confirm that a colonial framework was still operative, a framework also heavily informed by "the symbolism of the British game,"[71] and that efforts to cover the USA would follow its strictures and dictates when constructing the ethnic identities of those outside the Anglo-Saxon elite.

Returning to Eskenazi, it should be noted that he specifically used the word *partisans* to describe the people who chased Goldstein around the field. Whether borrowed directly from Eskenazi or not, Glick also consciously chose to utilize the word *partisan*, writing that Goldstein was chased by "a group of Cagliari partisans."[72] Openly and repeatedly associating Italian players and fans with the word *partisan* is another subtly loaded word choice that seemed to imply rabid, brainless barbarism, or, perhaps even worse in one of the headiest periods of the Cold War, communism. The OED defines partisan as "one exhibiting blind, prejudiced, and unreasoning allegiance,"[73] a pitch-perfect description of those who would physically terrorize a referee in blind sway to primordial tribal loyalties.

The use of the word *prejudice* to define the characteristics of *partisan* is interesting considering its use in this context. Delving a little deeper, though, Merriam-Webster defines a partisan as "a member of a body of detached light troops making forays and harassing an enemy"[74] and as "a member of a guerrilla band operating within enemy lines," ascribing a level of sociopolitical heft to the term, specifically a vague sense of creeping communism at the height of the Cold War crucible. The notion that these "partisan" Italian Americans were in some sense "operating behind enemy lines" is another demonstration of how "the most trenchant expressions of exceptionalism and exclusion were directed at those posited outside this hierarchy altogether."[75]

The press was beginning to use soccer to divide, exclude, and reinforce existing prejudices.

This language illustrates rather plainly the subtle, sophisticated contours of these "trenchant expressions of exclusion" while providing a snapshot of who was to be excluded from the mainstream and, by extension, from what it meant to be American. The *OED* goes even further, defining partisan as a "guerilla or resistance fighter, esp. in Italy or Eastern Europe in the Second World War" and, of course, as a member of "the communist-led resistance forces in Yugoslavia." There were numerous, varied Italian partisan groups in the war and many of the socialist-tinged groups were aligned with the Allies, forming a resistance against the forces of fascism. Yet just more than two decades later during the Cold War period, the Italian partisans' anarchist and socialist leanings would likely color their remembrance in the American collective conscious.

As an example, a context-specific reference point for literary Americans in the postwar era would be something like the *Partisan Review*, a "Trotskyite" journal started in the 1930s as an outgrowth of the John Reed Club, the "arts branch" of the American Communist Party.[76] The *Partisan Review* publicly renounced the Soviet project during the ascendancy of Josef Stalin. As shown, the conscious use of the word *partisan* in connection with the Italians has a negative (or, at the very least, an ominous or questionable) sociopolitical connotation, serving to add a layer of menace and suspicion while also reinforcing their foreignness as a suitable reason for the concerted efforts to exclude them from assimilation and "legitimate notions of citizenship and national identity."[77]

Another instance of curious language usage was introduced into the discourse by USA president and longtime United States Soccer Football Association (USSFA) member James P. McGuire, who told the *Washington Post* that "the American public has to be indoctrinated to the sport."[78] "Indoctrination" was a curious way to depict the familiarization process related to something benign, such as a wholesome, start-up sports league that you'd conceivably want curious newspaper readers to shell out money to take their families to. It is a word that both exudes and reinforces the foreign, alien nature of the game. It has a sinister connotation that imparts a sense of coercion, forced exposure, and imposition. Even worse (perhaps because of the above-mentioned examples) it was commonly used in conjunction with exposure to communism.

Indeed, one of the *OED*'s entries for "indoctrinate" reads: "To imbue *with* a doctrine, idea or opinion"[79] or, more specifically, "To imbue with Communist ideas." The *OED* then supplies three separate instances of usage since 1945 wherein "indoctrinate" is tied specifically to depicting the stigma of communism, including one from H. L. Mencken. What would make McGuire deliberately choose this word over others? Obviously he wouldn't try to purposely sabotage his soccer league by linking it, however subliminally, to communism. Is it possible that the use of words like *indoctrinate* had become so commonplace during the Cold War that the full range and gravity of their symbolic meaning had become muted or lost? Whatever the reason McGuire settled on "indoctrinate" to describe the public's consumptive learning curve, the reporters covering the USA/NPSL began regularly utilizing the word in their own writing.

Two days after its first appearance in the *Washington Post* on October 2, 1966, the same paper ran a story by staff writer Dave Brady, who wrote that "the North American [league] plans to begin next spring with exhibition matches involving some of the best teams from abroad, to indoctrinate U.S. fans before starting formal play in 1968."[80] It appeared again not long after in a *Post* column written by Bob Addie, who observed that "the new soccer leagues—the National Professional Soccer League and the North American Soccer League—have big money behind them and are determined to indoctrinate the American public."[81] This is an instructive example of the full force of the word's myriad negative connotations being expressed simultaneously. The wealthy owners are characterized as "determined" to inflict soccer upon and thus forcibly "indoctrinate" the American public to its alien charms.

A final example can glimpsed in a February 1967 column by the *New York Times'* Joseph Durso, who wrote that "from [Dick] Walsh on down, the owners of the 12 teams in the new 'major league' are hurrying to indoctrinate Americans to the glories of soccer."[82] Again the full range of the coercive nature of this specific word in this particular context is on display as the owners "hurry" to indoctrinate Americans "to the glories of soccer." The repetitive, unfailingly sinister use of "indoctrination" stands as another example of the subtle yet purposeful linguistic choices systematically made by reporters to cast these new soccer leagues and the game itself as foreign at best and insidious, communistic, and antithetical to American values at worst. "Partisan" and "indoctrinate"—words that explicitly invoke or imply communism—were used to impart a sense of alien menace to the game of soccer.

In his column a week after the tempestuous Yankee Stadium match, Glanville trained a critical eye on the poor quality of the refereeing (a recurring theme throughout all extant writings on the USA/NPSL), writing "at the bottom of the trouble, apart from unpardonable violence of the fans, was poor refereeing, two bad fouls by Cerro players and astonishingly feeble police work."[83] Glanville described the scene in this way: "One looked on, incredulous, when the first spectator was allowed to climb the railings, run on the field, take a kick at Goldstein, then return unmolested to his position, still in full public view. Two policemen strolled over and appeared to have a friendly chat with him."[84]

The shockingly lax police work emphasized by Eskenazi was confirmed by Glanville. Returning to the apparent lack of control, Glanville wrote that "though one had great sympathy" for "Little Leo Goldstein" during "his ordeal" the official "refereed without authority, trotting amiably about the field, hearing, seeing and speaking no evil." Glanville places a level of culpability on Goldstein that doesn't appear in other known accounts of the event. The poor quality of American officiating in 1967 is a recurring motif that is never far from the surface in a memoir, an interview, or a match recap from this era. The saddest part is that team owners and their handpicked administrators like Dick Walsh knew so little about the game that they could not realize or identify the fact that weak officiating was a danger that resonated far beyond a bad call that nullified a goal. The caliber of officiating can be traced to the core of every violent incident that occurred.

Glanville then poses an interesting question: Why did the fans assault the referee and not the player guilty of the rash, violent tackle? He received an interesting answer from Cerro/Skyliners boss Ondino Viera, who attributed the violent reaction to "ancestralism." Viera further said "they attacked the authority." The muddy indefinable nexus between raw, inchoate tribalism and a rising sense of antiauthoritarian sentiment that was becoming pervasive in many segments of American life seemed to coalesce here in an ugly flashpoint that generated troubling smoke signals of the violence to come. Or perhaps the incident can be viewed as a symptomatic reflection of the violence that had already begun rocking America that "long hot summer," as a nasty urban riot in Cincinnati that saw 900 national guard troops called to the scene had been contained mere days before the match at Yankee Stadium.

The Yankee Stadium incident is also emblematic of the incredible tangle of identities at play within the USA and their often uneasy coexistence. Near the end of the USA season, Gerald Eskenazi noted that "it is now obvious that the crowds that have turned out have been more eager to see the opposition than the home team."[85] Eskenazi observed that "most of the crowd leaned towards the Irish team" and that the "same thing happened when the Skyliners faced teams from Sardinia, Scotland and the Netherlands." The New York audience initially instigated the violence because they felt the referee had wronged the *visiting* team. The entire ugly incident kicked off because residents of New York City, most likely of Italian ancestry, were furious about the treatment of a team from Sardinia that was in the Bronx representing Chicago.

Glanville's *Times* of London colleague Geoffrey Green was also in attendance at Yankee Stadium and attributed the "flare up" to a combination of a "night temperature of 85 degrees and laced with Latin blood."[86] The use of the phrase *Latin blood*—which has a long tradition of usage in the discourse of British football and is a reference to the "Latin temperament"[87] residing within Argentines—can be found as far back as 1925 in the *Times* of London and can again be read as a subtle othering, perhaps used to subliminally impart the stigma of erratic barbarism and savagery upon the instigators of the aforementioned "flare up." (Daley offered proof earlier in this chapter that American writers did not shy from its use, either.) Green noted that "the Italian element in the crowd invaded the pitch and attacked the harmless little American referee."[88] His account restores the terror missing from Eskenazi's carnivalesque retelling, portraying it as life-and-death chase with "Goldstein fleeing for his life like some rabbit caught in the headlights of a car." Green too would characterize the incident as "a small grotesque riot."

And just as the Santos–Benfica match in New York the previous summer provided early warning of the latent tribally tinged violence somehow endemic to large gatherings of American soccer fans, Green observed that "the match was abandoned while the subway trains rumbled by and the music blared out 'the Stars and Stripes' to restore order."[89] The patriotic anthem added an extra layer of irony to a narrative designed to exclude "the Italian element" from mainstream definitions of American life and as stakeholders in the creation of an authentic "American" identity.

Amazingly, on June 14, two nights night before the bizarre and troubling events unfolded at Yankee Stadium, another "player riot" occurred during the second half of the Detroit Cougars match against the Houston Stars. The match was halted with more than seventeen minutes remaining after referee Eddie Clemons awarded Detroit a free kick ten yards outside Houston's penalty area. This decision prompted a fight that "erupted before 7,196 fans"[90] in the Motor City, another city that was little more than a month away from the harrowing violence and civil unrest of the Twelfth Street Riots. Were these soccer "riots"—which occurred in the same two metropolitan areas that would also erupt with the most intensity during the long hot summer period—just outrageous coincidences? Or were they ominous premonitions, spontaneous eruptions of a latent, barely controlled violence just beneath the surface?

The *New York Times* ran a somewhat lengthier AP account of the match that included direct quotes from Detroit's publicity director Gordon Preston. Preston told the AP that the fight erupted because "Houston's fullback, Luiz Alberto, laid out Detroit's Tommy Jackson cold with a kick to the kidney." Preston maintained that after this happened "players from both teams swung into the melee." The AP pointed out that "officials of both teams rushed into the fighting" as well as "about 20 of the 7,196 fans."[91] The day this piece ran in the *Times* would be the first of nearly two weeks of almost daily coverage of soccer "riots" occurring all over North America.

An interesting parallel to the AP's role in reporting the riots occurring in the USA can be viewed a month later in the scrutiny of its role in reporting on Newark and other "long hot summer" incidents. James H. Couey Jr., publisher of the *Tampa Tribune*, addressed the Alabama Press Association days after Newark and said that "colored and inaccurate reports of violence in one city can increase tension and cause violence in others."[92] Couey used the recent civil disturbance in Tampa as an example of the distortions wire service reports were capable of promoting and perpetuating, saying, "Tampa's problems were serious, but not serious enough to justify the scare heads and explosive objectives used by the writers." He termed wire service reporting on Tampa's situation "highly inaccurate" and responsible for "inflating it far beyond the truth."[93]

These are revealing glimpses behind the veil at structural tensions within the interplay between local and wire service reports. Couey's comments also provide a revealing look at the psychology of newspaper publishers during this era. The comments provide a probable explanation as to why the AP's accounts of the Yankee Stadium incident are so sterile and bloodless, so as to avoid increasing tension in other USA/NPSL cities around the nation. The tension Couey cites "between overplaying stories and underplaying them" can definitely be viewed in the USA's press narrative.

The Detroit Cougars were represented in the USA by Glentoran FC of Northern Ireland. Supporters of the hardscrabble Belfast club have created a beautiful website with detailed match recaps of Glentoran's 1967 tour as the Cougars, such is the pride that the team still inspires. There the ill-fated Houston–Bangu contest is described as a "rough-house of a match"[94] that "almost inevitably exploded into a free for all with some of the Brazilians using corner-flag poles as spears." The recap further states that events in this match "caused a stir in the American Press with a special feature being shown on nationwide NBC television."

Detroit was second only to Chicago in the controversy sweepstakes, setting the tone for what was to come when player-coach Johnny Colrain was suspended for allegedly punching linesman Bobby Jack in the face for disallowing a goal in a heated match against Dublin's Shamrock Rovers, also known as the Boston Rovers. Dick Walsh suspended Colrain for the offense even though he steadfastly maintained his innocence, as accounts of the events on this fateful evening seem to vary. The Glentoran FC website describes the Rovers match as "robbery with violence,"[95] omitting any mention of Colrain's punch and playing up mistakes made by the "rookie linesman who had very limited knowledge of the game."

Despite the levels of subjectivity in such reports, one recurring theme emerges clearly: poor refereeing was somewhere to be found amid all of these incidents, precipitating the unacceptable levels of violence that plagued the USA. The incompetence of the officials mirrored perfectly the incompetence of the USA owners' vision and execution, as well as the futile incompetence that many residents of overcrowded urban cities dealt with each day in attempting to mitigate their mounting grievances. It is remarkable how much the USA—a hastily assembled league in its debut season—was able, when viewed as cultural text, to reflect "quite intimately,"[96] as Glanville put it, the chaos, violence, prejudice, and creeping bureaucratic incompetence so indicative of this stage of American history.

A few nights later on June 18, the Chicago Mustangs would again be at the center of a violent maelstrom that thankfully didn't end in serious injuries or worse. This time the setting was Toronto's Varsity Stadium and once again a referee was the flashpoint. The official, Art King, awarded Toronto a free kick in the eighty-second minute of the match. Toronto quickly took the kick and Colin Grant scored from ten yards out, which prompted an outpouring of outrage from the Mustangs who vehemently asserted that King never blew the whistle twice to officially restart play.

According to the *Chicago Tribune*, in an account published with no byline, after the "Chicago players realized that they lost their argument to King, one of them picked up the ball and waved his teammates off the field."[97] This provocation prompted "the spectators, about 3,000 of a crowd of 15,178" to swarm "onto the field." Again violence was visited upon the referee as "King was punched in the body and kicked several times on the legs." There are many things related to this account worthy of further investigation.

First, as with the riot in New York (and perhaps mindful of Couey's warnings to Southern newspaper publishers), the *Tribune* decided to take a bloodless, sterile approach to its coverage of this event. In fact, the only time the *Tribune* injected any vitality into or attached bylines to its coverage of the Mustangs was during moments of derision and mockery like Condon's. Thousands of spectators invading the field during a sporting event (albeit a nontraditional one) in North America merit only a brief unsigned recap? It's stunning that the paper didn't use the occasion to ridicule the sport further while ratcheting up its exclusionary language.

The *Baltimore Sun* and *Washington Post* each carried similar versions of events from the AP, which characterized the event as a "riot with thousands of fans swarming on the field."[98] Interestingly the word *riot* does not appear in the *Tribune*'s initial report about the incident, but—perhaps taking its cues from the AP—all subsequent mentions of the incident depict it as such. USA commissioner Dick Walsh suspended three members of the Mustangs for their part in the incident, with Adriano Reginato, Mario Tiddia, and Guiseppi Longoni being disciplined for "helping start a riot in Toronto."[99]

This specific *Tribune* piece added the detail that "some 3,000 fans, many of them local Italians, charged onto the field."[100] Apparently in their zeal to devise special promotions in hopes of drawing fans to the stadiums by any means necessary, many teams, Toronto included, decided to promote Cagliari's appearance as part of an "Italian heritage night"; ancestralism indeed. USA owners and promoters, in their incompetence and haste, were obviously not fully aware (despite obvious precedents) of the volatile tribal sensibilities such events had the potential to arouse, nor how easy a target these events would be for those eager to use "trenchant expressions of exceptionalism and exclusion"[101] to define and control them.

When the violence started in Newark less than a month after the Yankee Stadium incident, it was termed an "insurrection" by New Jersey Governor Richard J. Hughes, who also characterized the events as an "open rebellion." Buried underneath the headlines was a lengthier statement Hughes made, wherein he stated that "the line between the jungle and the law might as well be drawn here as any place in America."[102] This statement contains a not-so-subtle othering of the rioters, primarily African Americans, as uncivilized animals or more specifically inhabitants of the "jungle." It is interesting how similarly charged language delivering "trenchant expressions of exceptionalism and exclusion" was used to depict the agents of both the disturbance at Yankee Stadium and the events in Newark.

Hughes' inflammatory reference to the jungle recalls Daley's aforementioned comparison of Maracana Stadium to a zoo, and again people of color are subtly but purposely conflated with animals. Both Daley and Hughes stop short of using the word *animals*, as Sir Alf Ramsey did when describing the Argentine national team, but the implication is clear. Former president Dwight Eisenhower had no such restraint and lamented the "animal ferocity"[103] exhibited by those in Newark who were looting and attacking "our police." The phrase *our police* demonstrated the naked psychology of American power while also delineating the yawning gap of exclusion and marginalization African Americans would have to traverse—clearly "our police" were not their police.

The word "animals" was, as noted, retroactively injected into the narrative that emerged from the Yankee Stadium riot, and it's interesting (and sad) to see it in the discourse surrounding the Newark riot. Particularly so because in June 1924, a baseball game between the New York Yankees and Detroit Tigers ended in a riot "when 18,000 spectators stormed the field and started a riot which involved the police, the players and the employees of the park."[104] The sheer number of participants, as well as the openly acknowledged involvement of the police, would surely elevate this incident beyond what occurred forty-three years later, almost to the day, in Yankee Stadium, prompting severe rebukes in severely trenchant language.

Yet the most charged word used to describe the events of that day was a reference to the frenzied, battling crowd as a "mob," even though the participants "tried to break through the rear of the Tiger dugout and get at the players" while "the whole field now, viewed from the lofty press box, was a surging mass of bobbing straw hats and swinging fists." This is an astonishing scene that almost seems to be relayed with a tinge of frontier theory, rough-and-tumble, American-style romanticism that masks the underlying severity of the incident, which ultimately led the police "to make menacing gestures with their clubs, and threaten to pull their guns."[105]

By any measure this riot was larger and more violent than the Skyliners–Mustangs incident, but since it erupted from within America's "national pastime" and featured legendary, iconic white players such as Babe Ruth and Bob Meusel and most likely a majority white crowd, the edge and menace in the account is missing. There is no insidious or charged language likening the participants to "animals" or "partisans." There is no distancing, no exclusionary language, no attempt to "other" participants in what was a far more explosive and dangerous incident. The comparison between the two riots nearly fifty years apart definitely shows the degree to which the teams in the USA, and soccer in general, were depicted and constructed as foreign with subversive language marshaled stringently against them.

The spectators that tussled at Yankee Stadium in the summer of 1967 were painted as "partisans" and "animals" completely separate from the mainstream American body politic expressly due to their ethnic status and consumption of a soccer match, whereas the baseball players and fans were depicted as participating in a manly punch-up à la Doc Holliday and the boys in some dusty Tombstone saloon. A much more violent situation is emphatically not placed outside the bounds of mainstream civilization where, presumably, the "animals" and "partisans" reside nor are the participants constructed with exclusionary language.

The players and fans attending the USA match were others to be isolated, studied, condemned, ridiculed, but, most importantly, excluded. And this is why it's important to note that similar linguistic choices and strategies were then applied to the violence in Newark and on through the rest of the long hot summer. It was language that clearly constructed African Americans as others. The word *animal*, in particular, remained so charged that both sides of the divide recognized its power, prompting Albert Black, head of the Newark Commission on Human Rights, to depict the Newark police as "animals,"[106] othering and dehumanizing the police.

The *Chicago Tribune* jumped into the breach with a full-throttled linguistic assault. The paper ran an excerpt from a piece originally published in *Barron's Weekly* entitled "Poverty Warriors," which asserted that the long hot summer riots were not spontaneous and were funded by groups such as the Office for Economic Opportunity, before noting that "like the poor, slums and rats have always been with us."[107] This marked an explicit conflation of the urban poor with rats, which encapsulates the tenor of discourse at this specific moment in American history when the USA was being interpreted to fans in language similar to the language used to describe systemically poor, desperate people of color in large urban cities. The dehumanizing bestialization of both groups was reaching a fever pitch.

Barron's salvo also contains similarities to and echoes of Daley's earlier comparison of the Maracana to a zoo. As we've seen, there were many reasons the USA failed, but perhaps one worth considering is the level of otherness with which it was depicted through the only medium it had access to: newspapers. It was relentlessly described in terms that were foreign and alien during a violent, uncertain time in American history where to be those things was dangerous—and definitely not profitable.

Not being profitable, of course, would have been the final straw for professional soccer in America, its last chance to prove a significant level of economic and cultural viability in American life. The "trenchant expressions of exceptionalism and exclusion"[108] wielded by powerful, reactionary forces successfully managed to construct the USA as equally foreign and isolated from the American establishment as the poor urban minorities that were moved after years of prejudice, neglect, and decay to wreck their own communities.

The USA was culpable in that its haste to start operating a year ahead of schedule forced it to rely on undertrained referees unprepared for the rigors of officiating games between professional teams from all over the globe. Language barriers made communication among all parties on the field next to impossible, so players inevitably began responding in the language of "the reducer": crunching tackles that only elevated the bad blood in dismal, empty baseball stadiums on steamy, uncomfortable nights. Referees quickly lost control of these matches, and the violence spread like a contagion into the stands. The fans' culpability must be acknowledged, too. Poor refereeing or not, there was no excuse for the number and intensity of the pitch invasions that occurred that summer. These actions perpetuated and gave flesh, blood, and sinew to the narratives that Arthur Daley and others had been pushing for years about soccer fans and the game's endemic violence. It made using exclusionary rhetoric and subversive language that much easier. This rhetoric's ease of use compounded efforts already underway in newspapers to make the game appear alien and exotic.

These systematic efforts coupled with the self-inflicted wounds of zealous fan behavior helped consign the early years of the rebirth of professional soccer in America to ignominy and failure. However, soccer administrators from the NASL through Major League Soccer (MLS) learned these lessons quickly and harshly, and, thankfully, there hasn't been a hint of violence comparable to what happened in the USA since that time.

One of the ways NASL administrators tried to combat this rot was to consciously shift the game away from the very constituents—inner-city ethnic communities and "hyphenated Americans"—who had nurtured the American game and provided its vitality throughout the dark days of the mid-twentieth century. It was an incredible paradox that the game had to be taken from those who loved it best and awkwardly repackaged and reconstituted in the image of people like David Condon and William Cutler to achieve any level of positive mainstream acknowledgment.

THE ANATOMY OF AN "IMAGE"

The *image* of soccer in this country has changed, has been made to change, and the change in image, like so much else in America, has brought success. —Lowell Miller[109]

Miller went on to illustrate exactly what he meant by this, describing the crowd at a 1977 New York Cosmos match in the following manner: "The crowd at Meadowlands is surprising in its composition—not the predominantly male, immigrant or ethnic crowd you'd expect." It is this very image—male, immigrant, ethnic—that was rigidly fixed in the minds of the men who launched the USA/NPSL enterprise in 1967, and many of their failures and shortcomings can be traced to that image.

To be completely clear, ethnicity was undoubtedly on the minds of NPSL owners, as their public relations people at Grey Public Relations would so publicly attest, telling the *New York Times*: "It's a very definite fact that there is in the United States a tremendous hardcore interest in soccer among ethnic groups."[110] Despite being obsessed with this demographic image, the owners, execs, and admen seemed to lack the proper language, psychology, and tactical outreach to grab these particular consumers, since they were not typically a coveted demographic. As we've seen, these consumers (even had they been reached effectively) would not accept just any product haphazardly thrown out on the field; they were prepared and willing to consume high-caliber soccer of the kind the USA/NPSL/NASL was ill suited to immediately produce.

Cosmos coach Gordon Bradley told Lowell Miller that "we had to create an image to get Americans—the most sports-minded people—to accept soccer." Although neither says it explicitly, it's easy to infer that the "image" they are referring to that needed to be changed was the consumer: soccer was the exclusive preserve of ethnic and immigrant men. The game's image had to be reconstructed and rebuilt to resemble the more "clean-cut" and "all-American" archetype Bob Kap envisioned when fashioning the Dallas Tornado from scratch.

A clean-cut and affluent Anglo-American image—like the one projected by Chicago Spurs co-owner Will Cutler or New York Generals director Eugene Scott—coincidentally mirrored the class demographic that the original architects of the USA/NPSL seemed to concede was initially out of reach. It is interesting to consider who they thought had enough disposal income to buy the proposed Milton Bradley NPSL board games and toys.[111]

Miller noted breathlessly that the stands at the Cosmos match were "full of All-American suburban kids" and that many of them were girls. In fact, he writes "women account for some 45 percent of league attendance." Although "soccer's new audience is clean-cut, affluent, 'upscale'—as Madison Avenue puts it,"[112] it is certainly not a coincidence that "clean cut" and "all-American" were the words used to describe this new audience. Palpable connections can be discerned between the conscious ethnic and racial composition of the 1968 Tornado and the audience NASL teams like them began drawing in the intervening ten years, partially due to the subtle, persistent uniformity of language in evidence. By 1983 St. Louis Steamers owner Bob Kerner felt emboldened enough to proclaim "Ethnic? It's nothing ethnic. No more. The Italians, the Germans, they're part of America now. It's a night out."[113]

It is interesting to see journalists acknowledge that the game began to succeed and be taken seriously by the establishment once it was played by and sold, almost exclusively, to white, upper-middle-class Americans. It's sadly ironic that the ethnic communities that truly loved and nurtured American soccer throughout the twentieth century were systematically excluded from constructing and controlling the game's new identity in the '70s. The use of the word "image" as a euphemistic cover is in itself fascinating, particularly when concepts of identity are such an intrinsic part of this story. Phil Woosnam preferred the word "tradition," and the NASL commissioner voiced similar thoughts through the years, referring to the league's necessary struggle to "break down the barriers and the traditions."[114]

Did men like Hunt, Robert Hermann, and Jack Kent Cooke know all along that shifting soccer's image would be the only path to success? Did they try (and fail miserably) to initially market the game to urban, male immigrant audiences because they truly felt that was the game's only audience in 1967? Their utter inability to communicate effectively to those very audiences—despite the overwhelming effectiveness of the one-size-fits-all advertising strategies of the time—goes a long way toward explaining what on the surface seems to be a baffling display of incompetence by competent men. In effect, they didn't know how to reach communities excluded from the mainstream narrative. Or did they think that the game could not reach or appeal to the affluent, suburban "clean-cut, all-American" (read: white) men and women, who constituted the prized consumer demographic for every other product in American life, without being recast?

The desperate, frenzied appeal to this prized demographic goes a long way toward explaining certain facets of "Americanization," such as those awkwardly undertaken by the Dallas Tornado in the late '60s, which appeared to be attempts to have the players mirror the prized "clean-cut" and "all-American" audience in a bid for mainstream acceptance. Not only did it exclude ethnic and minority communities, the image was shifted ever so gently upward, with class now a newly implemented lever of exclusion, whereas before race and ethnicity were the primary sites for negotiation. This shift was evident in the treatment of Baltimore Bays coach Doug Millward, also couched as a matter of "image."

Steve Cady's fawning *American Psycho*-esque catalog of New York Generals director Eugene Scott's status symbols in the *Times* (strikingly similar to Condon's portrait of Cutler) was a way of broaching the class divide on a subconscious level.[115] Miller's piece represents one of the first times the word *affluent* explicitly creeps into the discourse and is a harbinger of the rampant suburbanization of the game that would essentially become a cliché by the year 2000. Now the class issue was out in the open, a perfect example of "soccer as a point of intersection between class and race."[116]

Soccer's newly constructed image depicted the identity and portraiture of America that was sold as a readymade lifestyle by corporations, partially because it was the world inhabited by the executives of those corporations. This image also provided to the outside world an officially sanctioned snapshot of a carefully constructed American likeness: white, affluent, and suburban. It was also an attempted negation of the power soccer contained as a cultural agent able to provide access into the American mainstream so that "ethnic Americans," minorities, and women could begin contributing their voices and likenesses to the American narrative.

The countervailing influence of conservative voices in the newspapers and their sophisticated, effective use of subversive language to stymie and distort soccer's American rebirth must be considered here as well. Different motives can be examined as to why. The innately conservative nature of many sportswriters has been examined by researchers such as Chris Lamb, who did excellent work demonstrating that conservatism informed how these men covered and constructed Major League Baseball.

The innate conservatism of sports journalists and the already established narrative that soccer was "foreign" and even "socialist" conspired to make many reporters gleefully subvert the efforts of the USA/NPSL in a subtle yet concerted fashion, using linguistic strategies of subversion that othered the game and the players, particularly those with brown skin. They so rigidly set the parameters of the "image" and identity that Bradley and Miller publicly acknowledged needed changing before soccer could be accepted on a large scale.

Woosnam returned to the word *image* numerous times throughout the '70s, telling the *Baltimore Sun* "image is what professional sports is all about"[117] and that at the absolute lowest point in the NASL's existence in 1969 prior to the International Cup the preeminent question in his mind was "could we recover our image?"[118] The AP couldn't agree with Woosnam fast enough, opining that "with an image, Madison Avenue cannot be far behind."[119] Madison Avenue's shiny new "open for business" sign with regard to soccer was another indication that the game's new image was predicated on issues of class as well as ethnicity.

Woosnam subtly acknowledged the media's voice and role in the debacle of the late '60s, saying euphemistically, "the media didn't understand. If they believe, then everyone believes."[120] Was it a question of simply not believing or one of outright sabotage? Derek Liecty, general manager of the Oakland Clippers, confirmed two long-held suspicions when I spoke to him while researching this book: one was that most sports editors were openly anti-soccer from the outset, and he experienced this firsthand with the *San Francisco Chronicle*, whose editor admitted as much to him when he started working for Oakland.[121]

The second thing was that newspapers assigned their newest, most inexperienced cub reporters to the soccer beat. The inexperience is also a major reason why British narratives and symbolism were so privileged and prevalent in the discourse, as we've seen with the examples of the word *animal* and the phrase *Latin blood*. So in nearly every city, apathy, antagonism, and inexperience collided with the USA/NPSL, coloring its respective narratives with ominous shades of grey before a ball was even kicked. It was almost a self-fulfilling prophecy that the USA's image became one associated with foreigners, deception, and violence.

Woosnam said that the NASL was "overcoming a 60-year background of identifying soccer as an immigrant sport and the pastime of a few Ivy League schools"[122] before noting proudly that it had evolved to where "it has become the sport of suburbia." Once the transition was made into suburbia and its corresponding image of white picket fence Americana, then the game could be taken seriously by advertisers and investors, partially because its power, vitality, and what it represented to the colored, colonized people of the world could be neutralized, neutered, and otherwise controlled, its journey over the class divide complete.

Miller observes that soccer's "converts do not exactly hail from the nation's inner cities" and that "the new base for soccer is in the suburbs,"[123] surrounding what NASL commissioner Phil Woosnam termed "all-American cities" like Dallas, Los Angeles, and Seattle. Again, the specific descriptor *all-American* is used to depict the new image of the game. It is interesting to note that subversive language was used continually to exclude the game from taking root when it was specifically perceived to be and actually marketed exclusively to the "nation's inner cities." This is also why similarities can be detected between the language used to interpret the USA/NPSL and the riots that occurred during the long hot summer: it was marshaled to exclude agency on behalf of precisely the same residents of the nation's inner cities.

To emphasize beyond doubt what this image shift consisted of, Miller asks, "How did soccer move from the sandlots of immigrant areas into the razzle-dazzle mainstream of major league professionalism?" As long as it was viewed as something exclusively for immigrants, the game was something to be feared, hated, and excluded from entering the mainstream by all those who were able to utilize "subversive language to deny opportunities."[124] Once the image was shifted into the mainstream, subversive language was not deployed in quite the same manner. It's telling that the ethnic component essentially had to be erased, the game's image recast, for this transition to respectability and acceptance to occur. It speaks volumes about American society and psychology at a time that "ethnicity" was still viewed as an insurmountable obstacle for mainstream inclusion and, of course, profitability.

As a native Welshman and newcomer to American society, Woosnam had an interesting vantage point of what was taking place. He immediately discerned that the game's connection to "ethnicity" in America was a serious problem. Woosnam told the *Baltimore Sun* that "the biggest negative factor we have to overcome is tradition,"[125] a word carefully chosen to address the "ethnic question" that haunted the league. It is telling that Woosnam immediately assessed this problem as being more acute than other vexing and legitimate problems, such as television exposure and quality of play on the pitch.

Woosnam accurately noted that "people here have the impression that soccer is strictly for foreigners or ethnic groups. Once we break those prejudices down, we will succeed."[126] He explicitly labeled these antagonistic feelings "prejudice," which can be viewed as proof that perceptive minds, even at the time, were able to pick up on the level of linguistic subversion that the press marshaled against the league. It was also another way of confirming the degree to which subversive language was used to systemically exclude ethnics, women, and people of color from the mainstream.

The shift of soccer's image in America from representing ethnic groups and inner cities to one closely associated with suburbs and whiteness was as pronounced as it was sudden. Just as white Americans fled the same inner cities in droves after World War II, the game of soccer followed a similar trajectory, migrating to the suburbs. It was this relocation that made the game acceptable to mainstream voices and less susceptible to the types of rhetorical and linguistic subversion we've seen throughout this book. And as Franklin Foer and many others have written, relatively affluent, white, middle-class suburbanites then unquestionably adopted the game as their own for a variety of reasons.

As per Foer's observation, the recalibration and relocation of the game's image definitely had a modicum of validity, but even that must be questioned as it still largely ignored Latinos, a burgeoning community that helped drive the growth of the game in a direct parallel with its growth in the suburbs. Latinos would become more central and visible in the 1990s, when MLS explicitly decided to build the new league relying specifically on the economic power of the Latino and suburban constituencies. The lily-white suburban image gushed over by Miller in the *New York Times* was itself an act of negation, as it immediately used the game's fresh new image to exclude.

The pitchside American soccer identity was painstakingly constructed to project determination, strength, vigor, and hard work. But this construction was done in such a discursive fashion as to also simultaneously define people of color, particularly South Americans, using a negative reductive grammar of stereotypes that seemed to imply that determination, strength, vigor, and hard work were the exclusive preserve of Americans.

Taken together, after all this effort, the American soccer identity was that of hard work, determination, and definitive notions of strength and masculinity, while the game's image was dominated by "clean-cut," white, "All-American" suburbanites, with the only positive development being the acknowledgment of women in the construction of said image. The image itself increasingly became an act of subversion because it gave a distorted and inaccurate picture of the game it was supposed to represent, visually and symbolically concealing the vast progressive zones erected through the game's agency in the United States behind a carefully constructed veil of whiteness.

Chapter Five

California Clippers

Barnstorming on the Bay

The California/Oakland Clippers remain the most elusive and intriguing of phantoms amid the many ghostly franchises that strode through the United Soccer Association (USA), the National Professional Soccer League (NPSL), and the North American Soccer League (NASL) in the late '60s. In their brief history, the Clippers were the inaugural—and ultimately the sole—NPSL champion, defeated the Israeli national team, and scored a 3–0 victory over Manchester City (then reigning champions of England), all before officially becoming the first side to host a Soviet team on American soil when they squared off with the legendary Viktor Maslov's powerful Dynamo Kiev at Kezar Stadium.

The Clippers were owned by the trio of Joseph O'Neill, H. T. Hilliard, and William Brinton. O'Neill and Hilliard were oilmen with sports in their blood (O'Neill played football for Notre Dame in the '30s[1]) and deep connections to the Midland, Texas, petroleum set, including the social tableaux inhabited by former president George H. W. Bush. In retrospect, these unassuming businessmen managed to assemble what was unquestionably the shrewdest, most competent, yet least acclaimed NPSL organization.

In *Distant Corners*, David Wangerin refers to their entire frantic, frenetic existence as a "peculiar fantasy,"[2] which fittingly came close to never occurring at all. The franchise that ultimately became the Clippers was initially awarded to interests in Boston that were forced to relinquish it to O'Neill and company's California Professional Soccer Inc. in October 1966 when they couldn't find a suitable place to play.[3] This footnote serves as yet another example of how venue policy has haunted and shaped the course of

American soccer, remaining problematic throughout the game's development in the twentieth century.

The outfit began and ended playing under the California Clippers moniker, officially changing (in typical NPSL fashion) their name to the Oakland Clippers in June 1967 due to "local pressure" midway through the NPSL season.[4] The team was selected by executive vice president and general manager Derek Liecty and former Red Star Belgrade manager Dr. Aleksander Obradovic. Liecty starred for Stanford's soccer team in the early '50s before spending two seasons working for Bill Cox's International Soccer League (ISL) from 1961 to 1962.

Obradovic, a fascinating man who initially joined Red Star as a physiotherapist, was in football purgatory after falling out with the Communist Committee of Belgrade in 1966—presumably due to his lifetime suspension from the Yugoslavian Football Federation for publicly admitting receipt of illegal payments from Red Star, according to the *Baltimore Sun.*[5] Obradovic gave the Clippers a seasoned, sophisticated football mind possessed of perhaps the rarest commodity in NPSL administrative circles: the ability to locate, assess, and evaluate talent. Liecty had actually met Obradovic years earlier when Red Star came to the United States to compete in the 1961 ISL tournament.

Despite their previous acquaintance, though, Hollywood forces would intervene, and Dan Tana, a fellow Yugoslav and Los Angeles Toros investor, would recommend the doctor for the Clippers job. Liecty recalls Obradovic eagerly accepting the Clippers job after "Mr. O'Neill . . . got on a plane and flew over to Belgrade and had all the usual drinks and throwing the glasses in the fireplace and all that stuff and came back and said, 'well, he's going to come and he's promised to bring a whole bunch of players that will not need to have any transfers paid.'"[6] Obradovic quickly obtained the services of Ivan Toplak, another former Red Star man, to help coach the team. Toplak had been a Red Star captain as well as a Yugoslav international during his playing days. The two men would form a formidable technical partnership, one that was certainly unmatched in North America at that time. Toplak would go on to coach the Yugoslavian national team after his Clippers adventure, as well as undertaking an NASL return engagement with the San Jose Earthquakes.

Obradovic then made good on his promise, using his connections and cache to poach a surprising number of quality first division players willing to roll the dice in America, including NPSL-leading goalkeeper Mirko Stojanovic and leading scorer Illija Mitic. Mitic, a former Partizan Belgrade player, would become an NASL fixture, later starring for the Dallas Tornado and ultimately finishing seventh on the league's all-time scoring list with 101 goals. Both Stojanovic and fullback Milan Cop were full Yugoslavian internationals, while Mitic and Momcilo Gavric had deputized for the U-23 side.

The Clippers started with this solid, impressive Yugoslavian core, and Liecty—in one of the many fascinating intrusions of ethnic identity into the USA/NPSL story—publicly attributed their immediate effectiveness and success to this "single ethnic base."[7] Liecty's quote ran in a *Washington Post* article by Andrew Beyer that argued that the Whips should "profitably study"[8] the Clippers' example. As future developments in Washington would bear out, a case could be made that the Whips were influenced by the Clippers, particularly with regard to building a team along similar ethnic lines or a "single ethnic base." The Whips' early attempts to build their team with a Scandinavian or "Nordic" core come immediately to mind as an example.

Liecty and Obradovic were subtle and intelligent enough in their vision for the Clippers and in their understanding of the game to realize that beyond a "single ethnic base," a cohesive team was built on a consistent, coherent style of play in which all players combined to complement each another. To achieve this Liecty and the Clippers signed only players who were comfortable with and could function within the "short passing game that the Yugoslavs favored,"[9] ensuring a philosophical chemistry and unity of vision, a necessity that was either lost on most neophyte American front offices or nearly impossible to achieve due to the onerous restrictions stemming from the NPSL's "outlaw status" and the overall haste with which NPSL sides were built.

According to Canada's Tele Sport, Obradovic knew exactly what he wanted, which was "the nucleus of Oakland to play the same type of soccer with no possibility of language barriers hampering coordination; he wanted a capable assistant to execute his shrewd ideas; he wanted a flexible 4–2–4 pattern."[10] Liecty emphasized the value of Obradovic's uncanny ability to assess "a player's skills and how they might fit into the strategy that he would put together."[11] Two major contributors from outside Yugoslavia were William Quiros and Edgar Marin, Costa Rican internationals and Club Saprissa teammates who would mesh well within the Clippers' tactical and philosophical framework. Marin in particular would pop up again and again, scoring timely goals for the Clippers. Wangerin dubbed this "peculiar Tico-Slavic nucleus" a "first in world football."[12]

Liecty noted that Obradovic could not only find good players all over the world, but perhaps more impressively, he was able to negotiate clean, legal releases and transfers despite operating outside FIFA's umbrella, just as he had boasted to O'Neill.[13] One of the final pieces of the puzzle was Obradovic's recruitment of star-crossed English center-half Mel Scott. Scott was a highly touted young talent playing for Chelsea when his career was suddenly interrupted by a stint of military service. After returning from service, Scott played for second-division Brentford for four years before receiving Obradovic's call. Obradovic immediately converted the twenty-seven-year-old to fullback and Scott became the anchor of the NPSL's stingiest defense.

The Clippers fielded a smartly assembled, smoothly functioning squad that stormed to the NPSL's Western Division title, scoring sixty-four goals in thirty-two matches. The Clippers' clinical, confident swagger led them to almost immediately break the fourth wall and challenge their reluctant neighbors, the USA's San Francisco Golden Gate Gales to "a game to decide the professional soccer championship of Northern California."[14] The Eredivisie's ADO Den Haag was, of course, starring as the Golden Gales, and Obradovic brashly stated, "I am certain we would win over the ADO team."[15]

At this stage the Clippers were 4–1–1 and already regarded as one of the NPSL's best defensive teams, causing Obradovic to emphasize "what we are saying to them [ADO] is that we are Northern California's first and best professional soccer team and as far as we are concerned, we can prove it on the field of play."[16] Even though ADO were never dominant in Holland like Ajax or Feyenoord, they were amid a renaissance under highly regarded Austrian coach Ernst Happel, finishing as high as third in 1965 and subsequently making the domestic KNVP Cup final in 1966. ADO would ultimately claim the KNVP Cup in 1968—the year after they returned home from the USA—with a 2–1 victory over Ajax.

In context, Obradovic was boldly challenging an established team achieving decent results in a respected European league with his newly assembled squad of short-passing Yugoslavian and Central American castaways. ADO declined, citing their membership in FIFA, a fact but also a slight that members of the USA never tired of delivering to their NPSL counterparts. This challenge set the tone for the Clippers' season and, along with their fine-tuned short-passing game, became a hallmark of their identity.

The Clippers were also uniquely positioned from a communications standpoint, in that NFL and NCAA Hall of Famer Ernie Nevers served on their board of directors. As team vice president he became a valuable, effective advocate for the Clippers and the league. Nevers' background as a decorated, authentic American sportsman made him a credible figure that newspaper reporters accorded a level of respect, his credibility removing their leverage and ability to take subliminal or overt cheap shots at the game when he spoke of it.

This provided Nevers an important platform to promote soccer's intrinsic sense of physical democracy. It was a platform he used to say things like "modern football demands a regiment of giants. The little guy is being shut out. But he can always play soccer"[17] and "I believe in soccer. Soccer doesn't require a lot of weight or a lot of height but only speed and guts. A soccer player needs more stamina than any other athlete today."[18]

Nevers touched on two extremely relevant concepts: soccer's democracy of the body, which allowed men and women of all shapes and sizes to play, as well as the extreme level of conditioning and stamina required by the game. Both were important to note because doing so, particularly in Nevers' voice, helped to elevate the game above the petty attempts in the American press to cast it as soft and unmanly.

Nevers was virtually alone among the American sports hierarchy in his public advocacy and support for the game, and it must be emphasized that another figure voicing these opinions would likely have been undermined by subversive language to some degree. "I think Ernie truly became a soccer fan,"[19] Liecty said as he fondly recalled Nevers' hard work on behalf of the Clippers.

Finally, through Liecty's connections at Stanford, the Clippers hired Dr. Leo Weinstein to serve as their official publicity director. Weinstein, a German Jew who fled to America in 1938, was a lifelong soccer fan obsessed with tactics and blessed with an encyclopedic knowledge of the game. Liecty remembered meeting Weinstein "at Stanford in 1951 when he was a graduate student and we played one season of soccer together and the next season he became my coach."[20]

The two remained lifelong friends and Weinstein seemed a natural fit as Clippers publicity director. Weinstein's brief was to educate the local press and public about the game, a job he performed with relish. According to Liecty, Weinstein "would literally hold classes in the press box,"[21] painstakingly reconstructing the mechanics of scoring plays and outlining tactical strategies unfamiliar to the journalists. Weinstein's gregarious nature and infectious soccer zeal won over the local press core, in Liecty's view, making them more sympathetic to the Clippers than reporters in other cities.

As we've seen, a sympathetic (Dallas) or at least a nonadversarial (Los Angeles) local press relationship worked wonders. Even in the Bay area, this was a gargantuan task. Liecty remembers taking a trip with Clippers ownership "to see the sports editor of the *San Francisco Chronicle*, and he was and had always been anti-soccer, so I'll never forget him sitting there and saying 'all you guys are doing is bringing me more work.'"[22] This was another glaring indication of the contempt many newsrooms had for soccer in the United States and the uphill battle the owners faced trying to sell it. The conservative nature of sportswriters at this time was summed up in a contemporaneous *New York Times* article written by Phillip H. Dougherty, who noted that "soccer has not yet won wide acceptance among newspaper sports editors, who seem to be a bit timid about something so new."[23]

Hiring an advocate as dynamic as Dr. Weinstein to counteract this lack of acceptance was yet another innovative, intelligent move made by the franchise. Finally, Liecty views the decision to invite the local press to an exhibition the NPSL was sponsoring in Los Angeles between Santos and River Plate as pivotal. Liecty characterized the trip as "extremely successful," demonstrating with certainty that the Clippers "knew how to treat the media well."[24]

Tactically, the Clippers played tenacious defense and used their deadly short-passing game to control the tempo of a match. They could also shift gears suddenly, frantically pressing and overwhelming the opposing team's penalty area when their patience or resolve wore down, particularly when facing tired road teams toiling in humid Bay area climes. After a convincing 3–1 home victory against the Baltimore Bays in June, the *Baltimore Sun* remarked that "Dr. Alek Obradovic's strategy of flooding the penalty zone with seven or eight players paid off"[25] almost immediately when Marin scored less than a minute into the match. Not long after that, the Clippers blanked the Atlanta Chiefs 2–0 in front of a disappointing 3,818 Oakland fans to register their season-high eighth straight victory.

However, the Clippers' short-passing game could occasionally sputter, as it did when they lost 1–0 to the Bays in Baltimore in front of an above-average 7,108 fans, causing Ken Nigro of the *Baltimore Sun* to note that the Clippers "seemed content passing the ball" and relied heavily "on a patient style of play that sometimes included as many as six passes."[26] Nonplussed by the Bays stifling his possession-based tactics, the always brash Obradovic ruthlessly called the Bays out after the match, saying, "The Baltimore players, all they do is lay on the grass with injuries every two seconds. How can we put the pressure on when they do that? If they try that in Europe they must leave the game but here, no."[27] If his thoughts weren't already clear, Obradovic concluded thunderously, "If we played them ten times, we would beat them nine."[28]

What emerges in the aftermath of this showdown with the Bays is a confirmation of all the following characteristics of the Clippers identity:

- Confidence. Obradovic loved issuing colorful, mildly belligerent public challenges to teams anywhere in the world
- Short-passing game. Nigro mildly mocks the short-passing game, exasperatingly counting out the "six passes" the Clippers utilized to get from point A to point B on the pitch but his account offers confirmation that the Clippers rarely deviated from a ball-control, short-passing attack.
- Pressing. Obradovic referred to it directly after ripping the Bays for diving, asking how his team could properly apply pressure with so many players lying on the grass.

It is remarkable that a team built under such onerous restrictions and in a drastically compressed time frame was able to assume and project such a distinct identity so quickly. The Clippers may have had no Americans on their roster, but perhaps they alone in these early days were building a truly "American" team: brash, confident, sturdy, clinical, efficient, and media savvy.

While the Whips and others attempted to construct the American soccer identity on shortsighted conceptions of dull drudgery, fruitless industry, empty energy, and vapid vigor, the Clippers were authentically channeling the inspired polyglot frenzy of an emerging America. They were pointing the way toward the future and embodying soccer's ability to challenge and ultimately change fixed conceptions of identity.

When the dust settled from the Clippers–Bays midseason clash, both teams seemed to acknowledge that they could see each other again in the playoffs. This awareness could be glimpsed in Obradovic's gruff prediction, as well as in Bays coach Doug Millward's comments that victory over the Clippers gave "us a psychological lift. We know we can beat Oakland now and that's important since we might eventually meet them for the championship."[29] Both statements seem to forecast the immediate future.

As a sort of subliminal response to Obradovic, Millward also would say of the Clippers, "Oakland is a very consistent team. The only thing they lack which we have is a bit of spark and explosiveness."[30] Millward then referred directly to Obradovic's short-passing game, saying, "They seem to want to push the ball around in the first half, hoping to tire you out and then turn on the power in the second half."[31] Despite Millward's characterization of the Clippers as predictable, the Clippers would respond by playing well after this loss, immediately restoring their rhythm and pace over the next few weeks with a run that culminated in a 9–0 demolition of the division rival St. Louis Stars in front of nearly 10,000 fans who gave the Clippers a standing ovation.[32]

The Clippers home form was dominant but their road form was definitely a concern, as they would win only six of their sixteen matches away from the Coliseum. The Clippers clinched the Western Division title in Oakland on August 16 with a surprisingly comfortable 3–1 win against the punchless Chicago Spurs, who couldn't take advantage of a Clippers side reduced to ten men in the first half.[33] The Clippers' relatively easy trek through the NPSL's Western Division did indeed put them in the NPSL finals against none other than Clive Toye's Baltimore Bays. The Bays had barely snagged first place in the Eastern Division over the Philadelphia Spartans.

The NPSL had devised a home-and-home total goals championship series modeled on a European Cup tie. Shortly before the series Phil Woosnam analyzed the matchup, confirming Millward's assessment of the Clippers with his view that "they don't have as much reliance on individual skill as Baltimore does."[34] Woosnam also confirmed the Clippers' superior level of organization, telling the *Sun* "there aren't too many weaknesses in the Oakland team and if they make a mistake anywhere, someone will always cover it up."

The first leg took place in front of 16,619 crazed Baltimore fans. The raucous hometown supporters saw ex–Manchester United sniper Dennis Viollet score the lone goal of the match on a volley after some nice interplay with Juan Santisteban, handing the Bays a 1–0 victory. Viollet, who had admittedly struggled to find form throughout the contest, was there to pounce when needed, proving that a natural goal scorer's instincts are impervious to rust. Baltimore had "outplayed" the Clippers and "deserved to win, possibly by even more than the one-goal margin,"[35] according to the *Sun*.

The reason they didn't, however, was thanks to a stellar performance from the Clippers' Mirko Stojanovic. The keeper, who had accumulated ten regular-season clean sheets, made numerous "brilliant" and outstanding saves to prevent the Bays from building a more comfortable lead heading into Oakland. The Bays had now twice ground out 1–0 victories against the Clippers on their home pitch. But as had happened earlier in the summer, not only did the Bays' victory earn them no respect from the Clippers, it actually prompted a member of the team, this time Stojanovic, to publicly claim, "We have a better team than the Bays."[36] Perhaps it was a fitting message to be delivered by the man who had kept the tie within the Clippers' reach.

Despite being outworked by the Bays, the Clippers remained supremely confident heading home to the Oakland Coliseum, where they hadn't lost all season. Obradovic said 77-degree temperatures prevented his players from running before conceding "the team didn't play up to normal in Baltimore."[37] Interestingly, the width of the Coliseum's pitch would be truncated from seventy-two to sixty-six yards to accommodate an Oakland Raiders game the next day, making the field far more narrow than usual. Obradovic devilishly noted that it gave the Bays "six yards less to defend."

Before the match, Toby Hilliard publicly appealed to fans to help the Clippers surpass the impressive 16,619 attendance figure turned out by Baltimore, asking the locals to "compete and get people in the stadium."[38] Up until that point, the Clippers' best gate of the season was the previously mentioned 9,771, and Hilliard was "prepared to pay for a few thousand tickets out of his own pocket and distribute them to friends if it will help the attendance surpass that of Baltimore."[39]

As an added draw, the Clippers secured the halftime services of the Guckenheimer Sour Kraut Band and a hot air balloonist named Bill Berry.[40] Sadly, the drawing power of the Guckenheimer Sour Kraut Band was limited even in the psychedelic '60s and the lure of watching the Clippers secure the NPSL title enticed just over 9,000 to the Coliseum. In an even more ominous move, it was announced "half an hour before the start of the second game of the championship" that the "NPSL had filed an $18 million lawsuit against the USSFA, FIFA and just about every other soccer organization going."[41]

Those not in the stadium would miss seeing the Clippers storm to a 3–0 lead on the strength of a first-half hat trick by Dragan Djukic (a midseason pickup from the Los Angeles Toros) and never look back. After a competent, cohesive performance in Baltimore, the "outclassed"[42] Bays disintegrated into a fragile, ill-disciplined morass that ultimately saw Juan Santisteban ejected near the end of the first half. *The Sun*'s Ken Nigro described it as "a riotous scene" where "the Bays forgot completely about the match and turned it into a circus."[43] Things deteriorated rapidly when Sele Milosevic was awarded a penalty after an obvious foul by the Bays' Badu da Cruz.

According to Nigro, it would be "almost ten minutes" before Djukic would take the penalty as Santisteban, the stylish ex-Madrista, and Gaucho Tejada relentlessly charged after referee Mike Askenazi, with Tejada apparently even grabbing his shirt. Another member of the Bays, Uriel da Veiga, went "completely berserk" and was "snorting around the field"[44] before kicking the ball off the penalty spot and into the stands. Eventually, after kicking Djukic as he waited to take the spot kick, Santisteban was finally sent off and the Bays were down to ten men.

Nigro was incredulous about how long Askenazi allowed Santisteban and da Veiga to wreak havoc, snidely commenting on the referees' "endless patience" and amazing propensity to "overlook."[45] This is another of the many examples of poor refereeing that plagued the USA/NPSL and added a dangerously combustible element to the matches. In fact, each league's final contest saw the losing side have a man sent off: Santisteban for the Bays and Jimmy Smith for the Whips. Illija Mitic would set up Edgar Marin's goal thirteen minutes into the second half, sealing the tie and bringing the NPSL title to Oakland. Marin wasn't through scoring for the year, though, as he notched a hat trick in the Clippers' 6–3 victory in St. Louis against the Stars in the league's Challenge Cup, a bizarro world "community shield" that allowed the winner of the "second place playoff"[46] to take on the newly crowned champions.

When asked what stands out to him from these matches, Liecty replied, "the biggest memory I have of that is seeing the look on Mr. Toye's face when we won the Cup."[47] Liecty also recalled being excited about "how recognized we got by the local press, by the city of Oakland, by the chamber of commerce . . . and how great it was that we brought the first national professional championship in any sport to the city of Oakland."[48]

The Clippers ended the inaugural NPSL season either on top or ahead of essentially every metric and indicator, save for the one that mattered most: the bottom line. Hilliard publicly admitted that the organization had lost $400,000 in the days before the championship match with Baltimore.[49] It proved a sorrowful example that instant success and undeniable on-field quality weren't the magic elixirs or guarantors of profit that many in both leagues imagined they would be.

One of the major sticking points of the USA/NPSL merger was what to do with cities that had two franchises representing them, such as Chicago, New York, Toronto, Vancouver, and the Bay area. Luckily for the Clippers, their situation was resolved rather painlessly as the USA's San Francisco franchise decided to merge with its Vancouver counterpart, leaving northern California to its "first and best" soccer team. Clippers' co-owner Joseph O'Neill was elected deputy chairman of the NASL's executive committee, giving the team a voice in league governance. [50]

In March the team played the first of what would become another of their lasting legacies: an international friendly against Guadalajara in San Francisco, which they lost 1–0 in the second period of extra time. The match, held March 3, was a part of doubleheader that saw Racing Club handily defeat the Vancouver Royals 4–0. In the NASL that spring, the Clippers picked up right where they left off, winning their first three matches handily, including a 5–0 pasting of the hapless Washington Whips. Ever the perfectionist, Obradovic told the press he wasn't satisfied with his team's performance, saying "we are not yet stronger than last year." [51] He predicted they would need "another two or three weeks" to jell completely.

Less than two months later the Clippers played the reigning English Champions, Manchester City in Oakland. No public pleading or Sour Kraut string bands were needed to inflate the gate this time, as 25,237 fans came out to the stadium in what was then record attendance for a soccer match in California. The contest took place June 9, 1968, and Malcolm Allison's men, riding high off of their domestic triumph, likely expected only token resistance from a ragtag club barely a year old. They would be seriously mistaken.

The Clippers took a 1–0 lead in the thirty-second minute on a Mario Baesso strike. Shortly after, Tony Coleman and Mike Doyle were sent off in quick succession by referee Eddie Pearson. Down to nine men, the proud Englishmen battled as hard as they could before conceding two more goals and losing 3–0. The dismissals obviously slanted the game inexorably toward the Clippers, but it is worth considering that they allegedly "dominated" [52] the first half, allowing only three shots on goal.

The Mancunians were also shorthanded with three regulars back in England. It remains a watershed victory for the Clippers, although it was overshadowed by the shocking pair of victories the Atlanta Chiefs scored against Manchester City the same summer. Sadly, as Wangerin points out, "three days later, just 2,527 turned up for a league match with St. Louis" and even worse "the crowd for Manchester City would prove to be larger than those for Oakland's next eight home games put together." [53]

However, the Clippers rolled through July and August and a 4–2 victory against the Los Angeles Wolves in front of a paltry 1,719 spectators, marking six straight victories in league play. [54] Waves of off-the-field discontent would ripple to the surface near the end of August, as Hilliard told the *Oakland Tribune* that the team would consider relocation if they found a satisfactory deal elsewhere. Hilliard told the paper, "We don't want to leave Oakland, but this is a business. We've got to make this thing pay for itself, but if we're not going to get any help here, we'd be darn fools not to entertain other offers." [55]

Riding high in the NASL and cruising on the strength of their victory over Manchester City, it should be no surprise that the ultra-confident Clippers were one of the teams itching to face Pele and Santos during their American tour. The Brazilians shattered the weeks' old California attendance mark, drawing more than 29,000 fans to Oakland Coliseum on August 30, where they outclassed the Clippers 3–1. Pele scored twice, once in each half. Santos sliced through the humid American summer, losing only two of their thirteen matches overall and going a comfortable 6–2 against the NASL.

In hindsight, the mammoth gate coming just days after Hilliard's relocation warning probably did the franchise more harm than good, making subsistence entirely on international matches seem tantalizingly possible. Just a few weeks after the Santos match the Clippers hosted the Israeli national team in Oakland. Only 4,352 saw the Clippers grind out an impressive 2–1 win against the Israelis when Sele Milosevic scored the winning goal in the seventy-first minute.

As the inaugural NASL season wound down, the Clippers found themselves in a familiar place near the top of the league's Pacific Division. But the NASL's arcane and reviled point system, adopted from the NPSL, conspired to give the San Diego Toros the Pacific Division crown by one "bonus" point, even though the teams had identical 18–8–6 records. The Clippers were once again the highest scoring team in the league, notching seventy-one goals and conceding only thirty-eight. Wangerin singled out the damaging, ultimately decisive importance of a 1–1 draw against the lowly Dallas Tornado in the brutal Texas heat, a match that occurred during a run that saw Dallas outscored 38–6 in its previous seven matches. [56]

It is a mystery exactly what sort of "bonus" point or slip-up doomed the Clippers, but postwar American soccer lost a chance to see one of its brightest hopes defend their league title on a banal technicality. Sadly, after again leading the league in nearly every positive metric, the Clippers were once again near the bottom with an average attendance of 3,700. [57]

After the 1968 season, decimated by massive financial losses, many NASL franchises folded during the winter, including those in San Diego, Los Angeles, and Vancouver, leaving the Clippers isolated on the West Coast with the Dallas Tornado now their closest geographical rival. Liecty referred to the situation as a "geographic vacuum" [58] that created a huge dilemma for the owners, as travel would become economically unfeasible, not to mention exhausting for the players.

Despite hemorrhaging money, Liecty indicated that the ownership group definitely wanted to continue operating, though it must be noted that Toby Hilliard told United Press International (UPI) in early November that "there definitely would be no Clippers team" [59] in 1969, such was the uncertainty and despair surrounding the NASL. Hilliard also revealed that the team had lost more than $1 million and noted that "it was probably a mistake to play games exclusively in Oakland."[60]

The Clippers ultimately realized, as did the Generals and Whips, that there was money to be made playing international exhibitions against foreign teams. Hilliard put the situation in very stark, concise terms, noting that the club had "played 66 league matches over two years and lost money and played five with foreign teams and made money."[61] With that in mind, Liecty recalled that he and Dr. Obradovic came up with a plan to keep the Clippers in business without disbanding their excellent team or plunging headlong into bankruptcy due to travel expenses.

The plan "was to sit out the 1969 NASL season, keep our outstanding team together, and play a series of exhibition matches until the NASL had a chance to reorganize and regroup."[62] The hope was that in the interim the NASL would stabilize and ultimately reestablish teams on the West Coast. This was all happening amid the tumultuous background noise and mangled miscommunication regarding the rollout of the "all-American" single team plan, which eventually dissolved into acrimonious debate surrounding the International Cup.

Once Phil Woosnam won the internal power struggle and became executive director of the NASL, Liecty recalled that "he and the other league leaders looked upon our project as a threat to their reorganization, as they thought other teams would like to do the same and thus negate their efforts to reconstitute a viable league."[63] Again judging by the discourse between Woosnam and New York Generals director Eugene Scott, fears of other teams embarking on similar international schedules seemed a legitimate worry for NASL leaders at the time, as Scott and the Generals made numerous references to scheduling more international matches.

In fact, the very press release announcing the Generals' decision to cease operations specifically says that "the club may sponsor some visits by foreign teams."[64] The Generals had been trying to schedule friendlies since August 1967, while still operating as outlaws, they planned an exhibition against Atletica Portueguesa, which was canceled at the eleventh hour due to threats that the Brazilians would be sanctioned by the Brazilian Soccer Association.[65] The Washington Whips also embarked on a European tour in the fall of 1968 with the express intent of making money to offset their massive losses. The Cleveland Stokers opted out of the NASL at this time but retained their franchise rights—perhaps with the intent of staging independent exhibitions. The Stokers being one of many teams to enjoy a shattered attendance record the morning after a Santos visit. Amazingly, on the precipice of securing the NASL title in September, rumors began swirling of the Atlanta Chiefs' uncertain future, which prompted a report that suggested "there's talk that the Chiefs might stick together to play exhibitions with some of the better known foreign teams after quitting the NASL."[66] An astonishing piece of speculation in light of what would soon transpire.

Whatever the Clippers' intent, their decision created an acrimonious rupture, not only between themselves and the NASL, but, perhaps more importantly, between themselves and the United States Soccer Football Association (USSFA). According to Liecty, due to a pronounced and frustrating "lack of trust," the NASL and USSFA viewed the Clippers "as now being a hungry exploiter trying to capitalize by only playing foreign teams in the ways that some unscrupulous impresarios had done in the past."[67] Liecty lamented that "despite meetings, letters, telephone calls and other means, the Clippers management could not convince the NASL leaders nor the USSFA that our intentions were legitimate and, more important, designed to help reconstitute the NASL in the long run by having an established team already on the West Coast."

However, it is interesting to consider remarks made by Obradovic during this time, which would seem to contradict Liecty's assertions. According to Wangerin, "Obradovic expected 'eight or ten teams to follow our example by June,' then regional leagues with national playoffs."[68] It's not hard to imagine the shockwaves of fear these words stirred up at NASL headquarters in Atlanta, and this may have been why trust between the two groups was virtually nonexistent. The possibility of multiple unaffiliated teams, particularly one operating out of Manhattan, would certainly have been a nightmare scenario for the NASL.

Not only were Liecty's assurances unacknowledged, but the NASL and USSFA began to actively hinder and subvert the Clippers' efforts. To receive legal sanction for international matches now that they were outside the NASL, the Clippers became formally affiliated with the Peninsula Soccer League of the California Soccer Association. It was an arrangement initially supported by the USSFA, but that would soon come under intense scrutiny. While attempting to maintain civility and channels of communication with the NASL, the Clippers had begun inviting foreign teams to play in Oakland, San Francisco, Los Angeles, and Stanford.

Through Obradovic's connections, the Clippers were able to initiate negotiations with Valentin Granatkin of the Russian Federation in late 1968. Liecty recalled "Obradovic, sitting at midnight in my humble den in Oakland calling Moscow and convincing Mr. Granatkin that Dynamo Kiev should come to the United States."[69] Conducted during the height of the Cold War, these negotiations were already complicated and protracted, but Liecty asserts that USSFA intervened after Obradovic's breakthrough and attempted to sabotage them in the closing stages, telling the Clippers, "Your operation is hereby declared null and void. You cannot operate any further pending investigation by the USSFA."[70]

Liecty speculates that the association likely relented only due to fears of bad publicity, as dates were set and the Russians had already made travel arrangements. Interestingly enough, the *New York Times* noted that Dynamo's trip had been sponsored by the California Soccer Football Association, "which extended the invitation to the Ukrainians months ago" and that the "acceptance cable from Kiev arrived last Tuesday and clearance from the United States Soccer Football Association, the national governing body, was granted at once."[71] The emphasis on the clearance being "granted at once" seems jarring.

Liecty pointed out that the ability for the USSFA to "deny the Clippers' invitations to foreign teams" was their "biggest lever to put us out of business."[72] The USSFA's International Games Committee, which was responsible for facilitating invitations and permissions, was chaired by the long-tenured and suddenly powerful James P. McGuire. McGuire, who came to the United States from Scotland in 1926 and played for the Brooklyn Wanderers, was a fixture in the insulated world of postwar American soccer administration. In Liecty's view, McGuire already disliked the Clippers due to their association with the "outlaw" NPSL, but their groundbreaking, successful coup in bringing Dynamo to the states was a "blow to Mr. McGuire's pride and arrogance since he had always contended he would be the person to invite the first-ever Russian soccer team to visit the United States."[73]

Liecty remains convinced that this is the case, recalling McGuire boasting personally to him at a FIFA conference in Mexico in 1968 that he would certainly be the first to bring over a Russian team due to his close personal relationship with Granatkin.[74] McGuire's personal animus and bureaucratic interference severely damaged the Clippers' ability to properly promote their international matches, their efforts devoted instead to "a daily fight with administrative and bureaucratic problems of a Herculean nature put up by the USSFA and James McGuire,"[75] according to Liecty. McGuire becomes a subversive actor in Liecty's telling, not so much by using subversive language, but by utilizing bureaucratic machinations and quasi-legal manipulations.

According to Wangerin, "Obradovic told the *Oakland Tribune* that 'Baltimore, Atlanta and ourselves tried last year to get the Russians, but we went through other people. This time we tried to arrange the whole thing by ourselves, something I believe had never been done before, and this must have impressed the Russian Federation.'"[76] The "other people" Obradovic refers to most likely included McGuire, which makes it easier to understand why McGuire's ego was as bruised as Liecty contends. The draining, wearisome battles of bureaucratic attrition that helped sink the Clippers prompted Obradovic to forthrightly opine that "one of the problems here are the American soccer associations."[77] Ultimately, McGuire's actions would lead to antitrust litigation initiated by the Clippers' ownership group. When all of this is taken into consideration, it's truly amazing that the Clippers were able to schedule any matches, let alone a series of eleven exceedingly ambitious contests against top-tier international competition.

The slate started in late January when the Clippers, now once again the California Clippers, hosted the Mexican side Atlas in a rainy Kezar Stadium. The Clippers registered a comfortable 3–0 victory over the men from Guadalajara on a soggy pitch in front of 5,142 fans as they marched toward their historic clash with Dynamo Kiev. The poster for this event, archived at www.nasljerseys.com, says that match was presented in "cooperation" with the USSFA.[78]

The final break between the Clippers and USSFA to which Liecty refers apparently happened at some point between the Guadalajara match on January 26 and the date of the first Dynamo clash on February 23. Not only were the Dynamo matches a cultural and diplomatic coup, but they promised a fascinating tactical and aesthetic matchup between two grizzled technicians.

Jonathan Wilson referred to Viktor Maslov as "the father of modern football."[79] During his mid- to late '60s run with Dynamo Kiev he perfected many of his tactical innovations, solidifying his legacy as one of the most influential managers in football history. Dynamo had won three consecutive Soviet titles, including a domestic double in 1966, and was considered one of the best sides anywhere in the world when they headed to the states to meet the Clippers.

Maslov is credited with inventing the 4–4–2 formation, modifying the in vogue and widely used 4–2–4 in the early '60s by having his wingers drop back into the midfield, creating a flat, balanced bank of four. Dynamo used the new formation to devastating effect. Besides pioneering the 4–4–2, Maslov's Dynamo were also among the first sides to rely on zonal marking. In fact, Maslov once famously said that "man-marking humiliates, insults and even morally represses the players who resort to it."[80]

This insight into Maslov's psychology is invaluable and speaks to the emphasis on highly synchronized collective movement that defined his Dynamo sides. This finely honed collective mentality was sharpened further by Maslov's trailblazing emphasis on nutrition and conditioning, which elevated Dynamo's fitness levels beyond most, if not all, of their competitors. The superior fitness levels and collective mind-set allowed Dynamo to press relentlessly when defending, becoming one of the first teams to successfully utilize that tactic, as well.

Taken together, the sum of Maslov's tactical inventions is staggering, and this particular Dynamo squad became their fullest, deadliest instrument of expression. However, it was a testament to the tactical acumen of Obradovic that he'd actually fared extremely well against Maslov in their prior matchups. The coaches had met five times previously in their various stops throughout the Soviet Union and Yugoslavia, with Maslov's teams accruing just one victory and a draw.

The Associated Press (AP) interviewed Obradovic about this, and the coach specifically recalled a 1948 match in Moscow. Obradovic said, "It wasn't a game, it was a political match. We took a 5–1 lead and Stalin and the Russian leaders walked out of the stadium. He missed seeing the Russians catch up and tie, 5–5."[81] Perhaps engaging in some subtle psychological sparring with Obradovic, Maslov characterized his squad as playing a "defensive game primarily" ahead of their first meeting with the Clippers. Maslov also stressed the Dynamo's flexibility, telling the *New York Times* that "he uses a 4–2–4 or other formations when the situation warrants it."[82]

While the Clippers were taking on all comers in North America, Dynamo had ended Celtic's reign as European champions, winning 2–1 in Glasgow in front of 80,000 rabid Scots. The Clippers had missed out on the chance to defend their title by one point, while Dynamo surged to their third straight crown, losing only two of their thirty-eight league matches. The Clippers had placed five players on the NASL All-Star team, while Dynamo Kiev featured eight internationals and no less than four members of the Soviet Union's third-place 1966 World Cup squad, including halfback Iosif Sabo, keeper Viktor Bannikov, and forwards Valeriy Porkuyan and Viktor Serebryanikov. The stage was set for an intriguing battle.

The first match was scheduled at Kezar Stadium in San Francisco and took place on February 23, 1969. The Russians drew first blood, winning a rainswept match 3–2 on a soupy pitch pockmarked with gridiron markings. Perhaps couched in the fervor of wishful thinking (or perhaps not, as Santos drew nearly 30,000 without a burst of Cold War patriotism working in its favor), Clippers management was expecting a crowd of at least 15,000, but hopefully 18,000.

A disappointing 11,815 spectators were on hand to see Dynamo center-forward Anotolidy Puzach score three times on the damp, misty afternoon. A second-half downpour rendered Kezar's pitch all the more muddy and treacherous. The poor field conditions became a talking point after the game and Maslov explicitly said, "If you expect soccer to flourish in this country, you must show it on a better field."[83] Soviet Soccer Federation chairman Fedor Martynyuk emphasized that "We play in all kinds of weather, rain, snow and everything, but not a field like Kezar. It was difficult to display our talents."[84]

The tattered old stadium had also recently come under fire from Los Angeles Rams coach George Allen, who called it a "disgrace." The Soviets confirmed his assessment with zeal. According to Shav Glick, at kickoff time, the field "was such a quagmire that even the seagulls were bypassing it."[85] Incidentally, "horrible" Kezar was nearly the Clippers' full-time home, but Liecty advised ownership to meet with prominent real estate developer

Robert Nahas about playing in his brand-new Coliseum. A meeting was arranged and Liecty remembered "we all went down and saw the stadium and immediately said, 'This is it. This is where it's going to be.' No Kezar."[86]

Ghostly footage of this match exists, and it's worth watching not only to see how bad the pitch truly was, but also to witness the unquestionable moments of beauty and brilliance that emerge from the mire. Breathtakingly intricate, razor-sharp short-passing triangles erupt from Dynamo, which proved their skill translated on all continents, transcending terrible playing surfaces to shine like a beacon in the Bay, while the Clippers reveal a comparable level of creativity and guile that demonstrate their worthiness as opponents.

Unlike the substandard pitch, the Clippers had definitely earned Maslov's respect and he told reporters that "they could be compared in fairness to a very normal European team."[87] It's one thing for Derek Liecty to assert "that the Clippers could play in any First Division Professional League in the world," particularly "in such countries as Germany and England," but it's another thing entirely when that viewpoint is confirmed by the man credited with being "the father of modern football."

The second match took place in the Los Angeles Coliseum on March 2 in front of 10,287. The Dynamo needed a last-gasp equalizer from Iosif Sabo to salvage a 1–1 draw. Shav Glick covered the match for the *Los Angeles Times* and lauded the "amazing Californians, put together by Dr. Aleksandar Obradovic"[88] who were a mere six seconds from a remarkable victory. After predicting a Clippers victory before the match, Stojanovic was imperious in goal, successfully weathering a fierce Ukrainian storm until fullback Vasily Krulikovskiy blazed down the side of the pitch and lobbed a high cross into the box that was ultimately deflected onto Sabo's merciless boot from six yards out.

Stojanovic made eighteen saves and was awarded a trophy as the game's most valuable player. John Kowalik, former Chicago Mustang and NASL goal-scoring leader, had put the Clippers ahead in the fifty-ninth minute after a beautiful setup from Edgar Marin. The match quickly acquired an ill temper as Dynamo's Ferents Medvid and the Clippers' Cirilo "Pepe" Fernandez were sent off midway through the first after a skirmish erupted between the two.

Despite hoping for significantly larger crowds, the Clippers ownership, battered and bruised by "crowds of 2,000 and 3,000 for the last two years in Oakland," were encouraged by two successive crowds greater than 10,000 and spoke of their plans to return to Los Angeles "with a series of international matches this summer."[89] The Clippers were undeterred by their failure to secure the victory and gained a measure of confidence from their otherwise solid and impressive performance.

Obradovic gave the AP a window into his team's psychology after the draw, saying "our players think we can beat them this time."[90] Sadly for the Russians, the third match of the series would again be played on the gnarled Kezar Stadium turf. The pitch was also on Obradovic's mind, causing him to remark, "we'll have a dry field, which gives us the advantage."[91] The remark perfectly encapsulated the Clippers' remarkably assured nature.

Kezar was dry on March 9, but conditions were cold and wind whipped through the old, drafty stadium. Picking up where the last match left off, the two surprisingly even foes engaged in a tightly wound, back-and-forth struggle in front of 11,223 fans. The match-winning goal came off the head (once again) of John Kowalik, who scored on a play that was orchestrated (once again) by Edgar Marin and Frank Mesaros in the seventy-second minute. There would be no last-gasp equalizer from the Dynamo this time. The Clippers were victorious, 1–0.

After three matches, nothing really separated the two sides; each had scored and conceded four goals and had won, lost, and drawn a match against their opponent. The Clippers had fought one of the world's most dominant teams to a standstill; in this context it's easy to imagine why the NASL would have been upset at the prospect of the Clippers shining so brightly outside their dimly lit orbit. Perhaps this unhappiness, coupled with McGuire's vendetta, explains why overall press coverage of the series was so scant and abysmal, with only cursory wire service reporting delivering the results in many cities.

If the publicity were more widespread, the buzz more palpable, what would stop the New York Generals from independently scheduling a series of matches such as these? Or perhaps the silence was part of a larger strategy of subversion. It would seem, specifically within the context of the Cold War, that any sporting victory against the Soviets, particularly in a game like soccer, which they valued and excelled at, would garner some glowing, gloating coverage in the press. But the silence was deafening.

It is amazing how soccer so awkwardly and repeatedly collides with patriotism in the American psyche; such was the mistrust it engendered that the mainstream press wouldn't even use the Clippers' victory against the Soviets as cheap propaganda. Whatever the reason coverage of the Clippers–Dynamo series was so slight, the undeniable fact remains that Obradovic and Toplak's Clippers went toe-to-toe with the "father of modern football" at the height of his power and acquitted themselves quite nicely.

This represented a massive missed opportunity on the part of the NASL and all those who wanted the game to succeed in the United States. Historians such as Wangerin argue that American soccer history was plagued by shortsightedness, petty territorial squabbles, and inept management. This incident is emblematic of all three simultaneously. Why the USSFA and NASL couldn't subsume their jealousy, egos, and paranoia to help jointly promote these matches is mind-blowing.

No matter their league affiliation or primary national or ethnic constitution, the Clippers could have been collectively trumpeted as the winning face of American soccer (or simply as *a* face of American soccer) when no such signifier existed. This gift came at *precisely* the time it was most needed, as uncertainty and public bickering were all the pubic knew of the NASL, if they knew anything about the league at all. Previews of Dynamo's visit to the Bay ran within days of the New York Generals' folding in the *Times*.

If McGuire engaged in trite bureaucratic subversions to disrupt the Clippers, it should be viewed as a mistake more costly than the many other mistakes made during this time. The Clippers presented the American soccer hierarchy with a golden opportunity when soccer was floundering desperately. The question becomes, was this opportunity missed because of ineptitude or was it missed intentionally under the guise of petty, spiteful subversion?

In the end, Obradovic got his wish—a Clippers victory that he proudly hoped would "establish American soccer's reputation in world competition."[92] It was, however, a victory that occurred largely in the dark and on the margins, a victory denied its proper celebration and significance. Maslov and Dynamo Kiev earned respect as stoic sporting ambassadors who graciously invited a team from the American Youth Soccer Organization to play against Kiev's junior side in the Ukraine.

In a comical aside, the Ukrainians also "loaded their suitcases with rock 'n' roll records and autographed pictures of Lana Turner"[93] before leaving California. The Dynamo boys apparently remembered the actress fondly from *The Postman Always Rings Twice* and were desperate to meet her. Ms. Turner opted out, however, sending autographed pictures instead. Everyone left happy. For the Clippers that happiness would be short lived.

Next up was an April exhibition against the U.S. men's national team. At this time the U.S. team was in the Dark Ages and just beginning to search for a way to climb back into the light. Still, nadir or not, the Clippers embarrassed the national team 4–0 in what the AP termed a "lopsided game"[94] at Balboa Stadium. The Clippers effortlessly racked up a clean sheet with their second-string keeper Leonel Conde, sending an ominous, prescient message about the tenor of the United States' qualification prospects for the 1970 World Cup in Mexico.

Ever ambitious, the Clippers scheduled matches with Mexico's Club America and a Fiorentina squad that was amid securing only the second *scudetto* in team history. The club had also scheduled a tournament of sorts involving the motley assortment of West Bromwich Albion, Dukla Prague, and Vitoria Setubal of Portugal. These matches were scheduled for May and were in a sense competing directly with the NASL's International Cup.

Throughout the months of March, April, and May, the "daily fights" with the USSFA and McGuire's "Herculean" bureaucratic entanglements wore down Liecty and the Clippers ownership. Perhaps a huge gate or a solid Clippers win in the match against Club America on May 2 would have helped buoy spirits but neither occurred. The Clippers lost a match that was closer than the 3–1 scoreline would indicate, as Club America's Rene Trujillo scored twice in the last three minutes to secure the win. Unfortunately, only 3,666 were on hand to witness the proceedings in the gigantically empty Los Angeles Coliseum.

The Clippers squared off against Vitoria Setubal in Fresno on May 18, losing 2–0 to the proud Portuguese side in front of only 1,700 fans. Gusts of twenty-mile-per-hour wind made for treacherous conditions, and the Clippers came out flat, falling behind only seven minutes in, when Ernest Figueriredo banged home a rebound. Setubal tallied again on Jacinto Joao's header and the Clippers were down by two before the interval. In the second half the Clippers responded, surging into Setubal's end and launching shot after shot at Jinis Vital, the club's beleaguered keeper. Vital was forced to make twenty saves, but it was not enough and the Clippers lost their second straight.[95]

A few days later, the Clippers hosted West Bromwich Albion at the Coliseum, and it was the Clippers who stormed out in front with a 2–0 lead. Illija Mitic scored the Clippers' first goal on a coolly taken penalty and Mesaros provided the second. The Baggies, fresh from an FA Cup triumph, never lost their pace or resolve, rattling more than twenty shots at Stojanovic in a furious attempt to level the score.

Much like the second contest with Dynamo, the Clippers were a mere seconds from an extremely impressive victory when Tony Brown's twenty-five-yard strike inched inside the left goal post, securing a 2–2 draw and saving West Brom massive blushes. The Clippers' collapse was disheartening, as they conceded both goals after eighty-eight minutes had elapsed. Still, without such an incredible display from Stojanovic, the result likely would have been much different. Only 5,143 fans showed up to see this remarkable match, which was paired with a Dukla–Setubal contest that also ended in a draw, 1–1.[96] The buzzards were circling.

The buzz surrounding the Clippers' future was starting to rattle and hum a little louder, even as they played fascinating matches against a colorful cross-section of globally renowned opponents. The behind-the-scenes struggle with the USSFA, as described by Liecty, and subpar gates were starting to feel insurmountable to the ownership group. This was the atmosphere swirling around the team as it began its two-match series with Fiorentina, the reigning Serie A champions.

The Clippers and Fiorentina engaged in a taut, tactical struggle in Los Angeles, with the Clippers ultimately losing 2–1 to the Italians on the strength of Eraldo Mancin's goal in the seventieth minute. The goal developed from a free kick taken by Amarildo, who lashed the post with his shot, which then bounced right to the waiting Mancin. Stojanovic was out of position and unable to properly defend the rebound in what proved to be a rare mistake by the Yugoslavian international.

The Clippers, down 1–0 at the break, attacked ambitiously in the second while seeking an equalizer. It arrived in the sixty-fourth minute when Dave Davidovic blazed a shot past Franko Superchi. The gloom would only increase as a mere 4,212 showed up to watch what was a tense, legitimate topflight match. Undaunted, the Clippers would gain a measure of revenge, besting Fiorentina 4–2 in San Francisco in front of 7,356 fans and handing the *scudetto* holders their first loss in a span of more than thirty-one matches.

This would be the Clippers' last hurrah, but what a last gasp of class and exhilaration it was, a fine football epitaph that would stand the test of time. The Clippers bolted out to a 3–0 lead against the formidable Italians, prompting co-owner Toby Hilliard to tell reporters that "It's a helluva note to break up one of the great teams in the world."[97] Were the Clippers truly "one of the great teams in the world"? It's hard to say that with certainty, even though they could point to victories against the champions of England, Italy, and Russia in less than a year's time, not to mention decisive wins against two separate national teams.

What they definitively were was the best team produced during professional soccer's American relaunch in the late '60s. They were also the ultimate example that fan identification trumped on-field success as a recipe for acquiring profits and stability. During their three years of existence, the Clippers could not have performed better on the field, nor could they have been better citizens and members of the northern California community. Issues of identity and ethnicity aside for a moment, the Oakland Clippers of the NPSL/NASL should have have been promoted as the model of American soccer that they truly were in those early, desperate days.

If the USSFA subverted the Clippers' efforts behind the scenes due to petty jealousies and territorial disputes—and there are strong indications that was indeed the case—then the USSFA itself set soccer's growth back decades. What's even more ironic is that in a very real sense, the Clippers essentially became the "national" or "all-American team" that was clumsily mooted to the press by some NASL owners near the end of 1968. The owners woozily dreamed that this "all-American" team would take on established global giants like Real Madrid, Manchester United, and Santos in lieu of NASL league play in 1969. This feverish course of action became the Clippers' reality.

The Clippers finished their audacious exhibition schedule at a more-than-respectable 7–6–2. What was less respectable was that those matches averaged only 5,000 in attendance, which in context may have been slightly higher than NASL's average gate for the International Cup. In retrospect, it's hard to predict what legitimate attendance expectations should have been at the time. The enormous gates from the Santos and Manchester City matches seemed to suggest even then that there was an appetite for international competition on the West Coast.

Even if you throw out Santos, which drew large crowds everywhere thanks to Pele's presence, the Manchester City match could have (and rightly so) led the Clippers' owners to set their attendance sights higher than was likely achievable at the time. The Dynamo crowds, which were not terrible or insignificant, probably should have caused the owners to readjust their expectations. Perhaps there was no saving the Clippers at that point, regardless. The word went out not long after the Fiorentina match that the Clippers had announced a press conference for the following Wednesday, where, presumably, they would confirm their demise.

After some surprisingly successful (at least athletically and aesthetically) exhibition matches entirely outside the NASL's sphere, the California Clippers officially ceased operations on June 4, 1969, with team president William M. Brinton citing "lack of fan support and staggering financial losses for three years."[98] Brinton acknowledged that the club had lost $1.5 million and that the ownership group had "finally reached the end of our resources."[99] It was an ignominious end to a startlingly good franchise, both on and off the field.

Brinton singled out the USSFA as the primary cause of their troubles, setting the stage for the antitrust lawsuit he would lodge against them. Brinton ultimately initiated legal proceedings against the USSFA, NASL, and the California Soccer Association, among other parties. The Clippers alleged in their suit that the USSFA required the organization "to secure approval for further games under procedures which it deemed unreasonable and with which it cannot comply."[100]

These are the same allegations levied by Liecty in his published reminiscences. Liecty recalled that the Clippers' lawsuit, the third filed against the USSFA in less than five years (the NPSL and Bill Cox had filed the others), dragged on for eighteen months and was finally "settled on the court house steps at the 11th hour when the judge informed the defendants that they would lose the case if there was not a settlement."

In what was a strange coincidence, Cox lodged his suit against USSFA at almost the same time as the Clippers. Cox's lawsuit against the USSFA and the American Soccer League (ASL) charged the groups with "monopoly and restraint of trade."[101] His statements were also voiced in similarly exasperated language, as Cox told the press that "any team which is willing to comply with the general rules of international soccer should be allowed to compete with no opportunity for USSFA to block it."[102]

The legal aspect of this story is another strand worthy of further examination. In his *New York Times* op-ed Eugene Scott specifically referred to the situation developing between the USSFA and the Clippers as one of "two delicate problems" that should be recorded as "warnings for the future." Scott pointedly singled out what he termed the "disruptive situation regarding foreign games where USSFA, the governing amateur soccer body in this country, has the right, has the unchallenged right to determine under what circumstances foreign teams can play in the United States."[103]

He then mentions that the Clippers were "recently chastised by USSFA"[104] for their series of matches against Dynamo Kiev, independently confirming many of Liecty's contentions. Scott ends by ominously noting that these are facts "which a bright young man in the Justice Department some day might find curious."[105] In fact, it took only a few months before the USSFA was challenged in court on two separate but interrelated fronts. Here is an instance of Scott using his access to the *New York Times* to send a warning shot to the USSFA. These incidents contribute to the uneasy tangle with which antitrust laws have always intertwined with sports in the United States.

As with baseball, antitrust becomes in some instances a way to engage in subversive, hypocritical practices under cover of judicial obfuscation, as maverick baseball owner Bill Veeck so eloquently pointed out by quoting Justice Felix Frankfurter's minority opinion that "it would baffle the subtlest ingenuity to find a single differentiating factor between other sporting exhibitions . . . and baseball."[106] Frankfurter wrote those scathing words in a 1955 opinion after his colleagues on the Supreme Court denied boxing an antitrust exemption similar to Major League Baseball's.

Perhaps USSFA and the remaining baseball men among the NASL ownership were attempting to erect a similar framework of logically inconsistent legal protections. It's extremely telling that the two men who reacted most strongly to the USSFA's actions, Scott and Brinton, were both lawyers themselves. They were able to recognize legal subversion and react accordingly to it using the various means at their disposal as actors of privilege—Scott through channels such as the *New York Times* and Brinton through successful litigation in the courts.

Soccer was an even more complicated matter because no other American sports enterprise functioned within or were beholden to the rules of an international organization such as FIFA and, by extension, their national surrogate, USSFA. It's no surprise that this arrangement would chafe successful men who were not used to answering to such oversight, let alone foreign oversight. A pattern emerges of the USSFA as a hypocritical and vindictive actor, susceptible to acting upon personal slights and grudges but primarily acting to preserve its newly minted status as an important and prosperous organization.

Liecty touched on this previously, mentioning McGuire's personal dislike of the "outlaw" NPSL. The dislike was mutual and can be traced to the

NPSL's founding. In a profile of the USSFA on the eve of the 1967 "soccer war," Andrew Beyer observed that the NPSL owners considered the USS-FA's terms for sanction "a form of blackmail [that they] wouldn't pay" before noting that their objections had to be a matter of principle because $250,000 was "mere pocket money"[107] to some of the men involved. This turned out to be true.

Beyer's hunch was confirmed by NPSL vice president Charles Houghton, who told him "we didn't feel that any organization had the right to give an exclusive franchise to any one pro soccer league."[108] Houghton continued, saying that the NPSL had "appealed to FIFA to examine the conditions under which soccer was being run over here. It's not compatible with our way of life. We feel they have got to clean house." This was strong language that indicated an unresolved level of tension and animosity, as well as an inexorable march toward litigation between the NPSL and USSFA. Besides not being used to this form of regulation, what seemed to be at issue from the outset was the USSFA's exclusive jurisdiction over exhibitions and friendlies.

The issue of playing exhibitions apparently had been on the minds of NPSL executives from day one, and it surfaces in the *Washington Post*'s reporting on USA–NPSL merger talks a full year before the Clippers went rogue and the Generals began making noise about following suit. Beyer quoted NPSL commissioner Ken Macker as saying, "What we wanted was to be recognized now, so that our teams can play foreign teams."[109] Santos' lucrative 1968 summer tour of the states was barely half over before Macker announced the formation of a committee to expand the NASL's foreign schedule.[110] Interestingly enough, this ill-fated committee included none other than Bill Cox, then executive president of the St. Louis Stars, in addition to Lamar Hunt, George Flaherty (Vancouver), and Dick Cecil (Atlanta).

Many experts and observers felt that the USSFA's exclusive sanction of the USA likely would have been considered a clear-cut violation of antitrust law. Beyer spoke to an antitrust lawyer who said "the exclusivity would be very vulnerable under the antitrust law if this were another type of business."[111] The lawyer continued, "it would be a contract between a ruling body with one single competitor which excludes all other competitors from operating." In these terms, the stark monopolistic nature of the USA and USSFA's arrangement becomes clear, but as Beyer notes, "there is no neat formula to determine an antitrust violation."[112] The lawsuit was ultimately dropped amid the clamor about the merger.

The situation between Bill Cox and the USSFA went back to the latter days of the ISL. To receive sanction from FIFA to stage ISL matches, Cox formed a partnership with the ASL, which was officially recognized by the USSFA. A problem inevitably arose, according to Tom Dunmore of *Pitch Invasion*, because the ASL "had long been making its money by arranging exhibition tours with high-profile teams from overseas" and "this was precisely the market Cox was trying to corner."[113] The ISL quickly began to surpass the ASL, ultimately terminating their working relationship, which created enemies for Cox within the USSFA. Wangerin noted that the ISL's growing stature also began to rankle USSFA, "whose own leagues had been underwriting foreign tours for decades."[114]

This is an important point when considered along with the fact that the USA's decision to import foreign teams in 1967 was a continuation of "the very practice which helped to alienate Cox from the USSFA." This serves to underline the hypocritical, vindictive, and personal nature of USSFA's leadership, while also illustrating the complex knot of litigious grudges that emerged from under their jurisdiction in the late '60s.

Ed Levitt from the *Oakland Tribune* summed up the Clippers' entire inspired, unlikely, and barely believable voyage, writing: "Perhaps never before in sports history has there been a team like this: organized in Europe, financed in Texas, trained in Redwood City, home-based in Oakland, and winners of a US championship without one American player on the club."[115] And just like that, the Clippers were gone. The cost of their absence to the NASL's growth and to the development American soccer can never be measured adequately.

Read as a cultural text, Levitt's description of the Clippers accurately reflected a version of American identity and vitality more faithfully than the clumsy, racialized dreck that was purposefully constructed as "American" elsewhere in the NASL. The Clippers reflected good old-fashioned American ingenuity and adaptability, the best features of the melting pot ethos so integral to the nation's narrative, as well as a bold self-assuredness that allowed them to flourish on an increasingly interconnected global stage. The Clippers contained and reflected all of this in a bleak era of war, violence, and prejudice. Even their downfall, authored largely by a powerful and vindictive bureaucratic entity, was, sadly, an accurate depiction of modern America.

I asked Liecty directly what he thought the Oakland Clippers' true legacy was and he said:

> The Clippers had two legacies that live on. The California Youth Soccer Association was basically started because of the Clippers. It had started as a small entity in the mid-'60s run by a man by the name of Donald Greer. Greer was instrumental in starting this fledgling thing called the California Youth Soccer Association. Mr. Greer became a full-time employee of the Oakland Clippers whose only job was to develop his program: junior soccer. He developed the California Youth Soccer Association, and it became the model for all youth soccer as it's organized in the United States, with the exception of the

AYSO [American Youth Soccer Organization]. He is a key, critical person in terms of what I feel is part of our legacy in helping get that program going.

The other legacy concerns a man named Clay Berling. Clay Berling is a fellow my age who had five children and lived in Berkeley, California, at the time that the Clippers were starting to go into business. He found out that he could take his whole brood down to the Oakland Coliseum on a Sunday afternoon for one of these new Clipper things for next to nothing, so he would do that. As a result of all this, Mr. Berling became a total soccer nut. Shortly after we folded up he started a newspaper called *Soccer West*. And he put money into this . . . and then it eventually became a magazine called *Soccer America*, and he poured money into this, and it has now morphed into an online magazine. He's the one, who . . . after professional soccer got going, had any kind of magazine with a national basis that was worth a hill of beans. Mr. Berling is a member of the USSFA National Soccer Hall of Fame because of all of the promotional work that he's done for it. He's in the National Soccer Coaches of America Association Hall of Fame, where he attends their annual convention every year as he's done for forty years. I attribute his getting into soccer to the Clippers [which] was a spinoff from us helping promote soccer in the United States. [116]

Chapter Six

Dallas File

In contrast to what we've seen thus far, the *Dallas Morning News* did a great job covering the United Soccer Association (USA) and North American Soccer League (NASL), perhaps due to the outsized influence and pull of the venerable and beloved Lamar Hunt. To emphasize just how beloved, Hunt's partner, the fruitcake magnate Bill McNutt gushed to *Sports Illustrated*, "I'm convinced he's the nicest guy the lord ever put on this earth." [1] More than just being nice, Hunt was a rarity. A member of the Texas oil aristocracy, he was humble and self-conscious enough to say things like

> I do detest ostentation, big dealing, like using your name to get a better hotel reservation or good seat in a restaurant. I just can't stand to see people thinking they should get a better table because of some influence they think they might have. I believe in taking your turn. It's only fair. [2]

The oil business might have been in his blood, but sports were in his heart. Hunt acquired the nickname "Games" while growing up due to his compulsion to continually create new contests and competitions. Hunt acknowledged this, saying, "others paint or write, I make up games." [3] Born in Arkansas, Hunt settled in Dallas permanently after his college days playing football for the Southern Methodist University Mustangs, where men like future NFL legends Raymond Berry and Forrest Gregg were his teammates. Perhaps more than anything else, it was Hunt's deep unabashed love for Dallas specifically and Texas in general that helped facilitate the favorable coverage the Dallas Tornado would receive in their inaugural season. After all, this was a man who, when his Dallas Texans moved to Kansas City, had to be forcefully convinced that retaining the name *Texans* was "unfeasible and unrealistic." Hunt argued stubbornly "that there would have been nothing odd about calling a team the Kansas City Texans" [4] until cooler, more savvy heads prevailed. Hunt insisted that "it was strictly for Dallas to get a team that the AFL [American Football League] was started." Hunt's "hometown chauvinism"[5] was a catalyst that changed the course of American's sports history. Hunt's fortune, passion for sports, and drive "to get in at the bottom and build something new, from the ground up"[6] made him naturally suited to be a player in the rebirth of professional soccer in the United States.

It is somehow fitting that this brief contextual background depicting a man so deeply devoted to his home, his city, and his community serves as the introduction to an examination of the Dallas Tornado's sometimes messy yet surprisingly successful effort to establish an authentic connection to their local community and a legitimate sense of local fan identification. The tension between the contrasting philosophical approaches many franchise owners took regarding whether establishing a solid local connection with their community was more important than simply focusing on delivering a winning product is crucial to understanding the dynamics of the USA, the National Professional Soccer League (NPSL), and the NASL. Dallas provides an excellent case study of what a successful emphasis on building local connections and fan identification looked like. Paradoxically, it seems that Hunt, his own sense of local pride well-established, adhered more closely to the view that winning was more important.

In the run-up to USA's season, the *Morning News* (like the *Washington Post* and *New York Times*) made no secret of the fact that Scotland's Dundee United were "Representing owner Hunt's Tornado,"[7] lavishing praise on United and variously referring to them as "16 of Scotland's finest"[8] and "pretty much the Cinderella team in European play this past season."[9] Dundee's run to domestic glory was halted, however, by its USA compatriots, the Aberdeen Dons, who nipped them 1–0 in the Scottish Cup semifinals. Once the season started, though, these references were downplayed and employed by the paper only to signify community. Dundee United's rapid transformation into a "home" team was a remarkable example of the successful creation of a sense of fan identification within the USA enterprise, not to mention the indispensible role journalists had in that creation. The mechanics behind the creation can be glimpsed in a column Sam Blair wrote after the Tornado's nil–nil draw against Houston in their home debut.

Blair took great pains to convey the crowd's emotional attachment, artfully describing a Dallas goal that was ultimately waved off. The "fans exploded"[10] over the nullified goal and Blair noted "that a big scoring play by the home team can apparently ignite a grand display of emotion, no matter what the sport."[11] Immediately linking Dundee to "home" was a subtle and effective form of Americanization used to help solidify a tenuous communal connection. It is instructive to consider Blair's column in contrast to Andrew Beyer's observation that the marked statistical advantage enjoyed by home sides in the NPSL "could be that the NPSL has fans who can fire up a team, fans who have identified more readily with their home clubs than USA fans have been able to do with their foreign imports."[12] Blair's column should also briefly be considered in contrast to chapter 4's examples from the *Chicago Tribune*, which of course reflect the polar opposite in tone.

The efforts of the *Morning News* staff speak to the immense influence reporters had in their ability to practically translate this league into being for their readers. The *Dallas Morning News* reporters deliberately tried to establish, whether genuine (and there's no reason to believe it wasn't) or not, a connection between readers and team, instilling an overriding sense that this was "their" team, manufacturing a suspension of disbelief, or perhaps a benevolent "masquerading" of identity.

The *Morning News* continued to overtly label and include Dundee as members of its community, in part by almost always revealing that the other team was not who it appeared to be. They also accomplished this with very telling, precise word choices. For instance, the Houston Stars were uniformly referred to as "alias Bangu of Brazil"[13] or "alias Bangu of Rio de Janiero."[14] "Alias" is, of course, a "false or assumed name,"[15] according to the *Oxford English Dictionary (OED)*.

In the modern American lexicon, "alias" is most commonly connected with fugitives, criminal acts, and adultery. Not only does this "other" the rival team, it implies that they are to some degree dishonest, making them easier to dislike and facilitating the natural urge to connect with the Tornado. *Morning News* reporter Bob St. John does something truly remarkable, though, referring to the Tornado as "the Dallas Scotsmen"[16] in the same article that he outed Houston as being Bangu operating under an "alias."

So complete was the paper's absorption—and, by extension, the readers, fans, and the greater Dallas community—of Dundee United that their identity morphed into Dallas's own "Scotsmen," the two fundamental pieces of their identity reduced and reconstructed into a wholesome hybrid identity that transcended the sum of its parts. Dallas, through the powerful voice of the *Morning News*, had given of itself, had bestowed a piece of its own identity and self upon the young men of Dundee United. The newspaper's success in helping to manufacture this identity would actually come back to haunt Hunt during the International Cup just two years later.

The Dallas–Fort Worth community responded well and the team enjoyed a level of support that far outstripped the popularity of USA teams like the Chicago Mustangs and Boston Rovers, teams that were placed in markets, unlike Texas, where soccer had been played and consumed on some level for years. The Dallas example, described by Brian Glanville as an "enigma,"[17] is instructive for many reasons. When attempting to explain it, Tornado co-owner Bill McNutt said, "You see Dallas is benefiting from the very thing we thought would hurt us—the lack of an ethnic group. With us, the city is viewing the thing as the Dallas Tornado Soccer Club."[18]

Why exactly was this? The pleasant tone and persistent level of coverage from the *Morning News* definitely was a factor. Hunt had publicly voiced his fear that Dallas had "no large ethnic group to swell his attendance these first few years"[19] to the *Washington Post* in January 1967. But as McNutt would note, the lack of a tradition or foundation for the sport in Texas coupled with the lack of a ready-made ethnic fan base actually created a vacuum that Dundee United were able to fill right away in their role as the Dallas Tornado. It would be ridiculous to say that the Tornado didn't have any competition, though, as Texas' passion for and consumption of American football was and is a widely acknowledged obsession. Not only did Dallas' "lack of an ethnic group" actually help the team to succeed, but it served, in a sense, to illuminate why the existence of numerous bona fide soccer-loving "ethnic groups" in areas like New England and Chicago actually hurt league performance there.

Boston presents a fascinating case study, according to Steven Apostolov of the University of Massachusetts. Apostolov posits that deep ethnic connections to soccer, the kind both the USA and NPSL were counting on, may have been a factor behind the surprisingly low attendance at Boston Rovers matches and that Boston's rich tradition of popular, well-established "ethnic amateur and semi pro teams" with "tremendous followings"[20] likely conspired to depress turnout for the USA and NASL teams that tried to survive in Boston since the late '60s.

As evidence of this theory, Apostolov cites the flourishing Luso American Soccer Association (LASA), founded in 1973 (after the Rovers folded but during the reign of the NASL's short-lived Boston Minutemen), which after a few years of existence had an average of between 3,000 and 5,000 attendees at their matches.[21] Apostolov speculates that those numbers show that "the large Portuguese community of New Bedford, Fall River and Taunton preferred the intimate atmosphere at municipal stadiums to the professional games of NASL teams."[22]

Boston professional soccer franchises historically have had problems properly securing stadiums for their teams to play in, with the Minutemen playing in no less than six different venues in two years.[23] Incidentally, the entire existence of the Oakland Clippers is owed to the fact that the Boston interests that were initially awarded the franchise had to relinquish it due to a lack of proper venue. This problem impacts Apostolov's theory, but his numbers do present a striking contrast. The Rovers averaged a league-low 4,171, the Minutemen 4,442, right in the middle of what the LASA averaged. Due to savvy local promotion, a symbol of the close-knit bonds communities formed through the game, the American Soccer League's (ASL) Boston Astros, a team with Brazilian roots and connections to Atletico Mineiro, sometimes played to crowds of 15,000 in Boston's Nickerson Field.

Apostolov writes, "had these spectators [those who attended LASA games and Boston Astros matches] attended the matches of the Boston Minutemen or the New England Teamen [oh so subtly sponsored by Lipton Tea] instead, some of these NASL teams might have survived."[24] A similar trajectory can be glimpsed in sociologist David Trouille's research on soccer's history in Chicago. The sheer number and presence of long-established ethnically based teams such as Sparta A.B.A and Schwaben conspired to depress turnout for both Chicago entries (the Mustangs and Spurs, respectively) in the soccer war of 1967, with Spurs bottoming out at slightly more than 2,000 per match. By the crucial year of 1969, both of these cities would vanish entirely from the NASL map, as would New York.

This is evidence that ethnicity and soccer were bound together in an ever-more-complex series of relationships that USA executives were at a loss to properly understand. In another instance of class and ethnicity directly intersecting with the game, these men, due to their total unfamiliarity with both the product and the demographic, saw only a vast, undifferentiated potential audience constituted of people who were commonly referred to as "hyphenated Americans"—the Irish and Portuguese immigrants in Massachusetts and the Polish and Italian immigrants of Chicago, for example. Either they couldn't grasp or weren't fully aware of the level of attachment these passionate soccer fans had already forged with their local, ethnically constructed teams, bonds that could not be broken for, in many cases, inferior products. The sophistication of these so-called hyphenated Americans and their cultivated eye for the nuances of the game, sharpened after years of watching quality soccer played by their family, friends, and neighbors in their own neighborhoods, had made them accustomed to a certain level of class on the field that the ramshackle teams of the NPSL, in particular, were not initially able to provide.

Why were the Texans so quick to embrace the Scots? Definitely the deep Scottish roots of many Texans likely made it much easier and more natural than would have initially appeared with no established competition, like the LASA in Boston. But this identification cuts swiftly against the grain of Beyer's observation that fans in most cities seemed to be lukewarm, at best, to USA franchises precisely because they could not establish a sense of identification with teams that were foreign and temporary. The people in Dallas were eager to adopt the Tornado as their own rather quickly. Why or how they were so willing and able to see past Dundee United's caretaker role as "their" team and still embrace the squad as "locals" to the tune of more than 9,200 spectators per match in 1967 is remarkable. It was an embrace that would be tested almost immediately when Hunt and McNutt set about building the "real" Dallas Tornado from scratch.

THE BALLAD OF THE DALLAS TORNADO

In the wake of the chaotic and disastrous 1967 USA season, after Dundee United went home to resume its domestic duties in Scotland's topflight, Lamar Hunt and Bill McNutt hired a Yugoslavian businessman living in Toronto named Bob Kap (born Božidar Kapušto) to help them build a new franchise. After obtaining a law degree from the University of Belgrade, Kap played professionally in Europe before writing voluminously for the publication *Soccer Illustrated.* Legend has it that Kap was corresponding with Hunt for an article when he found out that the Tornado needed a manager.[25] Kap told Hunt that he had coached in England and had played for Manchester United. Kap's resume also included an apprenticeship under the legendary Ferenc Puskas at the Soccer Academy in Hungary before fleeing to Canada amid the 1956 Hungarian Revolution. As time wore on and Kap's behavior became more erratic and his methods more exposed, the contours of his career began to appear invented. Much of it likely was fabricated. It was a hire that certainly set the tone for things to come.

With Hunt duly convinced, Kap spent months in Europe scouting and ultimately selecting players to form the new-look Tornado. Curiously, all of the players selected were white and hailed from England, the Netherlands, or Scandinavia, with the mandate being to select players capable of projecting a clean-cut "all-American"[26] look. Besides resurrecting the same level and style of clumsy irony embodied by the now-discarded USA moniker, this provides revealing insight into what the Tornado front office viewed as "all-American." Seven of the eight Englishmen selected hailed from Liverpool and surrounding areas.

Kap was assisted by an Englishman named Dave Moorcroft, "a local amateur of some pedigree,"[27] who would ultimately go on to have a run with Tranmere Rovers. Moorcroft would also make the Tornado touring squad. A freshly recruited nineteen-year-old Tornado named Bill Crosbie's firsthand recollections of this voyage have been collected on the website nasljerseys.com, and they provide an engrossing one-of-a-kind insight into this period. The *Guardian* also published an expanded version of Crosbie's recollections with an assist from the *Liverpool Echo.* Crosbie said he could not recall whether the tour was Hunt's or Kap's idea,[28] while the *Baltimore Sun* later reported that the Central American leg of the tour was the brainchild of Tornado general manager Ed Fries.[29] Perhaps fittingly Fries resigned shortly after the battered, exhausted team returned from Costa Rica. Michael Mac-Cambridge, a Hunt biographer, remarked that tour idea was "so elaborately fanciful that no one claimed authorship of it after the fact."[30]

Crosbie provided an interesting example of Kap's recruiting methods, as he responded to an ad in the *Echo* seeking "top-class amateur footballers."[31] It was also Crosbie, a bus conductor, who confirmed that "the idea was to have a very young 'All-American' style look about us."[32] During the time of the shaggy, Sgt. Pepper–era Beatles, Crosbie, a proud Liverpudlian, recalled being told by Kap to "get a short back and sides before I see you again."[33] In Crosbie's telling, it was Kap who "wanted an All American look, crewcuts for everyone,"[34] but it isn't hard to imagine that this dictum was handed down from on high, largely since Kap wasn't American and likely had a completely different conception of what it meant.

Confirmation that the "all-American" dictum likely came from Hunt can be gleaned in his publicly stated desire for "a team to awaken the Texan's national and regional pride."[35] To complete the proudly regional "all-American" look, the team was "instructed to wear club suits complete with Stetson hats wherever they went."[36] The *Morning News'* Roy Edwards further spelled out the plan, writing "this was to be Dallas' own team, a group of 'typical American boys' with whom we could all identify and with whom the game could grow and flourish."[37]

Perhaps this particular Americanization strategy was undertaken to counteract the subversive language many franchises encountered trying to market brown-skinned athletes from Italy and South America. But as mentioned, Dallas did all right at the box office, considering the overall climate, and they benefitted greatly from gracious, friendly newspaper coverage. Perhaps also it was the clearest manifestation yet that the game could not flourish in the collective minds of Madison Avenue until it had marketable (read: white) faces to sell and was the opening salvo in a concerted attempt to reconstruct the league's murky image into something more recognizably American. But once again the ironies are layered. The Tornado selected foreigners to affect an "all-American" image, making the entire concept ludicrous—even if it were not explicitly racialized to some degree, as initially they were all pointedly Caucasian. This should doubtlessly be viewed as one of the NASL's first concrete steps taken toward an Americanization of the game that would shift its existing image along more desirable ethnic and class lines.

When all was said and done, the Tornado lasted until 1981 (longer than the New York Cosmos) and won an NASL title in 1971, but perhaps they remain most well known for their infamous world tour before the 1968 NASL season. Apparently Kap envisioned the tour as part boot camp, part team-building exercise for his young recruits, none of which had ever even set foot in Dallas. According to MacCambridge, Kap had convinced Hunt that the best way to build a team from scratch was to travel the earth, accumulating talent and cohesion as it went along.[38]

Accounts differ, but the newly formed club played somewhere between thirty-two and forty-eight matches (a full European season) in a grueling six-month global jaunt that saw it go from Europe through Asia and back again to Central America. Brian Harvey (now the Oklahoma City University men's soccer coach) recalled thirty-eight matches.[39] They played in Ceylon, Bombay, Auckland (drawing 2–2 against Canterbury), Fiji, Iran (losing 2–1 to the Iranian Air Force, a team that, according to Crosbie, contained no less than seven internationals[40]), and even appeared in Saigon a mere forty-five days before the Tet Offensive. The players were stoned in Singapore after losing 4–2 to Singapore's national team in December.

The team cancelled a second match as well as "a shopping tour of the scenic island city" after being pelted with rocks as it left the pitch, with one player, Jan Book, being "slightly injured by a stone that grazed his head."[41] Crosbie remembered Per Larsen fouling "one of theirs" prompting the enraged crowd to begin "throwing stones and other things on the pitch."[42] Larsen further "annoyed them by bowing," Crosbie said and then "we had to be escorted from the pitch."[43] Harvey remembered one Singaporean player attacking the Tornado with the corner flag and a crowd eager to get involved because "we were the Dallas Tornado, and we were associated with the assassination of President Kennedy."[44] This frenzied atmosphere demonstrated that politics and war hovered like a heavy fog in the background as the team traversed the globe. The Tornado wisely remained holed up in their dressing room for hours as tempers cooled.

A version of this scene repeated itself in Honduras, but the projectiles were orange rinds.[45] The Tornado registered a handful of triumphs along the way, including a 2–2 draw with Turkish giants Fenerbahce in front of a reported 25,000 in Istanbul on October 10.[46] The Tornado had actually forged a 2–0 lead against the reigning Turkish champs before ultimately settling for a respectable, hard-fought draw. While in Greece the team was initially scheduled to take a flight from Athens to Cyprus, but the awestruck young travelers spent so much time at the Acropolis they missed their flight.

In a chilling symbol of the war-torn global climate and an unmistakable omen representing the fraught, seat-of-the-pants nature of the Tornado's absurdist jaunt, that flight, British European Airways Flight CY284, exploded in midair, killing all sixty-three people aboard. It was and is still suspected that a bomb was planted in hopes of killing Greek general and guerilla fighter Georgios Grivas, who, like the young footballers, was unable to actually make that flight. Amazingly, the general would ultimately end up on the same flight to Cyprus as the terrified Tornado.

Besides menacing military squads and national teams, the Tornado played (and lost 2–1) against such oddities as a team representing Mitsubishi Heavy Industries in Tokyo on Christmas Eve. Although Crosbie recalled the aforementioned match as being against a Japanese national side that would go on to play in the 1968 Summer Olympics, the Associated Press (AP) account of the contest, which notes that the Mitsubishi Heavy Industries team actually came from behind to beat our heroes, ran in papers from Omaha to Oregon on Christmas Day 1967.[47] Records indicate that the Tornado actually played the Japanese national team in Osaka on Boxing Day; perhaps Crosbie mixed up the two dates in his mind.[48] Surprisingly, the *Dallas Morning News* paid scant attention to the barnstorming tour until the Central American leg, where Hunt, McNutt, and local journalists came aboard. Most available accounts prior to that emanated from wire service reports in other American newspapers.

By the time the team made it through the mountains of Iran and into Pakistan, their numbers had shrunk to just sixteen, with two of those remaining being goalkeepers. The squad had difficulty entering India and some players "were forced to spend two days waiting for their visas in a run-down hotel near the border."[49] Crosbie recalled that the miserable players complained of only having a "small chicken"[50] to eat during the wait. The AP characterized the players as having been "reported lost"[51] before Fries clarified that they had just been "delayed by red tape at a border check."[52] They didn't fare much better once in country, winning only one of the seven matches they played there before being detained due to political riots in Calcutta. Crosbie recalls the team hiding "in our hotel for two days, playing billiards and cards" before leaving "at 4 am to sneak out of India."[53]

The Tornado's surreal visit to Saigon happened in December 1967. Crosbie remembered "being well protected, with a police escort to the hotel" but, conversely, the team was also "allowed to walk around Saigon on our own as sightseers,"[54] earning the enmity and wrath of incredulous U.S. soldiers who warned them of "locals patrolling the area on scooters armed with hand grenades."[55] Harvey recalled a more sinister atmosphere, with "helicopters taking off and going more or less 24–7,"[56] as well as a white-knuckle helicopter ride down the Mekong Delta. Harvey also remembered playing against American military personnel. The Tornado actually emerged unbeaten from Vietnam, earning a 2–2 draw in their last match before leaving the war-torn nation.

The weary team finally returned to Dallas on February 15, where they were met with an "overwhelming reception from more than 1,000 fans."[57] That gesture of warmth and support humbled the globetrotting players and demonstrated the Dallas community's embrace of its Tornado. Forward Chris Tonning told the *Morning News*, "It was more than we could expect,"[58] before emphasizing how much the team "felt at home." Tonning went on to say "Everybody has been very kind to us. They have taken care of us very much. Many families want to help us."[59] It was a remarkable outpouring of support and commitment by a Dallas community already light-years beyond many of its peers in its willingness to accept the team and players as its own.

We've seen that the *Morning News* was instrumental in constructing and conveying a sense of community, a legitimate sense of home that was felt immediately by players who had never even been to Dallas. In an era and enterprise full of identity gyrations and distortions, Dallas' ability to establish this type of rapport with a team that was essentially a cipher filled with unknown young men from Europe was amazing. Poignantly, and strikingly, an unnamed player told the *Morning News* after the ill-fated '68 season, "We tried to be American."[60] It was a naked acknowledgement of the subtle yet acute pressure exerted on the young European men chosen to affect an "all-American" look and persona. The player went on to reaffirm that "we made so many friends" in the community and that "people took us into their homes,"[61] thus demonstrating again the community's willingness to bond with the Dallas Tornado, foreign or not, winners or not.

The players reciprocated in kind, participating in a unique, innovative "pick your seat" promotion at Turnpike Stadium, "meet the Tornado" days, and a match against the North Texas All-Stars, the existence of which in early 1968 is itself indicative of the stirrings of something far greater than the team's middling gate receipts the previous year would suggest. This level of connection seemed to be predicated on more than innovative promotions, but what underpinned it remains elusive. It appears unlikely that it was entirely due to the supposed "all-American" look, though it certainly played well in the 1960s South.

The Tornado were immediately thrust back into the maelstrom after their idyllic welcome to Texas in February. The squad was booked on a treacherous four-game (three in five days) jaunt through Central America. The best results they could scrape out were a pair of 3–3 draws with Club Saprissa and Puntarenas in San Jose, Costa Rica. They lost 2–1 to Olimpia in Tegucigalpa, Honduras, in what was characterized as an "extremely rough game,"[62] which may be why the 4,500 in attendance were so eager to pelt them with orange peels and reeds. Tonning opened the scoring with a header. Not long after, Brian Harvey was sent off for protesting a nasty tackle inflicted on fullback John Stewart. The Tornado were forced to play more than sixty minutes with ten men, conceding twice to ensure a narrow defeat.

At this point, Crosbie confirmed that "all of the players were completely exhausted both mentally and physically."[63] Sadly, like Bob Kap, sacked amid the doomed 1968 season to be replaced by Keith Spurgeon after it dawned on Hunt that his resume was likely the fiction of a con man,[64] Crosbie would not make it to the finish line, either, tearing his ankle ligaments "in a game on a baseball pitch in St. Louis."[65] He was forced to leave the squad after appearing in only six NASL matches. Crosbie's injury reflects a sorry picture of the state of NASL playing surfaces.

He recalled that "many times we played on baseball fields" and in this instance he was "on the shale part of the infield and turned to run back"[66] when his ligaments snapped. It was another unique confluence of politics and fate that would ultimately send Crosbie back to Liverpool, as his work visa only allowed him to play soccer, and during the Vietnam War "foreign nationals who were not using their work visas could be drafted to the U.S.

army."[67] Crosbie's draft status serves as an example that provides real-life context to perhaps the most outlandish rumor that emerged from the USA and NPSL's dirty war.

When the NPSL sued the USSFA and USA, one of its allegations was that those groups spread rumors that foreign players signing for the "outlaw" league were liable to be drafted to fight in Vietnam. This sounds outlandish and over the top, but the threat seems to have emerged from remarks made by Cliff Lloyd, then secretary of Britain's players union. Fearing the supposed economic power of the rogue NPSL and the potential threat it posed for poaching British talent, British administrators quickly and vociferously announced that any players or coaches opting for the NPSL would be banned for life.

Apparently not content with stopping there, Lloyd then invoked the specter of unsuspecting players being drafted to serve in Vietnam.[68] Crosbie's story illustrates the kernel of truth to be found in this dire-sounding scenario. It was not, however, the result of some malevolent plan hatched by the USA, but rather a real stipulation within American work visas at that time.

It was a tour and team completely of the early NASL era: ambitious to the point of naivete and foolishness, buffeted by the turbulent political nature and widespread global strife of a rapidly changing world, and ultimately caught between strange crosscurrents of identity, commerce, and power. Crosbie wondered if such a massive tour, even one that had undoubtedly brought the players closer together personally, was the best way to prepare for the first NASL season. Writing a postmortem of the 1968 campaign, Roy Edwards remarked that "in the history of American sports there may never have been a team like the Dallas Tornado." After cataloging the tour, the multiple coaches, general managers, front-office shakeups, and rapid player turnover, Edwards wrote, "I can only find one word to describe it: Incredible."[69]

NOTES ON 1969: "ALL ACROSS THE USA"

The complex issue of fan identification again reared its head in the wake of the paltry, deflating crowds drawn by the visiting squads from the United Kingdom, which included the Wolves, Dundee United, West Ham, Aston Villa, and Kilmarnock during the NASL's 1969 International Cup. As we've seen with the Dallas Tornado in 1967, many Americans unfamiliar with the game wanted to form bonds with teams they could rightly view as their own, even if that meant watching poorly assembled squads play low-quality soccer.

Most British and foreign observers—Brian Glanville included—incorrectly surmised that average Americans, accustomed to watching and producing the "best," could only latch onto the game if and when they were introduced to the highest quality soccer. ISL creator Bill Cox was another steadfast believer in this notion. The conundrum owners faced was the hard-earned, slowly dawning knowledge that ethnic or "hyphenated Americans," the built-in audience many in the USA/NPSL were absolutely counting on, *were* concerned with quality of play and had stayed away largely because it was initially so poor. This was a perfect storm.

Newly minted American fans were curious about the game but couldn't get behind or attached to foreign teams masquerading as locals. They pre-ferred to watch and support a genuinely local team, no matter how good or bad the team was. Second-generation Americans turned their noses up at the soccer on offer for a variety of reasons. In some instances, like we've seen with New England and Chicago, their solid ties to long-established local and semi-pro leagues offered a quality of play comparable and possibly superior to some of the fledgling professional soccer turned out by the NASL and the USA/NPSL before it.

Like Dallas, Atlanta was another place where soccer seemed to flourish organically, precisely because there was no infrastructure or history of local leagues to compete with or live up to. An unnamed Atlanta Chiefs official told the *New York Times* that "The soccer fans in the city are wanting to see their own favorites play world class sides, not someone else's favorites" and that Aston Villa, standing in as the Chiefs for the summer, were a "great side. But one finds it difficult to attach oneself to a club here on a five week visit."[70] The tournament had barely concluded before Lamar Hunt conceded that "very quickly the project with five British clubs turned sour on us and there is no doubt promotions of this kind are doomed."[71]

In retrospect, it is striking that Hunt and Bill McNutt had no inkling that their local populace, one they were so intimately connected with, would feel this way about an imported team, no matter how charming, talented, and familiar that team was. Dundee United took their role as ambassadors seri-ously, even more so due to the fact that they were very popular in the summer of 1967, and it was obvious that cordial relations between the two organizations continued to exist.

In fact, when speaking of plans for the International Cup to the *Dallas Morning News*, Bill McNutt went so far as to say, "it would be tragic for Dundee United to come to the United States and not come to Dallas."[72] McNutt characterized the Scots as "old friends" and noted "they were well received in their stay here the last time, and the fact that they signed up again knowing they were coming to Dallas speaks for itself."[73] McNutt's glowing remarks were echoed, almost uniformly, by the *Dallas Morning News*, as the paper supported the run-up to the International Cup with consistently sympa-thetic coverage that was singular in its tone and consideration.

Starting from the previously cited article in March 1969, the *Morning News* ran numerous articles touting the impending return of Dundee United. The paper took great pains to emphasize how "much improved" this version of United was, in particular advertising the torrid goal-scoring exploits of the "exciting new star"[74] Kenny Cameron (who had indeed notched an impressive thirty-six goals in thirty-four matches, the second highest total in Europe) throughout the spring. At the end of April the paper ran a handful of articles explicitly inviting the fans to greet United at Love Field at 7:30 pm the night of their arrival, even providing their flight number (American Airlines 069).[75]

Tornado executive director Paul Waters said, "we are not only inviting the public in general, we have also asked all of the Tornado Junior League members to appear in uniform so that the Scotsmen can see the soccer interest in our Dallas youth."[76] As can be seen, the owners and media were positively gushing in their promotion of United's second tenure representing Dallas. Perhaps this bullishness was emblematic of a dominant "win at all costs" strain of American business psychology, a psychology especially prevalent among eminent, successful Texans like McNutt and Hunt that held that the public wouldn't or couldn't fully embrace the "authentic" Dallas Tornado because of their abysmal performance on the pitch throughout 1968. Whatever the origins of such blinding optimism, there is no discernible trace from their public statements of the time that Hunt or McNutt had even the slightest inkling that Dundee United's second tour of duty would fail so spectacularly at the box office. The size and scope of the International Cup's failure was such that it led Hunt to pronounce unequivocally, barely two months after the *Morning News* was breathlessly relaying Dundee United's flight number, that such promotions were henceforth "doomed."[77]

Hunt provided a more detailed explanation to Roy Edwards, saying, "I think that we obviously made a mistake taking on the International Cup aspect."[78] Interestingly, Hunt then said that "it was not a unanimous opinion to take it on. But it was necessary to take it on to keep at least five teams in operation."[79] The Tornado owner then emphasized that "now the unanimous opinion is that if we were starting in 1970 we would not start with the International Cup but would have our own teams all the way."

Even more fascinating is Hunt's admission that the entire idea of importing teams was confusing to a public for whom the game was still largely alien. Hunt told Edwards that he "kept hearing it over and over" and that people were "very confused because we have a Scottish team [Dundee United] here, yet they understand our own team is practicing and they don't understand the relationship between the two. It is very confusing and I think this has contributed to the lack of interest."[80]

As if to underline the identity confusion further, Edwards dutifully informs readers that at halftime during Dundee United's last match as the

"Dallas Tornado," "members of the Dallas Tornado would be introduced."[81] This is the only time an owner of a USA or NASL team ever contemporaneously acknowledged the confusion endemic to the imported team format publicly. This acknowledgment of "confusion" is also an implicit acknowledgement of the bewildering tangle of identities that lies at the heart of the entire ordeal.

After Hunt went public with his thoughts on the rampant consumer confusion, the tone of the *Dallas Morning News* turned abruptly from friendship and warmth to open skepticism, noting that if "the Dallas Tornado has any ideas about taking this town by storm, it must first dispose of a team that didn't—Dundee United."[82] The paper then took up the confusion angle itself for the first time, observing that "an actual confrontation between the two clubs seems the best way of proving that Dundee United is *not* the Tornado. There has been some confusion on this point up until now,"[83] which is comical since the paper did more to solidify the ruse than any other media outlet or mouthpiece. The sudden shift in tone is jarring, as is the incredulous way it seemed to regard the fans' confusion.

Perhaps that confusion partially stemmed from paragraphs that characterized United as returning "home to Dallas from the highlands of Scotland," ready to appear "before the Texas home folk."[84] While recapping a match against Aston Villa in the same piece, the paper described a goal "that got the Dallas club within range."[85] It was the nature and tone of coverage like this that unquestionably helped spread a sense of confusion about exactly who the Dallas Tornado were, particularly after the team played as "itself" during 1968. But no matter the retroactive spin, the fact remained: during the team's three-year existence, its part was twice played by Dundee United, creating a dissonant knot of confused identities.

As the International Cup progressed and the team struggled while attendance sagged miserably, the *Morning News'* characterizations altered ever so slightly, referring to Dundee as "the adopted Texans"[86] before shifting to referring to them almost exclusively as "Dundee United" as the month wore on. Incidentally "the adopted Texans" characterization appeared in a recap of a 3–3 draw with Kilmarnock that was witnessed by less than 800 people. Not surprisingly, there is absolutely no mention of the crowd. On June 1 while recapping the final International Cup match, a 3–2 victory over International Cup champions Wolverhampton, the *Morning News* used no Dallas signifiers in reference to Dundee, repeatedly referring to them as the "Scotsmen"[87] instead.

The gradual shift of their identity, as constructed by the *Morning News* during the International Cup, particularly after Hunt spoke publicly, is fascinating to consider. Hunt still remained of the mind-set that winning and success were the only ingredients that would change the box-office fortunes of his beleaguered team, downplaying the powerful role identity and local connections played in the Tornado's reception by the community. Locals did respond to the Tornado. Locals did begin forming a bond with the historically bad yet authentically constructed 1968 "homegrown" version of the team, because ultimately the community viewed that team as theirs, whether they were truly homegrown or not.

Hunt continued to focus on winning, telling the *Morning News* "we're very much at the mercy of the team record" and that if the team "got off like last year and don't win a game until the latter part of the season we won't attract flies." It is difficult to see how promising signs of fan identification and loyalty were missed so thoroughly, but the philosophical divide between instant success and gradual solidification of local identification continued to manifest itself. This preoccupation would haunt American soccer executives for years.

Buried in the fine print in the story of the International Cup's decisive failure is the fact that nearly 500 people *did* show up at Love Field to greet the Scottish footballers. Roy Edwards wrote that "many of the welcomers were members of Dallas and suburban youth soccer teams, and they were attired in their uniforms."[88] No one could have have known it at the time, but the appearance of "Dallas and suburban youth soccer teams" would provide the foundation of a successful, profitable, and authentically American soccer enterprise.

When Dundee United were set to open their slate of "home" fixtures in Dallas against Villa, it was designated "junior soccer night, with all the Dallas county junior soccer teams in uniform for a pregame parade around the field."[89] The very existence of such junior soccer teams in Texas, a defiant gridiron bastion, in the late '60s was a miracle in and of itself, containing the blueprint for sustained and successful growth going forward. After the Villa match, the Tornado booster club held "a post-game get together" where fans were able to meet players, followed the next day by "a clinic for soccer coaches and game officials."[90] This gradual infrastructure creation was not sexy or profitable, but it was this hard work behind the scenes within local communities that ultimately enabled the game to thrive in the coming decades. Texas youth soccer is now so large and well established that the invitation-only Dallas Cup youth tournament is considered one of the most prestigious in the world, drawing teams from around the globe and adding millions of dollars into the local economy. Although Dundee United and all of the other foreign teams and players who passed through the United States in the late '60s deserve credit for helping spark the existence of youth leagues, it was the youth leagues themselves that would slowly build the game into the cultural and economic force it is today.

NASL owners were interested in having the players visit schools and sponsor clinics for promotional value and for long-term viability, but they could not let go of the idea that foreign teams were the ticket to immediate

success until the massive, embarrassing failure of the International Cup finally put it to rest. It is a testament to the immense wealth of Lamar Hunt, not to
mention his obvious love of sports, that he was willing and able to incur
substantial financial losses with the Tornado, and by extension the entire
NASL, in order to build the game from its grassroots once it became apparent
that short-term fixes like touring English and Scottish sides as stand-ins were
"doomed."

Dramatically, the citizens of Dallas, who so warmly embraced Dundee
United as their own in the summer of 1967, openly rebelled against the Scots
in a bare-knuckled consumerist sense when they returned to reprise their role
as the Dallas Tornado in 1969. Perhaps because in the interim the "real"
Dallas Tornado had been assembled and played an entire campaign in 1968,
a predictably treacherous one wherein they won only two of their thirty-six
league matches after their brutal preseason tour. The hapless Tornado finished the inaugural NASL season with an astonishing –81 (minus eighty-one)
goal differential, being outscored by a four-to-one average each time out. It
got so bad that right before his sacking, Kap was sent back to Europe to
recruit more players, leaving Hunt and McNutt to manage the team. The
team was so awful that the "all-American" look and concept were scrapped
and "foreign stars"[91] from Turkey and South American were drafted. As the
nightmare progressed and the Tornado were a garish, putrid 0–18–3, Hunt
dubbed them the "worst professional athletic team in North America."[92]

Undaunted, Tornado player Brian Harvey told reporters right from the
outset of the International Cup tournament in 1969 that "many Dallas people
who are genuinely interested in the sport made it plain they were not keen to
see a Scottish side ease us out to play for the city."[93] In Texas authentic local
identification proved far more crucial than quality, even when a team's ineptitude reached legendary proportions. After one year of the "real" Tornado,
Dundee United was now irretrievably "foreign," in what amounted to another
fascinating spin of the identity carousel.

This was evidenced by what was perhaps the nadir of the imported team
experiment, when less than 200 fans showed up to see Dundee United and
Kilmarnock play an exhilarating, wide-open 3–3 draw in Dallas that summer.
Harvey surmised correctly that even though the Tornado "had a poor season,
we have at least established an identity."[94] It was this identity predicated on
an invaluable connection with fans that would be clouded and largely undermined by the International Cup project.

New York Generals executive Eugene Scott also reinforced this point
regarding identity around this time. In a striking, nakedly honest fashion,
Scott wrote in the *Times* "that the NASL's plan of importing foreign teams
for adoption by member cities for five weeks in May would not satisfy local
desire for bona fide identification with a top quality soccer club in New
York."[95] It was a simple yet eloquent argument in favor of establishing

legitimate local ties with a franchise that was undercut by the short-term gains of imported teams. The irony is that Dallas easily established such "bona fide identification" whereas New York could not.

Less than two months into the NPSL season, Glanville made a similar observation in the *New York Times* when he noted, "there's not a glimmer yet of fan identification."[96] Always a perceptive observer, Glanville's column was subtitled "Fan identification is necessary to promote the new pro sport in the U.S."[97] This valuable advice was being screamed from the rooftops at the *New York Times*, making subsequent decisions by savvy businessmen such as Hunt and McNutt that much more incomprehensible, particularly when they, unlike most other owners, had a legitimate fan identification foundation.

New York, like Chicago and Boston, had a long historical relationship with the game and boasted well-established semi-professional leagues such as the German-American Soccer League (GASL). New York was also home to the International Soccer League (ISL), but the city would prove to be the hardest market to conquer in the early years of the NASL, even as execs saw Santos and Inter draw more than 41,000 fans to Yankee Stadium in 1966, whipping them into a frenzy as they glimpsed a tangible market that was achingly beyond their grasp.

Glanville, in full acknowledgement of this, remarked that "whatever club represents New York will find itself faced with a peculiar problem."[98] Glanville than asked a pertinent question: whether those representing the Generals "realized the nature of their problem."[99] Judging by Eugene Scott's comments less than a year later, it would appear that they may have realized the nature of their problem a bit too late. The bitter paradox here is that Hunt seemed to realize far too late that he had stumbled onto a solution or at the very least a foothold.

In 1983 Frank Deford observed that Major Indoor Soccer League's (MISL) New York Arrows, with a heavily foreign contingent led by Steve Zungul, had won four straight MISL titles yet were virtually ignored both at the box office and by the powerful and influential local media. Another MISL owner was quoted as saying "he would rather have the Arrows field a less successful team stocked with 'American heroes' than a perennial champion of alphabet unknowns." This strand of thinking is labeled "box-office xenophobia" by Deford, who notes that "there's a clear correlation between success at the gate and Americanization."[100] The fans in Dallas seemed to be of a similar mind in the late '60s, preferring a spectacularly unsuccessful team stocked with "locals" (who were entirely foreign) to a decent foreign team who had been systematically constructed as "local."

Nowhere else in the psychology and lexicon of American sports is losing considered preferable to winning other than in a context like this where dominant conceptions and interpretations of the American identity are challenged. Again we can also see a level of fear and skepticism regarding the game, because it allows foreigners representing the New York Arrows to prove themselves more formidable and more heroic than any random group of "American heroes." This was a symbolic battle that significant elements of American power were unprepared to lose or to suffer gladly.

It's obvious that masculine conceptions of heroism were a preeminent concern for those with the power to shape the construction of the American identity through soccer. These concerns were present from the very beginning of the game's reintroduction, as Andrew Beyer noted in January 1967: "what the league needs are heroes. More specifically, what it needs are American heroes."[101] Andrei Markovits and Steven Hellerman articulated the key stumbling block, which, of course, was that there were "not enough quality players of American origin to stock a first-rate top division soccer league in the U.S." at the time "hence, the problem of 'hero identification,' one of many problems that doomed the NASL, remains."[102]

Due to its lack of "American heroes," the United States appeared weak and exposed on a symbolic battlefield that the rest of the world took seriously. This was certainly an area where the game intersects with and becomes a locus for "contesting notions of masculinity and femininity."[103] It also provides insight into why other nations and ethnicities were systematically feminized in their construction within the USA narrative: it was another way to mask and counteract the glaring paucity of "American heroes" on the pitch.

Shav Glick also ran with this theme, writing a column titled "Pro Soccer Must Develop Heroes."[104] Glick noted that "close association with one's athletic heroes is one of the foundations in the success of sports as a business."[105] He cited an eternal American rite of passage—pretending to be Willie Mays batting in the ninth inning of the World Series in a Little League game—before remarking that "the lack of that association is the biggest single barrier to the success of professional soccer in Los Angeles."[106] No other professional sport in America had grappled with this problem, save perhaps hockey but even then most National Hockey League stars of that era were Canadian and not constructed as foreign or exotic. Glick openly wonders, "can the Los Angeles fan associate himself with Blagoje Vidinic" and others due to their explicit foreignness?

Perhaps it was Cold War stigma, perhaps a blatant example of "box-office xenophobia," but the stridently held assumption that Americans wouldn't get excited about someone with the last name "Vidinic," particularly when folks in America with similar last names were being counted on to float the new leagues, was insidious. This illustrates a dangerous, telling dichotomy: people with those sorts of last names were fit only to buy and not be sold. This connects with why the game's image was so strenuously and consciously manipulated during the early and mid-'70s.

Journalist Murray Olderman wrote a column arguing that one of these flush new outfits should back a truck full of money to Wilt Chamberlain's door and convince him to play goal, thus giving that team an "immediate identity."[107] Olderman also voiced skepticism about the marketability of Eastern Europeans, writing, "I mean, who ever heard of Dragutin Mehandic of the New York Generals" before returning to his feverish ideas of recruiting basketball and football players to speed up the necessary production of "a native hero."[108]

An even more interesting and reality-based take on the situation was provided by Lloyd Hogan of the *Chicago Defender*, who observed that "American sports buffs are a strange breed"[109] that "rarely cotton to any sports invented somewhere other than the good old U.S.A."[110] Hogan went on to note somewhat sarcastically that trying to suck sports-minded folks through the turnstiles was a fool's errand:

> without even offering them a couple of bona fide home state All-America selections for them to cheer on to victory. . . . Just gotta have those All-Americans, man. That "hometown hero" stuff may be a corny gimmick, but it never fails to bring that extra buck to the ticket window.[111]

Hogan acknowledged that Ken Macker had recently emphasized that "our goal is to develop native-born American players to compete in the World Cup,"[112] an authentic creation of "native-born American heroes" within which Dallas and Atlanta would ultimately figure largely.

Toros executive vice president Jack Tobin articulated the need to "eventually have young American boys on our rosters." What is worthy of further examination is the leap between "Americanization" and the desire for "young American boys on our rosters" to the rapid creation of "American heroes." The sloppy, frenzied rush to create such heroes instantly on a nationwide scale could perhaps be understood as part of the logic underpinning the decision to create an "All-American" or single league team at the end of the 1968 NASL season.

After the massive financial losses incurred by all franchises during the NASL's inaugural season, estimated to be between $250,000 and $500,000,[113] some owners and administrators put forth a "league" or "national team" plan. According to the *Washington Post*, "the plan calls for the creation of one team from the best players in the NASL" and that team "would tour the United States and play exhibitions against world-class opposition, such as Santos of Brazil, Manchester City of England and Real Madrid of Spain."[114] The plan also stipulated that league cities would continue to promote the game through clinics.

Backers of this plan seemed to be chasing the big money and big gates that had accompanied visits from globally renowned squads such as Santos,

AC Milan, and Manchester City that summer. The national team plan was also likely conceived as another desperate attempt to Americanize the game. Not only would the national team plan achieve a rapid, entirely symbolic Americanization, it would also serve to elevate such a team to "American hero" status instantaneously, whether actually American or not, were they to start scoring victories over global giants like AC Milan, Santos, and Real Madrid. Viewed through the prism of hero creation, this plan makes more sense contextually. The thorny identity tangle resulting from the fact that nearly all players selected for such a team would be foreign and not American remained but would be obscured by the team's symbolic shroud as a "national" or "All-American" side.

For his part, Washington Whips owner Earl Foreman voiced support for the national team idea, labeling it "attractive," but also admitting that he wasn't "at all sure what it means."[115] Foreman's remarks are a perfectly composed snapshot of NASL ownership's thinking in those early days. The *Post* reported that the "Whips joined seven other members of the North American Soccer League in Chicago in voting to suspend league competition for at least three years in favor of a single league team to play international league games."[116] Whips general manager Peter Haley characterized Foreman is "being a key man in making this decision."[117] It is striking to consider that a month before becoming a "key" decision maker in the process, Foreman was publicly admitting he wasn't sure what it even meant.

This harried, helter-skelter back and forth was indicative of the instinctively poor decision making that was the hallmark of the NASL. To further emphasize the chaotic incompetence of NASL leadership, the *Post* noted that "Dave Smoyer, an assistant to resigned commissioner Dick Walsh, was the only member of the league office at the meeting." That the NASL survived at all is a testament to the herculean efforts of men like Phil Woosnam and Lamar Hunt when only one member of the league office bothered to show up for a meeting that was held to decide the future of the entire enterprise.

Smoyer said the that league team would "compete in each of the participating cities at least three times a year" and that "competition would include such championship teams as Moscow Dynamo; Real Madrid; Santos, Brazil; Manchester United and Tottenham Hodspurs from England." Those in opposition to the national or single-league team idea hoped to operate the NASL as it was presently constituted but on a smaller scale in 1969. A big blow to those hopes was delivered by CBS, which informed the NASL at the November 1 meeting that it would not be renewing its option to televise games during the upcoming year.

The *New York Times* report about the meeting differed slightly in tone, characterizing ownership votes for the "single All-American team"[118] as a gambit to "revolutionize" soccer in America. The move was also depicted as a "glamour tactic to revive interest in the United States," with plans for the "single All-American team" becoming ever more ambitious amid dreams of "perhaps 60 matches next year against international champions."[119] It is notable how frequently the *Times* report uses the word "American," which would serve to underline the fact that the plan should be viewed as an attempt to establish identification with the game on a national scale.

As noted previously, were this team to achieve any measurable level of success, it could instantly create "American heroes"—likely to be foreign, of course, but symbolically American by virtue of being part of the "single All-American team."[120] This would give America some symbolic cachet and respectability in an area where it was sorely lacking. Consideration of this plan also demonstrates that rather than undertaking the hard, slow work of facilitating fan identification city by city, many of the remaining owners remained psychologically wedded to dead-end, short-term strategies.

The tension between the crucial need for cultivating fan identification and, ultimately, "American heroes" and the immediate overall quality of the on-field product so closely intertwined with the Dallas Tornado story was summed up perfectly by Neil Amdur in the *New York Times*, who wrote:

> If it took outstanding American players to interest fans, as many believed, the problem was insoluble, for no American stars were on the horizon. And if it was really good play that Americans wanted to see, that meant the increased use of foreign teams, without building up a following for the NASL clubs.[121]

Woosnam's vision for 1969 was to try and split the impenetrable difference outlined by Amdur and create two separate tournaments in which teams from the United Kingdom once again stood in for American franchises, playing home-and-home series against each other before the "real" NASL teams took over and began a scaled-down regular season on June 1. Woosnam dubbed the first part of the campaign the International Cup, a moniker that bore echoes of Bill Cox's pioneering International Soccer League.

At this point in the story Woosnam had a choice: to rebuild the five remaining teams' infrastructure for the future or to re-embrace foreign teams as a short-term fix. Financial considerations likely ruled the day, and he and other stakeholders probably felt that imported teams offered at least moderate financial gain. But, like Eugene Scott, Woosnam was perceptive enough to realize that local infrastructure building was inextricably linked to establishing firm, durable connections with a local fan base eager to embrace a team as its own. Being at ground zero in Atlanta, where, like Dallas, those very things were starting to occur, it is surprising that Woosnam pushed for and endorsed the International Cup.

Perhaps the most interesting display of the contrasting impulses between the need for local fan identification and the "show 'em the best" soccer mentality played out in Baltimore, where a West Ham United side loaded with no less than three 1966 World Cup stars, including Geoff Hurst and Bobby Moore, came to Maryland to impersonate the Baltimore Bays—or, as Ken Nigro of the *Baltimore Sun* would put it, simply become "West Ham of Baltimore,"[122] echoing the same identity amalgamation used by the *Dallas Morning News*. Nigro even admitted in the next paragraph that "it sounds strange."[123] No wonder the fans in International Cup cities were so confused, much to the chagrin of owners like Hunt.

Much has been written about the impact of the 1966 World Cup finals on the formation of the USA, NPSL, and, ultimately, NASL. The arrival of a loaded, topflight team that included the man who notched an amazing hat trick in front of a reputed twenty million American eyes could only test the strength of the World Cup effect as well as the theory that discerning American fans were staying away from NASL matches due only to the poor quality of play.

Nigro addressed this directly in the *Baltimore Sun*, writing that NASL officials initially "felt all they had to do was put 11 players on the field and crowds would swarm to them"[124] but that the public "refused to pay professional prices for less than professional soccer."[125] Nigro interviewed Bays coach Gordon Jago, who said "the fans have been asking us to get a better product"[126] and "we have one now and we'll see if these people are as keen as they make out to be."[127] This outcry from Bays fans for a higher standard of soccer not only underlines the tension between fan identification and quality, but it provides a direct contrast to the feelings of the Dallas Tornado fans, who wanted "their" team, no matter how historically poor and inept it performed.

Once implementation of the International Cup and the ascension of Phil Woosnam occurred simultaneously in the beginning of 1969, it becomes obvious that the NASL consciously decided to build the game at the grassroots levels, through clinics, at schools, and so forth. The necessity of players fluent in English and thus capable of communicating at said clinics and promotional events is a legitimate factor to be considered relative to why South American teams were not invited to participate in the International Cup.

Woosnam spoke directly about this issue to the *Baltimore Sun*, saying that he felt that one of the USA's "biggest weaknesses was importing teams from all over." Woosnam emphasized that "instead of looking for everything for the ethnic groups, I think it's about time we worry about what the Americans would like" and as a consequence of that "now all of our teams have English speaking players who understand our problems."[128] This adds further confirmation that British teams were chosen largely for the purposes of communication, but it also confirms that issues of ethnic identity were viewed as problematic even by sympathetic figures such as Woosnam. It—as did Glick's piece questioning whether Californians could relate to the Slavic

Toros—also seems to suggest and reaffirm the troubling psychological divide between ethnic groups and Americans, as if the two were mutually exclusive. Issues of ethnicity and identity would continue to be discussed going forward but often using euphemisms such as *image* and *tradition*.

Language barriers aside it still remains suspicious that under the guise of Americanization the Tornado openly and publicly sought an "all-American" look, exclusively recruiting Caucasian men from Liverpool and Denmark initially. Whether conscious or not, these decisions and statements add a racial dynamic to the creation of the NASL that must be considered, specifically when issues of ethnicity were being publicly addressed by Woosnam and others.

One thing the coverage of the 1969 International Cup emphasized was that the teams, West Ham in particular, were to act and to be viewed as footballing missionaries. By all accounts West Ham—and Dundee United, for that matter—took their roles as ambassadors seriously, playing a highflying, exciting, fluid brand of football that produced goals by the bushel. The Hammers had won the FA Cup in 1964 and followed that up with an impressive victory against Bayern Munich in the old, now defunct, European Cup Winners Cup the following season, a triumph the *Daily Mirror*'s Ken Jones described to *Baltimore Sun* readers as confirming "a new dimension of quality."[129] Jones noted that "since then ultimate success has eluded them; but it is their all around influence on the game that marks them as supreme ambassadors for British football."

This is the level of respect and acclaim West Ham United garnered as they made the trek to America that summer. Bay's coach Gordon Jago assured the *Sun* that West Ham "will be excellent sports ambassadors."[130] Woosnam piled the accolades on even further, saying, "they are probably the best missionary club in the world," and "they are first class disciples and will respond to anything asked of them."[131] Woosnam had a special connection to West Ham, playing for the legendary London side known even in the '50s for "attractive, precise play."[132] Woosnam, a stylish footballer with seventeen full international caps for Wales, signed with the Hammers in November 1958. Woosnam's signing prompted West Ham manager Ted Fenton to gush, "Phil is so West Ham he might have been moulded by us." Ron Greenwood, West Ham's manager in 1969, assured the American press that "we wouldn't be here without good intentions. We're here to entertain, to help sell football in America. If we don't do that then I guess we've failed."[133]

Yet, sadly, the Baltimore fans largely stayed away, with the biggest crowd at Memorial Stadium that summer a paltry 5,129. Attendance actually declined for each West Ham "home" match in the Charm City, bottoming out at 2,685. The team was so good that it actually inspired bitter, cranky, generally disinclined American sports columnists to write things like they "could hardly have played better or more attractive soccer"[134] and that the Hammers displayed "an attacking style which was fast moving and interesting to watch."

Those words were written by the *Sun*'s Bob Maisel, who went on to make a few other crucial observations, remarking on the sad fact "that West Ham hasn't even drawn as well as the old Bays did"[135] despite their ability to do things "the old Bays didn't know existed in the game of soccer."[136] Maisel noticed that "apparently, the people preferred to watch a team with which they could identify, a team which really represented the city, even though it played an inferior brand of soccer."[137] This comment encapsulates the tension between fan identification and on-field performance and provides a direct contrast to Jago's assertion that the public was clamoring for a "better product."

The meager attendance would seem to demonstrate rather definitively that fans in Baltimore—like their counterparts in Dallas—wanted above all to support a team they viewed as their own. Maisel also noted the "irony of the overall situation is that Geoff Hurst, the West Ham superstar who had the most to do with causing money people in this country to send up the trial soccer balloon, wasn't able to draw in person."[138] The public was interested in a high-quality product; they just seemed to prefer that such a product be legitimately local.

Hurst's form that summer inspired Tornado president Bill McNutt to exclaim, "I never saw a guy in any sport turn in a more superb performance."[139] He went on to say that Hurst "was fantastic—just a one-man gang," who was "an unselfish player" on top of everything else. McNutt surely would have known, as Dundee United played Hurst's Hammers three times in eight days that summer and were on the receiving end of 6–1 and 8–2 thrashings by the fluid, in-form East London side. All told West Ham hung seventeen goals on the overmatched Scots in slightly more than a week and scored thirty-three total goals in ten matches during their summer jaunt, with a young Trevor Brooking scoring an impressive six himself.

The Hammers ultimately played to only 18,783 paying customers during their five "home" matches in Baltimore. The *Morning News* interviewed West Ham's manager Ron Greenwood, and he told the paper that "football is as much an artistic expression as playing the violin"[140] and that his side approached the game accordingly. Greenwood said that "he saw the light" when he watched "the Hungarians play in 1954,"[141] referring to their epochal 7–1 destruction of England that ushered in the era of the 4–2–4 formation under Gusztav Sebes. Tornado assistant coach John Best remarked that he was "even more convinced that theirs is one of the most talented sides from the skillful and artistic point of view,"[142] stressing that "their goals looked easy" due to "sheer perfection and professionalism."[143]

Despite their magical play and blistering form, West Ham was not able to win the International Cup; that honor for the second time in three summers went to Wolverhampton, which was playing as the Kansas City Spurs. The Spurs/Wolves ended the International Cup unbeaten through eight matches, winning six and scoring a tidy twenty-five goals. Sadly, before the tournament was over and just as Lamar Hunt would do, Gordon Jago told the *Baltimore Sun* "we know now that this type of format is not right."[144] Nigro noted "artistically, West Ham and the other four foreign teams were successful," displaying "an attractive, attacking style" but that "no one has come out to see these clubs."[145] As the aforementioned testimonials reflect, there is nothing else West Ham could have done to draw fans. They sold the game admirably off the pitch and played magnificently on it. If this team, under these circumstances, couldn't win the argument that fans preferred quality, then who could?

This was an emphatic answer to Jago's earlier challenge for the fans to prove that quality was what they really were "keen" on. Nigro went on to observe that "there is no question that the format of adopting foreign teams will not be repeated."[146] It is a testament to the sheer magnitude of the International Cup's failure that many involved in the NASL's upper echelons were repudiating it before it was over. It proved to be the death knell of the strain of thinking that held that all the fans needed and wanted was true quality on the pitch. No one did or ever has doubted the quality and level of soccer that West Ham, the Wolves, Dundee, and the others played in cavernous, sparsely filled stadiums in sweltering heat; it took this much of a loss, this much of an abject failure to finally shift the psychology beyond foreign examples and placeholders.

SURVIVING THE '60S: DALLAS AND ATLANTA—ECHOES FROM THE PAST

As we've seen, the local community formed an emotional connection to the Tornado rather quickly, solidifying Dallas' place as an American soccer stronghold that continues to this day. Dallas-born Kyle Rote Jr. became the first legitimate local "American hero" after being discovered by the indefatigable Lamar Hunt in 1972. Rote was named the NASL's rookie of the year while starring for the Tornado in 1973 and perhaps more importantly became the league's first truly marketable American star, appearing on the cover of *Sports Illustrated* as "Soccer's Great American Hope." FC Dallas has become an MLS institution, carrying on a legacy begun by the loveable, ragtag, homegrown Tornado in 1968. But perhaps the true legacy of that team, and of the Dundee United squad that kick-started the Tornado franchise, is its role in establishing a globally respected youth soccer infrastructure in Dallas. This steady growth culminated with the establishment of the city's annual, incredibly prestigious, invitation-only Dallas Cup youth tournament.

The Dallas Cup was founded in 1980 and has hosted youth teams from more than 100 countries and produced more than 350 World Cup alumni, including Landon Donovan, Wayne Rooney, Javier "Chicharito" Hernandez, and Clint Dempsey. The establishment of the Dallas Cup was a pivotal point on Dempsey and Donovan's journey to international stardom, and thus we were finally able to witness the creation of authentic "American heroes," their creation made possible by events set in motion in the dark dusty days of the USA–NPSL skirmish.

The Dallas Cup draws more than 100,000 spectators annually and brings in nearly $12.6 million to the local economy,[147] sums only dreamed of in the late '60s as money flowed quickly into the red. The very idea of a city in Texas hosting an annual youth soccer tournament with a global reach would have been considered a harmless fantasy of the overstimulated psychedelic minds of the era.

To reinforce the Dallas Cup's direct connection to that time, one must only acknowledge the name of the tournament's elite U-19 Super Group, which is now known as the Gordon Jago Super Group.[148] Jago, the Dallas Cup's executive director from 2002 to 2012, first arrived on the American soccer scene in 1967 as the coach of the NPSL's Baltimore Bays. Jago toured the states as the manager of Fulham, making connections with the Oakland Clippers' ownership group before being hired by the Bays. During his playing career, Jago captained England's youth team a handful times against Holland, Switzerland, and Belgium, an honor that likely cemented his passion for youth soccer.[149] Jago also had a brief two-match stint coaching the U.S. men's national team in 1969 during the World Cup qualifiers before tours of duty with QPR, Millwall, the Tampa Bay Rowdies, and, finally, the Dallas Sidekicks.

Under his leadership and on the strength of his connections, youth squads representing global behemoths such as Manchester United, Real Madrid, and Arsenal have all played in the Dallas Cup. Jago was named a Member of the Order of the British Empire for his contributions to soccer worldwide, his undeniable impact on the game's growth at all levels in America bridging perfectly the past and present. It is only fitting that two of the "all-American cities" singled out by Woosnam all those years ago would thrive in this fashion.

It's amazing how durable and persistent the idea that instant success is more important than building or establishing a sense of fan identification is in American soccer psychology. This is again bleeding through the headlines in 2014. It can be glimpsed in an ESPNFC piece by British writer Iain Macintosh titled "MLS Miami Will Need Results, Not Becks' Star Power, to Succeed."[150] In it Macintosh—echoing Lamar Hunt, among others, in defiant proof that old ideas die hard—argues that David Beckham's newly proposed Miami MLS franchise will prosper only if it's successful on the pitch. Never mind that the Portland Timbers, a hugely successful franchise of recent vintage, has been a raging success without notable results on the pitch (until recently) due to their willingness to embrace the need of establishing solid fan identification first and foremost.

Macintosh argues that Miami is a tough sports market and notes that the MLS failed in it once before, not to mention the NASL, before writing that the Miami franchise "will be just another football team and their success or failure in the city will largely depend on how they perform on and off the pitch."[151] One wonders why off-pitch performance matters so much if what's truly important—as Macintosh's column seems to hold—is the team's success on it. Amazingly, in the next sentence, referring to the failure of the MLS's Miami Fusion, Macintosh observes that the Fusion's "demise was attributed, in part, to a lack of identification with local residents."[152]

The main thing that's changed during the past few decades is that at least now most writers and league brass are aware of the importance of local identification, even if they still prioritize it below success in importance. In the late '60s only a handful of executives and pundits seemed to truly recognize its importance. It is incredible that the tension and dynamic between these two philosophies are still in conflict decades later, as they so clearly were in the period between 1967 and 1969. It seems impossible that the MLS hasn't learned that the importance of establishing a sense of local fan identification and community far outstrips instant success. The Oakland Clippers should stand as a testimony that immediate success means nothing without the ability to forge legitimate connections to the local community.

It's also strange how, in paying lip service to "identification with local residents," Macintosh seemingly refuted or contradicted his entire argument on behalf of instant success by writing of Miami's need to "build loyalty before building revenue."[153] The refusal to acknowledge the pivotal importance of creating fan identification and the stubborn eagerness on the part of many American soccer stakeholders to steadfastly repeat past mistakes positively oozes from this column.

If lack of local fan identification doomed the Miami Fusion, why wouldn't it also doom David Beckham's franchise? Has the sterling, highly studied example of the Seattle Sounders not taught us anything? The Sounders established themselves as part of the identity of young, urban, multicultural Seattleites, which helped ensure and solidify their massive success before they started winning regularly on the field.

MLS marketing director Howard Handler gushed to ESPN after participating in the Emerald City Supporters' "mind-blowing"[154] procession to Qwest Field from Pioneer Park that after mingling with Sounders fans, "I realized that their support was an expression of their own identities—a reflection of who they are and what it means to be 20- and 30-year-olds in Seattle."[155] It is almost solely on the strength of this expression, this level of ironclad identification, that former National Basketball Association (NBA) commissioner David Stern called the Sounders "the most successful expansion team in the history of sports."[156] That success rests almost entirely on the level of fan identification that was created and nurtured before, and existed independently of, any tangible success the Sounders enjoyed on the pitch.

Even now as one of the MLS's marquee franchises, they have yet to win the MLS Cup. So why are people still obsessed with the notion that success on the pitch is the most important driver and signifier of success in American soccer? The example set by the Sounders, one so radiant and epic that the NBA and leagues around Europe were forced to take note and pay homage, is built on identifying and establishing an authentic bond with the local community. Luckily for the MLS and American soccer, the Sounders' owners are smart enough to know "we didn't create anything they did."[157] They're also "careful not to disrupt the organic growth and authenticity"[158] of what has developed in Seattle, something for which all American soccer fans should be grateful.

There is a direct line between the fan identification first conjured by the Tornado all the way through its fullest, most authentic and organic expression in Seattle with the Sounders. Dallas is the bridge that binds the story together temporally. Gordon Jago and the "Gordon Jago Super Group" demonstrates the impact Phil Woosnam and the NASL's decision to build the game through youth by creating a youth soccer infrastructure has had on the game's undeniable growth and positioning in American today. The concept of identity and local identification that was demonstrated dramatically within the ripples created by the 1968 Dallas Tornado continued to gather strength, with the crashing waves of the new millennium Seattle Sounders providing the fullest, most authentic expression of what that identification means and looks like in the modern era.

Outside of the Cosmos, a case can be made that the Atlanta Chiefs were the most influential team of the pre-MLS era. Some reasons for this: the Chiefs were Phil Woosnam's gateway to becoming one of the most pivotal figures in the development of postwar American soccer; they introduced the world to the NASL's inaugural rookie of the year, Kaizer "Boy Boy" Motaung, who would eventually form South Africa's wildly successful Kaizer Chiefs, their name itself a homage to Motaung's NASL beginnings; the Chiefs' two improbable victories against Malcolm Allison's Manchester City, then champions of England, victories that are still etched into American soccer lore. But perhaps the most important legacy of the Chiefs was their youth soccer programs, which "have mushroomed far beyond their in-town roots, yielding suburban stars like 2002 U.S. World Cup players Clint Mathis and Josh Wolff."[159] Again we glimpse the end product, the organic creation of "American heroes" after decades of painstaking work. This systemic ability to produce World Cup–caliber players was the ultimate fruition of the best laid plans of men like Woosnam and it is only fitting that the groundwork he painstakingly undertook would pay off in such spectacular fashion.

The full gravity and depth of this accomplishment sinks in even further when considering Woosnam's view of Atlanta when he arrived. The Welshman described Atlanta as "the least soccer-educated city in the league."[160] This comment was prompted by the observation that the 1967 Atlanta Chiefs were loaded with British players, which again brought up the language issue. Woosnam said "the game is hardly played in Atlanta so we felt we had to get players who could speak English"[161] so that they could "get out and try to build up the sport." This dramatically illustrates not only Atlanta's barrenness as a soccer city in 1967, but also serves as an important precedent for establishing Woosnam's views on the language barrier, which would be manifested in his selection of five U.K.-based teams for the International Cup.

But even in the span of one year, soccer grew tremendously in Atlanta, as did the Chiefs. Woosnam said "when we came to Atlanta nobody knew anything about our sport. Soccer was played in ten private schools. This year, 41 schools played it and next year 70, or 100% will play it."[162] If that wasn't encouraging enough, Woosnam noted that "Georgia Tech has just adopted it as a varsity sport, and the University of Georgia is taking it up."[163] Extremely impressive progress in the course of a year, particularly when considering the entire fulcrum of NASL power would shift to the city that same winter, giving Atlanta an elevated level of importance through the early '70s before league offices moved back to New York.

The New Georgia Encyclopedia has some other interesting numbers to put this growth in perspective, noting that the Georgia State Soccer Association (GSSA) was formed in 1967. Besides reacting to the galvanizing pull of the Chiefs, the GSSA was formed to provide structure to the "amateur teams consisting of Scottish and South American migrants"[164] who had been competing "informally with teams from Lockheed-Georgia (later Lockheed Martin)."[165] Lockheed had opened a plant in Marietta in 1951 and started "its own league,"[166] which ties it, and by extension the South, into the established American tradition of factory-sponsored soccer teams like Bethlehem Steel. Research has been done on factory teams in New England and Pennsylvania but little has been done at all on such teams in the South. Traces of company-sponsored teams also appear on the West Coast, with Boeing fielding two teams in Washington's State Soccer league as far back as 1968.[167] This suggests an area ripe for further research, particularly since the *New Georgia Encyclopedia* traces soccer in Georgia all the way back to the 1920s, when it was played by employees of the John H. Harland Company.[168]

The legendary matches between the Chiefs and Manchester City deserve a special mention as a galvanizing force in the Chiefs' ability to cast such a considerable shadow. The two contests drew crowds in excess of 23,000 and 25,000 fans. Woosnam cited these matches and the Chiefs' surprising ability to meet the Citizens on what he termed "equal footing" as crucial in getting fans "emotionally involved."[169] In remarks to the Sports Reporters Association (SRA), Woosnam again mentioned fan identification, stressing that it was "good for the fans who get emotionally involved with their team."[170]

It is striking that Woosnam would then become the driving intellectual and administrative force behind the International Cup (also known as the "Atlanta plan"), which would go a long way toward undermining the very emotional involvement that he was breathlessly describing to the gathered reporters. There was obviously no way for him to know the full extent of the catastrophe and sheer number of defections that would rock the NASL at the end of the season, but it was no secret even then, in the summer 1968, that many franchises were barely surviving. Woosnam alluded to it himself while addressing the SRA, saying, "we'll lose some more money and we'll lose some teams."[171] One can only assume that despite this bravado, he was not completely unprepared for the scale of the carnage and attrition that marked the end of the NASL's inaugural season, nor did he have any early inkling that he would be called upon to keep the league afloat.

Some insight into Woosnam's psychology as well as the general gloom that presided over the NASL in the winter of 1968–69 can be glimpsed in his comment that "It was a blank period in our life."[172] Such blankness and desperation were perhaps what led Woosnam to make such a major miscalculation wagering on the International Cup, particularly after he had publicly criticized the USA's format. The International Cup, along with everything else, dramatically short-circuited fan identification at a critical juncture for the NASL.

Amateur and youth soccer would flourish through the treacherous ebbs and flows of the professional game in Atlanta, and the Georgia Youth Soccer Association (GYSA) was formed in 1974 after the original incarnation of the Chiefs had morphed into the Atlanta Apollos. In its first year of operation the GYSA boasted "200 statewide registrants," a number that would balloon to a "peak of more than 80,000 in 2001."[173] Programs for women also started in earnest during the '70s, with the Decatur–Dekalb YMCA forming one of the first female recreational leagues.

Finally, in the fraught racial climate of the times, the Atlanta Chiefs provided a vision of a more harmonious future during the nation's darkest days. Woosnam noted that after he accepted the position with the Chiefs "the very next news item that came in showed the Mayor of Atlanta standing on top of a car in the midst of a riot."[174] This was the context in which the Chiefs found themselves operating. Besides fielding an unabashedly diverse, multiracial unit, the Chiefs' front office led by Atlanta Braves vice president Dick Cecil integrated the team's offices and facilities, no mean feat in the late-'60s South. The Chiefs and Braves also started neighborhood outreach programs, such as the Good Neighbor Program to address and assuage ill will and concerns over the contentious construction of Atlanta–Fulton County Stadium.

The stadium, like many during that era, was built in a longstanding African American neighborhood, displacing families and disrupting a community that had thrived for years. To make matters worse, Atlanta's mayor at that time, Ivan Allen, spoke of the stadium's location as part of his plan to create a "buffer zone" around the downtown area,[175] further inflaming tensions. Years later Cecil would recall threats to his home and family. Yet the Chiefs not only persevered, but flourished, providing an example of racial coexistence that was influential and inspirational. The team's 1968 NASL title also confirmed that racial harmony could power a collective to achieve considerable objectives.

It was ironic that before playing for Atlanta in the feverish '60s Kaizer Motaung had never played desegregated football at any level in his native South Africa. The irony was compounded when he was inspired partly by his time in America to form the Kaizer Chiefs in 1970 and to do so in hopes of establishing a "team that emphasized through words and deeds, on and off the pitch that soccer was about comradeship, about friendship, sportsmanship."[176] It's a testament to the unique blend of people and circumstances in Atlanta that those are the lessons and values Motaung was able to experience, internalize, and perpetuate from his sojourn in the states. The global legacy of the Chiefs serves as hopeful counterpoint to the unifying power of the game during an era where it was used to further exclude and divide a fractured America.

Chapter Seven

1968–1969

Scenes and Sketches from the American Frontier

MERGERS AND ACQUISITIONS

Merger talks between the warring United Soccer Association (USA) and National Professional Soccer League (NPSL) began heating up after USA's season ended in mid-July. By August confidence was high that the two leagues would officially merge. There were talks planned in Chicago for early September, when nearly all involved felt a merger would be finalized. Instead, on the eve of the second leg of its championship tie between the Oakland Clippers and Baltimore Bays, the NPSL announced an eighteen-million-dollar antitrust lawsuit in federal court against FIFA, United States Soccer Football Association (USSFA), and USA.

According to the *New York Times*, the suit alleged that "in violation of Federal antitrust laws, the defendants have entered into a conspiracy to drive the National Professional League out of soccer."[1] The suit also charged that the defendants "made a contract giving the United Soccer Association exclusive control for 10 years over who may operate pro soccer teams in the United States." The lawsuit sought damages and an injunction that would essentially prevent all USA teams from operating in America until "the National Pro League and its members are granted recognition."

NPSL commissioner Ken Macker told Andrew Beyer that the league felt it had to take this drastic step after the talks in Chicago disintegrated and problems between the groups appeared "insurmountable."[2] According to Beyer, the merger foundered on the rocks of the NPSL's television contract with CBS, which USA officials allegedly leaned heavily on the NPSL to renegotiate. The USA was also characterized as "intransigent" on the issue of cities where both leagues competed. Finally, USA demanded that its commissioner, Dick Walsh, assume the same role in the newly merged league. A USA official bleated to Beyer that it was "untenable and repugnant for them to think that Macker could become an official of a recognized league after heading up an outlaw league."[3]

This comment summed up the arrogant bluster the USA brought to the merger talks. Beyer observed that the NPSL seemed to have entered the negotiations "with self-deceptive optimism and a curious form of doublethink" because it tried to conduct itself as an equal. Perhaps this optimism stemmed from the fact that the organization was ready to play the antitrust suit stashed up their sleeve. Macker said the NPSL was ready to file the suit as early as August 16, but withheld believing then that a merger was imminent. It was a predictable denouement to a saga that couldn't have ended any other way.

The merger that created the North American Soccer League (NASL) was officially announced on December 7, 1967. Earl Foreman was a member of the USA committee that spent eighteen hours ironing out details during a frantic session in Cleveland. In typical stuttering, sketchy NASL fashion, the merger was publicly announced on December 7, but a closer look at the fine print revealed it was "contingent on the NPSL's resolving by December 31 its troubles with soccer's ruling bodies."[4] Ultimately, the merger was finalized but the decision to announce its passage publicly, when there was still a significant chance for it to be scuttled after many similar mishaps and false starts, was pure NASL. This pattern would repeat itself after the 1968 season with the bizarre, premature announcement of the NASL's suspension prior to the International Cup.

A compromise was reached that saw Ken Macker and Dick Walsh each preside over a conference in the new league. The Pittsburgh Phantoms and Philadelphia Spartans folded almost immediately. The thorny issue of cities with two teams was worked out in a largely bloodless fashion. Toronto City bowed out, leaving Ontario entirely to the Falcons. The Los Angeles Toros moved south to San Diego. The Boston Rovers vanished into thin air, leaving the Boston Beacons to represent Massachusetts soccer. The San Francisco Golden Gales melded into the Vancouver Royals, and the New York Skyliners were completely subsumed by the New York Generals. Finally, a group headed by attorney John Latshaw took over the Chicago Spurs and relocated them to Kansas City. When the smoke cleared, seventeen franchises remained to compete in the NASL's inaugural season.

SANTOS SCENES: SOUTH AMERICAN SOCCER TROUBADOURS STRIKE OUT

A reference to the existence of the Cleveland Stokers while researching the history of the Stoke City Potters for a blog post about the 2011 FA Cup final brought the USA era to my attention. I grew up in the rust belt and the thought of the Cleveland Stokers running onto the pitch of Municipal Stadium, tenderly known in some quarters as "the Mistake by the Lake," with English legend Gordon Banks in the net seemed too fantastic and outrageous to believe, a colorful scene so callously edited out of the grainy, sepia-toned American sports narrative.

Besides the fact that he managed to import one of the world's oldest club sides, the Stokers' original owner Vernon Stouffer (who also owned the Cleveland Indians) scored an undeniable coup—not to mention instant credibility for the USA—by bringing in Banks, who after winning the World Cup, was transferred to Stoke City from Leicester in April 1967, just in time to be shipped off to the shores of Lake Erie. Banks wasn't able to come to the States until June due to national team obligations, but he was there June 13, when he made his American debut in a 2–2 draw with the Washington Whips.

The 1967 Cleveland Stokers also boasted the services of Banks' World Cup–winning teammate George Eastham and other well-known English players such as Peter Dobing, Roy Vernon, and Maurice Setters. Sadly, the Stokers franchise would not survive the great purge of 1968–1969, folding at the end of the first NASL campaign. Cleveland narrowly missed contending for the USA title, finishing one point behind the Washington Whips. They would also lose a heart-stopping, extra time semifinal tie against the eventual NASL champion Atlanta Chiefs in 1968. After two seasons in Cleveland, the Stokers finished with nineteen wins, fifteen draws, and ten losses, good for fourth-highest winning percentage among NASL teams, according to the Ohio Historical Society. [5]

But the Stokers would not fall quietly through the cracks of history as a July 12, 1968, *Los Angeles Times* headline loudly attests: "Near Riot Follows Santos First Loss." [6] That headline hovered over a recap of the decidedly non–Stoke City yet still formidable homemade version of the Cleveland Stokers, which shockingly defeated Pele's Santos side, 2–1. The result almost instigated "Cleveland's first soccer riot" after the officials negated a Santos equalizer with an offside call near the end of the match.

This version of the Stokers was a ragtag amalgamation consisting of the nucleus of the NPSL's lovably bruising, now-defunct Philadelphia Spartans squad (who had finished in second place in the Eastern Division only five points behind Baltimore) and various other upstarts and journeymen. One of the players inherited from the Spartans was the NPSL's most valuable player,

Ruben "the Hatchet" Navarro, a wily veteran center-half who had assumed coaching duties for Philadelphia near the end of the season, acquitting himself brilliantly. Navarro was an Argentine international well acquainted with and known to torment the great Pele.

Navarro and Pele knew one other from many epic international and domestic South American battles during Navarro's time at Independiente, with the two sides warring regularly over the Copa Libertadores crown. Pele once called Navarro "the greatest defensive player in all of South America."[7] For his part, Navarro said, "I enjoy playing against him very much. Pele is a man who will play an honest game of soccer."[8] The Stokers also featured surprising firepower in the form of Enrique Mateos, a fixture on the legendary, dynastic Real Madrid squads of the 1950s.

Santos had just demolished the Boston Beacons 7–1. It had been a relatively easy ride through the States for the Brazilians up until that point. They were undefeated and racking up big-time box office numbers everywhere they went. As far as their NASL competition was concerned, Pele told the *Cleveland Plain Dealer* before the match that "St. Louis and Kansas City were the best teams we played so far."[9] Pele himself had to swoop in and rescue Santos with the winning strike against the St. Louis Stars in what turned out to be a tense, relatively difficult 3–2 victory for the Brazilians.

There were an amazing 16,205 supporters at Cleveland Municipal Stadium to witness this incredible, one-of-a-kind match. Mateos opened the scoring on a penalty that he deposited sharply into the upper right-hand corner. Dietrich Albrecht scored the winning goal with less than eight minutes remaining after Pele brilliantly orchestrated Toninho's equalizer. Santos appeared to have snatched a draw from the jaws of defeat on another Toninho strike with just more than a minute to play, but linesman Jack Connor signaled for offsides and Santos erupted in protest.

The *Plain Dealer* described the incident at the end of the match as a "melee,"[10] wherein the "Brazilian team swarmed over the officials and wound up arguing with fans." Bill Nichols wrote that when Toninho's face-saving equalizer was waved off, "the entire Santos team swarmed over the beleaguered official in protest." Some enraged Santos players "climbed on tarpaulin near the third base dugout and proceeded to yell and throw sand at the partisans, while time ran out." Nichols recalled that "Pele spit at fans in the lower seats" while teammates "climbed into the lower deck" and kicked at the linesmen. Referee Henry Landauer said, "I've refereed numerous international matches and never had anything like this occur."[11] It was Santos' first defeat in North America.

Two days later the New York Generals would register unquestionably the biggest result in their brief history when they also defeated Santos 5–3 in Yankee Stadium. Just as in Cleveland, Santos drew a fantastic crowd of more than 15,000 (15,645) that saw a charged-up, well-rested Generals squad blaze out of the gate. The Generals raced to 3–0 lead against the tiring Brazilians "with sheer power and doggedness they had never displayed before,"[12] according to Gerald Eskenazi. Generals coach Freddie Goodwin instructed his team to stop Pele from getting on the ball by pressing relentlessly, which they did, mounting a sustained attack the weary Santos players were unable to withstand.

As Eskenazi noted, "the New Yorkers had only played once in the previous 11 days and they were prepared to run through the tepid night." The speedy Warren Archibald scored twice for New York within the first seventeen minutes before future World Cup–winning manager Cesar "the Cannon" Menotti added a third with a close-range shot. Other notables on the pitch for the Generals included future Cosmos coach Gordon Bradley, "a heavy-footed powerful Briton" tasked with marking the one-and-only "Black Pearl." Bradley acquitted himself well against his future Cosmos charge, save for an own goal (OG) he was responsible for, which finally put the Brazilians on the board. Santos traveled to Washington, D.C., immediately afterward, where Pele recorded a hat trick in 3–1 victory over the Whips in what was Santos' fifth match in just nine days.

In the end, Santos went 6–2 against the NASL and made so much money (a reported $250,000) that they came back to America near the end of August for additional dates. The *Baltimore Sun* reported that they received $27,000 for every appearance.[13] They were such a huge, tantalizing draw that their success may have inadvertently sown the seeds for discord among NASL owners tired of losing money (like those of the Generals, Whips, and California Clippers) and those committed to building a domestic league infrastructure, no matter how painfully unprofitable it seemed at the time. This is one of a handful of factors that led the Clippers to break away and play an independent slate of friendlies, prompting (whether intentionally or not) others to give it serious consideration.

THE 1968 NASL CHAMPIONSHIP: ATLANTA CHIEFS VS. SAN DIEGO TOROS

Though much has been written about the Atlanta Chiefs, very little is known about the San Diego Toros. Original owner Dan Reeves lost interest in the Los Angeles Toros franchise and sold it to a group that included none other than Bill Cox. Cox was the co-owner and general manager of the San Diego Toros before abruptly selling his interest in the club on June 26, 1968—in the middle of the NASL season. Cox reportedly owned 20 to 25 percent of the Toros before selling to Emilio Azcarraga so he could immediately take an executive vice president position with the St. Louis Stars.[14] It was a curious move by an exceedingly curious figure.

The Toros operated out of Balboa Stadium and had a "distinct Latin/ South American bent to their roster."[15] The team was filled with considerable talent, including goalkeeper Ataulfo Sanchez, who had conceded only nineteen goals in twenty-two matches, including eight clean sheets. Sanchez, an Argentine, joined the Toros from the decorated Mexican side Club America, becoming a significant part of their surprising title challenge. Right-half Severo DeSales was also a Club America alum, suiting up more than 200 times for the club, including during their 1962 Mexican Cup run. Right-back Miroslav Milovanovic was a former Yugoslav Olympian. These men formed the core of a stingy unit that finished second in defense, behind only the Chiefs.[16]

Team captain Ron Crisp was a holdover from the Los Angeles Toros and had played one of the link positions in their 4–2–4 formation. The left-half played every minute of every match (the only Toro to do so) at such a high level in 1968 that he was named to the NASL All-Star team. Inside-left Vava featured for the legendary 1958 and 1962 Brazilian World Cup–winning sides, and at thirty-four years old had scored four goals during the NASL campaign. Forward Cirilo "Pepe" Fernandez tied for the NASL goal-scoring lead with Chicago's John Kowalik, netting thirty goals to help the Toros win the Western Conference by a razor-thin margin over the Oakland Clippers.[17]

Fernandez became an NASL fixture, starring for the 1969 NASL Champion Kansas City Spurs before a stint in the Eredivisie and a return to the states with the Seattle Sounders. During his torrid, prolific season, the Toros were forced to pay $25,000 to Club Emelec of Ecuador due to a dispute regarding the legality of his contract.[18] Fernandez helped pace a Toros attack that scored sixty-five times. The squad was coached by George Curtis, an Englishman who had managed Brighton & Hove Albion.

The NASL mandated an idea that the NPSL threatened to do once the 1967 season had began, which was to institute a two-legged semifinal aggregate tie between the division leaders in each conference to decide who would play in the finals. The Toros finished 18–8–6 (identical to the Oakland Clippers), good enough for first in the Pacific Division on the strength of a single point due to NASL's adoption of NPSL's bizarro scoring system, and a chance to meet the Gulf Division winners, the Kansas City Spurs.

The Spurs were also capable of filling the net, featuring noted target men such as Willie Roy, Eric Barber, and former Aberdeen goal poacher Ernie Winchester. The first leg of the tie played out as a tight 1–1 draw in Kansas City in front of 5,041 fans.[19] Ataulfo Sanchez would take care of the rest. The keeper shone throughout a gut-wrenching, scoreless contest in Balboa Stadium that the Toros finally won 1–0 in extra time. Only 6,271 were on hand to see San Diego clinch their place in the inaugural NASL championship.[20]

The Atlanta Chiefs picked up where they had left off the previous year, playing tight, aggressive defense—particularly in Atlanta, where they were nearly impenetrable—and then counterattacking with guile, precision, and pace. The Chiefs also got excellent goaltending from Vic Rouse, who, one-upping the dominant Sanchez, had conceded just twenty-five goals in twenty-six matches. The Chiefs' attack was not as potent as San Diego's. The Chiefs had scored just fifty goals, putting them thirteenth out of seventeen teams. They made up for their tepid scoring punch with a thumping physical style that saw them rack up 577 fouls throughout the NASL season.[21] The Chiefs generated their attack from the still-stylish and slick Woosnam, the ageless forward Peter McParland, who, like the Toros' Vava, was a veteran of the 1958 World Cup, and of course a young South African dynamo named Kaizer "Boy-Boy" Motaung. As Atlantic Division winners, Atlanta earned a date with the Cleveland Stokers to decide who would represent the Eastern Conference in the NASL title game.

Similar to what had transpired in Kansas City, the two teams battled to a cagey 1–1 draw in Cleveland. Atlanta struck first on a great individual effort by Willie McIntosh in the thirty-second minute. The Stokers countered near the end of the first half when Enrique Mateos lofted a beautiful cross to Amancio Cid to head home for his fourteenth goal of the season. This was all Atlanta needed to see, withdrawing into a massed, mobile bank of defense that the *Cleveland Plain Dealer*'s Dan Coughlin compared to Helenio Herrera's Inter Milan.[22] Saying "we would have liked to come out," Woosnam insisted that it was the Stokers who pushed them back into such a cautious, cynical posture. In testimony to why forms of *catenaccio* were so hated, the Stokers' exasperated Hank Liotart summed it up, saying "it was impossible to penetrate when they have eight men standing in a line."[23]

Atlanta withdrew, satisfied to frustrate the Stokers and play for a draw. Their 10–3–3 home record stood as a testament to how difficult it was for teams to win in Fulton County Stadium. The match turned out to be the Cleveland Stokers' Midwestern swan song, the last time they would play in Ohio. Only a miniscule 3,431 turned out, illuminating the writing on the wall with ominous force. It was a sad ending.

After ninety hair-raising minutes, the Eastern Conference championship remained deadlocked at 1–1 and it seemed like anything, including another match in Cleveland, was possible. It was Mateos again who influenced the match for the Stokers, scoring seven minutes into the first overtime period. The momentum shifted decisively to Cleveland. Woosnam admitted afterward that his "players packed it in,"[24] ready to concede defeat. The Stokers eased up ever so slightly, as well, and Cid spurned an excellent chance with less than five minutes to go in the first overtime. It was a reprieve Atlanta desperately needed and would seize fiercely. Suddenly Atlanta was ascendant.

Peter McParland was on the bench until the second overtime. He entered the match and with time draining from the clock, scored the equalizer with fifty-one seconds left. Vic Crowe managed to chip the ball to McParland through heavy traffic in front of Paul Shardlow's net and the old warhorse slid it home. The Stokers were devastated and would not recover. Kaizer Motaung scored the winning goal minutes later. [25]

As the Chiefs prepared to win the city of Atlanta's first professional sports title, the air of uncertainty swirling around the NASL's future began to seep into public reports. The *Marietta Journal* reported that the Chiefs were "desperately trying to keep from folding." [26] The *Journal* even hinted darkly that the Chiefs "might stick together to play exhibitions with some of the better known foreign teams after quitting the NASL." This again brought the ever-so-unfriendly topic of international friendlies back to the forefront.

The embarrassing attendance at Cleveland showed that there was clearly blood in NASL waters. To put the friendly issue in proper perspective, Atlanta averaged around 5,500 in attendance for NASL matches during its first-place season but averaged a staggering 25,000 spectators during the course of their three exhibitions with Manchester City and Santos. [27] Numbers like these were why NASL franchises jockeyed for and ultimately chased exhibition-heavy schedules like the Holy Grail. It was one of the underlying reasons they fought so hard to be recognized. It was the fissure at the center of so many problems, squabbles, and conflicts throughout this era, going back to the International Soccer League's (ISL) travails in the early '60s.

The championship series between the Toros and Chiefs had an anticlimactic feel after the high drama that occurred between Atlanta and Cleveland. The first match, held in front of 9,360 at Balboa Stadium, was a relatively drab affair highlighted by the heroics of Ataulfo Sanchez. The Chiefs attacked with ferocious intent, seeking an early advantage, only to have Sanchez make save after brilliant save in the opening half hour. The contest slipped into neutral and ended 0–0. [28] San Diego now faced the daunting trip to Atlanta.

A raucous crowd of 14,494 showed up to watch the Chiefs build a solid 2–0 lead in the first half. McParland struck again in the twenty-third minute on a nice pass from Brian Hughes. It was the first goal scored by either team in three head-to-head meetings. Motaung began to grow in stature, causing trouble in front of Sanchez, who spilled a rebound of Boy-Boy's header that Delroy Scott punched home for a two-goal advantage. The Chiefs clamped down and began playing defense with their normal ferocity, flustering the Toros, who seemed out of ideas. Motaung clinched the title in style for Atlanta, dribbling past markers like traffic cones before rifling a shot past Sanchez to make it 3–0. [29] The Chiefs were the first NASL Champions. The Toros would vanish without a trace.

Atlanta swept up postseason accolades just as they had swept through the NASL playoffs. Kaizer Motaung was named the NASL rookie of the year, the first step in an incredible voyage that would see him become a globally renowned sportsman. Phil Woosnam won the coach of the year award for guiding the Chiefs to the title.[30] Woosnam's resume was expanding rapidly, as he'd also been named coach of the U.S. Men's national team—such as it was in those dark days—in addition to his duties as player, coach, and general manager for the Chiefs. His resume would soon expand even further as the NASL stared into the abyss during the winter of 1968.

EUROPE '68

In the fall of 1968, the Washington Whips' very future hung in the balance, so naturally they did what any struggling American soccer franchise would do: take off on a European tour. The Whips left Dulles Airport at 2 pm on October 3, 1968, "with the survival of the North American Soccer League in serious doubt."[31] Team officials admitted that the tour was expected to generate "at least a modest profit for the financially troubled Whips," remarking to the *Post's* Andrew Beyer that "we definitely wouldn't have gone on the trip if we were going to lose money." Such was the sorry state of affairs in the states that the Whips were actually expected to draw more in Europe than they did in the in Washington, D.C.

The Whips' tour fits into a larger pattern of behavior. NASL teams like the New York Generals increasingly talked of adding more exhibitions as a viable revenue stream, since most teams drew their largest houses of the year by far when either playing against or hosting global giants like Santos. The Whips were no different, drawing more than 20,000 for Santos' visit in July.[32] The Oakland Clippers had already decided to break away from the league to play an independent exhibition slate after all of their geographical rivals folded. The *Post* reported that the Whips had matches scheduled in Germany, Sweden, and Denmark and that general manager Pete Haley was trying to arrange a friendly with the team's former alter ego, the Aberdeen Dons.

In typical Whips fashion, the ramshackle outfit left for their first match in Lubeck, Germany, without a manager. Fullback and team captain John Worbye was to manage to the team until arriving in Europe, where Dennis Viollet, "who has been rumored to be the next Whips manager . . . may join the team."[33] The whole thing had a farcical, wing-and-a-prayer feel befitting a last-gasp dash across the Atlantic. Viollet had just finished a successful tenure as captain of the Baltimore Bays and stands as another example of the many legendary soccer figures that quietly passed through the NASL in its early days.

On October 5 the Whips defeated perennial German minnows VfB Lubeck 2–1 on the strength of goals from Niels Huttel and Nana Gyau, with an
assist from the omnipresent Victorio Casa.[34] Viollet did indeed meet the
team in Hamburg, briefly assuming managerial duties before the franchise
folded for good at the end of the month. The Whips played again on October
12, registering a 2–2 tie against Holstein Kiel on a penalty in the final
minute, according to the Associated Press.[35] After this match, the Whips'
tour dissolves into static and ultimately radio silence. There is no discernible
record of and thus no likelihood that proposed matches in Gothenburg, Sweden, and Alborg, Denmark, ever took place. The Whips next surfaced again
on November 2 amid reports that the NASL was suspending operations for
three years.

DISCOURSES OF POWER

A vote was taken at a league meeting in Chicago to "temporarily disband the
14-team major league and concentrate instead on a single All-America
team."[36] The *New York Times* stressed that the decision to suspend league
play "was prompted by woes of attendance" and the teams averaged as few
as 3,000 fans and as many as 7,000. The formation of a single team, NASL
All-Star XI or "All-American" team, was apparently designed to meet the
dual objectives of "Americanizing" the game (although, of course, none of
these players would actually be American. Sound familiar?) while playing as
many international friendlies as possible in league cities against famous touring teams like Santos.

The New York Generals' chief operating officer Eugene Scott was quoted
as saying "Each member will own a part of this new team. If interest becomes big enough, local identity will become engendered and then local
operations will be started again."[37] This was curious because the Generals
reportedly "led opposition to the switch at the meeting," loudly voicing their
strong preference for the existing league format. The Generals' opposition to
the "All-American team" would remain strident. It would also be voiced
primarily through Eugene Scott's presence in the pages of the *Times*. Scott,
the "lawyer and sportsman," suddenly emerges as a pivotal figure here, becoming the most articulate public advocate of the importance of establishing
"local identity" (an authentic connection between city and franchise) as well
as a fierce adversary of Phil Woosnam and what would soon become known
as the "Atlanta plan."

The NASL's haphazardly announced suspension lingered uncertainly in
the air for more than a month. The owners waited for what they probably
assumed would be certain and automatic approval from USSFA. Until reports emerged in early December indicating that USSFA had "refused to

allow the North American Soccer League to disband or change its league structure unless the league guaranteed that the association would not be responsible for claims by dissident members."[38]

Ironically, it was the $250,000 in USA and NPSL fees and gate percentages that breathed life into the organization, expanding the USSFA's previously meager resources and giving it power and a level of status it wasn't prepared to relinquish for a harebrained idea to form a "single All-American" or national team. The denial of sanction was certainly a way for USSFA and its former president James P. McGuire to stay relevant and funded.

With the denial of sanction the owners hastily reconvened to figure out how or if they could salvage the 1969 season. An eerie press silence descended until early the next year while the remaining owners debated the league format. Woosnam would later refer to it as a "blank period"[39] in the lives of all involved. Details regarding the contours of and specific actors engaged in these debates emerged slowly, largely through the public discourse between Phil Woosnam and Eugene Scott.

On January 8, an Associated Press report announced the re-formation of an eight-team domestic league, news that was delivered to the wire service by Atlanta Chiefs officials,[40] itself an indication that power within the league had shifted dramatically. Not surprisingly, the statement also officially announced Woosnam's appointment as the NASL's executive director. Woosnam would waste no time in shifting league emphasis to "the development of soccer in each city" in addition to "bringing top European teams to the United States for a series of league sponsored exhibitions."

At this stage, Chicago and Oakland were still considered league cities, even though the Clippers had already begun planning their ambitious exhibition schedule, with their first match scheduled for January 26 against Club Atlas. Chicago would soon follow in New York's footsteps and cease operations. Details of the Atlanta plan,[41] or what would ultimately become the International Cup, began to surface almost immediately after Woosnam's promotion became public.

Gerald Eskenazi noted that five of the eight remaining NASL teams backed the plan and that the backers did so with hopes of making "the public quickly aware of good soccer." The thinking was that with appetites whetted by top-quality play, fans might then begin the process of establishing a connection with their local NASL teams, a connection deepened by the use of local players. As noted before, there were discernible signs that this connection was being forged contemporaneously in cities like Atlanta and Dallas. One city fielded the reigning NASL champions, the other a historically bad team sporting a jaw-dropping minus eighty-one goal differential, which indicated that identification was slowly being established at both extremes of the on-field performance spectrum.

Scott began questioning the logic of the plan from the pages of the *New York Times,* saying "they want to bring in foreign clubs that would be adopted by the local cities for a five week season. After that, the local talent would take over and play a home-and-home series with one another."[42] Scott cautioned that the "quality of play on the local level would be way below what it was last year" when the league had made "a tremendous jump on quality over the previous year." This was undeniably true with the Generals and Stokers both recording victories against Santos. Manchester City was also famously humbled a handful of times by NASL teams during its summer tour.

The word *local* in Scott's initial quote is key, though, because it points to yet another instance in which the NASL proved absolutely abysmal at messaging. The idea that the league-play phase of the 1969 NASL season would be played by local or semi-professional talent began to emerge from the already dense clouds of incompetence and confusion swirling around the league. Was it Woosnam's intent to stage the league phase of the upcoming season with amateur, local, or semi-pro players?

The Generals and Baltimore Bays were certainly under the impression that the 1969 NASL season was going to be a developmental league played by "semi-pro"[43] players. The *Baltimore Sun*'s Ken Nigro wrote that the new-look Bays "will be more like a semi-pro squad. The salaries will not be high and the players will work at their jobs during the day while practicing at night and playing on weekends."

The salary most bandied about was $75, as Gerald Eskenazi reported, "each member of a development team, which eventually would be a city's sole representative, would be limited to $75 a game."[44] To put this in context, that was the same sum paid to referees during the 1967 NPSL season. One of the reasons for doing this—besides alleviating the NASL's obvious financial ruin—was to ensure that the "majority of players will be young Americans."[45]

Continuing this particular strategy to "Americanize" the NASL, the *Sun* understood the plan as "NASL clubs will field teams with emphasis on development of local talent and will play once a week during summer months." Reviewing Phil Woosnam's public statements at the time yields plenty of comments such as, "First, we have some of the world's finest players flying in for the International Cup. Second we have more American players in the process of being signed ready to emerge in our regular season."[46] His adroit phrasing definitely invites ambiguity.

The New York Generals were convinced that league play would feature developmental talent. Scott referred again to the "local talent" who would "take over" after the International Cup before stating outright that the NASL told the Generals they would have to "scrap their 1968 team in order to stay in the league"[47] and that its "regular team" would not be allowed to enter league competition. This "Americanization" strategy seems to have come directly from the same dismal lineage as the "All-American" team farce. Scott characterized it as a "new system that would perpetuate a fraud on the public," stressing that "under no circumstances would the Generals play under the new format."

It seems almost unbelievable that this actually could have been Woosnam's intention, but just a week into league play, the Baltimore Bays lodged a formal protest over what Coach Gordon Jago "termed the use of 'professional' players by the Kansas City Spurs."48 This would further corroborate the Generals' discontented rumblings that professionalism was purposefully deemphasized under the Atlanta plan. Jago told the *Baltimore Sun* his understanding was that "the object of the league this year was to keep costs low and not have full time players."

According to Jago, this arrangement "would allow the club to keep the game alive and at the same time give the American boys a chance." The coach insisted that the Spurs "definitely have violated league rules which state that you cannot pay a player more than $75 per match." An agitated Jago noted that "the word development was bandied about by Mr. Woosnam and everybody quite freely. That's what I thought this league was supposed to be, a development league."49 This would seem to remove all doubt, if any lingered, that there was substance to the Generals' grievances and that, behind closed doors, part of the plan was to make the NASL semi-professional under cover of night. Interestingly, Jago remarked that the St. Louis Stars were the only other team "living up to the original intent of the league," which explained why they were so poor—and sadly why eventual champion Kansas City was so good.

As mentioned, Woosnam certainly left room for interpretation when he spoke of increased American presence in the league, but if the intent was to bring in top-shelf talent like West Ham to impersonate the Bays before turning the reins over to local amateur players, the drop in quality of play would be so vertiginous it would be hard to discern any conceivable advantage in doing so, save for economics. In hindsight, this is exactly what happened and it ended up being the worst possible move, something Woosnam, Hunt, and Jago all realized before the International Cup tournament was even over. It managed to sabotage a growing sense of local identity in places like Dallas, while massively lowering the quality of play when casual fans that may have been impressed by West Ham's free-flowing pyrotechnics were ready to start tuning in. This was a Catch-22 the NASL was never able to satisfactorily negotiate in the late '60s, even though on paper the International Cup concept initially seemed like an attempt to address both problems.

Eugene Scott touched perceptively on the conundrum of ethnicity, which had flummoxed ownership from day one, saying "the ethnic groups interested in soccer came to see the foreign teams" before noting that ethnic fans "still haven't been given enough time to identify with their local talent."[50] He remarked that these same fans largely "didn't think we were good enough so they watched their local semipro teams." This is precisely what was also happening in St. Louis and Chicago, cities that had well-established, often ethnically based, amateur and semi-professional leagues that offered a higher or at least a comparable level of play in those markets. So a choice between watching an amateur Generals side or the German-American Soccer League's Greek American AA, for example, was not much of a choice at all for many. So why discard a vastly improved Generals team reflecting flashes of genuine quality?

Scott is perhaps the only administrative figure within the entire USA/ NPSL/NASL apparatus to publicly make this connection at the time. The question is, how would NASL owners achieve an acceptable level of quality with their franchises in what appeared to be a rapidly shrinking window of time? Add to this equation considerations of "Americanization" and the NASL seemed to be presented with impossible odds. This was partially due—as were most, if not all of the league's problems—to lack of knowledge on the part of the owners. As Wangerin correctly observed, "America's new soccer executives might have been able to appreciate the genius of a Pele, yet their pitiful knowledge of the game soon left them embarrassingly exposed. Telling good players from ordinary ones proved beyond them"[51] and this damaged them severely in the large markets that they were absolutely counting on.

Woosnam ever so subtly defended his plan, as well as the creeping tide of NASL amateurism, lamenting that "the whole problem with soccer in this country goes deeper than playing a few professional games."[52] The word *professional* is telling and seems to signal a definitive shift away from full-fledged professionalism. Woosnam then articulated what would become his vision and plan of action for the NASL throughout the decade, saying, "You've got to build the pyramid from the bottom up. You don't start with pro soccer and wind up with 8-year-olds playing soccer in grammar school. You start with the 8-year-olds and end with highly competent professional teams."

Woosnam stressed that "Americans have got to learn the value of playing soccer before watching the finished article." If that was truly how he felt, the logic behind bringing in West Ham seemed even less sound, save for its role as ambassador and advocate. The International Cup tournament was Woosnam's first major chance to help "build the pyramid." This was the latest salvo in a discursive battle between Scott and Woosnam to define the fundamental nature of the NASL.

Following through on their threats, the New York Generals informed the NASL that they would not take part in the 1969 season but that they "hoped to maintain some contact with the game." General manager Bill Bergesch told the *Times* that the team's offices would remain open and that "the club may sponsor some visits by foreign teams."[53] Scott had also floated the idea of "increasing the number of special exhibitions or 'friendlies'" as a way to increase revenue. Two reasons could explain the Generals' eagerness to pursue these friendlies: first, the exhibitions starring Santos and Napoli had recently drawn in excess of 40,000 New York fans, and second, the Oakland Clippers had broken away from the NASL and began operating independently, establishing an important precedent.

The barnstorming Clippers were scheduled to host Dynamo Kiev in San Francisco on February 23, and the first stateside visit by a Soviet team was creating a modest buzz while these events were transpiring. There is no doubt that the Generals were watching Oakland's moves and likely considered themselves capable of scheduling similarly lucrative matches, perhaps on an even larger scale. At this stage Brian Glanville weighed in on NASL developments and the evolving dialogue between Woosnam and Scott via his *New York Times* column, writing that it was "legitimate to build more slowly, on a small scale, carefully integrating club with community"[54] rather than haphazardly "tempt spectators with the best," creating unsustainable demands.

The integration between club and community in Dallas was the most promising example of what the future could look like. Glanville wrote that "the vital process of interlocking professional clubs with the rapid growth of soccer in schools and colleges will go forward," echoing Woosnam's invocation of a pyramid. He makes a point of noting that the Generals "alienated" school and college soccer, which is perhaps one reason why their attempts to establish a local connection were so ineffectual and poorly received.

Glanville then commented on the shift of the league's power base to Atlanta, depicting it as "a city which wants the league, while New York could scarcely care less." There is no doubt that this sudden power shift ruffled feathers in New York, as Scott would soon make clear, injecting a level of acidity and a palpable sense of hard feelings to the discourse. Glanville conceded that "New York is vital to the whole operation" and that he was sorry to see the Generals, who were "showing signs of life under their young director Gene Scott,"[55] go.

Scott himself took to the *Times*, penning a column titled "Generals Fade Away"[56] on March 16, wherein he accused "the underfed remainder of the North American Soccer League" of forcing the Generals to "scrap their 1968 team in order to stay in the league." The freshly personal tone of the debate can be discerned in Scott's acerbic words. Scott publicly acknowledged the Generals' overriding interest in friendlies and the friction it caused in league meetings, writing that the Generals were "criticized because their participation in giant tour games between such teams as Santos and Napoli fattened gate receipts, which facilitated substantial expenditures for skilled South American players." The Generals had purchased Eliseu from Santos and a handful of other players who had contributed to their uptick in class. It's clear that they didn't want to relinquish these new resources.

It's interesting that, as always, friendlies were capable of playing such a contentious role in deliberations regarding the league's future, but their potential for creating an economic imbalance, as outlined, would've been a legitimate concern for cities not blessed with New York's cultural cachet and resources. Scott indignantly refuted the charge that the "fattened gate receipts" made the Generals a "big bucks" franchise, highlighting the team's progressive plans to operate a streamlined organization that functioned on a "moderate budget." Scott highlighted the Generals' proposed move to Downing Stadium as evidence, writing that the Generals had engineered the move by promising to make capital improvements to the stadium in lieu of rent.

Had the Generals survived to make this move, they could have set a crucial, innovative example with regard to stadium policy, an issue that has remained problematic within American soccer all the way through to the early Major League Soccer era. Scott then wrote "that the NASL's plan of importing foreign teams for adoption by member cities for five weeks in May would not satisfy local desire for bona fide identification with a top quality soccer club in New York." Besides once again making this case more perceptively and articulately than anyone else connected to the league, Scott would be proven right on this point almost immediately, as Lamar Hunt and Gordon Jago would both soon acknowledge that the concept of importing foreign teams was "doomed," never to be repeated again. Scott then delivered a parting shot to Woosnam, although without mentioning him by name, dismissively noting that "the Atlanta coach was selected as executive director of the league" before warning that "a power base has begun to be generated in Atlanta . . . that was felt to be unhealthy to league balance." Here were both sides of a philosophical and now a geographic divide that split along many jagged, contentious lines, including difficult questions of identity and professionalism.

INTERNATIONAL CUP REMEMBRANCES: ASTON VILLA

When Aston Villa were selected to represent the Atlanta Chiefs in the International Cup, like Wolverhampton before them, they were toiling in Britain's Second Division, thus causing handwringing and consternation. According to an aside in the *Baltimore Sun*, the reasons Aston Villa was picked to come to the United States were "rather obvious" because "at one time last year the Atlanta Chiefs of the North American Soccer League came close to buying Aston Villa and several of the Chiefs once had connections to this team."[57] One of those Chiefs with connections to the Birmingham outfit was, of course, Phil Woosnam, who had joined the team from West Ham in 1962. As a former Villan and league mouthpiece, Woosnam took great pains to ensure fans that despite their Second Division status Villa were a storied outfit filled with First Division quality and class.

In 2012 the *Birmingham Mail* published a recap of Aston Villa's summer odyssey through America that's filled with fascinating details. The players "vividly" remembered "a Cherokee Indian puffing clouds of smoke out the top of a giant teepee on a platform behind the goal every time Villa scored at their 'home' ground of Atlanta Stadium."[58] This conveys a sense of the surreal anarchic spirit of the times: British teams playing soccer in mostly empty baseball stadiums under assumed names, the tangled knot of identities spilling over into a hyperreal cloud of racial insensitivities and stereotypes, the whole thing adding another layer to the deadly racial realignment engulfing the nation. Villa started fast in the States, racing out to a 2–1–1 record and twenty-two points. They would fade dramatically, perhaps as a portent of things to come, finishing with those same two victories and only twenty-eight total points.

The NASL was so haphazard, poorly run, and chaotic that one of Villa's "fixtures was postponed because the venue had been double booked and priority was given to a boy scout's troup." It is worth noting that at this time the Atlanta Chiefs were the defending NASL champions; one would think that would theoretically give them precedence over a scout troop. In addition to Woosnam, the Atlanta Chiefs featured two former Villa players: Norman Ashe and Victor Crowe. Crowe would soon be called upon to relieve Tommy Docherty of his managerial duties.

It was a quick turnaround for Docherty, who upon taking over the club in 1969 engineered a run that saw them lose just three times in twenty-three matches to close out their Second Division campaign.[59] Docherty predicted First Division ascension in short order. Villa's players viewed the whirlwind trip wherein they logged thousands of air miles as "a great bonding experience" (à la Celtic in 1966) and looked forward to the upcoming Second Division season—a season that sadly would end with relegation, not promotion, leaving the proud Birmingham side to ring in the '70s mired in the third tier of English football, the curse of '69 biting them hard.

> Crass though their mistakes often were, it may be that it is wrong and unfair to blame the millionaires. Goodness knows they tried, even if they so often ignored good advice, listened to the untalented or the unscrupulous, and ultimately went out not with a bang but with a whisper. —Brian Glanville[60]

Notes

INTRODUCTION

1. Ernst Friedrich Schumacher, *Small Is Beautiful: A Study of Economics As if People Mattered* (New York: Harper Perennial, 1989).

2. Charles Parrish and John Nauright, "Darts, Whips and Dips: The Rollercoaster Ride of Professional Soccer in DC" (working paper, n.d.), accessed February 14, 2014, eref href="http://www.academia.edu/1962245/Darts_Whips_and_Dips_The_Rollercoaster_Ride_of_Professional_Soccer_in_Washington_D.C.

3. Parrish and Nauright, "Darts, Whips and Dips."

4. Parrish and Nauright, "Darts, Whips and Dips."

5. Gary Armstrong and James Rosbrook-Thompson, "Coming to America: Historical Ontologies and United States Soccer," *Identities: Global Studies in Culture and Power* 17, no. 4 (July 9, 2010): 367.

6. Andrei S. Markovits and Steven L. Hellerman, "Soccer in America: A Story of Marginalization," *University of Miami Entertainment and Sports Law Review* 13 (fall 1995–spring 1996): 226, accessed February 14, 2014, HeinOnline Law Journal Library.

7. Parrish and Nauright, "Darts, Whips and Dips."

8. Markovits and Hellerman, "Soccer in America," 227.

9. Armstrong and Rosbrook-Thompson, "Coming to America," 367.

10. Parrish and Nauright, "Darts, Whips and Dips."

11. Markovits and Hellerman, "Soccer in America," 227.

12. Frank Deford, "Show, Sex and Suburbs," *Sports Illustrated*, February 28, 1983, accessed November 24, 2013, http://sportsillustrated.cnn.com/vault/article/magazine/MAG1120568/index.htm.

13. Parrish and Nauright, "Darts, Whips and Dips."

14. Michael Oriard, *King Football: Sport and Spectacle in the Golden Age of Radio and Newsreels, Movies and Magazines, the Weekly and Daily Press* (Chapel Hill: University of North Carolina Press, 2003), 19.

15. David Trouille, "Association Football to Futbol: Ethnic Succession and the History of Chicago-area Soccer," *Soccer and Society* 10, no. 6 (November 2009): 802.

16. Parrish and Nauright, "Darts, Whips and Dips."

17. Geoffrey Green, "U.S. Kicks Off in World Soccer," *(London) Times*, February 25, 1967, accessed September 23, 2013, Times Digital Archive.

18. David Wangerin, *Distant Corners: American Soccer's History of Missed Opportunities and Lost Causes* (Philadelphia, PA: Temple University Press, 2011), 206–7.

19. Green, "U.S. Kicks Off in World."

20. Thomas Allen Nelson, *Kubrick: Inside a Film Artist's Maze* (Bloomington: Indiana University Press, 2000), 235.

21. Nelson, *Kubrick: Inside a Film*, 234.

22. Green, "U.S. Kicks Off in World."

23. Nelson, *Kubrick: Inside a Film*, 234.

24. Robert Johnson Jr., "Say It Ain't So, Jay: Fitzgerald's Use of Baseball in *The Great Gatsby*," *The F. Scott Fitzgerald Review* 1 (2002): 40.

25. Johnson, "Say It Ain't So, Jay," 40.

1. RISKY BUSINESS

1. Martin Kane, "The True Football Gets Its Big Chance," *Sports Illustrated*, March 27, 1967, accessed May 12, 2014, http://sportsillustrated.cnn.com/vault/article/magazine/MAG1079671/1/index.htm.

2. Dave Brady, "Football, Baseball Owners Show Interest in Major League Soccer," *Washington Post*, March 20, 1966, accessed May 9, 2014, ProQuest Historical Newspapers.

3. David Wangerin, *Soccer in a Football World* (Philadelphia: Temple University Press, 2008), 122.

4. Brady, "Football, Baseball Owners Show Interest," C3.

5. Brady, "Football, Baseball Owners Show Interest," C3.

6. Gwilym S. Brown, "What Will He Think of Next?" *Sports Illustrated*, May 4, 1970, accessed March 31, 2014, http://sportsillustrated.cnn.com/vault/article/magazine/MAG1083569/1/index.htm.

7. Derek Liecty, telephone interview by the author, Washington, D.C., March 22, 2014.

8. Jerome Holtzman, "Turn Back the Clock . . . 1943," *Baseball Digest* 63, no. 8 (August 2004): 76, accessed April 14, 2014, SPORTDiscus with Full Text.

9. Brown, "What Will He Think of Next?"

10. Holtzman, "Turn Back the Clock," 76.

11. Brown, "What Will He Think of Next?"

12. Brown, "What Will He Think of Next?"

13. Holtzman, "Turn Back the Clock," 76.

14. Robert McG. Thomas Jr., "William D. Cox, 79, Team Owner Who Was Banned from Baseball," *New York Times*, March 30, 1989, B8, accessed May 12, 2014, ProQuest Historical Newspapers.

15. Derek Liecty, e-mail message to author, March 23, 2014.

16. Wangerin, *Soccer in a Football World*, 122.

17. Arthur Daley, "On a Grandiose Scale," *New York Times*, February 9, 1960, 35, accessed April 14, 2014, ProQuest Historical Newspapers.

18. Daley, "On a Grandiose Scale," 35.

19. Tom Dunmore, "In Lieu of Giants: The International Soccer League, Part Two," *Pitch Invasion*, blog entry posted November 7, 2011, accessed March 24, 2014, http://pitchinvasion.net/blog/2011/11/07/in-lieu-of-giants-the-international-soccer-league-part-two.

20. Tom Dunmore, "They Even Cheered Technique: The International Soccer League, Part One," *Pitch Invasion*, blog entry posted November 4, 2011, accessed March 24, 2014, http://pitchinvasion.net/blog/2011/11/04/they-even-cheered-technique-the-1960-international-soccer-league-part-one.

21. Dunmore, "In Lieu of Giants."

22. Dunmore, "In Lieu of Giants."

23. Dunmore, "In Lieu of Giants."

24. Liecty, telephone interview by the author.

25. Kane, "The True Football."

26. Steve Holroyd and David Litterer, "The Year in American Soccer—1965," American Soccer History Archives, last modified February 17, 2008, accessed March 31, 2014, http://homepages.sover.net/~spectrum/year/1965.html.

27. Tom Dunmore, "Expanded Dreams: The International Soccer League, Part Three," *Pitch Invasion*, blog entry posted November 14, 2011, accessed March 24, 2014, http://pitchinvasion.net/blog/2011/11/14/expanded-dreams-the-international-soccer-league-part-three.

28. Brown, "What Will He Think of Next?"

29. Dean McGowen, "Plans for Nationwide 11-Team Pro Soccer League Formulated Here," *New York Times*, May 11, 1966, 83, accessed September 23, 2013, ProQuest Historical Newspapers.

30. McGowen, "Plans for Nationwide 11-Team," 83.

31. McGowen, "Plans for Nationwide 11-Team," 83.

32. McGowen, "Plans for Nationwide 11-Team," 83.

33. Associated Press, "3 Cities Given Soccer Spots," *Baltimore Sun*, August 24, 1966, C4, accessed May 12, 2014, ProQuest Historical Newspapers.

34. Andrew Beyer, "Amateurs Grab Soccer War Playoff," *Washington Post*, January 18, 1967, D1, accessed March 17, 2014, ProQuest Historical Newspapers.

35. Steve Holroyd and David Litterer, "The Year in American Soccer—1966," American Soccer History Archives, last modified February 17, 2008, accessed March 31, 2014, http://homepages.sover.net/~spectrum/year/1966.html.

36. Wangerin, *Soccer in a Football World*, 124.

37. Brian Glanville, "Two Soccer Leagues One Too Many," *New York Times*, April 16, 1967, S7, accessed October 29, 2013, ProQuest Historical Newspapers.

38. Associated Press, "Ten-Team Pro Soccer League Formed," *Cleveland (OH) Plain Dealer*, June 17, 1966, 37, accessed September 23, 2013, America's Historical Newspapers.

39. United Press International, "Two U.S. Soccer Groups Announce New Merger," *Springfield (MA) Union*, August 9, 1966, 27, accessed September 23, 2013, America's Historical Newspapers.

40. Holroyd and Litterer, "The Year in American Soccer—1966."

41. Holroyd and Litterer, "The Year in American Soccer—1966."

42. Andrew Beyer, "Soccer Moguls Boot a Big One," *Washington Post*, September 12, 1967, D3, accessed March 26, 2014, ProQuest Historical Newspapers.

43. Beyer, "Amateurs Grab Soccer War Playoff," D1.

44. Beyer, "Amateurs Grab Soccer War Playoff," D1.

45. David Wangerin, *Distant Corners: American Soccer's History of Missed Opportunities and Lost Causes* (Philadelphia: Temple University Press, 2011), 175.

46. Beyer, "Amateurs Grab Soccer War Playoff," D1.

47. Associated Press, "Two Leagues Ready to Go," *Baltimore Sun*, February 19, 1967, A8, accessed May 12, 2014, ProQuest Historical Newspapers.

48. Beyer, "Amateurs Grab Soccer War Playoff," D1.

49. Ken Nigro, "Washington Whips' Official Scoffs at Bays and N.P.S.L.," *Baltimore Sun*, March 26, 1967, A13, accessed May 12, 2014, ProQuest Historical Newspapers.

50. Kane, "The True Football."

51. David Litterer, "The Year in Soccer—1929," American Soccer History Archives, last modified February 4, 2006, accessed March 28, 2014, http://homepages.sover.net/~spectrum/year/1929.html.

52. Litterer, "The Year in Soccer—1929."

53. Lloyd E. Millegan, "Unsanctioned Pro Soccer Loop Plans to Make Debut Next April," *New York Times*, August 23, 1966, 46, accessed September 24, 2013, ProQuest Historical Newspapers.

54. Associated Press, "3 Cities Given Soccer," C4.

55. Associated Press, "Ten-Team Pro Soccer League," 37.

56. Daley, "On a Grandiose Scale," 35.

57. Dunmore, "Expanded Dreams."

58. Associated Press, "3 Cities Given Soccer," C4.

59. Associated Press, "3 Cities Given Soccer," C4.

60. "Sports over Lightly," *Cleveland (OH) Plain Dealer*, August 25, 1966, accessed September 23, 2013, America's Historical Newspapers.

61. Dunmore, "Expanded Dreams."

62. United Press International, "British Soccer Official Rejects $38,000 Post," *New York Times*, September 6, 1966, 30, accessed September 23, 2013, ProQuest Historical Newspapers.

63. Associated Press, "U.S. Soccer Loop Seeking British Official," *New York Times*, September 13, 1966, 61, accessed September 23, 2013, ProQuest Historical Newspapers.

64. Associated Press, "Graham Named Soccer Loop Director," *The State The Columbia (SC) Record*, October 9, 1966, 38, accessed May 12, 2014, America's Historical Newspapers.

65. Richard Williams, "Phil Woosnam: From West Ham and Villa to Realizing the American Dream," *Guardian*, July 26, 2013, accessed May 12, 2014, www.theguardian.com/football/blog/2013/jul/26/phil-woosnam-west-ham-aston-villa-america.

66. United Press International, "Welsh Soccer Star Defies Ban, Signs with U.S. Pro Team," *Springfield (MA) Union*, September 9, 1966, 52, accessed May 12, 2014, America's Historical Newspapers.

67. Nick Harris, "From £20 to £33,868 per Week: A Quick History of English Football's Top-Flight Wages," Sporting Intelligence, last modified January 20, 2011, accessed May 12, 2014, www.sportingintelligence.com/2011/01/20/from-20-to-33868-per-week-a-quick-history-of-english-footballs-top-flight-wages-200101.

68. United Press International, "Welsh Soccer Star Defies Ban," 52.

69. "Soccer Merger Is Planned," *New York Times*, September 21, 1966, 59, accessed September 23, 2013, ProQuest Historical Newspapers.

70. Associated Press, "Pro Soccer OKs Merger," *(Portland) Oregonian*, September 22, 1966, 64, accessed May 12, 2014, America's Historical Newspapers.

71. Associated Press, "NPSL Nixes Merger Plan," *(Portland) Oregonian*, September 25, 1966, 93, accessed May 2, 2014, America's Historical Newspapers.

72. Associated Press, "NPSL Nixes Merger Plan," 93.

73. Dave Brady, "TV Loot Is Newest Soccer Goal," *Washington Post*, October 2, 1966, C4, accessed November 11, 2013, ProQuest Historical Newspapers.

74. Brady, "TV Loot," C4.

75. Dave Brady, "'Outlaw' Soccer League Lands CBS TV Deal," *Washington Post*, October 4, 1966, D1, accessed May 7, 2014, ProQuest Historical Newspapers.

76. Brady, "'Outlaw' Soccer League," D1.

77. Wangerin, *Soccer in a Football World*, 121.

78. Brady, "'Outlaw' Soccer League," D1.

79. United Press International, "CBS Gains Right to Telecast New Soccer League Contests," *Trenton (NJ) Evening Times*, October 4, 1966, 31, accessed May 12, 2014, America's Historical Newspapers.

80. United Press International, "World Soccer May Retaliate against CBS," *Washington Post*, October 5, 1966, D5, accessed May 12, 2014, ProQuest Historical Newspapers.

81. George Langford, "World Soccer Stars to Play in U.S.," *Chicago Tribune*, October 13, 1966, F1, accessed September 23, 2013, ProQuest Historical Newspapers.

82. Langford, "World Soccer Stars to Play," F1.

83. Langford, "World Soccer Stars to Play," F1.

84. "Soccer Ball Sales Show Rise According to Survey," *Baltimore Sun*, December 20, 1966, C4, accessed May 12, 2014, ProQuest Historical Newspapers.

85. Associated Press, "New Soccer League Given Pro Sanction," *New York Times*, December 29, 1966, 38, accessed September 23, 2013, ProQuest Historical Newspapers.

86. Associated Press, "New Soccer League," 38.

87. Joseph Durso, "Merger Key Topic at Soccer Talks," *New York Times*, December 28, 1966, 50, accessed May 12, 2014, ProQuest Historical Newspapers.

88. United Press International, "Walsh Leaves Dodger Post to Head Soccer League," *New York Times*, December 30, 1966, 22, accessed May 12, 2014, ProQuest Historical Newspapers.

89. Andrew Beyer, "Children's Section of Public Library Gave Walsh Start As Soccer Boss," *Washington Post*, March 19, 1967, B5, accessed March 17, 2014, ProQuest Historical Newspapers.

90. Beyer, "Children's Section," B5.

91. Associated Press, "Dodge Official Walsh to Head Soccer League," *Los Angeles Times*, December 30, 1966, B3, accessed May 12, 2014, ProQuest Historical Newspapers.

92. Wangerin, *Soccer in a Football World*, 126.

93. Andrew Beyer, "Foreman Is Three-Letter Man," *Washington Post*, March 26, 1967, E4, accessed April 5, 2014, ProQuest Historical Newspapers.

94. Beyer, "Foreman Is Three-Letter Man," E4.

95. David Wangerin, *Distant Corners: American Soccer's History of Missed Opportunities and Lost Causes* (Philadelphia: Temple University Press, 2011), 206–7.

96. Beyer, "Foreman Is Three-Letter Man," E4.

97. "The Big Eye League," *Time*, August 21, 1964, 78, accessed December 7, 2013, Academic Search Premier.

98. Beyer, "Foreman Is Three-Letter Man," E4.

99. Andrew Beyer, "Cooper Passes Test, Talks Good Game," *Washington Post*, February 12, 1967, C4, accessed April 5, 2014, ProQuest Historical Newspapers.

100. Andrew Beyer, "Cooper Starts Search for 7 Soccer Teams," *Washington Post*, January 3, 1967, D3, accessed March 17, 2014, ProQuest Historical Newspapers.

101. Andrew Beyer, "D.C. Entry Hopes to Educate Fans to Top Brand of Soccer," *Washington Post*, January 5, 1967, C3, accessed April 5, 2014, ProQuest Historical Newspapers.

102. Andrew Beyer, "12 Foreign Teams Set for Soccer," *Washington Post*, January 13, 1967, C3, accessed April 5, 2014, ProQuest Historical Newspapers.

103. Paul Days, *Stars in Stripes; Sunderland AFC As the Vancouver Royal Canadians* (Blue House Field, 2012), digital file.

104. Beyer, "Cooper Starts Search," D3.

105. "Sports over Lightly," *Cleveland (OH) Plain Dealer*, January 31, 1967, 31, accessed May 12, 2014, America's Historical Newspapers.

106. Joseph Durso, "Local Pro Soccer Teams May Share Stadium with Yanks in the Spring," *New York Times*, February 12, 1967, 196, accessed May 7, 2014, ProQuest Historical Newspapers.

107. Durso, "Local Pro Soccer Teams," 196.

108. "Pinto: New Salesman for Soccer," *New York Times*, March 5, 1967, 204, accessed May 12, 2014, ProQuest Historical Newspapers.

109. Associated Press, "Two Leagues Ready to Go," *Baltimore Sun*, February 19, 1967, A8, accessed May 12, 2014, ProQuest Historical Newspapers.

110. Pinto: New Salesman for Soccer," 204.

111. United Press International, "Commissioner Announced for Soccer," *Marietta (GA) Journal*, February 23, 1967, 15, accessed May 12, 2014, America's Historical Newspapers.

112. United Press International, "Filipino Chosen to Chair New Soccer League," *Trenton (NJ) Evening Times*, February 23, 1967, 32, accessed May 12, 2014, America's Historical Newspapers.

113. Associated Press, "Macker Gets Soccer Post," *Springfield (MA) Union*, February 23, 1967, 45, accessed May 12, 2014, America's Historical Newspapers.

114. United Press International, "Filipino Chosen to Chair," 32.

115. United Press International, "Commissioner Announced for Soccer," 15.

116. "Pro Soccer League Adopts New Name," *Washington Post*, March 10, 1967, D3, accessed May 12, 2014, ProQuest Historical Newspapers.

117. "Pro Soccer League Adopts New Name," D3.

118. Associated Press, "Stu Holcomb Joins Soccer," *Baltimore Sun*, August 12, 1966, C4, accessed September 24, 2013, ProQuest Historical Newspapers.

119. "Rival Soccer League Heads Talk Merger," *Los Angeles Times*, March 28, 1967, B4, accessed May 12, 2014, ProQuest Historical Newspapers.

120. Associated Press, "Two Leagues Ready to Go," A8.

121. "Merger," *Baltimore Sun*, March 28, 1967, C1, accessed May 12, 2014, ProQuest Historical Newspapers.

122. "Merger," C1.

123. Associated Press, "Soccer Loops Face Pressure," *Springfield (MA) Union*, March 29, 1967, 48, accessed May 12, 2014, America's Historical Newspapers.

124. "Sports over Lightly," *Cleveland (OH) Plain Dealer*, April 8, 1967, 39, accessed May 12, 2014, America's Historical Newspapers.

125. Andrew Beyer, "Hopes Dim for USA's TV Contract," *Washington Post*, March 23, 1967, H7, accessed May 12, 2014, ProQuest Historical Newspapers.

126. Beyer, "Hopes Dim," H7.

127. Kane, "The True Football."

128. Beyer, "Hopes Dim," H7.

129. Associated Press, "Soccer TV Is Called Good Risk," *Chicago Tribune*, February 28, 1967, C1, accessed May 12, 2014, ProQuest Historical Newspapers.

130. Associated Press, "CBS Officials Back Risk in TV Soccer," *(Portland) Oregonian*, February 28, 1967, 31, accessed May 12, 2014, America's Historical Newspapers.

131. Nigro, "Washington Whips' Official Scoffs," A13.

132. Associated Press, "Big Money Backs Fledgling Soccer League," *Springfield (MA) Union*, April 15, 1967, 14, accessed April 5, 2014, America's Historical Newspapers.

2. 1967, PART 1

1. Brian Glanville, "A Soccer Revolution," *New York Times*, July 23, 1967, 147, accessed October 27, 2013, ProQuest Historical Newspapers.

2. Chris Hunt, "Local Heroes: The Lisbon Lions," editorial, last modified June 2007, accessed April 7, 2014, www.chrishunt.biz/features40.html.

3. Glanville, "A Soccer Revolution," 147.

4. Rob Phillips-Knight, "Jock Stein's Lisbon Lions Shock Inter Milan," ESPN UK Football, last modified May 19, 2010, accessed April 7, 2014, www.espn.co.uk/football/sport/story/23486.html.

5. Brian Glanville, "Of Soccer and Madness," *New York Times*, June 18, 1967, 178, accessed October 27, 2013, ProQuest Historical Newspapers.

6. Glanville, "Of Soccer and Madness," 178.

7. Glanville, "Of Soccer and Madness," 178.

8. Glanville, "Of Soccer and Madness," 178.

9. Andrew Beyer, "New System Helps Eintracht Rebound," *Washington Post*, May 2, 1967, D3, accessed May 13, 2014, ProQuest Historical Newspapers.

10. Andrew Beyer, "Soccer Is Land and Sea of Schwartz's World," *Washington Post*, May 7, 1967, D4, accessed May 13, 2014, ProQuest Historical Newspapers.

11. Beyer, "Soccer Is Land and Sea," D4.

12. "Mirror Football Archive: Jock Stein," Mirror Football, accessed October 27, 2013, www.mirrorfootball.co.uk/archive/Jock-Stein-article147465.html.

13. Brian Glanville, "Two Soccer Leagues One Too Many," *New York Times*, April 16, 1967, S7, accessed October 29, 2013, ProQuest Historical Newspapers.

14. David Wangerin, *Soccer in a Football World* (Philadelphia: Temple University Press, 2008), 128.

15. Andrew Beyer, "Bag Pipes Blare As Dons Arrive to Play Soccer for Washington," *Washington Post*, May 24, 1967, D1, accessed May 13, 2014, ProQuest Historical Newspapers.

16. Chris Hunt, "Local Heroes: The Lisbon Lions."

17. *The Encyclopaedia of Scottish Football* (n.p.: Pitch Publishing, 2011), 164.

18. Paul Days, *Stars in Stripes; Sunderland AFC As the Vancouver Royal Canadians* (Blue House Field, 2012), digital file.

19. Andrew Beyer, "Soccer Team No Longer an It, Club Picks Whips as Nickname," *Washington Post*, March 9, 1967, E1, accessed May 13, 2014, ProQuest Historical Newspapers.

20. Beyer, "Soccer Team No Longer an It," E1.

21. "President Receives Whip Season Pass," *Washington Post*, May 27, 1967, E1, accessed May 13, 2014, ProQuest Historical Newspapers.

22. Andrew Beyer, "Whips Meet Cleveland Here Tonight," *Washington Post*, May 26, 1967, D1, accessed May 13, 2014, ProQuest Historical Newspapers.

23. "Legends Profile: Martin Buchan," Manchester United website, accessed May 13, 2014, www.manutd.com/en/Players-And-Staff/Legends/Martin-Buchan.aspx?pageNo=2.

24. Dave Morton, "Remember When: Newcastle United Icon Jinky Jimmy Turns 67 Today," *Newcastle (UK) Chronicle*, January 20, 2014, accessed April 26, 2014, www.chroniclelive.co.uk/lifestyle/nostalgia/newcastle-united-icon-jinky-jimmy-6528372.

25. Beyer, "Whips Meet Cleveland," D1.

26. Andrew Beyer, "Bag Pipes Blare."

27. Steve Holroyd, "The Year in American Soccer—1967," American Soccer Archives, accessed May 13, 2014, http://homepages.sover.net/~spectrum/year/1967.html.

28. James Fitzgerald, "Dallas Subs Win Soccer Opener, 1–0," *Chicago Tribune*, May 29, 1967, B5, accessed May 7, 2014, ProQuest Historical Newspapers.

29. Andrew Beyer, "Cleveland Plays without Ace Goalie," *Washington Post*, May 25, 1967, C5, accessed May 13, 2014, ProQuest Historical Newspapers.

30. Dan Coughlin, "Banks 'Aid' for Stokers," *Cleveland (OH) Plain Dealer*, June 13, 1967, 33, accessed May 13, 2014, America's Historical Newspapers.

31. Beyer, "Whips Meet Cleveland," D1.

32. "The Stokers Summer," The Oatcake–Stoke City FC Fanzine, last modified July 20, 2012, accessed May 13, 2014, http://theoatcake.wordpress.com/2012/07/20/the-stokers-summer-2/comment-page-1.

33. Andrew Beyer, "Young Whips Relish Contact, Play Uncomplicated Soccer," *Washington Post*, May 28, 1967, D6, accessed March 16, 2014, ProQuest Historical Newspapers.

34. Beyer, "Whips Meet Cleveland," D1.

35. Dan Coughlin, "Stokers Win Opener, 2–1," *Cleveland (OH) Plain Dealer*, May 27, 1967, 46, accessed May 13, 2014, America's Historical Newspapers.

36. Andrew Beyer, "All Soccer Styles Familiar to Storrie," *Washington Post*, May 30, 1967, C3, accessed May 13, 2014, ProQuest Historical Newspapers.

37. "Jim Storrie—the Laughing Cavalier," The Mighty Mighty Whites: The Definitive History of Leeds United, accessed May 13, 2014, www.mightyleeds.co.uk/players/storrie.htm.

38. Coughlin, "Stokers Win Opener, 2-1," 46.

39. Beyer, "Young Whips Relish Contact," D6.

40. Andrew Beyer, "Whips, Old Rivals Clash in Toronto," *Washington Post*, May 31, 1967, D4, accessed May 13, 2014, ProQuest Historical Newspapers.

41. Andrew Beyer, "Whips Expect Aggressive Offense by New York Tonight at Stadium," *Washington Post*, June 7, 1967, D1, accessed May 13, 2014, ProQuest Historical Newspapers.

42. Gerald Eskenazi, "Skyliners, Toronto a 1–1 Tie in Soccer League Opener," *New York Times*, May 29, 1967, 45, accessed May 13, 2014, ProQuest Historical Newspapers.

43. Eskenazi, "Skyliners, Toronto a 1–1 Tie in Soccer," 45.

44. Beyer, "Whips Expect Aggressive Offense," D1.

45. Richard Whittall, "When Toronto Pulled in the Stars," A More Splendid Life, last modified July 9, 2008, accessed May 13, 2014, www.amoresplendidlife.com/2008/07/when-toronto-pulled-in-stars.html.

46. Whittall, "When Toronto Pulled in the Stars."

47. Andrew Beyer, "Goalie Clarke's Play Saved So-So Game by Other Whips," *Washington Post*, June 2, 1967, D4, accessed May 13, 2014, ProQuest Historical Newspapers.

48. Beyer, "Goalie Clarke's Play," D4.

49. Andrew Beyer, "Whips Meet Chicago, Seek Second Victory," *Washington Post*, June 4, 1967, D1, accessed May 13, 2014, ProQuest Historical Newspapers.

50. Andrew Beyer, "Scoreless Tie Is Wrong Method to Whip up U.S. Soccer Interest," *Washington Post*, June 4, 1967, D4, accessed May 13, 2014, ProQuest Historical Newspapers.

51. Andrew Beyer, "Whips Hampered by Heat but Gain Stalemate, 1–1," *Washington Post*, June 5, 1967, D1, accessed May 13, 2014, ProQuest Historical Newspapers.

52. Beyer, "Whips Hampered by Heat," D1.

53. Associated Press, "Mustangs Tie," *Chicago Tribune*, June 5, 1967, C5, accessed May 13, 2014, ProQuest Historical Newspapers.

54. Andrew Beyer, "New York Blanked by Whips, 3–0," *Washington Post*, June 8, 1967, E1, accessed May 13, 2014, ProQuest Historical Newspapers.

55. Andrew Beyer, "Whips Play Cougars in Try for Top," *Washington Post*, June 11, 1967, D1, accessed May 13, 2014, ProQuest Historical Newspapers.

56. Dan Coughlin, "Stokers in 2nd Place," *Cleveland (OH) Plain Dealer*, July 5, 1967, 36, accessed May 13, 2014, America's Historical Newspapers.

57. Beyer, "Whips Play Cougars," D1.

58. "Introduction: The Story of One of Glentoran's Greatest Achievements," Glentoran Football Club website, accessed May 13, 2014, www.glentoran-fc.co.uk/cougars.htm.

59. "Rookie Linesman Robs Glentoran," Glentoran Football Club website, accessed March 29, 2014, www.glentoran-fc.co.uk/cougars%20shamrock%20rovers.htm.

60. Rich Passan, "Stokers and Mustangs Tie," *Cleveland (OH) Plain Dealer*, June 1, 1967, 70, accessed May 13, 2014, America's Historical Newspapers.

61. *Belfast (UK) Telegraph*, January 6, 2010, accessed May 13, 2014, http://www.belfasttelegraph.co.uk/sport/football/local/down-memory-lane-big-trevs-golden-goals-earn-him-deserved-oval-accolade-28510120.html.

62. "Penalty Controversy As Glens Win," Glentoran Football Club website, accessed May 13, 2014, www.glentoran-fc.co.uk/cougars%20shamrock%20rvrs.htm.

63. Andrew Beyer, "Whips Battle to Deadlock with Detroit," *Washington Post*, June 12, 1967, D1, accessed May 13, 2014, ProQuest Historical Newspapers.

64. Andrew Beyer, "Britain's Leading Goalie Faces Whips on Wednesday," *Washington Post*, June 13, 1967, D3, accessed May 13, 2014, ProQuest Historical Newspapers.

65. Dan Coughlin, "Vernon Is Soccer King," *Cleveland (OH) Plain Dealer*, June 6, 1967, 33, accessed May 13, 2014, America's Historical Newspapers.

66. Dan Coughlin, "Stokers Tie Wolves," *Cleveland (OH) Plain Dealer*, June 8, 1967, 76, accessed May 13, 2014, America's Historical Newspapers.

67. Coughlin, "Stokers Tie Wolves," 76.

68. Coughlin, "Stokers Tie Wolves," 76.

69. Andrew Beyer, "High Scoring Gales, Whips Clash Today," *Washington Post*, June 25, 1967, D3, accessed May 13, 2014, ProQuest Historical Newspapers.

70. Stephen Uersfeld, "Greatest Managers, #14: Ernst Happel," ESPNFC.com, last modified August 6, 2013, accessed May 13, 2014, www.espnfc.com/news/story/_/id/1511243/ernst-happel?cc=5901.

71. Uersfeld, "Greatest Managers."

72. Dan Coughlin, "Stokers Host Gales, Promise More Goals," *Cleveland (OH) Plain Dealer*, June 11, 1967, 55, accessed May 13, 2014, America's Historical Newspapers.

73. Coughlin, "Stokers Host Gales," 55.

74. Dan Coughlin, "Stokers Romp, 4–1," *Cleveland (OH) Plain Dealer*, June 12, 1967, 65, accessed May 13, 2014, America's Historical Newspapers.

75. Coughlin, "Stokers Romp, 4–1," 65.

76. Andrew Beyer, "Whips Tie Cleveland in Last Minutes," *Washington Post*, June 15, 1967, K21, accessed May 13, 2014, ProQuest Historical Newspapers.

77. Beyer, "Whips Tie Cleveland," K21.

78. Dan Coughlin, "Stokers Play 2–2 Tie," *Cleveland (OH) Plain Dealer*, June 15, 1967, 60, accessed May 13, 2014, America's Historical Newspapers.

79. Coughlin, "Stokers Play 2–2 Tie," 60.

80. Andrew Beyer, "Aberdeen's Turnbull Gets Kicks Whipping Youngsters into Shape," *Washington Post*, May 28, 1967, D4, accessed May 13, 2014, ProQuest Historical Newspapers.

81. Kenneth Denlinger, "Pele Dazzles Whips As 20,189 See Santos Win," *Washington Post*, July 15, 1968, D1, accessed May 13, 2014, ProQuest Historical Newspapers.

82. Coughlin, "Stokers Play 2–2 Tie," 60.

83. Coughlin, "Stokers Play 2–2 Tie," 60.

84. "Calm before the Storm," Glentoran Football Club website, accessed March 29, 2014, www.glentoran-fc.co.uk/cougars%20bangu.htm.

85. Associated Press, "Fight by Players Ends Soccer Game," *New York Times*, June 15, 1967, 65, accessed May 7, 2014, ProQuest Historical Newspapers.

86. "Calm before the Storm."

87. Brian Glanville, "Soccer Plays It Safe," *New York Times*, May 28, 1967, S9, accessed October 29, 2013, ProQuest Historical Newspapers.

88. Andrew Beyer, "Whips Play Undefeated L.A.," *Los Angeles Times*, June 20, 1967, D1, accessed May 13, 2014, ProQuest Historical Newspapers.

89. Brian Glanville, "Obituary: Ronnie Allen," *Guardian*, June 12, 2001, accessed May 13, 2014, www.theguardian.com/news/2001/jun/12/guardianobituaries.football.

90. Brian Glanville, "How I Gave Wolves the Chance to Conquer America," *(London) Times*, September 27, 2003, Sport, 45, accessed November 10, 2013, The Times Digital Archive.

91. Glanville, "How I Gave Wolves," 45.

92. "Zorros Change Official Name to Zorros," *Los Angeles Times*, March 14, 1967, C3, accessed May 13, 2014, ProQuest Historical Newspapers.

93. Shav Glick, "Wagstaffe of Wolves Idol of Fans," *Los Angeles Times*, July 13, 1967, B5, accessed May 13, 2014, ProQuest Historical Newspapers.

94. Jim Heath, "USA, 1967: Life in the Fast Lane," Wolves Heroes, last modified May 4, 2009, accessed May 13, 2014, www.wolvesheroes.com/2009/05/04/usa-1967.

95. Shav Glick, "Quick Lead, Rugged Defense Give Wolves Soccer Win, 2–1," *Los Angeles Times*, June 5, 1967, B1, accessed May 13, 2014, ProQuest Historical Newspapers.

96. Brian Glanville, "Bareno of Losers Gets First Score," *New York Times*, June 5, 1967, 1, accessed October 30, 2013, ProQuest Historical Newspapers.

97. Glanville, "Bareno of Losers," 1.

98. Beyer, "Whips Play Undefeated L.A.," D1.

99. Shav Glick, "Wolves Belt Vancouver Kids, 5–1," *Los Angeles Times*, June 15, 1967, C6, accessed May 7, 2014, ProQuest Historical Newspapers.

100. Glanville, "Bareno of Losers," 1.

101. Shav Glick, "Wolves' Coach Applauds 4–1 Win: Soccer at Its Best, Crowd Pleaser," *Los Angeles Times*, June 19, 1967, C2, accessed May 7, 2014, ProQuest Historical Newspapers.

102. Andrew Beyer, "USA Head Will Investigate Whips' Protest over Subs," *Washington Post*, June 22, 1967, C7, accessed May 13, 2014, ProQuest Historical Newspapers.

103. Beyer, "USA Head Will Investigate," C7.

104. Andrew Beyer, "Whips, Gales Struggle to Scoreless Tie," *Washington Post*, June 26, 1967, D1, accessed May 13, 2014, ProQuest Historical Newspapers.

105. Beyer, "Whips, Gales Struggle," D1.

106. Days, *Stars in Stripes*.

107. Patrick Glenn, "Obituary: Jim Baxter," *Guardian*, April 15, 2001, accessed May 13, 2014, www.theguardian.com/news/2001/apr/16/guardianobituaries.football.

108. Glenn, "Obituary: Jim Baxter."

109. Roy Jukich, "Leaky Defense Plagues McColl," *Toronto Sun*, June 22, 1967, accessed May 13, 2014, http://news.google.com/newspapers?id=kZplAAAAIBAJ&sjid=uIoNAAAAIBAJ&pg=4636%2C2364565.

110. Jukich, "Leaky Defense Plagues McColl."

111. "Stout Defence Earns a Draw," *Vancouver Sun*, June 29, 1967, accessed May 13, 2014, http://news.google.com/newspapers?id=l5plAAAAIBAJ&sjid=uIoNAAAAIBAJ&pg=5308%2C4853382.

112. Dan Coughlin, "Burrows Is Ready to Spark Stokers," *Cleveland (OH) Plain Dealer*, June 24, 1967, accessed May 13, 2014, America's Historical Newspapers.

113. Coughlin, "Burrows Is Ready," 37.

114. Dan Coughlin, "N.Y. Booters Play Here," *Cleveland (OH) Plain Dealer*, June 25, 1967, 44, accessed May 13, 2014, America's Historical Newspapers.

115. Dan Coughlin, "Stokers Lose First, 2–1," *Cleveland (OH) Plain Dealer*, June 26, 1967, 51, accessed May 13, 2014, America's Historical Newspapers.

116. Coughlin, "Stokers Lose First, 2–1," 51.

117. Coughlin, "Stokers Lose First, 2–1," 51.

118. Dan Coughlin, "Stokers in 'Dome' for Crucial Test," *Cleveland (OH) Plain Dealer,* June 27, 1967, 33, accessed May 13, 2014, America's Historical Newspapers.

119. Coughlin, "Stokers in 'Dome,'" 34.

120. Liz Smith, "Giltfinger's Golden Dome," *Sports Illustrated,* April 12, 1965, accessed May 13, 2014, http://sportsillustrated.cnn.com/vault/article/magazine/MAG1077072.

121. Smith, "Giltfinger's Golden Dome."

122. Days, *Stars in Stripes.*

123. Dan Coughlin, "Stokers Fall, 2–1; Lead by 2 Points," *Cleveland (OH) Plain Dealer,* June 28, 1967, 38, accessed May 13, 2014, America's Historical Newspapers.

124. Coughlin, "Stokers Fall, 2–1," 38.

125. Andrew Beyer, "Whips Face Key Test in Cotton Bowl," *Washington Post,* July 1, 1967, D3, accessed May 13, 2014, ProQuest Historical Newspapers.

126. Bill Lace, "Stokers Deflate Tornado," *Fort-Worth Star Telegram,* June 18, 1967, 27, accessed May 13, 2014, America's Historical Newspapers.

127. Bob St. John, "Stoke Smoke Chokes Dallas," *Dallas Morning News,* June 18, 1967, B1, America's Historical Newspapers.

128. Archie Macpherson, "Obituary: Jerry Kerr," *Independent,* November 11, 1999, accessed May 13, 2014, www.independent.co.uk/arts-entertainment/obituary-jerry-kerr-1125033.html.

129. Macpherson, "Obituary: Jerry Kerr."

130. Bob St. John, "Gusty Tornado Blows over Rovers, 4–1," *Dallas Morning News,* June 22, 1967, B1, accessed May 13, 2014, America's Historical Newspapers.

131. Bob St. John, "Gusty Tornado Blows over Rovers, 4–1," *Dallas Morning News,* June 22, 1967, B1, accessed May 13, 2014, America's Historical Newspapers.

132. St. John, "Dundee Blows Another One," B1.

133. Andrew Beyer, "Whips Won on Superb Condition," *Washington Post,* July 3, 1967, D4, accessed May 13, 2014, ProQuest Historical Newspapers.

134. "Introduction," Glentoran Football Club.

135. Dan Coughlin, "Stokers Face Irish Tonight," *Cleveland (OH) Plain Dealer,* June 4, 1967, 51, accessed May 13, 2014, America's Historical Newspapers.

136. Michael Lewis, "Remembering the Lancers," *Sports Illustrated,* December 5, 2000, accessed May 13, 2014.

137. Andrew Beyer, "Whips Invade Houston, Try to Grab Lead," *Washington Post,* July 4, 1967, D3, accessed May 13, 2014, ProQuest Historical Newspapers.

138. Andrew Beyer, "Whips Won by Relying on Strength," *Washington Post,* July 6, 1967, C3, accessed March 17, 2014, ProQuest Historical Newspapers.

139. Dan Coughlin, "Stokers in 2nd Place," *Cleveland (OH) Plain Dealer,* July 5, 1967, 33, accessed May 13, 2014, America's Historical Newspapers.

140. Coughlin, "Stokers in 2nd Place," 36.

141. "Glens Hold Stoke as Trainor Sent Off," Glentoran Football Club website, accessed May 13, 2014, www.glentoran-fc.co.uk/cougars%20stoke%20city.htm.

142. Andrew Beyer, "USA Allows Whips' Protest of L.A. Game," *Washington Post,* July 5, 1967, D2, accessed May 13, 2014, ProQuest Historical Newspapers.

143. Andrew Beyer, "Whips Need 5 or 6 Goals Tonight in Match against Unimposing Boston," *Washington Post,* July 8, 1967, D3, accessed May 13, 2014, ProQuest Historical Newspapers.

144. Beyer, "Whips Need 5 or 6 Goals," D3.

145. Andrew Beyer, "Whips Can Take Eastern Title Tonight," *Washington Post,* July 10, 1967, D1, accessed May 13, 2014, ProQuest Historical Newspapers.

146. "Hibs Face Saved by Late Goal," Glentoran Football Club website, accessed May 13, 2014, www.glentoran-fc.co.uk/cougars%20hibs.htm.

147. Dan Coughlin and Harold Greenberg, "Stokers Lose, but Still Alive,"*Cleveland (OH) Plain Dealer,* July 10, 1967, 32, accessed May 13, 2014, America's Historical Newspapers.

148. Gerald Eskenazi, "Skyliners and Stars Play to 2–2 Here in Final Game of Their Season," *New York Times,* July 9, 1967, 156, accessed May 13, 2014, ProQuest Historical Newspapers.

149. Eskenazi, "Skyliners and Stars Play," 156.

150. Shav Glick, "'Waggy' and Wolves Play to 2–2 Draw with Chicago," *Los Angeles Times*, July 6, 1967, B6, accessed November 7, 2013, ProQuest Historical Newspapers.

151. Roy Edwards, "Tornado Funnels Gale," *Dallas Morning News*, July 6, 1967, B3, accessed May 13, 2014, America's Historical Newspapers.

152. Bob St. John, "Another Tie for Tornado," *Dallas Morning News*, July 9, 1967, B1, accessed May 13, 2014, America's Historical Newspapers.

153. Andrew Beyer, "Whips Top L.A., 3–0, Win Title," *Washington Post*, July 11, 1967, D1, accessed May 13, 2014, ProQuest Historical Newspapers.

154. Andrew Beyer, "Whips, Los Angeles Collide Tonight for First U.S. Pro Soccer Crown," *Washington Post*, July 14, 1967, D1, accessed April 6, 2014, ProQuest Historical Newspapers.

155. "Former Don Goes to Washington," Aberdeen Football Club website, last modified June 27, 2011, accessed April 6, 2014, www.afc.co.uk/articles/20110627/former-don-goes-to-washington_2212158_2382701.

156. Beyer, "Whips, Gales Struggle," D1.

157. Beyer, "Whips Won by Relying," C3.

158. Andrew Beyer, "Turnbull Says Wolves Were Trying," *Washington Post*, July 12, 1967, D1, accessed April 6, 2014, ProQuest Historical Newspapers.

159. Andrew Beyer, "LA Says Referee Must Watch Whips," *Washington Post*, July 13, 1967, C3, accessed April 6, 2014, ProQuest Historical Newspapers.

160. United Press International, "West Ham Star Tells of Woes in Soccer Loop," *Springfield Union*, June 27, 1965, 37, accessed May 13, 2014, America's Historical Newspapers.

161. Holroyd, "The Year in American Soccer."

162. "Former Don Goes to Washington."

163. Andrew Beyer, "Whips Made Valiant Bid for USA Title Despite Smith's Ejection in First Half," *Washington Post*, July 16, 1967, C3, accessed April 6, 2014, ProQuest Historical Newspapers.

164. Beyer, "Whips Made Valiant Bid," C3.

165. Beyer, "LA Says Referee Must Watch," C3.

166. Beyer, "LA Says Referee Must Watch," C3.

167. "Former Don Goes to Washington."

168. Beyer, "Whips Made Valiant Bid," C3.

169. Associated Press, "English Soccer Team Rejects Bid by Cooke," *Washington Post*, July 19, 1967, D5, accessed March 9, 2014, ProQuest Newspapers.

170. Rich Roberts, "Jack Kent Cooke: Successful Owner Has Acquiring Mind," *Los Angeles Times*, January 22, 1984, B1, accessed May 14, 2014, ProQuest Historical Newspapers.

171. Bob Addie, "Attendance Figures Ominous," *Washington Post*, July 15, 1967, D1, accessed March 9, 2014, ProQuest Historical Newspapers.

172. "Merger Talk Incidental," *Los Angeles Times*, July 18, 1967, B2, accessed May 14, 2014, ProQuest Historical Newspapers.

173. Associated Press, "USA Reports Averaging 8850 a Game," *Washington Post*, June 21, 1967, D3, accessed May 14, 2014, ProQuest Historical Newspapers.

174. Associated Press, "Big Money Backs Fledgling Soccer League," *Springfield (MA) Union*, April 15, 1967, 14, accessed April 5, 2014, America's Historical Newspapers.

175. Glick, "Quick Lead, Rugged Defense," B1.

176. Addie, "Attendance Figures," D1.

177. Brian Glanville, "Soccer Success Visible," *New York Times*, June 4, 1967, S4, accessed October 29, 2013, ProQuest Historical Newspapers.

3. 1967, PART 2

1. Dave Brady, "TV Loot Is Newest Soccer Goal," *Washington Post*, October 2, 1966, C4, accessed November 11, 2013, ProQuest Historical Newspapers.

2. Derek Liecty, telephone interview by the author, Washington, D.C., March 22, 2014.

3. "D.C. Voted Second Pro Soccer Team," *Washington Post*, September 23, 1966, D3, accessed May 15, 2014, ProQuest Historical Newspapers.

4. Mark Asher, "Swede to Coach D.C. Soccer Team," *Washington Post*, October 23, 1966, C9, accessed May 14, 2014, ProQuest Historical Newspapers.

5. "The Art of Soccer," *Washington Post*, October 31, 1966, A20, accessed May 14, 2014, ProQuest Historical Newspapers.

6. "Soccer Decision Deferred," *Washington Post*, November 3, 1966, C1, accessed May 14, 2014, ProQuest Historical Newspapers.

7. Dave Brady, "Soccer Lease Goes to Foreman Group," *Washington Post*, November 10, 1966, C1, accessed May 14, 2014, ProQuest Historical Newspapers.

8. Andrew Beyer, "Whips Seek Cut in Stadium Rent," *Washington Post*, January 17, 1968, C1, accessed May 14, 2014, ProQuest Historical Newspapers.

9. Brady, "Soccer Lease Goes to Foreman," C1.

10. Dave Brady, "Soccer Team May Play in Baltimore," *Washington Post*, November 17, 1966, C6, ProQuest Historical Newspapers.

11. "Orioles May Back Booters," *Baltimore Sun*, November 18, 1966, C7, accessed May 14, 2014, ProQuest Historical Newspapers.

12. Doug Brown, "How Soccer Came to Baltimore," *Baltimore Sun*, April 16, 1967, SM14, accessed May 14, 2014, ProQuest Historical Newspapers.

13. Brown, "How Soccer Came to Baltimore," SM14.

14. Dave Brady, "Washington Soccer Group Nearing Deal with Orioles," *Washington Post*, November 25, 1966, D3, accessed May 14, 2014, ProQuest Historical Newspapers.

15. Ken Nigro, "Soccer Team May Locate in Baltimore," *Baltimore Sun*, November 24, 1966, C1, accessed May 14, 2014, ProQuest Historical Newspapers.

16. Ken Nigro, "Orioles Obtain Pro Soccer Club," *Baltimore Sun*, November 29, 1966, C1, accessed May 14, 2014, ProQuest Historical Newspapers.

17. Brown, "How Soccer Came to Baltimore," SM14.

18. Ken Nigro, "City's Soccer Team Names Toye As General Manager," *Baltimore Sun*, December 30, 1966, C3, accessed May 7, 2014, ProQuest Historical Newspapers.

19. Brown, "How Soccer Came to Baltimore," SM14.

20. Andrew Beyer, "Whips Must Build Team in Hurry, Can Profit by Mistakes of Others," *Washington Post*, January 14, 1968, D4, accessed March 1, 2014, ProQuest Historical Newspapers.

21. Andrew Beyer, "Ex-Reporter Pleased by His Soccer Team," *Washington Post*, April 13, 1967, C7, accessed May 14, 2014, ProQuest Historical Newspapers.

22. Ken Nigro, "Bays to Open Play April 16th," *Baltimore Sun*, January 11, 1967, C1, accessed May 14, 2014, ProQuest Historical Newspapers.

23. Beyer, "Ex-Reporter Pleased," C7.

24. Ken Nigro, "Bays Sign Two Forwards Playing for Spanish Teams," *Baltimore Sun*, February 5, 1967, A1, accessed May 14, 2014, ProQuest Historical Newspapers.

25. Beyer, "Ex-Reporter Pleased," C7.

26. Ken Nigro, "Bays Caused Israeli Furor by Signing Cohen, Primo," *Baltimore Sun*, March 14, 1967, C5, accessed May 14, 2014, ProQuest Historical Newspapers.

27. Nigro, "Bays Caused Israeli Furor," C5.

28. Nigro, "Bays Sign Two Forwards," A1.

29. Ken Nigro, "First Players Signed by Bays," *Baltimore Sun*, January 29, 1967, A1, accessed May 14, 2014, ProQuest Historical Newspapers.

30. Ken Nigro, "Taxes and Salaries Are Knotty Problems for Pro Soccer Teams," *Baltimore Sun*, January 23, 1967, C2, accessed May 14, 2014, ProQuest Historical Newspapers.

31. Ken Nigro, "Bays Introduce British Coach," *Baltimore Sun*, February 4, 1967, B1, accessed May 14, 2014, ProQuest Historical Newspapers.

32. Nigro, "Bays Introduce British Coach," B1.

33. Ken Nigro, "Bays Trials Rescheduled," *Baltimore Sun*, February 26, 1967, A9, accessed May 14, 2014, ProQuest Historical Newspapers.

34. Ken Nigro, "N.P.S.L. Adopts Revolutionary Scoring System," *Baltimore Sun*, March 21, 1967, C1, accessed May 14, 2014, ProQuest Historical Newspapers.

35. Nigro, "N.P.S.L. Adopts Revolutionary Scoring," C1.

36. Ken Nigro, "Bays, Generals Battle to Tie," *Baltimore Sun*, March 30, 1967, C1, accessed May 7, 2014, ProQuest Historical Newspapers.

37. Nigro, "Bays, Generals Battle to Tie," C1.

38. Ken Nigro, "Bays and Chiefs Vie in Richmond Struggle Today," *Baltimore Sun*, April 2, 1967, A1, accessed March 13, 2014, ProQuest Historical Newspapers.

39. Ken Nigro, "Atlanta Has Budding Star in Young Trinidad Kicker," *Baltimore Sun*, April 15, 1967, B1, accessed May 14, 2014, ProQuest Historical Newspapers.

40. Nigro, "Atlanta Has Budding Star," B1.

41. Gerald Eskenazi, "The Turnstiles Click," *New York Times*, April 17, 1967, 50, accessed May 14, 2014, ProQuest Historical Newspapers.

42. Eskenazi, "The Turnstiles Click," 50.

43. Ken Nigro, "Bays Beat Chiefs, 1–0, in Opener," *Baltimore Sun*, April 17, 1967, C1, accessed May 14, 2014, ProQuest Historical Newspapers.

44. Nigro, "Bays Beat Chiefs," C1.

45. "CBS Prepares for Bays Game," *Baltimore Sun*, March 24, 1967, C5, accessed May 14, 2014, ProQuest Historical Newspapers.

46. Bob Maisel, "The Morning After," *Baltimore Sun*, April 17, 1967, C1, accessed May 14, 2014, ProQuest Historical Newspapers.

47. Maisel, "The Morning After," C1.

48. Danny Blanchflower, "Just One Truth for Me," *Sports Illustrated*, June 10, 1968, accessed May 8, 2014, http://sportsillustrated.cnn.com/vault/article/magazine/MAG1081255/index.htm.

49. Ken Nigro, "Stars Have Tough Boss," *Baltimore Sun*, April 19, 1967, C1, accessed May 14, 2014, ProQuest Historical Newspapers.

50. Nigro, "Stars Have Tough Boss," C1.

51. "Willie Roy—USMNT," U.S. National Soccer Players, accessed May 14, 2014, www.ussoccerplayers.com/player/roy-willy.

52. "Willie Roy—USMNT."

53. Ken Nigro, "Stars Hand Bays First Defeat, 3–1," *Baltimore Sun*, April 20, 1967, C1, accessed May 14, 2014, ProQuest Historical Newspapers.

54. Ken Nigro, "Bays Coach Thinks Team is Progressing on Schedule," *Baltimore Sun*, April 10, 1967, C6, accessed May 14, 2014, ProQuest Historical Newspapers.

55. "Chyzowych Set As Bays Scout," *Baltimore Sun*, February 11, 1968, A10, accessed May 14, 2014, ProQuest Historical Newspapers.

56. "Spartan Booters in Bow," *Trenton Evening Times*, April 16, 1967, 65, accessed May 14, 2014, America's Historical Newspapers.

57. Ken Nigro, "Bays Battle Spartans to 0–0 Deadlock," *Baltimore Sun*, April 24, 1967, C1, accessed May 14, 2014, ProQuest Historical Newspapers.

58. Shav Glick, "Englishmen Is Leader of Multi-Lingual Toros," *Los Angeles Times*, July 22, 1967, A5, accessed October 27, 2013, ProQuest Historical Newspapers.

59. Tex Maule, "Kickoff for a Babel of Booters," *Sports Illustrated*, April 24, 1967, accessed October 27, 2013, http://si.com/vault/article/magazine/MAG1135457/index.htm.

60. Maule, "Kickoff for a Babel,"

61. Ken Nigro, "Bays to Battle Spurs Tonight," *Baltimore Sun*, April 28, 1967, C1, accessed May 14, 2014, ProQuest Historical Newspapers.

62. Nigro, "Bays to Battle Spurs," C1.

63. Gerald Eskenazi, "New York Eleven Will Play Spurs," *New York Times*, April 22, 1967, 23, accessed May 14, 2014, ProQuest Historical Newspapers.

64. Nigro, "Bays to Battle Spurs," C1.

65. Ken Nigro, "Bays Triumph on Two Goals by Chilinque," *Baltimore Sun*, April 29, 1967, B1, accessed May 14, 2014, ProQuest Historical Newspapers.

66. Associated Press, "Pittsburgh Not Taking to Soccer," *Washington Post*, May 24, 1967, D2, accessed May 14, 2014, ProQuest Historical Newspapers.

67. Ken Nigro, "Real Troubles Experienced by Phantom-Like Phantoms," *Baltimore Sun*, February 2, 1967, C3, accessed May 14, 2014, ProQuest Historical Newspapers.

68. Nigro, "Real Troubles," C3.

69. David Wangerin, *Soccer in a Football World* (Philadelphia: Temple University Press, 2008), 137.

70. Associated Press, "Loop-Leading Boot Team Fires Coach," *The Seattle (WA) Times*, May 1, 1967, 47, accessed October 28, 2013, America's Historical Newspapers.

71. Ken Nigro, "Phantoms Visit Bays Tonight," *Baltimore Sun*, May 3, 1967, C1, accessed May 14, 2014, ProQuest Historical Newspapers.

72. Nigro, "Phantoms Visit Bays," C1.

73. Ken Nigro, "Phantoms Beat Bays by 5 to 3," *Baltimore Sun*, May 4, 1967, C1, accessed May 14, 2014, ProQuest Historical Newspapers.

74. Wangerin, *Soccer in a Football World*, 131.

75. James Roach, "Soccer Players Have Spring Training, Too," *New York Times*, March 12, 1967, 209, accessed October 28, 2013, ProQuest Historical Newspapers.

76. Brian Glanville, "A Briton Takes a Kick at U.S. Soccer," *Washington Post*, June 25, 1967, D4, accessed October 28, 2013, ProQuest Historical Newspapers. "Bays Suffer First Loss on Road, 3–1," *Baltimore Sun*, June 19, 1967, C1, ProQuest Historical Newspapers.

77. Ken Nigro, "Bays Game Rained Out," *Baltimore Sun*, May 7, 1967, A9, accessed May 14, 2014, ProQuest Historical Newspapers.

78. Nigro, "Bays Game Rained Out."

79. Ken Nigro, "Bays Earn Tie with Spurs, 2–2," *Baltimore Sun*, May 14, 1967, SA1, accessed May 14, 2014, ProQuest Historical Newspapers.

80. Ken Nigro, "Speca's Last Minute Goal Gives Bays 3-to-2 Victory," *Baltimore Sun*, May 20, 1967, B1, accessed May 14, 2014, ProQuest Historical Newspapers.

81. Ken Nigro, "Bays Meet Generals in N.Y. Tonight," *Baltimore Sun*, May 24, 1967, C1, accessed May 14, 2014, ProQuest Historical Newspapers.

82. "Generals Rally in Second Half to Chief in Soccer, 2–2," *New York Times*, May 22, 1967, 55, accessed May 14, 2014, ProQuest Historical Newspapers.

83. Nigro, "Bays Meet Generals," C1.

84. Nigro, "Bays Meet Generals," C1.

85. "Bergesch Will Direct New Soccer Club Here," *New York Times*, February 19, 1967, 199, accessed May 14, 2014, ProQuest Historical Newspapers.

86. Gerald Eskenazi, "Yankees Bar Pro Soccer Game to Protect Stadium Turf," *New York Times*, April 25, 1968, 60, accessed May 14, 2014, ProQuest Historical Newspapers.

87. Eskenazi, "Yankees Bar Pro Soccer," 60.

88. Nigro, "Bays Meet Generals," C1.

89. Ken Nigro, "Bays and N.Y. Play to Dull 0–0 Deadlock," *Baltimore Sun*, May 25, 1967, C1, accessed May 14, 2014, ProQuest Historical Newspapers.

90. "TV Game Slated for Philadelphia," *New York Times*, April 30, 1967, 223, accessed May 14, 2014, ProQuest Historical Newspapers.

91. "Ferdinand Daucik (1950–1954)," FC Barcelona Web site, accessed May 14, 2014, www.fcbarcelona.com/club/history/detail/card/ferdinand-daucik-1950-1954.

92. Brian Glanville, "Obituary: Ladislao Kubala," *Guardian*, May 20, 2002, accessed May 14, 2014, www.theguardian.com/news/2002/may/21/guardianobituaries.brianglanville.

93. "Legends: Ladislao Kubala," FC Barcelona Web site, accessed May 14, 2014, www.fcbarcelona.com/club/history/detail/card/ladislao-kubala.

94. Jon Carter, "Rewind to 1961—Ladislao Kubala's Legacy at Barcelona," ESPNFC.com, last modified October 13, 2011, accessed May 14, 2014, www.espnfc.com/columns/story/_/id/967644/rewind-to-1961:-ladislao-kubala's-legacy-at-barcelona?cc=5901.

95. Glanville, "Obituary: Ladislao Kubala."

96. Roy Edwards, "Tough Kick from Abroad," *Dallas Morning News*, July 2, 1967, B2, accessed May 14, 2014, America's Historical Newspapers.

97. Ken Nigro, "Bays May Lose Israeli Players," *Baltimore Sun*, June 6, 1967, C1, accessed May 14, 2014, ProQuest Historical Newspapers.

98. Ken Nigro, "Bays Face Chiefs Here," *Baltimore Sun*, June 7, 1967, C1, accessed May 14, 2014, ProQuest Historical Newspapers

99. Ken Nigro, "Bays Edge Chiefs, 2–1 at Stadium," *Baltimore Sun*, June 8, 1967, C1, accessed May 14, 2014, ProQuest Historical Newspapers.

100. Ken Nigro, "Bays Seek First Place vs. Toronto," *Baltimore Sun*, June 10, 1967, B1, accessed May 14, 2014, ProQuest Historical Newspapers.

101. Ken Nigro, "Bays Beat Toronto by 3–2 Count," *Baltimore Sun*, June 11, 1967, SA1, accessed May 14, 2014, ProQuest Historical Newspapers.

102. Ken Nigro, "Bays Play Phantoms at Stadium Tonight," *Baltimore Sun*, June 14, 1967, C1, accessed May 14, 2014, ProQuest Historical Newspapers.

103. Nigro, "Bays Play Phantoms," C1.

104. "Bays Suffer First Loss on Road, 3–1," *Baltimore Sun*, June 19, 1967, C1, accessed May 14, 2014, ProQuest Historical Newspapers.

105. Ken Nigro, "Bays Defeat Los Angeles by 1–0 Score," *Baltimore Sun*, June 22, 1967, C1, accessed May 14, 2014, ProQuest Historical Newspapers.

106. Ken Nigro, "New Bonus Scoring System, May Return to Haunt Bays," *Baltimore Sun*, June 26, 1967, C6, accessed May 14, 2014, ProQuest Historical Newspapers.

107. Ken Nigro, "Phantoms Act Like Mets of Soccer League," *Baltimore Sun*, June 27, 1967, C1, accessed May 14, 2014, ProQuest Historical Newspapers.

108. Ken Nigro, "Bays Stage Rally, Gain 2-to-2 Tie," *Baltimore Sun*, June 28, 1967, C1, accessed May 14, 2014, ProQuest Historical Newspapers.

109. Ken Nigro, "Falcons Star Set for Bays Tonight," *Baltimore Sun*, June 30, 1967, C1, accessed May 14, 2014, ProQuest Historical Newspapers.

110. Ken Nigro, "Bays Lose in Toronto by 2 to 1," *Baltimore Sun*, July 1, 1967, B1, accessed May 14, 2014, ProQuest Historical Newspapers.

111. Ken Nigro, "Falcons Host Bays Tonight," *Baltimore Sun*, July 11, 1967, C1, accessed May 14, 2014, ProQuest Historical Newspapers.

112. Ken Nigro, "Generals Down Bays by 2 to 1," *Baltimore Sun*, July 17, 1967, C1, accessed May 14, 2014, ProQuest Historical Newspapers.

113. Nigro, "Generals Down Bays," C1.

114. Nigro, "Generals Down Bays," C1.

115. Ken Nigro, "Soccer Playoffs May Be Revised," *Baltimore Sun*, July 17, 1967, C5, accessed May 14, 2014, ProQuest Historical Newspapers.

116. Ken Nigro, "Coaching Change Spurs on Spurs," *Baltimore Sun*, July 23, 1967, SA1, accessed May 14, 2014, ProQuest Historical Newspapers.

117. Nigro, "Coaching Change."

118. Ken Nigro, "Bays Rally to Nip Spurs by 2–1 Count," *Baltimore Sun*, July 24, 1967, C1, accessed May 14, 2014, ProQuest Historical Newspapers.

119. Ken Nigro, "Bays, Toros Vie Tonight in Tilt Here," *Baltimore Sun*, July 26, 1967, C1, accessed May 14, 2014, ProQuest Historical Newspapers.

120. Ken Nigro, "Bays Beat Toros, 3–2, in Thriller," *Baltimore Sun*, July 27, 1967, C1, accessed May 14, 2014, ProQuest Historical Newspapers.

121. Nigro, "Bays Beat Toros," C1.

122. Ken Nigro, "Atlanta Kickers Tough As Hosts," *Baltimore Sun*, August 1, 1967, C1, accessed May 14, 2014, ProQuest Historical Newspapers.

123. Ken Nigro, "Bays Knot Chiefs, 2–2, in Atlanta," *Baltimore Sun*, August 6, 1967, A1, accessed May 14, 2014, ProQuest Historical Newspapers.

124. Ken Nigro, "Deleon Is New Ace of Generals," *Baltimore Sun*, August 7, 1967, C1, accessed May 14, 2014, ProQuest Historical Newspapers.

125. Ken Nigro, "Bays Near Title with 1–0 Victory," *Baltimore Sun*, August 10, 1967, C1, accessed May 14, 2014, ProQuest Historical Newspapers.

126. Ken Nigro, "Stars Visit Bays Sunday," *Baltimore Sun*, August 11, 1967, C3, accessed May 14, 2014, ProQuest Historical Newspapers.

127. Ken Nigro, "Bays Score 3–1 Victory to Near Title," *Baltimore Sun*, August 14, 1967, C1, accessed May 14, 2014, ProQuest Historical Newspapers.

128. Ken Nigro, "Bays Hope to Wrap up Title Here," *Baltimore Sun*, August 16, 1967, C1, accessed May 14, 2014, ProQuest Historical Newspapers.

129. Ken Nigro, "Bays Flag Delayed by Spartans," *Baltimore Sun*, August 17, 1967, C1, accessed May 14, 2014, ProQuest Historical Newspapers.

130. Nigro, "Bays Flag Delayed," C1.

131. Ken Nigro, "Bays Aim to Nab Pennant Today," *Baltimore Sun*, August 20, 1967, A1, accessed May 14, 2014, ProQuest Historical Newspapers.

132. Ken Nigro, "Bays Clinch Title in 0–0 Deadlock," *Baltimore Sun*, August 21, 1967, C1, accessed May 14, 2014, ProQuest Historical Newspapers.

133. Associated Press, "Navarro Named Top N.S.L. Player," *Baltimore Sun*, September 2, 1967, B3, accessed May 14, 2014, ProQuest Historical Newspapers.

134. "Spartans Quit Pro Boot Loop," *Pittsburgh Post-Gazette*, January 8, 1968, accessed May 14, 2014, http://news.google.com/newspapers?id=L51RAAAAIBAJ&sjid=b2wDAAAAIBAJ&dq=npsl&pg=7210%2C1312210.

135. Associated Press, "Pittsburgh Not Taking to Soccer," *Washington Post*, May 24, 1967, D2, accessed May 14, 2014, ProQuest Historical Newspapers.

136. Ken Nigro, "What Next? Bays in 1968 May Play without Coach," *Baltimore Sun*, September 5, 1967, C1, accessed May 14, 2014, ProQuest Historical Newspapers.

137. Ken Nigro, "Millward Ousted as Bay Coach," *Baltimore Sun*, September 5, 1967, C1, accessed May 14, 2014, ProQuest Historical Newspapers.

138. Nigro, "Millward Ousted," C1.

139. Nigro, "Millward Ousted," C1.

140. Bob Maisel, "The Morning After," *Baltimore Sun*, September 7, 1967, C1, accessed May 14, 2014, ProQuest Historical Newspapers.

141. Maisel, "The Morning After," C1.

142. Maisel, "The Morning After."

143. Ken Nigro, "Bays Name Englishman New Coach," *Baltimore Sun*, October 24, 1967, C1, accessed May 14, 2014, ProQuest Historical Newspapers.

144. Ken Nigro, "Ex-Coach Millward Raps Bays: Blames Soccer Team's Low Estate on Jago and Toye," *Baltimore Sun*, August 21, 1968, C1, accessed October 28, 2013, ProQuest Historical Newspapers.

145. Danny Blanchflower, "Just One Truth for Me," *Sports Illustrated*, June 10, 1968, accessed May 8, 2014, http://sportsillustrated.cnn.com/vault/article/magazine/MAG1081255/index.htm.

146. Blanchflower, "Just One Truth."

147. Nigro, "Ex-Coach Millward Raps Bays," C1

148. Blanchflower, "Just One Truth."

149. Georg N. Meyers, "TV Invents a Sport, Call It Soccer," *Seattle (WA) Daily Times*, March 14, 1967, accessed December 10, 2013, America's Historical Newspapers.

150. Associated Press, "Big Money Backs Fledgling Soccer League," *Springfield (MA) Union*, April 15, 1967, 14, accessed April 5, 2014, America's Historical Newspapers.

151. Ivor Davis, "The Latest Kick in Sport," *Los Angeles Times*, August 27, 1967, M44, accessed April 8, 2014, ProQuest Historical Newspapers.

152. Associated Press, "Foul Calls for Commercials Admitted by Soccer Referee," *New York Times*, May 15, 1967, 59, accessed April 8, 2014, ProQuest Historical Newspapers.

153. Associated Press, "Fake Fouls Called for TV Commercials," *Baltimore Sun*, May 15, 1967, C3, accessed April 8, 2014, ProQuest Historical Newspapers.

154. Associated Press, "Fake Fouls Called for TV Commercials," C3.

155. "Soccer League Confirms TV Ads Link," *New York Times*, May 16, 1967, 56, accessed April 8, 2014, ProQuest Historical Newspapers.

156. "Soccer League Confirms TV Ads Link," 56.

157. "Soccer League Confirms TV Ads Link," 56.

158. Associated Press, "Atlanta Chiefs' Coach Denies Phony Fouls," *Washington Post*, May 19, 1967, D3, accessed April 8, 2014, ProQuest Historical Newspapers.

159. Robert E. Dallos, "TV Soccer Charge Denied by C.B.S.," *New York Times*, June 7, 1967, 95, accessed April 9, 2014, ProQuest Historical Newspapers.

160. Dallos, "TV Soccer Charge Denied," 95.

161. Milton Richman, "Ref Toted a Gun," *St. Albans (VT) Messenger*, May 16, 1967, 6, accessed April 9, 2014, America's Historical Newspapers.

162. Robert Johnson Jr., "Say It Ain't So, Jay: Fitzgerald's Use of Baseball in 'The Great Gatsby,'" *The F. Scott Fitzgerald Review* 1 (2002): 40, accessed December 3, 2013, JSTOR.

163. Bill Veeck and Ed Linn, "Octopus under the Big Eye," *Sports Illustrated*, May 24, 1965, accessed December 7, 2013, http://sportsillustrated.cnn.com/vault/article/magazine/ MAG1077251/index.htm.

164. Johnson, "Say It Ain't So," 38.

165. William Barry Furlong, "A Sad Day for Baseball," *Sports Illustrated*, September 21, 1964, accessed December 7, 2013, http://si.com/vault/article/magazine/MAG1076373/index.htm.

166. Brian Glanville, "Soccer Plays It Safe," *New York Times*, May 28, 1967, S9, accessed October 29, 2013, ProQuest Historical Newspapers.

167. Charles Parrish and John Nauright, "Darts, Whips and Dips: The Rollercoaster Ride of Professional Soccer in DC" (working paper, n.d.), accessed February 14, 2014, http://www.academia.edu/1962245/Darts_Whips_and_Dips_The_Rollercoaster_Ride_of_Professional_ Soccer_in_Washington_D.C.

168. Wangerin, *Soccer in a Football World*, 122.

169. Associated Press, "Sports Pages Sure Tip to Orioles Stock Trend," *Springfield (MA) Union*, April 13, 1967, 3, accessed April 5, 2014, America's Historical Newspapers.

170. Brown, "How Soccer Came to Baltimore," SM14.

171. "Birds Plus Bays Equals $57,412," *Baltimore Sun*, December 24, 1967, A1, accessed April 5, 2014, ProQuest Historical Newspapers.

172. "Birds Plus Bays," A1.

173. "Birds Plus Bays," A1.

174. "Birds Plus Bays," A1.

175. Bob Addie, "Expensive Subsidiary," *Washington Post*, December 27, 1967, D1, accessed April 5, 2014, ProQuest Historical Newspapers.

176. Addie, "Expensive Subsidiary," D1.

177. Associated Press, "CBS Exonerated of Charges on Phony Timeouts," *Washington Post*, August 3, 1967, F6, accessed April 9, 2014, ProQuest Historical Newspapers.

178. Leonard Shecter, "Why It's Better to Watch the Game on TV," *New York Times*, March 3, 1968, SM32, accessed May 15, 2014, ProQuest Historical Newspapers.

179. Andrew Beyer, "Hopes Dim for USA's TV Contract," *Washington Post*, March 23, 1967, H7, accessed May 12, 2014, ProQuest Historical Newspapers.

180. William C. MacPhail, letter to the editor, *New York Times*, March 31, 1968, SM88, accessed April 9, 2014, ProQuest Historical Newspapers.

181. MacPhail, letter to the editor, SM88.

182. MacPhail, letter to the editor, SM88.

4. PRESS PLAY

1. Michael Maccambridge, "Director's Cut: 'Always Leave 'Em Laughing by Thomas Boswell," Grantland.com, last modified June 11, 2013, accessed May 8, 2014.

2. Jan Pinkerton and Randolph H. Hudson, "Chicago Tribune," in *Encyclopedia of the Chicago Literary Renaissance*, accessed May 7, 2014, Bloom's Literature.

3. Jan Pinkerton and Randolph H. Hudson, "Ring Lardner," in *Encyclopedia of the Chicago Renaissance*, accessed May 7, 2014, Bloom's Literature.

4. Robert Markus, "Obituary: David Condon, *Tribune* Columnist," *Chicago Tribune*, December 6, 1994, accessed January 26, 2014, http://articles.chicagotribune.com/1994-12-06/ news/9412060256_1_churchill-downs-chicago-tribune-tribune-columnist.

5. Markus, "Obituary: David Condon."

6. David Condon, "In the Wake of the News," *Chicago Tribune*, April 14, 1967, accessed January 26, 2014, ProQuest Historical Newspapers.

7. Condon, "In the Wake of the News," April 14, 1967.

8. David Trouille, "Association Football to Futbol: Ethnic Succession and the History of Chicago-area Soccer," *Soccer and Society* 10, no. 6 (November 2009): 796, accessed March 28, 2014, Taylor & Francis Social Sciences and Humanity Library.

9. Trouille, "Association Football to Futbol," 796.

10. Condon, "In the Wake of the News," April 14, 1967.

11. Vadim Furmanov, "A Sardinian Summer: The Forgotten Story of the Chicago Mustangs," In Bed With Maradona, blog entry posted August 20, 2013, accessed January 26, 2014, http://inbedwithmaradona.com/journal/2013/8/20/a-sardinian-summer-the-forgotten-story-of-the-chicago-mustangs.

12. Condon, "In the Wake of the News," April 14, 1967.

13. Furmanov, "A Sardinian Summer."

14. Condon, "In the Wake of the News," April 14, 1967.

15. Trouille, "Association Football to Futbol," 796.

16. Gary Armstrong and James Rosbrook-Thompson, "Coming to America: Historical Ontologies and United States Soccer," *Identities: Global Studies in Culture and Power* 17, no. 4 (July 9, 2010): 351, accessed March 28, 2014, Taylor & Francis Social Sciences and Humanities Library.

17. David Condon, "In the Wake of the News," *Chicago Tribune*, May 27, 1967, C1, accessed November 11, 2013, ProQuest Historical Newspapers.

18. Condon, "In the Wake of the News," C1.

19. Condon, "In the Wake of the News," May 27, 1967, C1.

20. Thomas M. Keefe, "The Catholic Issue in the *Chicago Tribune* before the Civil War," *Mid-America: An Historical Review* 57, no. 4 (1975): 242.

21. David Condon, "In the Wake of the News," *Chicago Tribune*, March 13, 1967, E1, accessed March 30, 2014, ProQuest Historical Newspapers.

22. Armstrong and Rosbrook-Thompson, "Coming to America," 367.

23. James Fitzgerald, "Dallas Subs Win Soccer Opener, 1–0," *Chicago Tribune*, May 29, 1967, B5, accessed May 7, 2014, ProQuest Historical Newspapers.

24. Fitzgerald, "Dallas Subs Win Soccer," B5.

25. Roy Edwards, "Tornado Roaring Success in Opener, 1–0," *Dallas (TX) Morning News*, May 29, 1967, B1, accessed May 7, 2014, America's Historical Newspapers.

26. "Nee," *Oxford English Dictionary*, accessed May 7, 2014, Oxford English Dictionary Online.

27. "Nee," *Oxford English Dictionary*.

28. "Nee," *Oxford English Dictionary*.

29. Shav Glick, "Wolves' Coach Applauds 4–1 Win: Soccer at Its Best, Crowd Pleaser," *Los Angeles Times*, June 19, 1967, C2, accessed May 7, 2014, ProQuest Historical Newspapers.

30. Shav Glick, "English Soccer Players Eye U.S.," *Los Angeles Times*, June 18, 1967, H13, accessed November 6, 2013, ProQuest Historical Newspapers.

31. Shav Glick, "Wolves Open at Home Against N.Y. Today," *Los Angeles Times*, June 4, 1967, H1, accessed November 6, 2013, ProQuest Historical Newspapers.

32. Shav Glick, "Wolves Leave . . . Title Stays Here," *Los Angeles Times*, July 16, 1967, H2, accessed March 30, 2014, ProQuest Historical Newspapers.

33. Shav Glick, "Wolves Belt Vancouver Kids, 5–1," *Los Angeles Times*, June 15, 1967, C6, accessed May 7, 2014, ProQuest Historical Newspapers.

34. Brian Glanville, "Bareno of Losers Gets First Score," *New York Times*, June 5, 1967, accessed October 30, 2013, ProQuest Historical Newspapers.

35. "Mask," *Merriam-Webster Thesaurus* (Springfield, MA: Merriam-Webster, 1989), 359.

36. Shav Glick, "Wolves, 'Fighting' Cagliari to Play," *Los Angeles Times*, July 5, 1967, B7, accessed November 9, 2013, ProQuest Historical Newspapers.

37. Gerald Eskenazi, "Skyliners Down Dallas Here, 4–1," *New York Times*, June 28, 1967, 50, accessed November 9, 2013, ProQuest Historical Newspapers.

38. Gerald Eskenazi, "Skyliners Oppose Mustangs Tonight," *New York Times*, June 16, 1967, S54, accessed May 7, 2014, ProQuest Historical Newspapers.

39. Gerald Eskenazi, "Referee Chased by Soccer Fans," *New York Times*, June 17, 1967, S23, accessed November 7, 2013, ProQuest Historical Newspapers.

40. Eskenazi, "Referee Chased," S23.

41. Gerald Eskenazi, "Skyliners Battle to 2–2 Soccer Tie with San Francisco at Yankee Stadium," *New York Times*, June 14, 1967, 56, accessed November 7, 2013, ProQuest Historical Newspapers.

42. Eskenazi, "Referee Chased," S23.

43. Scott Murray, Georgina Turner, and Sean Ingle, "The Greatest-ever European Cup Thrashings," *Guardian*, November 6, 2003, accessed November 9, 2013, www.theguardian.com/football/2003/nov/06/theknowledge.sport.

44. "Ken Aston—Inventor of Red and Yellow Cards," WineCape's Referee Blog, last modified February 23, 2010, accessed May 7, 2014, http://refarbiter.wordpress.com/2010/02/23/ken-aston-inventor-of-the-yellow-and-red-cards.

45. "Ken Aston," *The (London) Times*, October 25, 2001, Obituaries, 25, accessed November 7, 2013, The Times Digital Archive.

46. Murray, Turner, and Ingle, "The Greatest-ever European Cup Thrashings."

47. Eskenazi, "Referee Chased," S23.

48. Eskenazi, "Referee Chased," S23.

49. William J. Briordy, "Fans Riot As English Team Takes League Soccer Final at Downing Stadium," *New York Times*, August 5, 1963, 43, accessed November 9, 2013, ProQuest Historical Newspapers.

50. Gary Cartwright, "Spaniards Sparkle in the Astrodome," *Dallas (TX) Morning News*, April 20, 1967, B2, accessed November 22, 2013, America's Historical Newspapers.

51. Associated Press, "Fans Assault Referee in Mustang Duel," *Chicago Tribune*, June 17, 1967, D2, accessed November 11, 2013, ProQuest Historical Newspapers.

52. Gladys L. Knight, *Encyclopedia of American Race Riots*, Greenwood Milestones in African American History, ed. James N. Upton and Walter C. Rucker (Westport, CT: Greenwood Press, 2007), 365, accessed November 22, 2013, EBSCO eBook Collection (224792).

53. Knight, *Encyclopedia*, 365.

54. Gerald Eskenazi, "Santos of Brazil Tops Benfica, 4–0," *New York Times*, August 22, 1966, 46, accessed November 7, 2013, ProQuest Historical Newspapers.

55. Eskenazi, "Santos of Brazil," 46.

56. Brian Glanville, "How I Gave Wolves the Chance to Conquer America," *The (London) Times*, September 27, 2003, 45, accessed November 10, 2013, The Times Digital Archive.

57. Brian Glanville, "Soccer Plays It Safe," *New York Times*, May 28, 1967, S9, accessed October 29, 2013, ProQuest Historical Newspapers.

58. Glanville, "How I Gave Wolves."

59. Gerald Eskenazi, "Generals Turn Back Falcons in Soccer, 5–3, before 2,047 at Yankee Stadium," *New York Times*, June 18, 1967, 178, accessed November 9, 2013, ProQuest Historical Newspapers.

60. "England's World Cup Victory Strained Relations with Argentina," *The (London) Times*, January 1, 1997, 5, accessed November 8, 2013, The Times Digital Archive.

61. Brian Glanville, "Replaying Controversy and the Day Fate Took a Hand," *The (London) Times*, June 29, 1998, 27, accessed November 8, 2013, The Times Digital Archive.

62. Glanville, "Replaying Controversy," 27.

63. Brian Glanville, "A Misbegotten Series," *New York Times*, September 22, 1968, 204, accessed November 24, 2013, ProQuest Historical Newspapers.

64. Brian Glanville, "Hard-headed Soccer," *New York Times*, June 22, 1969, S9, accessed November 24, 2013, ProQuest Historical Newspapers.

65. Ken Nigro, "Press Meets Toye of Bays," *Baltimore Sun*, January 28, 1967, B1, accessed May 7, 2014, ProQuest Historical Newspapers.

66. Ken Nigro, "City's Soccer Team Names Toye As General Manager," *Baltimore Sun*, December 30, 1966, C3, accessed May 7, 2014, ProQuest Historical Newspapers.

67. Ken Nigro, "Bays, Generals Battle to Tie," *Baltimore Sun*, March 30, 1967, C1, accessed May 7, 2014, ProQuest Historical Newspapers.

68. Arthur Daley, "On a Grandiose Scale," *New York Times*, February 9, 1960, 34, accessed April 14, 2014, ProQuest Historical Newspapers.

69. Furmanov, "A Sardinian Summer."

70. Brian Glanville, "Two Soccer Leagues One Too Many," *New York Times*, April 16, 1967, S7, accessed October 29, 2013, ProQuest Historical Newspapers.

71. Armstrong and Rosbrook-Thompson, "Coming to America," 351.

72. Shav Glick, "Wolves, 'Fighting' Cagliari to Play," *Los Angeles Times*, July 5, 1967, B7, accessed November 9, 2013, ProQuest Historical Newspapers.

73. "Partisan," n. 2 and adj., *Oxford English Dictionary*, 3rd ed., accessed November 11, 2013, Oxford English Dictionary Online.

74. "Partisan," *The Merriam-Webster Thesaurus* (Springfield, MA: Merriam-Webster, 1989), 410.

75. Armstrong and Rosbrook-Thompson, "Coming to America," 351.

76. Sam Tanenhous, "Hello to All That: The Irony behind the Demise of the Partisan Review," Slate, last modified April 16, 2003, accessed November 23, 2013, www.slate.com/articles/arts/culturebox/2003/04/hello_to_all_that.html.

77. Armstrong and Rosbrook-Thompson, "Coming to America," 367.

78. Dave Brady, "TV Loot Is Newest Soccer Goal," *Washington Post*, October 2, 1966, C4, accessed November 11, 2013, ProQuest Historical Newspapers.

79. "Indoctrinate," *Oxford English Dictionary*, accessed May 7, 2014, Oxford English Dictionary Online.

80. Dave Brady, "'Outlaw' Soccer League Lands CBS TV Deal," *Washington Post*, October 4, 1966, D1, accessed May 7, 2014, ProQuest Historical Newspapers.

81. Bob Addie, "The Right Time," *Washington Post*, November 4, 1966, D4, accessed May 7, 2014, ProQuest Historical Newspapers.

82. Joseph Durso, "Local Pro Soccer Teams May Share Stadium with Yanks in the Spring," *New York Times*, February 12, 1967, accessed May 7, 2014, ProQuest Historical Newspapers.

83. Brian Glanville, "A Briton Takes a Kick at U.S. Soccer," *Washington Post*, June 25, 1967, D4, accessed October 28, 2013, ProQuest Historical Newspapers.

84. Glanville, "A Briton Takes a Kick," D4

85. Gerald Eskenazi, "Cougars Down Skyliners, 1–0, before 3,517," *New York Times*, July 3, 1967, 22, accessed April 3, 2014, ProQuest Historical Newspapers.

86. Geoffrey Green, "Conflict between Leagues Confuses Americans," *The (London) Times*, June 19, 1967, 13, accessed May 7, 2014, The Times Digital Archive.

87. Harold Torre, "A Sport-loving Nation," *The (Times) of London*, August 17, 1925, 17, accessed May 7, 2014, The Times Digital Archive.

88. Green, "Conflict between Leagues," 13.

89. Green, "Conflict between Leagues," 13.

90. Associated Press, "Houston Wins, 2–0, As Riot Halts Game," *Washington Post*, June 15, 1967, K27, accessed May 7, 2014, ProQuest Historical Newspapers.

91. Associated Press, "Fight by Players Ends Soccer Game," *New York Times*, June 15, 1967, 65, accessed May 7, 2014, ProQuest Historical Newspapers.

92. "Worldwide Comment on Newark," *Trenton (NJ) Evening Times*, July 16, 1967, 14, accessed November 23, 2013, America's Historical Newspapers.

93. "Worldwide Comment," 14.

94. "Calm before the Storm," Glentoran Football Club website, accessed March 29, 2014, www.glentoran-fc.co.uk/cougars%20bangu.htm.

95. "Rookie Linesman Robs Glentoran," Glentoran Football Club website, accessed March 29, 2014, www.glentoran-fc.co.uk/cougars%20shamrock%20rovers.htm.

96. Glanville, "Soccer Plays It Safe," S9.

97. "Mustangs in Huff; Fans Swarm Field," *Chicago Tribune*, June 19, 1967, C6, accessed November 11, 2013, ProQuest Historical Newspapers.

98. Associated Press, "Fans Riot As Chicago Loses, 2–1," *Washington Post*, June 19, 1967, D4, accessed May 7, 2014, ProQuest Historical Newspapers.

99. Associated Press, "Mustang Trio Suspended by Soccer League," *Chicago Tribune*, June 23, 1967, C4, accessed November 11, 2013, ProQuest Historical Newspapers.

100. Associated Press, "Mustang Trio," C4.

101. Armstrong and Rosbrook-Thompson, "Coming to America," 351.

102. John Wefing, *The Life and Times of Richard J. Hughes: The Politics of Civility* (New Brunswick, NJ: Rutgers University Press, 2009), 171.

103. United Press International, "Ike Would Restore 'Powers of Police,'" *Springfield (MA) Union*, July 26, 1967, 2, accessed November 23, 2013, America's Historical Newspapers.

104. "Baseball Game in Detroit Ends in a Riot; 18,000 Rush Field," *New York Times*, June 14, 1924, 1, accessed November 23, 2013, ProQuest Historical Newspapers.

105. "Baseball Game in Detroit," 1.

106. Aldo Beckman, "Newark Rioting Traced to Hate Campaign," *Chicago Tribune*, August 8, 1967, 1, accessed November 23, 2013, ProQuest Historical Newspapers.

107. "Riots Are Subsidized As Well As Organized," *Chicago Tribune*, August 6, 1967, 24, accessed November 23, 2013, ProQuest Historical Newspapers.

108. Armstrong and Rosbrook-Thompson, "Coming to America," 351.

109. Lowell Miller, "The Selling of Soccer-Mania," *New York Times*, August 28, 1977, 187, accessed January 2, 2014, ProQuest Historical Newspapers.

110. Philip H. Dougherty, "Advertising: Soccer Promotion Kicked Off," *New York Times*, April 17, 1967, 54, accessed December 10, 2013, ProQuest Historical Newspapers.

111. Dougherty, "Advertising," 54.

112. Miller, "The Selling of Soccer-Mania," 187.

113. Frank Deford, "Show, Sex and Suburbs," *Sports Illustrated*, February 28, 1983, accessed November 24, 2013, http://sportsillustrated.cnn.com/vault/article/magazine/MAG1120568/index.htm.

114. Ken Nigro, "Woosnam Eyes Soccer Success," *Baltimore Sun*, April 15, 1969, C1, accessed January 5, 2014, ProQuest Historical Newspapers.

115. Steve Cady, "U.S. Soccer, Losing Its Shirt, Told to Tighten Its Belt," *New York Times*, January 12, 1969, S12, accessed February 9, 2014, ProQuest Historical Newspapers.

116. David L. Andrews, Robert Pitter, Detlev Zwick, and Darren Ambrose, "Soccer's Racial Frontier: Sport and the Suburbanization of Contemporary America," in *Entering the Field New Perspectives on World Football*, ed. Gary Armstrong and Richard Guilanotti (Oxford: Berg, 1997), 263.

117. Associated Press, "Whither Soccer? To the Top, Woosnam Believes," *Baltimore Sun*, July 27, 1975, B6, accessed January 5, 2014, ProQuest Historical Newspapers.

118. Ken Nigro, "Baltimore Returns to Soccer League," *Baltimore Sun*, December 5, 1973, C1, accessed March 12, 2014, ProQuest Historical Newspapers.

119. Associated Press, "Whither Soccer?" B6.

120. Associated Press, "Whither Soccer?" B6.

121. Associated Press, "Whither Soccer?" B6.

122. Seymour Smith, "Woosnam Optimistic about Soccer's Future," *Baltimore Sun*, May 27, 1974, C4, accessed January 9, 2014, ProQuest Historical Newspapers.

123. Miller, "The Selling of Soccer-Mania," 187.

124. Robert Johnson Jr., "Say It Ain't So, Jay: Fitzgerald's Use of Baseball in 'The Great Gatsby,'" *The F. Scott Fitzgerald Review* 1 (2002): 40, accessed December 3, 2013, JSTOR.

125. Ken Nigro, "Woosnam Eyes Soccer Success," *Baltimore Sun*, April 15, 1969, C1, accessed January 5, 2014, ProQuest Historical Newspapers.

126. Nigro, "Woosnam Eyes Soccer Success," C1.

5. CALIFORNIA CLIPPERS

1. Associated Press, "SF Gets Soccer Franchise," *(Portland) Oregonian*, October 26, 1966, 35, accessed April 6, 2014, America's Historical Newspapers.

2. David Wangerin, *Distant Corners: American Soccer's History of Missed Opportunities and Lost Causes* (Philadelphia: Temple University Press, 2011), 192.

3. Associated Press, "SF Gets Soccer Franchise," 35.

4. United Press International, "Oakland's Own Now," *Washington Post*, June 11, 1967, D5, accessed March 1, 2014, ProQuest Historical Newspapers.

5. Ken Nigro, "Oakland Is Foe of Bays Tonight," *Baltimore Sun*, July 3, 1967, C1, accessed March 2, 2014, ProQuest Historical Newspapers.

6. Derek Liecty, telephone interview by the author, Washington, D.C., March 22, 2014.

7. Andrew Beyer, "Whips Must Build Team in Hurry, Can Profit by Mistakes of Others," *Washington Post*, January 14, 1968, D4, accessed March 1, 2014, ProQuest Historical Newspapers.

8. Beyer, "Whips Must Build Team," D4.

9. Beyer, "Whips Must Build Team," D4.

10. Wangerin, *Distant Corners*, 189.

11. Liecty, telephone interview by the author.

12. Wangerin, *Distant Corners*, 189.

13. Derek Liecty, "Comments by Derek Liecty, Former General Manager, Oakland Clippers Professional Soccer Team, National Professional Soccer League" (unpublished manuscript, n.d.).

14. United Press International, "Pro Soccer Challenge Turned Down," *Washington Post*, May 22, 1967, D6, accessed March 1, 2014, ProQuest Historical Newspapers.

15. United Press International, "Pro Soccer Challenge," D6.

16. United Press International, "Pro Soccer Challenge," D6.

17. Bob Addie, "Nevers Sees Merger," *Washington Post*, August 31, 1967, C4, accessed March 1, 2014, ProQuest Historical Newspapers.

18. Associated Press, "Football's Ernie Nevers Now Pumps for Soccer," *Washington Post*, May 25, 1967, C5, accessed March 1, 2014, ProQuest Historical Newspapers.

19. Liecty, telephone interview by the author.

20. Liecty, telephone interview by the author.

21. PAC-12 Conference, "Stanford Soccer's Renaissance Man: Leo Weinstein, 1921–2009," PAC-12 News, last modified May 12, 2009, accessed March 2, 2014, http://pac-12.com/article/2009/05/12/stanford-soccers-renaissance-man-leo-weinstein-1921-2009.

22. Liecty, telephone interview by the author.

23. Philip H. Dougherty, "Advertising: Soccer Promotion Kicked Off," *New York Times*, April 17, 1967, 54, accessed December 10, 2013, ProQuest Historical Newspapers.

24. Liecty, "Comments by Derek Liecty."

25. "Bays Suffer First Loss on Road, 3–1," *Baltimore Sun*, June 19, 1967, C1, ProQuest Historical Newspapers.

26. Ken Nigro, "Bays Edge Clippers by 1–0," *Baltimore Sun*, July 4, 1967, B1, accessed March 26, 2014, ProQuest Historical Newspapers.

27. Nigro, "Bays Edge Clippers," B1.

28. Nigro, "Bays Edge Clippers," B1.

29. Ken Nigro, "A Few Bays Nurse Bumps," *Baltimore Sun*, July 5, 1967, C4, accessed March 2, 2014, ProQuest Historical Newspapers.

30. Nigro, "A Few Bays," C4.

31. Nigro, "A Few Bays," C4.

32. Associated Press, "Clippers Blitz Stars, 9–0," *Baltimore Sun*, July 27, 1967, C4, accessed March 26, 2014, ProQuest Historical Newspapers.

33. Associated Press, "Clippers Beat Spurs, Win West Title," *Chicago Tribune*, August 17, 1967, E2, accessed April 6, 2014, ProQuest Historical Newspapers.

34. Ken Nigro, "Clippers Given Edge over Bays," *Baltimore Sun*, August 31, 1967, C1, accessed March 13, 2014, ProQuest Historical Newspapers.

35. Bob Maisel, "The Morning After," *Baltimore Sun*, September 4, 1967, C1, accessed March 3, 2014, ProQuest Historical Newspapers.

36. Maisel, "The Morning After," C1.

37. Ken Nigro, "Clipper's Coach Studies Weather," *Baltimore Sun*, September 7, 1967, C1, accessed May 9, 2014, ProQuest Historical Newspapers.

38. Ken Nigro, "Clippers Hope to Outdraw Bays in Oakland Tomorrow," *Baltimore Sun*, September 8, 1967, C1, accessed March 3, 2014, ProQuest Newspapers.

39. Nigro, "Clippers Hope to Outdraw," C1.

40. Nigro, "Clippers Hope to Outdraw," C1.

41. Wangerin, *Distant Corners: American Soccer's*, 193.

42. "Clippers Top Bays in Title Series, 4–2," *New York Times*, September 10, 1967, 242, accessed March 3, 2014, ProQuest Historical Newspapers.

43. Ken Nigro, "Clippers Rout Bays, 4–1, in Hectic Climax to Soccer Playoffs," *Baltimore Sun*, September 10, 1967, SP1, accessed March 26, 2014, ProQuest Historical Newspapers.

44. Nigro, "Clippers Rout Bays, 4–1," SP1.

45. Nigro, "Clippers Rout Bays, 4–1," SP1.

46. Associated Press, "Clippers Win Challenge Cup," *Baltimore Sun*, September 19, 1967, C2, accessed March 3, 2014, ProQuest Historical Newspapers.

47. Liecty, telephone interview by the author.

48. Liecty, telephone interview by the author.

49. Nigro, "Clippers Hope to Outdraw," C1.

50. Associated Press, "Pro Soccer Planned in Kansas City," *Baltimore Sun*, January 5, 1968, C1, accessed March 3, 2014, ProQuest Historical Newspapers.

51. Ken Nigro, "'New Look Bays Open Here Today," *Baltimore Sun*, April 21, 1968, A1, accessed March 3, 2014, ProQuest Historical Newspapers.

52. Associated Press, "Kansas City Tops Houston," *Baltimore Sun*, June 10, 1968, C9, accessed March 3, 2014, ProQuest Historical Newspapers.

53. Wangerin, *Distant Corners*, 196.

54. "Clippers Top Wolves, 4–2," *Los Angeles Times*, August 19, 1968, E2, accessed March 26, 2014, ProQuest Historical Newspapers.

55. Associated Press, "Crowds Off, Clippers Eye New Home," *Washington Post*, August 27, 1968, C5, accessed March 4, 2014, ProQuest Historical Newspapers.

56. Wangerin, *Distant Corners*, 199.

57. Steve Holroyd and David Litterer, "The Year in American Soccer—1968," American Soccer History Archives, last modified January 31, 2010, accessed February 5, 2014, http://homepages.sover.net/~spectrum/year/1968.html.

58. Liecty, "Comments by Derek Liecty."

59. United Press International, "Pro Soccer Was a Costly Lesson," *Seattle (WA) Daily Times*, November 5, 1968, 27, accessed March 4, 2014, America's Historical Newspapers.

60. United Press International, "Pro Soccer," 27.

61. Wangerin, *Distant Corners*, 200.

62. Liecty, "Comments by Derek Liecty."

63. Liecty, "Comments by Derek Liecty."

64. "Generals Soccer Team Won't Operate This Year," *New York Times*, February 19, 1969, 54, accessed March 26, 2014, ProQuest Historical Newspapers.

65. Associated Press, "Soccer Exhibition in N.Y. Ruled Out," *Baltimore Sun*, August 4, 1967, C1, accessed May 9, 2014, ProQuest Historical Newspapers.

66. United Press International, "Title Bid Farewell to Chiefs?" *Marietta (GA) Journal*, September 25, 1968, accessed April 11, 2014, America's Historical Newspapers.

67. Liecty, "Comments by Derek Liecty."

68. Wangerin, *Distant Corners*, 201.

69. Derek Liecty, e-mail message to author, March 23, 2014.

70. Liecty, "Comments by Derek Liecty."

71. "Soviet Eleven Arrives for U.S. Debut," *New York Times*, February 18, 1969, 49, accessed March 5, 2014, ProQuest Historical Newspapers.

72. Liecty, "Comments by Derek Liecty."

73. Liecty, "Comments by Derek Liecty."

74. Derek Liecty, e-mail message to author.

75. Liecty, "Comments by Derek Liecty."

76. Wangerin, *Distant Corners*, 203.

77. Wangerin, *Distant Corners*, 205.

78. "Oakland Clippers Friendlies," NASL Jerseys, accessed March 1, 2014, www.nasljerseys.com/Friendlies/Teams/Clippers%20Friendlies.htm.

79. Jonathan Wilson, *Inverting the Pyramid: The History of Football Tactics* (London: Orion, 2009), 154.

80. Chris Mann, "Football's Greatest Managers: #2 Viktor Maslov," The Equaliser, blog entry posted October 22, 2010, accessed March 13, 2014, http://equaliserblog.wordpress.com/2010/10/22/2-maslov.

81. Associated Press, "Russian Club Makes U.S. Soccer Bow," *Washington Post*, February 23, 1969, 53, accessed March 5, 2014, ProQuest Historical Newspapers.

82. "Soviet Eleven," 49.

83. Shav Glick, "George Allen Has Ally, Soviets Rap Kezar, Too," *Los Angeles Times*, February 25, 1969, E1, accessed March 5, 2014, ProQuest Historical Newspapers.

84. Glick, "George Allen," E1.

85. Glick, "George Allen," E1.

86. Liecty, telephone interview by the author.

87. Glick, "George Allen," E1.

88. Shav Glick, "Russians Gain 1–1 Tie with Clippers in Last 6 Seconds," *Los Angeles Times*, March 3, 1969, F1, accessed March 26, 2014, ProQuest Historical Newspapers.

89. Glick, "Russians Gain 1–1 Tie," F1.

90. Associated Press, "Clippers, Russ in Final Match of Soccer Series," *Seattle (WA) Daily Times*, March 9, 1969, 30, accessed March 5, 2014, America's Historical Newspapers.

91. Associated Press, "Clippers, Russ in Final," 30.

92. Associated Press, "Clippers, Russ in Final," 30.

93. Glick, "Russians Gain 1–1 Tie," F1.

94. Associated Press, "Clippers Top U.S. Kickers," *Los Angeles Times*, April 14, 1969, E3, accessed March 6, 2014, ProQuest Historical Newspapers.

95. Associated Press, "Clippers Bow by 2–0 Score," *Los Angeles Times*, May 19, 1969, B4, accessed March 6, 2014, ProQuest Historical Newspapers.

96. Shav Glick, "Soccer Duels at Coliseum End in Ties," *Los Angeles Times*, May 24, 1969, C3, accessed March 6, 2014, ProQuest Historical Newspapers.

97. "Oakland Clippers Friendlies."

98. United Press International, "California Clippers Go Out of Business," *Washington Post*, June 5, 1969, H2, accessed March 1, 2014, ProQuest Historical Newspapers.

99. United Press International, "California Clippers Go Out of Business," H2.

100. California Clippers, Inc. v. United States S.F. Assn., 314 F. Supp., 9th Cir. 1970. www.leagle.com/decision/19701371314FSupp1057_11156.xml/CALIFOR-NIA%20CLIPPERS,%20INC.%20v.%20UNITED%20STATES%20S.%20F.%20ASS'N.

101. "3 Soccer Groups Charged in Suit," *New York Times*, October 15, 1969, 54, accessed March 26, 2014, ProQuest Historical Newspapers.

102. "3 Soccer Groups Charged," 54.

103. Eugene L. Scott, "Generals Fade Away: Decision to Abandon League Play Forced out New York," *New York Times*, March 16, 1969, S6, accessed February 8, 2014, ProQuest Historical Newspapers.

104. Scott, "Generals Fade Away," S6.

105. Scott, "Generals Fade Away," S6.

106. Bill Veeck and Ed Linn, "Octopus under the Big Eye," *Sports Illustrated*, May 24, 1965, accessed December 7, 2013, http://sportsillustrated.cnn.com/vault/article/magazine/MAG1077251/index.htm.

107. Andrew Beyer, "Amateurs Grab Soccer War Playoff," *Washington Post*, January 18, 1967, D1, accessed March 17, 2014, ProQuest Historical Newspapers.

108. Beyer, "Amateurs Grab Soccer War Playoff," D1.

109. Andrew Beyer, "Soccer Moguls Boot a Big One," *Washington Post*, September 12, 1967, D3, accessed March 26, 2014, ProQuest Historical Newspapers.

110. "NASL to Expand Foreign Schedule," *Dallas (TX) Morning News*, July 11, 1968, B5, accessed April 13, 2014, America's Historical Newspapers.

111. Beyer, "Soccer Moguls," D3.

112. Beyer, "Soccer Moguls," D3.

113. Tom Dunmore, "Expanded Dreams: The International Soccer League, Part Three," Pitch Invasion, blog entry posted November 14, 2011, accessed March 24, 2014, http://pitchinvasion.net/blog/2011/11/14/expanded-dreams-the-international-soccer-league-part-three/.

114. David Wangerin, *Soccer in a Football World* (Philadelphia: Temple University Press, 2008), 123.

115. Wangerin, *Distant Corners*, 192.

116. Liecty, telephone interview by the author.

6. DALLAS FILE

1. Jack Olsen, "Biggest Cheapskate in Big D," *Sports Illustrated*, June 19, 1972, accessed April 1, 2014, http://sportsillustrated.cnn.com/vault/article/magazine/MAG1086220/1/index.htm.

2. Olsen, "Biggest Cheapskate in Big D."

3. Olsen, "Biggest Cheapskate in Big D."

4. Olsen, "Biggest Cheapskate in Big D."

5. Olsen, "Biggest Cheapskate in Big D."

6. Olsen, "Biggest Cheapskate in Big D."

7. "Tornado Blows In," *Dallas (TX) Morning News*, May 23, 1967, 3, accessed November 7, 2013, America's Historical Newspapers.

8. "Tornado Blows In," 3.

9. "Tornado Blows In," 3.

10. Sam Blair, "A New Way to Get Kicks," *Dallas (TX) Morning News*, June 5, 1967, 2, accessed April 1, 2014, America's Historical Newspapers.

11. Blair, "A New Way to Get Kicks," 2.

12. Andrew Beyer, "Home Pitch No Edge in USA," *Washington Post*, June 20, 1967, D3, accessed November 6, 2013, ProQuest Historical Newspapers.

13. Roy Edwards, "Tornado, Stars Tie as Goal Disallowed," *Dallas (TX) Morning News*, June 4, 1967, B1, accessed April 1, 2014, America's Historical Newspapers.

14. Bob St. John, "Tornado Sweeps into Astrodome," *Dallas (TX) Morning News*, June 10, 1967, B2, accessed April 1, 2014, America's Historical Newspapers.

15. "Alias," *Oxford English Dictionary*, accessed April 1, 2014, Oxford English Dictionary Online.

16. St. John, "Tornado Sweeps into Astrodome," B2.

17. Brian Glanville, "Pro Soccer's Enigma," *New York Times*, July 2, 1967, 104, accessed November 24, 2013, ProQuest Historical Newspapers.

18. Glanville, "Pro Soccer's Enigma," 104.

19. Andrew Beyer, "New Soccer League Sees American Players in Future," *Washington Post*, January 29, 1967, C4, accessed April 2, 2014, ProQuest Historical Newspapers.

20. Steven Apostolov, "Everywhere and Nowhere: The Forgotten Past and Clouded Future of American Professional Soccer from the Perspective of Massachusetts," *Soccer and Society* 13, no. 4 (July 2012): 526, accessed April 1, 2014, Academic Search Premier.

21. Apostolov, "Everywhere and Nowhere," 526.

22. Apostolov, "Everywhere and Nowhere," 526.

23. Andy Crossley, "1974–1976 Boston Minutemen," Fun While It Lasted: Lively Tales about Dead Teams, last modified August 25, 2013, accessed April 1, 2014, www.funwhileitlasted.net/tag/boston-minutemen.

24. Apostolov, "Everywhere and Nowhere," 527.

25. United Press International, "Soccer Writer Solicits Article, Ends Up As Coach," *Washington Post*, July 21, 1967, D4, accessed March 9, 2014, ProQuest Historical Newspapers.

26. Neil Jones, "The Forgotten Story . . . of the Dallas Tornado's 1967–68 World Tour," *Guardian*, January 9, 2014, accessed January 20, 2014, www.theguardian.com/sport/blog/2014/jan/09/forgotten-story-of-dallas-tornado.

27. Jones, "The Forgotten Story."

28. Jones, "The Forgotten Story."

29. Ken Nigro, "Dallas and Bays Collide Tonight: Tornado's Woes Began with Central American Tour," *Baltimore Sun*, May 18, 1968, B1, accessed January 3, 2014, ProQuest Historical Newspapers.

30. Michael MacCambridge, *Lamar Hunt: A Life in Sports* (Riverside, NJ: Andrews McMeel, 2012), 175.

31. Jones, "The Forgotten Story."

32. Jones, "The Forgotten Story."

33. Jones, "The Forgotten Story."

34. Jones, "The Forgotten Story."

35. Beyer, "New Soccer League," C4.

36. Jones, "The Forgotten Story."

37. Roy Edwards, "Sour Cream for Tornado," *Dallas (TX) Morning News*, May 31, 1968, B3, accessed April 12, 2014, America's Historical Newspapers.

38. MacCambridge, *Lamar Hunt*, 175.

39. "Harvey Saw the World with Dallas Tornado," Oklahoma City University Sports, last modified January 21, 2014, accessed April 2, 2014, www.ocusports.com/news/2014/1/21/MSOC_0121143535.aspx?path=msoc.

40. "Dallas Tornado 1967–68 World," NASL Jerseys, accessed December 17, 2013, www.nasljerseys.com/Misc/Tornado%2067-68%20World%20Tour2.htm.

41. Associated Press, "Fans Stone U.S. Kickers," *Baltimore Sun*, December 5, 1967, C6, accessed December 31, 2013, ProQuest Historical Newspapers.

42. Jones, "The Forgotten Story."

43. Jones, "The Forgotten Story."

44. "Harvey Saw the World," Oklahoma City University Sports.

45. Nigro, "Dallas and Bays Collide," B1.

46. Reuters, "Tornados in Soccer Tie," *New York Times*, October 12, 1967, 62, accessed December 31, 2013, ProQuest Historical Newspapers.

47. Associated Press, "Dallas Soccer Team Loses," *New York Times*, December 25, 1967, 41, accessed December 31, 2013, ProQuest Historical Newspapers.

48. "Dallas Tornado 1967–68 World," NASL Jerseys.

49. Jones, "The Forgotten Story."

50. Jones, "The Forgotten Story."

51. Associated Press, "Lost Soccer Stars Arrive in Calcutta," *Washington Post*, November 6, 1967, D8, accessed April 2, 2014, ProQuest Historical Newspapers.

52. Associated Press, "Lost Soccer Stars," D8.

53. Jones, "The Forgotten Story."

54. Jones, "The Forgotten Story."

55. Jones, "The Forgotten Story."

56. "Harvey Saw the World," Oklahoma City University Sports.

57. Roy Edwards, "Good to Be Home," *Dallas (TX) Morning News*, March 17, 1968, B3, accessed April 1, 2014, America's Historical Newspapers.

58. Edwards, "Good to Be Home," B3.

59. Edwards, "Good to Be Home," B3.

60. Roy Edwards, "Hail, and Farewell," *Dallas (TX) Morning News*, September 9, 1968, B2, accessed April 13, 2014, America's Historical Newspapers.

61. Edwards, "Hail, and Farewell," B2.

62. Edwards, "Good to Be Home," B3.

63. Dallas Tornado 1967–68 World," NASL Jerseys.

64. MacCambridge, *Lamar Hunt*, 184.

65. Jones, "The Forgotten Story."

66. Dallas Tornado 1967–68 World," NASL Jerseys.

67. Jones, "The Forgotten Story."

68. Andrew Beyer, "Amateurs Grab Soccer War Playoff," *Washington Post*, January 18, 1967, D1, accessed March 17, 2014, ProQuest Historical Newspapers.

69. Edwards, "Hail, and Farewell," B2.

70. Fraser Elder, "Soccer with an International Flavor Leaves a Sour Taste in American Cities," *New York Times*, June 1, 1969, S8, accessed December 31, 2013, ProQuest Historical Newspapers.

71. Elder, "Soccer with an International Flavor," S8.

72. "Dundee United: Old Soccer Team Back," *Dallas (TX) Morning News*, March 4, 1969, B8, accessed January 23, 2014, America's Historical Newspapers.

73. "Dundee United," B8.

74. "Dundee United Opens Local Season May 10," *Dallas (TX) Morning News*, March 11, 1969, B3, accessed January 23, 2014, America's Historical Newspapers.

75. "Tornado to Blow in on Love Field Ramp," *Dallas (TX) Morning News*, April 29, 1969, B3, accessed January 23, 2014, America's Historical Newspapers.

76. "Tornado to Blow," B3.

77. Elder, "Soccer with an International Flavor," S8.

78. Roy Edwards, "Cup Play Ending. Regular Slate Near," *Dallas (TX) Morning News*, May 29, 1969, B3, accessed January 29, 2014, America's Historical Newspapers.

79. Edwards, "Cup Play," B3.

80. Edwards, "Cup Play," B3.

81. Edwards, "Cup Play," B3.

82. "Against Dundee: Tornado Debut," *Dallas (TX) Morning News*, June 4, 1969, B2, accessed January 31, 2014, America's Historical Newspapers.

83. "Against Dundee," B2.

84. "Dundee Ties Villa, Plays Here Tonight at Cobb," *Dallas (TX) Morning News*, May 10, 1969, B4, accessed January 31, 2014, America's Historical Newspapers.

85. "Dundee Ties Villa," B4.

86. Roy Edwards, "Dundee Gets 3–3 Tie: Late Rally Erases 2-Goal Deficit," *Dallas (TX) Morning News*, May 15, 1969, B2, accessed February 2, 2014, America's Historical Newspapers.

87. Roy Edwards, "Dundee Nips Champs, 3–2," *Dallas (TX) Morning News*, June 1, 1969, B5, accessed February 2, 2014, America's Historical Newspapers.

88. Roy Edwards, "Dundee United Back: Soccer Team Back for 2nd Year," *Dallas (TX) Morning News*, May 2, 1969, B3, accessed January 23, 2014, America's Historical Newspapers.

89. "Dundee Ties Villa, Plays Here Tonight at Cobb," *Dallas (TX) Morning News*, May 10, 1969, B4, accessed January 31, 2014, America's Historical Newspapers.

90. "Dundee Ties Villa," B4.

91. Edwards, "Sour Cream for Tornado," B3.

92. MacCambridge, *Lamar Hunt*, 184.

93. Elder, "Soccer with an International Flavor," S8.

94. Elder, "Soccer with an International Flavor," S8.

95. Eugene L. Scott, "Generals Fade Away: Decision to Abandon League Play Forced out New York," *New York Times*, March 16, 1969, S6, accessed February 8, 2014, ProQuest Historical Newspapers.

96. Brian Glanville, "Soccer Success Visible," *New York Times*, June 4, 1967, S4, accessed October 29, 2013, ProQuest Historical Newspapers.

97. Glanville, "Soccer Success Visible," S4.

98. Brian Glanville, "U.S. Soccer on the Brink," *New York Times*, April 21, 1968, S9, accessed November 24, 2013, ProQuest Historical Newspapers.

99. Glanville, "U.S. Soccer on the Brink," S9.

100. Frank Deford, "Show, Sex and Suburbs," *Sports Illustrated*, February 28, 1983, accessed November 24, 2013, sportsillustrated.cnn.com/vault/article/magazine/MAG1120568/index.htm.

101. Beyer, "New Soccer League," C4.

102. Andrei S. Markovits and Steven L. Hellerman, "Soccer in America: A Story of Marginalization," *University of Miami Entertainment and Sports Law Review* 13 (fall 1995–spring 1996): 254, accessed February 14, 2014, HeinOnline Law Journal Library.

103. Gary Armstrong and James Rosbrook-Thompson, "Coming to America: Historical Ontologies and United States Soccer," *Identities: Global Studies in Culture and Power* 17, no. 4 (July 9, 2010), accessed March 28, 2014, Taylor & Francis Social Sciences and Humanities Library.

104. Shav Glick, "Pro Soccer Must Develop Heroes," *Los Angeles Times*, March 7, 1967, C2, accessed April 4, 2014, ProQuest Historical Newspapers.

105. Glick, "Pro Soccer Must Develop," C2.

106. Glick, "Pro Soccer Must Develop," C2.

107. Murray Olderman, "Soccer Woes Would Wilt with the Stilt," *St. Albans (VT) Messenger*, June 26, 1967, accessed April 6, 2014, America's Historical Newspapers.

108. Olderman, "Soccer Woes."

109. Lloyd Hogan, "Will Soccer Make It?" *Chicago Daily Defender*, August 19, 1969, 25, accessed April 6, 2014, ProQuest Historical Newspapers.

110. Hogan, "Will Soccer Make It?" 25.

111. Hogan, "Will Soccer Make It?" 25.

112. Hogan, "Will Soccer Make It?" 25.

113. Kenneth Denlinger, "Earl Foreman Promises Decision on Future of Whips by Thursday," *Washington Post*, October 2, 1968, D3, accessed February 8, 2014, ProQuest Historical Newspapers.

114. Denlinger, "Earl Foreman Promises Decision," D3.

115. Denlinger, "Earl Foreman Promises Decision," D3.

116. "North American League Suspends for 3 Years," *Washington Post*, November 2, 1968, D1, accessed April 4, 2014, ProQuest Historical Newspapers.

117. "North American League," D1.

118. "Pro Soccer Plans One-Team League," *New York Times*, November 2, 1968, 48, accessed February 8, 2014, ProQuest Historical Newspapers.

119. "Pro Soccer Plans One-Team League," 48.

120. "Pro Soccer Plans One-Team League," 48.

121. Neil Amdur, "Tennis," *New York Times*, December 22, 1968, accessed April 4, 2014, ProQuest Historical Newspapers.

122. Ken Nigro, "West Ham Eleven Plays at the Stadium Tonight," *Baltimore Sun*, May 2, 1969, accessed February 5, 2014, ProQuest Historical Newspapers.

123. Nigro, "West Ham Eleven Plays," C4.

124. Ken Nigro, "Soccer Fans on the Spot with Top Teams Due Here," *Baltimore Sun*, March 8, 1969, B4, accessed January 3, 2014, ProQuest Historical Newspapers.

125. Nigro, "Soccer Fans on the Spot," B4.

126. Nigro, "Soccer Fans on the Spot," B4.

127. Nigro, "Soccer Fans on the Spot," B4.

128. Ken Nigro, "NASL Takes New Outlook," *Baltimore Sun*, March 30, 1969, A10, accessed March 12, 2014, ProQuest Historical Newspapers.

129. Ken Jones, "High Praise for West Ham," *Baltimore Sun*, April 23, 1969, C3, accessed February 5, 2014, ProQuest Historical Newspapers.

130. Ken Nigro, "Gem for Bays in West Ham," *Baltimore Sun*, March 9, 1969, A10, accessed February 5, 2014, ProQuest Historical Newspapers.

131. Nigro, "Gem for Bays in West Ham," A10.

132. Ivan Ponting, "Phil Woosnam," *(London) Independent*, August 1, 2013, 50, accessed February 17, 2014, ProQuest Newsstand.

133. Nigro, "West Ham Eleven Plays," C1.

134. Bob Maisel, "The Morning After," *Baltimore Sun*, May 30, 1969, C1, accessed January 3, 2014, ProQuest Historical Newspapers.

135. Maisel, "The Morning After," C1.

136. Maisel, "The Morning After," C1.

137. Maisel, "The Morning After," C1.

138. Maisel, "The Morning After," C1.

139. Roy Edwards, "Dundee Faces Uphill Battle," *Dallas (TX) Morning News*, May 21, 1969, B1, accessed February 2, 2014, America's Historical Newspapers.

140. Roy Edwards, "A Game of Skill," *Dallas (TX) Morning News*, May 23, 1969, B2, accessed February 2, 2014, America's Historical Newspapers.

141. Edwards, "A Game of Skill," B2.

142. Edwards, "A Game of Skill," B2.

143. Edwards, "A Game of Skill," B2.

144. Ken Nigro, "Kilmarnock vs. West Ham at the Stadium," *Baltimore Sun*, May 30, 1969, C1, accessed February 5, 2014, ProQuest Historical Newspapers.

145. Nigro, "Kilmarnock vs. West Ham," C1.

146. Nigro, "Kilmarnock vs. West Ham," C1.

147. "Dallas Cup Quick Facts," Dallas Cup, accessed April 4, 2014, www.dallascup.com/about/overviewquickfacts/index_E.html.

148. "Elite Super Group Now the 'Gordon Jago Super Group,'" Dallas Cup, accessed March 10, 2014, www.dallascup.com/home/514101.html.

149. "Bays' Jago Named Coach of U.S. World Cup Squad," *Baltimore Sun*, March 7, 1969, C4, accessed March 13, 2014, ProQuest Historical Newspapers.

150. Iain Macintosh, "MLS Miami Will Need Results, Not Becks' Star Power, to Succeed," The Boot Room, blog entry posted February 6, 2014, accessed March 18, 2014, http://espnfc.com/blog/_/name/bootroom/id/677?cc=5901.

151. Macintosh, "MLS Miami."

152. Macintosh, "MLS Miami."

153. Macintosh, "MLS Miami."

154. Roger Bennett, "MLS Takes in the Big Picture," ESPN Soccer, last modified July 24, 2012, accessed February 6, 2014, http://espnfc.com/blog/_/name/bootroom/id/677?cc=5901.

155. Bennett, "MLS Takes in the Big Picture."

156. Doug McIntyre, "Reigning in Seattle," *ESPN The Magazine*, May 16, 2012, accessed February 6, 2014, http://espn.go.com/sports/soccer/story/_/id/7929299/soccer-seattle-sounders-prove-mls-put-fans-seats-espn-magazine.

157. McIntyre, "Reigning in Seattle."

158. McIntyre, "Reigning in Seattle."

159. Wendy Parker, "Atlanta Pro Soccer Always on Its Heels," *Atlanta (GA) Journal-Constitution*, June 13, 2004, E1, accessed February 6, 2014, ProQuest Newsstand.

160. Ken Nigro, "Bays and Chiefs Vie in Richmond Struggle Today," *Baltimore Sun*, April 2, 1967, A1, accessed March 13, 2014, ProQuest Historical Newspapers.

161. Nigro, "Bays and Chiefs Vie in Richmond," A1.

162. Maisel, "The Morning After," C1.

163. Maisel, "The Morning After," C1.

164. John Turnbull, "Soccer," *New Georgia Encyclopedia* (Georgia Humanities Council), last modified August 29, 2013, accessed April 4, 2014, www.georgiaencyclopedia.org/articles/sports-outdoor-recreation/soccer#Amateur-Teams.

165. Turnbull, "Soccer."

166. Turnbull, "Soccer."

167. "Bellevue, Boeing B in Big Boot Battle," *Seattle (WA) Daily Times*, February 25, 1968, 31, accessed April 13, 2014, America's Historical Newspapers.

168. Turnbull, "Soccer."

169. Maisel, "The Morning After," C1.

170. Maisel, "The Morning After," C1.

171. Maisel, "The Morning After," C1.

172. Nigro, "NASL Takes New Outlook," A10.

173. Turnbull, "Soccer."

174. Maisel, "The Morning After," C1.

175. John Turnbull, "Soccer Fields, for King and Atlanta, Lent Space to Move beyond Vietnam," The Global Game, blog entry posted February 5, 2008, accessed March 18, 2014, www.theglobalgame.com/blog/2008/02/soccer-fields-for-king-and-atlanta-lent-space-to-move-beyond-vietnam.

176. Turnbull, "Soccer Fields."

7. 1968–1969

1. "National Pro Soccer League Sues to End 'Conspiracy' against It," *New York Times*, September 10, 1967, 242, accessed May 9, 2014, ProQuest Historical Newspapers.

2. Andrew Beyer, "Soccer Moguls Boot a Big One," *Washington Post*, September 12, 1967, D3, accessed March 26, 2014, ProQuest Historical Newspapers.

3. Beyer, "Soccer Moguls Boot a Big One," D3.

4. Andrew Beyer, "Soccer Merger Becomes Official, Whips Prepare to Stock Squad," *Washington Post*, December 8, 1967, D8, accessed May 9, 2014, ProQuest Historical Newspapers.

5. Ohio Historical Society, "Cleveland Stokers," Ohio History Central, accessed January 25, 2014, www.ohiohistorycentral.org/w/Cleveland_Stokers.

6. United Press International, "Near Riot Follows Santos' First Loss," *Los Angeles Times*, July 12, 1968, D3, accessed May 15, 2014, ProQuest Historical Newspapers.

7. Ken Nigro, "Bays Hope to Wrap up Title Here," *Baltimore Sun*, August 16, 1967, C1, accessed May 14, 2014, ProQuest Historical Newspapers.

8. Bill Nichols, "Pele Is an Old Rival of Stokers' Navarro," *Cleveland (OH) Plain Dealer*, July 9, 1968, 31, accessed May 15, 2014, America's Historical Newspapers.

9. Bill Nichols, "Pele Is Magnet for Soccer Fans Tonight," *Cleveland (OH) Plain Dealer*, July 10, 1967, 32, accessed May 15, 2014, America's Historical Newspapers.

10. Bill Nichols, "Stokers Win in Near Riot," *Cleveland (OH) Plain Dealer*, July 11, 1968, 69, accessed April 6, 2014, America's Historical Newspapers.

11. Nichols, "Stokers Win in Near Riot," 69.

12. Gerald Eskenazi, "Generals Upset Santos Club, 5–3," *New York Times*, July 13, 1968, 21, accessed April 6, 2014, ProQuest Historical Newspapers.

13. Ken Nigro, "Pele to Perform for Fans Today in Washington," *Baltimore Sun*, July 14, 1968, A1, accessed May 15, 2014, ProQuest Historical Newspapers.

14. Associated Press, "Toros' Co-owner Sells Out, Resigns," *Seattle (WA) Times*, June 27, 1968, accessed May 9, 2014, America's Historical Newspapers.

15. "April 3rd, 1968—San Diego Toros vs. Boston Beacons," Fun while It Lasted, accessed May 9, 2014, www.funwhileitlasted.net/2012/12/17/april-3-1968-san-diego-toros-vs-boston-beacons.

16. "Chiefs Face San Diego in Finale," *Marietta (GA) Daily Journal*, September 25, 1968, 13, accessed May 15, 2014, America's Historical Newspapers.

17. "Chiefs Face San Diego," 13.

18. "Chiefs Face San Diego," 13.

19. Associated Press, "Stu Holcomb Joins Soccer," *Baltimore Sun*, August 12, 1966, B4, accessed September 24, 2013, ProQuest Historical Newspapers.

20. *Omaha World Herald*, September 17, 1968, 19, accessed May 15, 2014, America's Historical Newspapers.

21. "Chiefs Face San Diego," 13.

22. Dan Coughlin, "Stokers, Chiefs Tie, 1 to 1," *Cleveland (OH) Plain Dealer*, September 12, 1968, 62, accessed May 15, 2014, America's Historical Newspapers.

23. Coughlin, "Stokers, Chiefs Tie," 62.

24. Dan Coughlin, "Stokers Ousted," *Cleveland (OH) Plain Dealer*, September 15, 1968, 53, accessed May 15, 2014, America's Historical Newspapers.

25. United Press International, "Victorious Chiefs Await West Champs," *Marietta (GA) Journal*, September 16, 1968, 5, accessed May 15, 2014, America's Historical Newspapers.

26. United Press International, "Title Bid Farewell to Chiefs?" *Marietta (GA) Journal*, September 25, 1968, 13, accessed May 15, 2014, America's Historical Newspapers.

27. United Press International, "Title Bid Farewell to Chiefs?" 13.

28. Associated Press, "Tie in N.A. Soccer Series," *Trenton (NJ) Evening Times*, September 22, 1968, 61, accessed May 15, 2014, America's Historical Newspapers.

29. Associated Press, "Tie in N.A. Soccer Series," 61.

30. United Press International, "Phil Woosnam Selected As Coach of Year," *Marietta (GA) Journal*, September 18, 1968, accessed May 15, 2014, America's Historical Newspapers.

31. Andrew Beyer, "Whips off for Tour of Europe," *Washington Post*, October 4, 1968, D2, accessed February 8, 2014, ProQuest Historical Newspapers.

32. Kenneth Denlinger, "Pele Dazzles Whips As 20,189 See Santos Win," *Washington Post*, July 15, 1968, D1, accessed May 13, 2014, ProQuest Historical Newspapers.

33. Beyer, "Whips off for Tour," D2.

34. "Whips Defeat Germans in Tour Opener," *Washington Post*, October 6, 1968, C2, accessed February 8, 2014, ProQuest Historical Newspapers.

35. Associated Press, "Whips Gain Tie on Penalty Shot," *Washington Post*, October 13, 1968, C3, accessed February 8, 2014, ProQuest Historical Newspapers.

36. "Pro Soccer Plans One-Team League," *New York Times*, November 2, 1968, 48, accessed February 8, 2014, ProQuest Historical Newspapers.

37. "Pro Soccer Plans One-Team League," 48.

38. "Sanction withheld from U.S. Soccer Plan," *New York Times*, December 12, 1968, 68, accessed February 9, 2014, ProQuest Historical Newspapers.

39. Ken Nigro, "NASL Takes New Outlook," *Baltimore Sun*, March 30, 1969, A10, accessed March 12, 2014, ProQuest Historical Newspapers.

40. Associated Press, "Pro Soccer League Will Field 8 Clubs," *New York Times*, January 8, 1969, 55, accessed February 8, 2014, ProQuest Historical Newspapers.

41. Gerald Eskenazi, "Soccer Generals Warn of Pull-out," *New York Times*, January 16, 1969, 53, accessed May 16, 2014, ProQuest Historical Newspapers.

42. Steve Cady, "U.S. Soccer, Losing Its Shirt, Told to Tighten Its Belt," *New York Times*, January 12, 1969, S12, accessed February 9, 2014, ProQuest Historical Newspapers.

43. Ken Nigro, "Bays Ready Kick Slate," *Baltimore Sun*, February 16, 1969, A1, accessed May 16, 2014, ProQuest Historical Newspapers.

44. Eskenazi, "Soccer Generals Warn of Pull-out," 53.

45. Nigro, "Bays Ready Kick Slate," A1.

46. "NASL Teams Slate Eight Home Matches," *Marietta (GA) Journal*, April 6, 1969, 10, accessed January 24, 2014, America's Historical Newspapers.

47. Eugene L. Scott, "Generals Fade Away: Decision to Abandon League Play Forced out New York," *New York Times*, March 16, 1969, S6, accessed February 8, 2014, ProQuest Historical Newspapers.

48. Ken Nigro, "Jago Protests 'Pros' in Lineup: Bay's Coach Asks Woosnam to Study Situation," *Baltimore Sun*, June 10, 1969, C1, accessed March 20, 2014, ProQuest Historical Newspapers.

49. Nigro, "Jago Protests 'Pros' in Lineup," C1.

50. Cady, "U.S. Soccer, Losing Its Shirt," S12.

51. David Wangerin, *Soccer in a Football World* (Philadelphia: Temple University Press, 2008), 127.

52. Steve Cady, "U.S. Soccer, Losing Its Shirt," S12.

53. "Generals Soccer Team Won't Operate This Year," *New York Times*, February 19, 1969, 54, accessed March 26, 2014, ProQuest Historical Newspapers.

54. Brian Glanville, "Soccer to Try Again," *New York Times*, March 2, 1969, S23, accessed May 16, 2014, ProQuest Historical Newspapers.

55. Glanville, "Soccer to Try Again," S23.

56. Eugene L. Scott, "Generals Fade Away: Decision to Abandon League Play Forced out New York," *New York Times*, March 16, 1969, S6, accessed February 8, 2014, ProQuest Historical Newspapers.

57. Ken Nigro, "Aston Villa Team Plays Top Soccer," *Baltimore Sun*, May 19, 1969, C1, accessed May 16, 2014, ProQuest Historical Newspapers.

58. Mat Kendrick, "The Doc Made First Tour So Memorable," *Birmingham (UK) Mail*, July 16, 2012, 46, accessed February 6, 2014, ProQuest Newsstand.

59. Nigro, "Aston Villa Team Plays," C1.

60. Brian Glanville, "Final Boot for Soccer?" *New York Times*, November 10, 1968, S27, accessed September 14, 2014, ProQuest Historical Newspapers.

Selected Bibliography

I list here only the writings that have been most useful in constructing the foundation and structure of this book. This bibliography is not a comprehensive record of all of the resources I have compiled and consulted. It does, however, indicate the substance and range of materials I've read that have contributed to the formation of my ideas, and I intend for it to serve as a convenient access point for those who wish to pursue the postwar history of soccer in the United States, particularly that of the United Soccer Association and the National Professional Soccer League. All specific sources that have informed and ultimately been incorporated into the book are documented in the endnotes. Those notes provide a detailed roadmap for this fascinating period of American sports history.

Addie, Bob. Selected columns. *Washington Post*, 1958–1970. ProQuest Historical Newspapers.

Amdur, Neil. "Tennis." *New York Times*, December 22, 1968, S5. Accessed April 4, 2014. ProQuest Historical Newspapers.

Andrews, David L., Robert Pitter, Detlev Zwick, and Darren Ambrose. "Soccer's Racial Frontier: Sport and the Suburbanization of Contemporary America." In *Entering the Field: New Perspectives on World Football*. Edited by Gary Armstrong and Richard Guilanotti. Oxford: Berg, 1997.

Apostolov, Steven. "Everywhere and Nowhere: The Forgotten Past and Clouded Future of American Professional Soccer from the Perspective of Massachusetts." *Soccer and Society* 13, no. 4 (July 2012): 510–35. Accessed April 1, 2014. Academic Search Premier.

"April 3rd, 1968—San Diego Toros vs. Boston Beacons." Fun while It Lasted. Accessed May 9, 2014. www.funwhileitlasted.net/2012/12/17/april-3-1968-san-diego-toros-vs-boston-beacons.

Armstrong, Gary, and James Rosbrook-Thompson. "Coming to America: Historical Ontologies and United States Soccer." *Identities: Global Studies in Culture and Power* 17, no. 4 (July 9, 2010): 348–71. Accessed March 28, 2014. Taylor & Francis Social Sciences and Humanities Library.

Asher, Mark. "Swede to Coach D.C. Soccer Team." *Washington Post*, October 23, 1966, C9. Accessed May 14, 2014. ProQuest Historical Newspapers.

Associated Press. "Atlanta Chiefs' Coach Denies Phony Fouls." *Washington Post*. May 19, 1967, D3. Accessed April 8, 2014. ProQuest Historical Newspapers.

———. "Big Money Backs Fledgling Soccer League." *Springfield (MA) Union*, April 15, 1967, 14. Accessed April 5, 2014. America's Historical Newspapers.

———. "CBS Exonerated of Charges on Phony Timeouts." *Washington Post*, August 3, 1967, F6. Accessed April 9, 2014. ProQuest Historical Newspapers.

———. "CBS Officials Back Risk in TV Soccer." *(Portland) Oregonian*, February 28, 1967, 31. Accessed May 12, 2014. America's Historical Newspapers.

———. "Chiefs Blank Toros for Title." *Augusta Chronicle*, September 29, 1968, 3. Accessed May 15, 2014. America's Historical Newspapers.

———. "Clippers Beat Spurs, Win West Title." *Chicago Tribune*, August 17, 1967, E2. Accessed April 6, 2014. ProQuest Historical Newspapers.

———. "Clippers Blitz Stars, 9–0." *Baltimore Sun*, July 27, 1967, C4. Accessed March 26, 2014. ProQuest Historical Newspapers.

———. "Clippers Bow by 2–0 Score." *Los Angeles Times*, May 19, 1969, B4. Accessed March 6, 2014. ProQuest Historical Newspapers.

———. "Clippers, Russ in Final Match of Soccer Series." *Seattle (WA) Daily Times*, March 9, 1969, 30. Accessed March 5, 2014. America's Historical Newspapers.

———. "Clippers Stun Italians." *Los Angeles Times*, June 2, 1969, B5. Accessed March 6, 2014. ProQuest Historical Newspapers.

———. "Clippers Top U.S. Kickers." *Los Angeles Times*, April 14, 1969, E3. Accessed March 6, 2014. ProQuest Historical Newspapers.

———. "Clippers Triumph." *Fort Worth (TX) Star-Telegram*, January 27, 1969, 17. Accessed March 4, 2014. America's Historical Newspapers.

———. "Clippers Win Challenge Cup." *Baltimore Sun*, September 19, 1967, C2. Accessed March 3, 2014. ProQuest Historical Newspapers.

———. "Crowds Off, Clippers Eye New Home." *Washington Post*, August 27, 1968, C5. Accessed March 4, 2014. ProQuest Historical Newspapers.

———. "Dallas Soccer Team Loses." *New York Times*, December 25, 1967, 41. Accessed December 31, 2013. ProQuest Historical Newspapers.

———. "Dodger Official Walsh to Head Soccer League." *Los Angeles Times*, December 30, 1966, B3. Accessed May 12, 2014. ProQuest Historical Newspapers.

———. "English Soccer Team Rejects Bid by Cooke." *Washington Post*, July 19, 1967, D5. Accessed March 9, 2014. ProQuest Newspapers.

———. "Fake Fouls Called for TV Commercials." *Baltimore Sun*, May 15, 1967, C3. Accessed April 8, 2014. ProQuest Historical Newspapers.

———. "Fans Assault Referee in Mustang Duel." *Chicago Tribune*, June 17, 1967, D2. Accessed November 11, 2013. ProQuest Historical Newspapers.

———. "Fans Riot As Chicago Loses, 2–1." *Washington Post*, June 19, 1967, D4. Accessed May 7, 2014. ProQuest Historical Newspapers.

———. "Fans Stone U.S. Kickers." *Baltimore Sun*, December 5, 1967, C6. Accessed December 31, 2013. ProQuest Historical Newspapers.

———. "Fight by Players Ends Soccer Game." *New York Times*, June 15, 1967, 65. Accessed May 7, 2014. ProQuest Historical Newspapers.

———. "Football's Ernie Nevers Now Pumps for Soccer." *Washington Post*, May 25, 1967, C5. Accessed March 1, 2014. ProQuest Historical Newspapers.

———. "Foul Calls for Commercials Admitted by Soccer Referee." *New York Times*, May 15, 1967, 79. Accessed April 8, 2014. ProQuest Historical Newspapers.

———. "Get a Kick out of This." *(Portland) Oregonian*, May 2, 1969, 66. Accessed April 3, 2014. America's Historical Newspapers.

———. "Graham Named Soccer Loop Director." *The State: The Columbia (SC) Record*, October 9, 1966, 38. Accessed May 12, 2014. America's Historical Newspapers.

———. "Guard Takes Hard Look at Riot Control Methods." *Augusta (GA) Chronicle*, July 28, 1967, 9A. Accessed November 23, 2013. America's Historical Newspapers.

———. "Houston Wins, 2–0, As Riot Halts Game." *Washington Post*, June 15, 1967, K27. Accessed May 7, 2014. ProQuest Historical Newspapers.

————. "Kansas City Tops Houston." *Baltimore Sun*, June 10, 1968, C9. Accessed March 3, 2014. ProQuest Historical Newspapers.

————. "Loop-leading Boot Team Fires Coach." *The Seattle (WA) Times*, May 1, 1967, 47. Accessed October 28, 2013. America's Historical Newspapers.

————. "Lost Soccer Stars Arrive in Calcutta." *Washington Post*, November 6, 1967, D8. Accessed April 2, 2014. ProQuest Historical Newspapers.

————. "Macker Gets Soccer Post." *Springfield (MA) Union*, February 23, 1967, 45. Accessed May 12, 2014. America's Historical Newspapers.

————. "Mustang Trio Suspended by Soccer League." *Chicago Tribune*, June 23, 1967, C4. Accessed November 11, 2013. ProQuest Historical Newspapers.

————. "Mustangs Tie." *Chicago Tribune*, June 5, 1967, C5. Accessed May 13, 2014. ProQuest Historical Newspapers.

————. "Navarro Named Top N.S.L. Player." *Baltimore Sun*, September 2, 1967, B3. Accessed May 14, 2014. ProQuest Historical Newspapers.

————. "New Soccer League Given Pro Sanction." *New York Times*, December 29, 1966, 38. Accessed September 23, 2013. ProQuest Historical Newspapers.

————. "NPSL Nixes Merger Plan." *(Portland) Oregonian*, September 25, 1966, 93. Accessed May 2, 2014. America's Historical Newspapers.

————. "Pittsburgh Not Taking to Soccer." *Washington Post*, May 24, 1967, D2. Accessed May 14, 2014. ProQuest Historical Newspapers.

————. "Pro Soccer League Will Field 8 Clubs." *New York Times*, January 8, 1969, 55. Accessed February 8, 2014. ProQuest Historical Newspapers.

————. "Pro Soccer OKs Merger." *(Portland) Oregonian*, September 22, 1966, 64. Accessed May 12, 2014. America's Historical Newspapers.

————. "Pro Soccer Planned in Kansas City." *Baltimore Sun*, January 5, 1968, C1. Accessed March 3, 2014. ProQuest Historical Newspapers.

————. "Russian Club Makes U.S. Soccer Bow." *Washington Post*, February 23, 1969, 53. Accessed March 5, 2014. ProQuest Historical Newspapers.

————. "SF Gets Soccer Franchise." *(Portland) Oregonian*, October 26, 1966, 35. Accessed April 6, 2014. America's Historical Newspapers.

————. "Soccer Exhibition in N.Y. Ruled Out." *Baltimore Sun*, August 4, 1967, C1. Accessed May 9, 2014. ProQuest Historical Newspapers.

————. "Soccer Loops Face Pressure." *Springfield (MA) Union*, March 29, 1967, 48. Accessed May 12, 2014. America's Historical Newspapers.

————. "Soccer TV Is Called Good Risk." *Chicago Tribune*, February 28, 1967, C1. Accessed May 12, 2014. ProQuest Historical Newspapers.

————. "Spartan Booters in Bow." *Trenton (NJ) Evening Times*, April 16, 1967, 65. Accessed October 28, 2013. America's Historical Newspapers.

————. "Sports Pages Sure Tip to Orioles Stock Trend." *Springfield (MA) Union*, April 13, 1967, 3. Accessed April 5, 2014. America's Historical Newspapers.

————. "Spurs, Toros Deadlock, 1–1." *Dallas (TX) Morning News*, September 12, 1968, B4. Accessed May 15, 2014. America's Historical Newspapers.

————. "Stu Holcomb Joins Soccer." *Baltimore Sun*, August 12, 1966, C4. Accessed September 24, 2013. ProQuest Historical Newspapers.

————. "Ten-Team Pro Soccer League Formed." *Cleveland (OH) Plain Dealer*, June 17, 1966, 37–39. Accessed September 23, 2013. America's Historical Newspapers.

————. "3 Cities Given Soccer Spots." *Baltimore Sun*, August 24, 1966, C4. Accessed May 12, 2014. ProQuest Historical Newspapers.

————. "Tie in N.A. Soccer Series." *Trenton (NJ) Evening Times*, September 22, 1968, 61. Accessed May 15, 2014. America's Historical Newspapers.

————. "Toros' Co-Owner Sells Out, Resigns." *Seattle (WA) Times*, June 27, 1968. Accessed May 9, 2014. America's Historical Newspapers.

————. "Two Leagues Ready to Go." *Baltimore Sun*, February 19, 1967, A8. Accessed May 12, 2014. ProQuest Historical Newspapers.

————. "U.S. Soccer Loop Seeking British Official." *New York Times*, September 13, 1966, 61. Accessed September 23, 2013. ProQuest Historical Newspapers.

———. "USA Reports Averaging 8,850 a Game." *Washington Post*, June 21, 1967. Accessed May 14, 2014. ProQuest Historical Newspapers.

———. "Whips Change Officials." *Baltimore Sun*, June 22, 1968, B3. Accessed April 13, 2014. ProQuest Historical Newspapers.

———. "Whips Gain Tie on Penalty Shot." *Washington Post*, October 13, 1968, C3. Accessed February 8, 2014. ProQuest Historical Newspapers.

———. "Whither Soccer? To the Top, Woosnam Believes." *Baltimore Sun*, July 27, 1975, B6. Accessed January 5, 2014. ProQuest Historical Newspapers.

Baltimore Sun. Selected articles. 1966–1969. ProQuest Historical Newspapers.

BBC. "Celtic Win European Cup 1967." BBC Scotland. Accessed October 27, 2013. www.bbc.co.uk/scotland/sportscotland/asportingnation/article/0045/print.shtml.

Beckman, Aldo. "Newark Rioting Traced to Hate Campaign." *Chicago Tribune*, August 8, 1967, 1. Accessed November 23, 2013. ProQuest Historical Newspapers.

Belfast Telegraph, January 6, 2010. Accessed May 13, 2014. www.belfasttelegraph.co.uk/sport/football/local/down-memory-lane-big-trevs-golden-goals-earn-him-deserved-oval-accolade-28510120.html.

Bennett, Roger. "MLS Equals MLB in Popularity with Kids." ESPNFC.com. Last modified March 7, 2014. Accessed March 11, 2014. http://espnfc.com/news/story/_/id/1740529/mls-catches-mlb-espn-sports-poll?cc=5901.

———. "MLS Takes in the Big Picture." ESPN Soccer. Last modified July 24, 2012. Accessed February 6, 2014. http://espnfc.com/blog/_/name/bootroom/id/677?cc=5901.

Beyer, Andrew. Selected columns. *Washington Post*, 1967–1968. ProQuest Historical Newspapers.

"The Big Eye League." *Time*, August 21, 1964, 78. Accessed December 7, 2013. Academic Search Premier.

"The Big Sellout." *Sports Illustrated*, August 24, 1964. Accessed December 7, 2013. http://sportsillustrated.cnn.com/vault/article/magazine/MAG1076264/index.htm.

Blair, Sam. "A New Way to Get Kicks." *Dallas (TX) Morning News*, June 5, 1967, 2. Accessed April 1, 2014. America's Historical Newspapers.

Blanchflower, Danny. "Just One Truth for Me." *Sports Illustrated*, June 10, 1968. Accessed May 8, 2014. http://sportsillustrated.cnn.com/vault/article/magazine/MAG1081255/index.htm.

Boswell, Thomas. "Bangu Offers Darts, Chance to Open Up." *Washington Post*, August 8, 1971, C7. Accessed May 8, 2014. ProQuest Historical Newspapers.

Brady, Dave. Selected columns. *Washington Post*, 1966. ProQuest Historical Newspapers.

Briordy, William J. "Fans Riot As English Team Takes League Soccer Final at Downing Stadium." *New York Times*, August 5, 1963, 43. Accessed November 9, 2013. ProQuest Historical Newspapers.

Brown, Doug. "How Soccer Came to Baltimore." *Baltimore Sun*, April 16, 1967, SM14. Accessed May 14, 2014. ProQuest Historical Newspapers.

Brown, Gwilym S. "What Will He Think of Next?" *Sports Illustrated*, May 4, 1970. Accessed March 31, 2014. http://sportsillustrated.cnn.com/vault/article/magazine/MAG1083569/1/index.htm.

Bryan, Hank. "Generals 'Roughed Up.'" *Trenton (NJ) Evening Times*, May 1, 1967, 30. Accessed October 28, 2013. America's Historical Newspapers.

Cady, Steve. "U.S. Soccer, Losing Its Shirt, Told to Tighten Its Belt." *New York Times*, January 12, 1969, S12. Accessed February 9, 2014. ProQuest Historical Newspapers.

California Clippers, Inc. v. United States S.F. Association, 314 F. Supp. (9th Cir. 1970). www.leagle.com/decision/19701371314FSupp1057_11156.xml/CALIFORNIA%20CLIPPERS,%20INC.%20v.%20UNITED%20STATES%20S.%20F.%20ASS'N.

"Calm before the Storm." Glentoran Football Club. Accessed March 29, 2014. www.glentoranfc.co.uk/cougars%20bangu.htm.

Carter, Jon. "Rewind to 1961—Ladislao Kubala's Legacy at Barcelona." ESPNFC.com. Last modified October 13, 2011. Accessed May 14, 2014. www.espnfc.com/columns/story/_/id/967644/rewind-to-1961:-ladislao-kubala's-legacy-at-barcelona?cc=5901.

Cartwright, Gary. "Spaniards Sparkle in the Astrodome." *Dallas (TX) Morning News*, April 20, 1967, 2. Accessed November 22, 2013. America's Historical Newspapers.

Chicago Tribune. Selected articles. 1966–1968. ProQuest Historical Newspapers.

Cleveland (OH) Plain Dealer." Sports over Lightly." August 25, 1966. Accessed September 23, 2013. America's Historical Newspapers.

———. Sports over Lightly." January 31, 1967, 31. Accessed May 12, 2014. America's Historical Newspapers.

———. Sports over Lightly." April 8, 1967, 39. Accessed May 12, 2014. America's Historical Newspapers.

Condon, David. "In the Wake of the News." *Chicago Tribune*, April 14, 1967, C1. Accessed January 26, 2014. ProQuest Historical Newspapers.

———. "In the Wake of the News." *Chicago Tribune*, March 13, 1967, E1. Accessed March 30, 2014. ProQuest Historical Newspapers.

———. "In the Wake of the News." *Chicago Tribune*, May 27, 1967, C1. Accessed November 11, 2013. ProQuest Historical Newspapers.

Coughlin, Dan. Selected columns. *Cleveland (OH) Plain Dealer*, 1967–1968. America's Historical Newspapers.

Dallas Cup. "Elite Super Group Now the 'Gordon Jago Super Group.'" Dallascup.com. Accessed March 10, 2014. www.dallascup.com/home/514101.html.

"Dallas Cup Quick Facts." Dallas Cup. Accessed April 4, 2014. www.dallascup.com/about/overviewquickfacts/index_E.html.

"Dallas Tornado 1967–68 World Tour." NASL Jerseys. Accessed April 1, 2014. www.nasljerseys.com/Misc/Tornado%2067-68%20World%20Tour2.htm.

Dallas (TX) Morning News. Selected articles. 1967–1969. America's Historical Newspapers.

Dallos, Robert E. "TV Soccer Charge Denied by C.B.S." *New York Times*, June 7, 1967, 95. Accessed April 9, 2014. ProQuest Historical Newspapers.

Davis, Ivor. "The Latest Kick in Sport." *Los Angeles Times*, August 27, 1967, M44. Accessed April 8, 2014. ProQuest Historical Newspapers.

Days, Paul. *Stars in Stripes; Sunderland AFC As the Vancouver Royal Canadians*. Illustrated by Jaime Collins. Blue House Field, 2012. Digital file.

Deford, Frank. "Show, Sex and Suburbs." *Sports Illustrated*, February 28, 1983. Accessed November 24, 2013. http://sportsillustrated.cnn.com/vault/article/magazine/MAG1120568/index.htm.

Denlinger, Kenneth. Selected columns. *Washington Post*, 1968. ProQuest Historical Newspapers.

Dougherty, Philip H. "Advertising: Soccer Promotion Kicked Off." *New York Times*, April 17, 1967, 54. Accessed December 10, 2013. ProQuest Historical Newspapers.

Duke University. "Ghana." Soccer Politics/The Politics of Football. Accessed May 8, 2014. http://sites.duke.edu/wcwp/research-projects/africa/the-politics-of-african-soccer/ghana.

Dunmore, Tom. "Expanded Dreams: The International Soccer League, Part Three." Pitch Invasion. Blog entry posted November 14, 2011. Accessed March 24, 2014. http://pitchinvasion.net/blog/2011/11/14/expanded-dreams-the-international-soccer-league-part-three/.

———. "In Lieu of Giants: The International Soccer League, Part Two." Pitch Invasion. Blog entry posted November 7, 2011. Accessed March 24, 2014. http://pitchinvasion.net/blog/2011/11/07/in-lieu-of-giants-the-international-soccer-league-part-two/.

———. "They Even Cheered Technique: The International Soccer League, Part One." Pitch Invasion. Blog entry posted November 4, 2011. Accessed March 24, 2014. http://pitchinvasion.net/blog/2011/11/04/they-even-cheered-technique-the-1960-international-soccer-league-part-one.

Durso, Joseph. "Local Pro Soccer Teams May Share Stadium with Yanks in the Spring." *New York Times*, February 12, 1967, 196. Accessed May 7, 2014. ProQuest Historical Newspapers.

———. "Merger Key Topic at Soccer Talks." *New York Times*, December 28, 1966, 50. Accessed May 12, 2014. ProQuest Historical Newspapers.

Edwards, Roy. Selected Columns. *Dallas (TX) Morning News*, 1967–1969. America's Historical Newspapers.

Elder, Fraser. "Soccer with an International Flavor Leaves a Sour Taste in American Cities." *New York Times*, June 1, 1969, S8. Accessed December 31, 2013. ProQuest Historical Newspapers.

The Encyclopaedia of Scottish Football. N.p.: Pitch Pub, 2011.

Eskenazi, Gerald. Selected columns. *New York Times*, 1967–1969. ProQuest Historical Newspapers.

"Ferdinand Daucik (1950–1954)." FC Barcelona.com. Accessed May 14, 2014. www.fcbarcelona.com/club/history/detail/card/ferdinand-daucik-1950-1954.

FIFA. "1962 FIFA World Cup Chile, Match Report: Chile-Italy." FIFA.com. Accessed November 9, 2013. www.fifa.com/worldcup/archive/edition=21/results/matches/match=1472/report.html.

Fitzgerald, James. "Dallas Subs Win Soccer Opener, 1–0." *Chicago Tribune*, May 29, 1967, B5. Accessed May 7, 2014. ProQuest Historical Newspapers.

"Former Don Goes to Washington." Aberdeen Football Club. Last modified June 27, 2011. Accessed April 6, 2014. www.afc.co.uk/articles/20110627/former-don-goes-to-washington_2212158_2382701.

Furlong, William Barry." A Sad Day for Baseball." *Sports Illustrated*, September 21, 1964. Accessed December 7, 2013. http://si.com/vault/article/magazine/MAG1076373/index.htm.

Furmanov, Vadim. "A Sardinian Summer: The Forgotten Story of the Chicago Mustangs." In Bed with Maradona. Blog entry posted August 20, 2013. Accessed January 26, 2014. http://inbedwithmaradona.com/journal/2013/8/20/a-sardinian-summer-the-forgotten-story-of-the-chicago-mustangs.

Glanville, Brian. Selected columns. *New York Times*, 1967–1969. ProQuest Historical Newspapers.

Glenn, Patrick. "Obituary: Jim Baxter." *Guardian*, April 15, 2001. Accessed May 13, 2014. www.theguardian.com/news/2001/apr/16/guardianobituaries.football.

"Glens Hold Stoke as Trainor Sent Off." Glentoran Football Club. Accessed May 13, 2014. www.glentoran-fc.co.uk/cougars%20stoke%20city.htm.

Glick, Shav. Selected columns. 1967–1969. *Los Angeles Times*. ProQuest Historical Newspapers.

Green, Geoffrey. "Conflict between Leagues Confuses Americans." *(London) Times*, June 19, 1967, 13. Accessed May 7, 2014.The Times Digital Archive.

———. "U.S. Kicks off in World Soccer." *(London) Times*, February 25, 1967, 10. Accessed September 23, 2013.The Times Digital Archive.

Harris, Nick. "From £20 to £33,868 per Week: A Quick History of English Football's Top-Flight Wages." Sporting Intelligence. Last modified January 20, 2011. Accessed May 12, 2014. www.sportingintelligence.com/2011/01/20/from-20-to-33868-per-week-a-quick-history-of-english-footballs-top-flight-wages-200101.

Heath, Jim. "USA, 1967: Life in the Fast Lane." Wolves Heroes. Last modified May 4, 2009. Accessed May 13, 2014. www.wolvesheroes.com/2009/05/04/usa-1967.

"Hibs Face Saved by Late Goal." Glentoran Football Club. Accessed May 13, 2014. www.glentoran-fc.co.uk/cougars%20hibs.htm.

Hogan, Lloyd. "Will Soccer Make It?" *Chicago Daily Defender*, August 19, 1969, 25. Accessed April 6, 2014. ProQuest Historical Newspapers.

Hollander, Zander. *The American Encyclopedia of Soccer*. New York: Everest House Publishers, 1980.

Holroyd, Steve, and David Litterer." The Year in American Soccer—1965–1969." American Soccer Archives. Accessed May 13, 2014. http://homepages.sover.net/~spectrum.

Holtzman, Jerome. "Turn Back the Clock . . . 1943." *Baseball Digest* 63, no. 8 (August 2004): 74–77. Accessed April 14, 2014. SPORTDiscus with Full Text.

Hunt, Chris. "Local Heroes: The Lisbon Lions." Editorial. Last modified June 2007. Accessed April 7, 2014. www.chrishunt.biz/features40.html.

"Introduction: The Story of One of Glentoran's Greatest Achievements." Glentoran Football Club. Accessed May 13, 2014. www.glentoran-fc.co.uk/cougars.htm.

"Jim Storrie—The Laughing Cavalier." The Mighty Mighty Whites: The Definitive History of Leeds United. Accessed May 13, 2014. www.mightyleeds.co.uk/players/storrie.htm.

John, Bob St. "Another Tie for Tornado." *Dallas (TX) Morning News*, July 9, 1967, B1. Accessed May 13, 2014. America's Historical Newspapers.

———. "Dundee Blows Another One; Kerr Raps Ref." *Dallas (TX) Morning News*, June 26, 1967, B1. Accessed May 13, 2014. America's Historical Newspapers.

———. "Gusty Tornado Blows over Rovers, 4–1." *Dallas (TX) Morning News*, June 22, 1967, B1. Accessed May 13, 2014. America's Historical Newspapers.

———. "Stoke Smoke Chokes Dallas." *Dallas (TX) Morning News*, June 18, 1967, B1. America's Historical Newspapers.

Johnson, Robert, Jr. "Say It Ain't So, Jay: Fitzgerald's Use of Baseball in 'The Great Gatsby.'" *The F. Scott Fitzgerald Review* 1 (2002): 30–44. Accessed December 3, 2013. JSTOR.

Jones, Ken. "High Praise for West Ham." *Baltimore Sun*, April 23, 1969, C3. Accessed February 5, 2014. ProQuest Historical Newspapers.

Jones, Neil. "The Forgotten Story . . . of the Dallas Tornado's 1967–68 World Tour." *Guardian*, January 9, 2014. Accessed January 20, 2014. www.theguardian.com/sport/blog/2014/jan/09/forgotten-story-of-dallas-tornado.

Jukich, Roy. "Leaky Defense Plagues McColl." *Toronto Sun*, June 22, 1967. Accessed May 13, 2014. http://news.google.com/newspapers?id=kZplAAAAIBAJ&sjid=uIoNAAAAIBAJ&pg=4636%2C2364565.

Kane, Martin. "The True Football Gets Its Big Chance." *Sports Illustrated*, March 27, 1967. Accessed May 12, 2014. http://sportsillustrated.cnn.com/vault/article/magazine/MAG1079671/1/index.htm.

Keefe, Thomas M. "The Catholic Issue in the Chicago Tribune before the Civil War." *Mid-America: An Historical Review* 57, no. 4 (1975): 227–45.

"Ken Aston—Inventor of Red and Yellow Cards." WineCape's Referee Blog. Last modified February 23, 2010. Accessed May 7, 2014. http://refarbiter.wordpress.com/2010/02/23/ken-aston-inventor-of-the-yellow-and-red-cards/.

Kendrick, Mat. "The Doc Made First Tour So Memorable." *Birmingham (UK) Mail*, July 16, 2012, 46. Accessed February 6, 2014. ProQuest Newsstand.

Knight, Gladys L. *Encyclopedia of American Race Riots*. Edited by James N. Upton and Walter C. Rucker. Milestones in African American History. Westport, CT: Greenwood Press, 2007. Accessed November 22, 2013. EBSCO eBook Collection (224792).

Korsower, Abe. "Pro Soccer Suspended; Mustangs May Disband." *Chicago Tribune*, November 2, 1968, G1. Accessed February 8, 2014. ProQuest Historical Newspapers.

Kubrick, Stanley, Michael Herr, and Gustav Hasford. *Full Metal Jacket*. New York City: Alfred A. Knopf, 1987.

Lace, Bill. "Stokers Deflate Tornado." *Fort Worth Star-Telegram*, June 18, 1967, 27. Accessed May 13, 2014. America's Historical Newspapers.

Lamb, Chris. *Conspiracy of Silence: Sportswriters and the Long Campaign to Desegregate Baseball*. Lincoln: University of Nebraska Press, 2012.

Langford, George. "World Soccer Stars to Play in U.S." *Chicago Tribune*, October 13, 1966, F1. Accessed September 23, 2013. ProQuest Historical Newspapers.

"Legends: Ladislao Kubala." FC Barcelona. Accessed May 14, 2014. www.fcbarcelona.com/club/history/detail/card/ladislao-kubala.

"Legends Profile: Martin Buchan." Manchester United. Accessed May 13, 2014. www.manutd.com/en/Players-And-Staff/Legends/Martin-Buchan.aspx?pageNo=2.

Lewis, Michael. "Remembering the Lancers." *Sports Illustrated*, December 5, 2000. Accessed May 13, 2014. http://sportsillustrated.cnn.com/inside_game/michael_lewis/news/2000/12/05/Lewis_column_cnnsi/.

Liecty, Derek. "Comments by Derek Liecty Former General Manager, Oakland Clippers Professional Soccer Team, National Professional Soccer League." Unpublished manuscript, n.d.

———. E-mail message to author. March 23, 2014.

———. Telephone interview by the author. Washington, DC. March 22, 2014.

Lindner, Andrew M., and Daniel N. Hawkins. "Globalization, Culture Wars, and Attitudes Towards Soccer in America: An Empirical Assessment of How Soccer Explains the World."

Sociological Quarterly 53, no. 1 (Winter 2012): 68–91. Accessed April 5, 2014. Wiley Online Library.

Litterer, David. "The Year in Soccer—1929." American Soccer History Archives. Last modified February 4, 2006. Accessed March 28, 2014. http://homepages.sover.net/~spectrum/year/1929.html.

Los Angeles Times. Selected articles. 1966–1969. ProQuest Historical Newspapers.

MacCambridge, Michael. "Director's Cut: 'Always Leave 'Em Laughing' by Thomas Boswell." Grantland. Last modified June 11, 2013. Accessed May 8, 2014.

MacCambridge, Michael. *Lamar Hunt: A Life in Sports.* Riverside, NJ: Andrews McMeel, 2012.

———. "More Than a Game." In *A New Literary History of America.* Edited by Greil Marcus and Werner Sollors, 890–94. Cambridge, MA: Belknap Press, 2009.

Macintosh, Iain. "MLS Miami Will Need Results, Not Becks' Star Power, to Succeed." The Boot Room. Blog entry posted February 6, 2014. Accessed March 18, 2014. http://espnfc.com/blog/_/name/bootroom/id/677?cc=5901.

MacPhail, William C. Letter to the editor. *New York Times,* March 31, 1968, SM88. Accessed April 9, 2014. ProQuest Historical Newspapers.

Macpherson, Archie. "Obituary: Jerry Kerr." *Independent,* November 11, 1999. Accessed May 13, 2014. www.independent.co.uk/arts-entertainment/obituary-jerry-kerr-1125033.html.

Maisel, Bob. Selected columns. *Baltimore Sun,* 1967–1969. ProQuest Historical Newspapers.

Mann, Chris. "Football's Greatest Managers: #2 Viktor Maslov." The Equaliser. Blog entry posted October 22, 2010. Accessed March 13, 2014. http://equaliserblog.wordpress.com/2010/10/22/2-maslov.

Marcus, Joe. "Difficulties Face Soccer: Near-Defunct NASL Fights Apathy in the U.S." *Baltimore Sun,* April 27, 1969, A12. Accessed January 21, 2014. ProQuest Historical Newspapers.

Marietta (GA) Daily Journal. "Chiefs Face San Diego in Finale." September 25, 1968, 13. Accessed May 9, 2014. America's Historical Newspapers.

Marietta (GA) Journal. "NASL Teams Slate Eight Home Matches." April 6, 1969, 10. Accessed January 24, 2014. America's Historical Newspapers.

Markovits, Andrei S., and Steven L. Hellerman. "Soccer in America: A Story of Marginalization." *University of Miami Entertainment and Sports Law Review* 13 (fall 1995–spring 1996): 225–55. Accessed February 14, 2014. HeinOnline Law Journal Library.

Markus, Robert. "Obituary: David Condon, Tribune Columnist." *Chicago Tribune,* December 6, 1994. Accessed January 26, 2014. http://articles.chicagotribune.com/1994-12-06/news/9412060256_1_churchill-downs-chicago-tribune-tribune-columnist.

———. "$tu Learns That $occer Language." *Chicago Tribune,* November 4, 1967, D3. Accessed April 3, 2014. ProQuest Historical Newspapers.

Maule, Tex. "Kickoff for a Babel of Booters." *Sports Illustrated,* April 24, 1967. Accessed October 27, 2013. http://si.com/vault/article/magazine/MAG1135457/index.htm.

McGowen, Dean. "Plans for Nationwide 11-Team Pro Soccer League Formulated Here." *New York Times,* May 11, 1966, 83. Accessed September 23, 2013. ProQuest Historical Newspapers.

McIntyre, Doug. "Reigning in Seattle." *ESPN the Magazine,* May 16, 2012. Accessed February 6, 2014. http://espn.go.com/sports/soccer/story/_/id/7929299/soccer-seattle-sounders-prove-mls-put-fans-seats-espn-magazine.

McKinnon, Dave. "Dallas Tornado 1967–68 World Tour." North American Soccer League Jerseys. Accessed January 2, 2014. www.nasljerseys.com/Misc/Tornado%2067-68%20World%20Tour2.htm.

Meyers, Georg N. "TV Invents a Sport, Call It Soccer." *Seattle (WA) Daily Times,* March 14, 1967. Accessed December 10, 2013. America's Historical Newspapers.

Millegan, Lloyd E. "Unsanctioned Pro Soccer Loop Plans to Make Debut Next April." *New York Times,* August 23, 1966, 46. Accessed September 24, 2013. ProQuest Historical Newspapers.

Miller, Lowell. "The Selling of Soccer-Mania." *New York Times,* August 28, 1977, 187. Accessed January 2, 2014. ProQuest Historical Newspapers.

Moore, Jack. "Cold Mountain." The Classical. Blog entry posted January 23, 2013. Accessed January 3, 2014. http://theclassical.org/articles/cold-mountain.

Morton, Dave. "Remember When: Newcastle United Icon Jinky Jimmy Turns 67 Today." *Newcastle (UK) Chronicle*, January 20, 2014. Accessed April 26, 2014. www.chroniclelive.co.uk/lifestyle/nostalgia/newcastle-united-icon-jinky-jimmy-6528372.

Murray, Scott, Georgina Turner, and Sean Ingle. "The Greatest-Ever European Cup Thrashings." *Guardian*, November 6, 2003. Accessed November 9, 2013. www.theguardian.com/football/2003/nov/06/theknowledge.sport.

Nee, Chris. "The Summer of '69 and Stateside Silverware for Wolverhampton Wanderers." In Bed with Maradona. Blog entry posted July 3, 2012. Accessed January 26, 2014. http://inbedwithmaradona.com/journal/2012/7/3/the-summer-of-69-and-stateside-silverware-for-wolverhampton.html.

Nelson, Thomas Allen. *Kubrick: Inside a Film Artist's Maze*. Bloomington: Indiana University Press, 2000.

New York Times. Selected articles. 1924–1970. ProQuest Historical Newspapers.

Nichols, Bill. Selected columns. *Cleveland (OH) Plain Dealer*, 1967–1968. America's Historical Newspapers.

Nigro, Ken. Selected columns. *Baltimore Sun*, 1967–1969. ProQuest Historical Newspapers.

"Oakland Clippers Friendlies." NASL Jerseys blog. Accessed March 1, 2014. www.nasljerseys.com/Friendlies/Teams/Clippers%20Friendlies.htm.

Ohio Historical Society. "Cleveland Stokers." Ohio History Central. Accessed January 25, 2014. www.ohiohistorycentral.org/w/Cleveland_Stokers.

Oklahoma City University. "Harvey Saw the World with Dallas Tornado." Oklahoma City University Sports. Last modified January 21, 2014. Accessed April 2, 2014. www.ocusports.com/news/2014/1/21/MSOC_0121143535.aspx?path=msoc.

Olderman, Murray. "Soccer Woes Would Wilt with the Stilt." *St. Albans (VT) Messenger*, June 26, 1967. Accessed April 6, 2014. America's Historical Newspapers.

Olsen, Jack. "Biggest Cheapskate in Big D." *Sports Illustrated*, June 19, 1972. Accessed April 1, 2014. http://sportsillustrated.cnn.com/vault/article/magazine/MAG1086220/1/index.htm.

Omaha World Herald, September 17, 1968. Accessed May 15, 2014. America's Historical Newspapers.

Oriard, Michael. *King Football: Sport and Spectacle in the Golden Age of Radio and Newsreels, Movies and Magazines, the Weekly and Daily Press*. Chapel Hill: University of North Carolina Press, 2003.

PAC-12 Conference. "Stanford Soccer's Renaissance Man: Leo Weinstein, 1921–2009." PAC-12 News. Last modified May 12, 2009. Accessed March 2, 2014. http://pac-12.com/article/2009/05/12/stanford-soccers-renaissance-man-leo-weinstein-1921-2009.

Parker, Wendy. "Atlanta Pro Soccer Always on Its Heels." *Atlanta (GA) Journal-Constitution*, June 13, 2004, E1. Accessed February 6, 2014. ProQuest Newsstand.

Parrish, Charles, and John Nauright. "Darts, Whips and Dips: The Rollercoaster Ride of Professional Soccer in DC." Working paper, n.d. Accessed February 14, 2014. http://www.academia.edu/1962245/Darts_Whips_and_Dips_The_Rollercoaster_Ride_of_Professional_Soccer_in_Washington_D.C.

Passan, Rich. "Stokers and Mustangs Tie." *Cleveland (OH) Plain Dealer*, June 1, 1967, 66–70. Accessed May 13, 2014. America's Historical Newspapers.

"Penalty Controversy As Glens Win." Glentoran Football Club. Accessed May 13, 2014. www.glentoran-fc.co.uk/cougars%20shamrock%20rvrs.htm.

Phillips-Knight, Rob. "Jock Stein's Lisbon Lions Shock Inter Milan." ESPN UK Football. Last modified May 19, 2010. Accessed April 7, 2014. www.espn.co.uk/football/sport/story/23486.html.

Pinkerton, Jan, and Randolph H. Hudson. "Chicago Tribune." In *Encyclopedia of the Chicago Literary Renaissance*. Accessed May 7, 2014. Bloom's Literature.

———. "Ring Lardner." In *Encyclopedia of the Chicago Renaissance*. Accessed May 7, 2014. Bloom's Literature.

Pittsburgh (PA) Post-Gazette. "Spartans Quit Pro Boot Loop." January 8, 1968. Accessed May 14, 2014. http://news.google.com/newspapers?id=L51RAAAAIBAJ& sjid=b2wDAAAAIBAJ&dq=npsl&pg=7210%2C1312210.

Ponting, Ivan. "Phil Woosnam." *(London) Independent*, August 1, 2013, 50. Accessed February 17, 2014. ProQuest Newsstand.

Reuters. "Tornados in Soccer Tie." *New York Times*, October 12, 1967, 62. Accessed December 31, 2013. ProQuest Historical Newspapers.

Richman, Milton. "Ref Toted a Gun." *St. Albans (VT) Messenger*, May 16, 1967, 6. Accessed April 9, 2014. America's Historical Newspapers.

Roach, James. "Soccer Players Have Spring Training, Too." *New York Times*, March 12, 1967, 209. Accessed October 28, 2013. ProQuest Historical Newspapers.

Roberts, Rich. "Jack Kent Cooke: Successful Owner Has Acquiring Mind." *Los Angeles Times*, January 22, 1984, B1. Accessed May 14, 2014. ProQuest Historical Newspapers.

"Rookie Linesman Robs Glentoran." Glentoran Football Club. Accessed March 29, 2014. www.glentoran-fc.co.uk/cougars%20shamrock%20rovers.htm.

Schumacher, Ernst Friedrich. *Small Is Beautiful: A Study of Economics As if People Mattered.* New York: Harper Perennial, 1989.

Scott, Eugene L. "Generals Fade Away: Decision to Abandon League Play Forced out New York." *New York Times*, March 16, 1969, S6. Accessed February 8, 2014. ProQuest Historical Newspapers.

———. "Jimmy Bostwick Upsets Brother." *New York Times*, January 19, 1969, S3. Accessed May 16, 2014. ProQuest Historical Newspapers.

Seattle (WA) Daily Times. "Bellevue, Boeing B in Big Boot Battle." February 25, 1968, 31. Accessed April 13, 2014. America's Historical Newspapers.

Shecter, Leonard. "Why It's Better to Watch the Game on TV." *New York Times*, March 3, 1968, SM32. Accessed May 15, 2014. ProQuest Historical Newspapers.

Smith, Liz. "Giltfinger's Golden Dome." *Sports Illustrated*, April 12, 1965. Accessed May 13, 2014. http://sportsillustrated.cnn.com/vault/article/magazine/MAG1077072.

Smith, Red. "Red Smith's Views: Pro Teams Now Run by Ad Men." *Washington Post*, February 13, 1966, C3. Accessed December 10, 2013. ProQuest Historical Newspapers.

Smith, Seymour. "Woosnam Optimistic about Soccer's Future." *Baltimore Sun*, May 27, 1974, C4. Accessed January 9, 2014. ProQuest Historical Newspapers.

St. John, Bob. "Tornado Sweeps into Astrodome." *Dallas (TX) Morning News*, June 10, 1967, B2. Accessed April 1, 2014. America's Historical Newspapers.

Stokers Play 2–2 Tie. Cleveland (OH) Plain Dealer, June 15, 1967. Accessed May 13, 2014. America's Historical Newspapers.

"The Stokers Summer." The Oatcake–Stoke City FC Fanzine. Last modified July 20, 2012. Accessed May 13, 2014. http://theoatcake.wordpress.com/2012/07/20/the-stokers-summer-2/comment-page-1.

Tanenhous, Sam. "Hello to All That: The Irony behind the Demise of the Partisan Review." Slate. Last modified April 16, 2003. Accessed November 23, 2013. www.slate.com/articles/arts/culturebox/2003/04/hello_to_all_that.html.

Thomas, Robert Mcg. Jr. "William D. Cox, 79, Team Owner Who Was Banned from Baseball." *New York Times*, March 30, 1989, B8. Accessed May 12, 2014. ProQuest Historical Newspapers.

The (London) Times. "England's World Cup Victory Strained Relations with Argentina." January 1, 1997, News, 5. Accessed November 8, 2013. The Times Digital Archive.

———. "Ken Aston." October 25, 2001, Obituaries, 25. Accessed November 7, 2013. The Times Digital Archive.

Torre, Harold. "A Sport-loving Nation." *(London) Times*, August 17, 1925. Accessed May 7, 2014. The Times Digital Archive.

Trenton (NJ) Evening Times." Spartan Booters in Bow." April 16, 1967, 65. Accessed May 14, 2014. America's Historical Newspapers.

———. "Worldwide Comment on Newark." July 16, 1967. Accessed November 23, 2013. America's Historical Newspapers.

Trouille, David. "Association Football to Futbol: Ethnic Succession and the History of Chicago-area Soccer." *Soccer and Society* 10, no. 6 (November 2009): 795–822. Accessed March 28, 2014. Taylor & Francis Social Sciences and Humanity Library.

Turnbull, John. "Soccer." In *New Georgia Encyclopedia*. Georgia Humanities Council. Last modified August 29, 2013. Accessed April 4, 2014. www.georgiaencyclopedia.org/articles/sports-outdoor-recreation/soccer#Amateur-Teams.

———. "Soccer Fields, for King and Atlanta, Lent Space to Move beyond Vietnam." The Global Game. Blog entry posted February 5, 2008. Accessed March 18, 2014. www.theglobalgame.com/blog/2008/02/soccer-fields-for-king-and-atlanta-lent-space-to-move-beyond-vietnam.

Uersfeld, Stephen. "Greatest Managers, #14: Ernst Happel." ESPNFC.com. Last modified August 6, 2013. Accessed May 13, 2014. www.espnfc.com/news/story/_/id/1511243/ernst-happel?cc=5901.

United Press International. "British Soccer Official Rejects $38,000 Post." *New York Times*, September 6, 1966, 30. Accessed September 23, 2013. ProQuest Historical Newspapers.

———. "California Clippers Go out of Business." *Washington Post*, June 5, 1969, H2. Accessed March 1, 2014. ProQuest Historical Newspapers.

———. "CBS Gains Right to Telecast New Soccer League Contests." *Trenton (NJ) Evening Times*, October 4, 1966, 31. Accessed May 12, 2014. America's Historical Newspapers.

———. "Commissioner Announced for Soccer." *Marietta (GA) Journal*, February 23, 1967, 15. Accessed May 12, 2014. America's Historical Newspapers.

———. "Filipino Chosen to Chair New Soccer League." *Trenton (NJ) Evening Times*, February 23, 1967, 32. Accessed May 12, 2014. America's Historical Newspapers.

———. "Ike Would Restore 'Powers of Police.'" *Springfield (MA) Union*, July 26, 1967. Accessed November 23, 2013. America's Historical Newspapers.

———. "Near Riot Follows Santos First Loss." *Los Angeles Times*, July 12, 1968, D3. Accessed May 15, 2014. ProQuest Historical Newspapers.

———. "Oakland's Own Now." *Washington Post*, June 11, 1967, D5. Accessed March 1, 2014. ProQuest Historical Newspapers.

———. "Phil Woosnam Selected As Coach of Year." *Marietta (GA) Journal*, September 18, 1968. Accessed May 15, 2014. America's Historical Newspapers.

———. "Pro Soccer Challenge Turned Down." *Washington Post*, May 22, 1967, D6. Accessed March 1, 2014. ProQuest Historical Newspapers.

———. "Pro Soccer Loop Becomes Reality." *Marietta (GA) Daily Journal*, June 17, 1966, 12. Accessed September 23, 2013. America's Historical Newspapers.

———. "Pro Soccer Was a Costly Lesson." *Seattle (WA) Daily Times*, November 5, 1968, 27. Accessed March 4, 2014. America's Historical Newspapers.

———. "Russians Defeat U.S. in Soccer, 3–2." *Washington Post*, February 24, 1969, D6. Accessed March 5, 2014. ProQuest Historical Newspapers.

———. "Soccer League Will Pay $400 Bonus per Victory." *Washington Post*, March 3, 1967, D5. Accessed May 13, 2014. ProQuest Historical Newspapers.

———. "Soccer Writer Solicits Article, Ends up As Coach." *Washington Post*, July 21, 1967, D4. Accessed March 9, 2014. ProQuest Historical Newspapers.

———. "Title Bid Farewell to Chiefs?" *Marietta (GA) Journal*, September 25, 1968, 13. Accessed April 11, 2014, and May 15, 2014. America's Historical Newspapers.

———. "Two U.S. Soccer Groups Announce New Merger." *Springfield (MA) Union*, August 9, 1966, 27. Accessed September 23, 2013. America's Historical Newspapers.

———. "Victorious Chiefs Await West Champs." *Marietta (GA) Journal*, September 16, 1968, 5. Accessed May 15, 2014. America's Historical Newspapers.

———. "Walsh Leaves Dodger Post to Head Soccer League." *New York Times*, December 30, 1966, 22. Accessed May 12, 2014. ProQuest Historical Newspapers.

———. "Welsh Soccer Star Defies Ban, Signs with U.S. Pro Team." *Springfield (MA) Union*, September 9, 1966, 52. Accessed May 12, 2014. America's Historical Newspapers.

———. "West Ham Star Tells of Woes in Soccer Loop." *Springfield (MA) Union*, June 27, 1965, 37. Accessed May 13, 2014. America's Historical Newspapers.

————. "World Soccer May Retaliate against CBS." *Washington Post*, October 5, 1966, D5. Accessed May 12, 2014. ProQuest Historical Newspapers.

Vancouver Sun. "Stout Defence Earns a Draw." June 29, 1967. Accessed May 13, 2014. http://news.google.com/newspapers?id=l5plAAAAIBAJ&sjid=uIoNAAAAIBAJ&pg=5308%2C4853382.

Veeck, Bill, and Ed Linn. "Octopus under the Big Eye." *Sports Illustrated*, May 24, 1965. Accessed December 7, 2013. http://sportsillustrated.cnn.com/vault/article/magazine/MAG1077251/index.htm.

Veve, Thomas D. "Before the Boss: Mike Burke and the CBS Yankees." In *Baseball/Literature/Culture: Essays 2006–2007*. Edited by Ronald E. Kates and Warren Tormey, 150–59. Jefferson, NC: McFarland, 2008. Accessed January 2, 2014. www.daltonstate.edu/faculty-staff/tveve/hist1051%20bridge/The%20Business%20of%20Sport%20I/Before_The_Boss.pdf.

Wangerin, David. *Distant Corners: American Soccer's History of Missed Opportunities and Lost Causes*. Philadelphia: Temple University Press, 2011.

————. *Soccer in a Football World*. Philadelphia: Temple University Press, 2008.

Washington Post. Selected articles. 1958–1969. ProQuest Historical Newspapers.

Wefing, John. *The Life and Times of Richard J. Hughes: The Politics of Civility*. New Brunswick, NJ: Rutgers University Press, 2009.

Whittall, Richard. "When Toronto Pulled in the Stars." A More Splendid Life. Last modified July 9, 2008. Accessed May 13, 2014. www.amoresplendidlife.com/2008/07/when-toronto-pulled-in-stars.html.

Williams, Richard. "Phil Woosnam: From West Ham and Villa to Realizing the American Dream." *Guardian*, July 26, 2013. Accessed May 12, 2014. www.theguardian.com/football/blog/2013/jul/26/phil-woosnam-west-ham-aston-villa-america.

"Willie Roy-USMNT." U.S. National Soccer Players. Accessed May 14, 2014. www.ussoccerplayers.com/player/roy-willy.

Wilson, Jonathan. *Inverting the Pyramid: The History of Football Tactics*. London: Orion, 2009.

Index

About the Author

Dennis J. Seese is a research librarian at American University and a freelance writer/journalist based in Washington, D.C. He was born and raised in Pittsburgh, where he earned a BA in English literature and MLIS from the University of Pittsburgh. It was there that a mad band of Russians and Turks, with some assistance from Thierry Henry, introduced Seese to the beauties of the Beautiful Game during the 2006 World Cup. He's been a devoted, obsessive fan ever since, always seeking to grasp the history and gain a deeper understanding of the world's finest game. Seese's soccer musings have been published on *ESPN FC*, *In Bed with Maradona*, and *SB Nation*, and he's currently a staff writer/editor for *Managing Madrid*, an acclaimed Real Madrid blog with a global following. When not watching or writing about soccer, Seese is thinking, researching, and/or writing about music, oral history, film, American studies, housing policy, citizen journalism, information literacy, service learning, literature, and creative nonfiction. Other outlets that have featured Seese's writing include the monograph *Soccer Culture in America: Essays on the World's Sport in Red, White and Blue* as well as the *Huffington Post*, *Library Journal*, *Educational Media Review Online (EMRO)*, and *Education Review*. Seese lives in Silver Spring, Maryland, with his beautiful wife, Alison, their amazing son, Miles, and fluffy orange cat, Jo-Jo.